React 18 Design Patterns and Best Practices

Fourth Edition

Design, build, and deploy production-ready
web applications with React by leveraging
industry-best practices

Carlos Santana Roldán

BIRMINGHAM—MUMBAI

React 18 Design Patterns and Best Practices
Fourth Edition

Senior Publishing Product Manager: Suman Sen
Acquisition Editor – Peer Reviews: Saby Dsilva
Project Editor: Parvathy Nair
Content Development Editor: Shazeen Iqbal
Copy Editor: Safis Editor
Technical Editor: Srishty Bhardwaj
Proofreader: Safis Editor
Indexer: Rekha Nair
Presentation Designer: Rajesh Shirsath
Developer Relations Marketing Executive: Priyadarshini Sharma

First published: January 2017
Second published: March 2019
Third published: May 2021
Fourth edition: July 2023

Production reference: 3070823

Published by Packt Publishing Ltd.
Grosvenor House
11 St Paul's Square
Birmingham
B3 1RB, UK.

ISBN 978-1-80323-310-9

www.packt.com

I would like to dedicate this book to my lovely daughter, Victoria.

— Carlos Santana Roldán

Contributors

About the author

Carlos Santana Roldán is a software engineer with over 16 years of experience in the industry. He is the author of the books *React Cookbook* and *React Design Patterns and Best Practices* – Second, Third, and Fourth Editions. Carlos is also the founder of one of the most renowned developers' communities in Latin America, Series Frontend, where he trains individuals in various web technologies (https://www.youtube.com/@SeriesFrontend).

About the reviewers

Roy Derks has been working in web development for the past 15 years. He has founded multiple startups, and worked as a startup CTO and developer advocate for numerous startups. Roy has been using GraphQL, React, and TypeScript since the early days and is seen as a thought leader in the space. In recent years he has published multiple books with Packt Publishing such as *React Projects* (First and Second Editions) and *React and React Native* (Third and Fourth Editions).

Jonathan Reeves is a software engineer with over five years of experience. Jonathan has used JavaScript and/or TypeScript for most of his development career, which has included extensive usage of React, GraphQL, and Node with Express. Currently, he is working as a mid-level software engineer in the video game industry using C++ and the .NET tech stack.

First, I would like to thank my wife. Without her patience and help with our children, I would not have been able to review this book in the amount of time necessary. I love you. I would also like to thank my kids for allowing me to review this book in the hopes that sometime soon they will start their journey of learning software development. Ava, and Grayson, Daddy loves you very much.

Join our community on Discord

Join our community's Discord space for discussion with the author and other readers:

https://packt.link/React18DesignPatterns4e

Table of Contents

Chapter 3: Cleaning Up Your Code   29

Preface

React is a revolutionary, open-source JavaScript library that breathes life into web applications by constructing intricate user interfaces from small, isolated chunks known as components. This book serves as a roadmap, guiding you through the wonders of React and enhancing your productivity by introducing an efficient workflow without compromising on quality.

Our journey begins by delving deep into the core of React, gaining a thorough understanding of its internal mechanisms and architecture. With this strong foundation in place, we will guide you towards writing clean and maintainable code, breaking down complex concepts into digestible and manageable chunks.

Continuing our journey, we will uncover the art of building components that aren't just one-off entities but reusable pieces across your application. We'll illuminate the path to structuring your applications, making them more organized and manageable. The seemingly daunting task of creating functional forms will become a breeze as we equip you with strategies and techniques to do so effectively.

As we ascend further, we'll immerse ourselves in styling React components. You'll learn how to bring your applications to life with aesthetic appeal while ensuring they remain swift and responsive. Moreover, you'll discover the secrets of enhancing application performance, fine-tuning your components for speed and efficiency.

In the final phase of our journey, we'll delve into testing methodologies effectively, refining the quality and reliability of your applications. You'll also gain insight into contributing to React and its thriving ecosystem, joining the ranks of developers who continually drive its evolution.

By the end of this book, the trial-and-error process, the developmental hurdles, and guesswork will be things of the past. You will have harnessed the power of React, equipped with the skills necessary to construct and deploy real-world React web applications with confidence and finesse.

Who this book is for

This book is for web developers who want to increase their understanding of React and apply it to real-life app development. Intermediate-level experience with React and JavaScript is assumed.

What this book covers

In *Chapter 1, Taking Your First Steps with React*, we start our journey to understand React by learning to write declarative code and distinguishing between our components and React's elements. We also discuss why we combine logic and templates in React, a decision that was controversial initially but ultimately beneficial. Recognizing the potential for feeling overwhelmed in the rapidly evolving world of JavaScript, we suggest taking small, manageable steps to avoid fatigue. We wrap up by introducing the new `create-vite` tool, preparing you for hands-on coding experience in React.

In *Chapter 2, Introducing TypeScript*, we'll learn the basics of TypeScript, including creating simple types, interfaces, using enums, namespaces, and template literals. We'll also figure out how to set up our first TypeScript configuration file (`tsconfig.json`) and divide it into two parts - a common part and a specific part, which is particularly handy when working with MonoRepos. After this chapter, you'll be all set to delve into using JSX/TSX code and explore ways to make your code better in the next chapter. Get ready to use TypeScript to make your React apps easy to work with and maintain.

In *Chapter 3, Cleaning Up Your Code*, we'll get to know JSX, including how it's written and what it can do. We'll also set up Prettier and ESLint to keep our code neat and prevent mistakes. Plus, we'll learn about functional programming, which makes our code easier to manage and test. After tidying up our code, we'll be prepared to go deeper into React and learn how to make components that we can use repeatedly in the next chapter. By adopting good habits, we can build React apps that are simple to manage, grow, and check.

In *Chapter 4, Exploring Popular Composition Patterns*, we'll learn how to use "props" to make our reusable components work together better. Using props helps keep our components separate and welldefined. We'll look at two common ways to organize components: the container and presentational pattern, which keeps the rules and looks of our components separate. We'll also learn about **Higher Order Components (HOCs)** for dealing with context without making our components too dependent, and the Function as Child pattern for creating components on-the-fly.

In *Chapter 5, Writing Code for the Browser*, we'll look at how React can be used in a web browser to create forms, handle events, and animate SVGs. We'll learn about the `useRef` Hook, which is an easy way to reach DOM nodes.

With React's simple, straightforward approach, managing complex web apps becomes easier. Plus, React allows us to access DOM nodes directly if we need to, which makes it simple to use React with other libraries.

In *Chapter 6, Making Your Components Look Beautiful*, we'll dive into styling in React. We'll start by looking at the problems with making CSS work for big projects, using the experiences of Meta as an example. We'll learn about how we can write styles directly inside our React components, which keeps our code tidy and easy to read. But we'll also learn about the limitations of this method and explore another way of styling, called CSS modules, that lets us write CSS in separate files but keep the styles scoped to individual components. Finally, we'll get to know `styled-components`, a popular library for styling in React. By the end of this chapter, you'll have many tools for making your React apps look great.

In *Chapter 7, Anti-Patterns to Be Avoided.*, we'll talk about four ways of using components that could slow down or mess up our web apps. For each problem, we'll use an example to show what goes wrong and how to fix it. We'll learn why using properties to set up the state can cause problems between the state and the properties. We'll also see how using the wrong "key" attribute can mess up the way React updates components. Lastly, we'll learn why spreading non-standard properties to DOM elements is a bad idea. Understanding these issues will help us use React more effectively and avoid common mistakes.

In *Chapter 8, React Hooks*, we'll have a lot of fun learning about the new React Hooks. We'll learn how they work, how to use them to get data, and how to change a class component into a Hooks one. We'll also learn about effects and the differences between `memo`, `useMemo`, and `useCallback`. Finally, we'll see how the `useReducer` Hook works and how it's different from `react-redux`. All of this will help us make our React components faster and better.

In *Chapter 9, React Router*, we'll learn about React Router, a tool we use with React to move between pages in a single-page application. React doesn't do this on its own, so we use React Router. We'll find out how to use it to make our app respond to different URLs and manage navigation. By the end of this chapter, you'll know how React Router works and how to use it in your projects. We'll learn the differences between the `react-router`, `react-router-dom`, and `react-router-native` packages, how to set up React Router, how to add the `<Routes>` component, and how to add parameters to the routes.

In *Chapter 10, React 18 New Features*, we'll explore the new and improved React 18. It has loads of features that make building cool, interactive apps even easier.

With automatic state update grouping, concurrent rendering, Suspense for getting data, better error handling, and new component types, you can create engaging and fast apps. If you work with React, it's a good idea to consider upgrading to React 18. We'll also look at some of the big new features in Node 18 and 19, which can make our web projects even better.

In *Chapter 11, Managing Data*, we'll learn about the React Context API and how to use React Suspense with SWR. We'll learn the basics of the Context API, including creating and using contexts and how the useContext hook makes this even easier. We'll also look at React Suspense and how it helps us handle loading states better for a smoother user experience. We'll also learn about SWR, which makes it easier to fetch and cache data with React Suspense. Lastly, we'll learn how to use the new Redux Toolkit. All these tools will help us build faster and more user-friendly React apps.

In *Chapter 12, Server Side Rendering*, we'll finish our journey through **server-side rendering (SSR)** with React. Now you'll know how to create an app that uses SSR, and why it can be useful for things like **search engine optimization (SEO)**, social sharing, and improving performance. We'll learn how to load data on the server and put it into the HTML template so it's ready for the client-side app when it starts up in the browser. Lastly, we'll see how tools like Next.js can make setting up SSR in React a lot easier by reducing the amount of extra code and hiding some of the tricky parts.

In *Chapter 13, Understanding GraphQL with a Real Project*, we're going to learn about GraphQL, a cool tool that helps us work with APIs and our data more efficiently. Unlike regular REST APIs, GraphQL lets us ask for exactly what we need and nothing more. We're going to use it to make a simple login and user registration system for a real project. We'll learn how to install PostgreSQL, set up environment variables with an .env file, set up Apollo Server, make GraphQL queries and mutations, work with resolvers, create Sequelize models, use JWTs, play with the GraphQL Playground, and do authentication. By the end, you'll know how to use GraphQL in your own projects.

In *Chapter 14, MonoRepo Architecture*, we'll talk about something called a "MonoRepo." Normally, when we build apps, we have one app, one git repository, and one build output. But many organizations use a single repository for all their apps, components, and libraries to make development easier. This is what we call a monorepository. It's like keeping all your code in one big basket instead of having many little baskets. This makes it easier to keep everything updated and it can save time. We'll also discuss how a MonoRepo can make it easier to refactor code, improve teamwork, and speed up the process of updating a package dependency without having to publish a new version every time there's an update.

Chapter 15, Improving the Performance of Your Applications, we will explore techniques to make your apps run smoother and quicker for a better user experience. We'll delve into how React updates your app's display and how using keys can aid in this process for improved efficiency. We will discover the importance of well-structured, task-focused components in boosting app performance. We will discuss the concept of immutability and its significance in helping `React.memo` and `shallowCompare` work effectively. Toward the end, we will introduce various tools and libraries that can further speed up your applications. This chapter aims to equip you with valuable knowledge to enhance the speed and performance of your apps.

In *Chapter 16, Testing and Debugging,* we're going to learn all about testing. You'll find out why testing is important and explore different tools and techniques for checking if our React components are working as they should. We'll work with libraries like React Testing Library and Jest to write and run tests, and even see how to test complex parts of our application like high-order components or forms with lots of fields. Plus, we'll learn how to use tools like React DevTools and Redux DevTools to help us develop better apps. By the end of this chapter, you'll have a solid grasp of how to keep your app working well through effective testing.

In *Chapter 17, Deploying to Production,* we're going to take the React app you've built and share it with the world! We'll use a cloud service called DigitalOcean to do this. You'll learn how to use Node.js and nginx to get your app up and running on a server, and we'll use an Ubuntu server from DigitalOcean for this purpose. We'll walk you through how to set up a DigitalOcean Droplet, configure it, and link it to your domain. We're also going to introduce you to CircleCI, which is a tool that helps you automatically make sure your app is always ready for users, no matter how many changes you make. By the end of this chapter, you'll have your app live on the internet for everyone to see!

To get the most out of this book

To master React, you need to have a fundamental knowledge of JavaScript and Node.js. This book is mostly targeted at web developers, and, at the time of writing, the following assumptions were made of the reader:

- The reader knows how to install the latest version of Node.js.
- The reader is an intermediate developer who can understand JavaScript ES6 syntax.
- The reader has some experience of CLI tools and Node.js syntax.

Download the example code files

The code bundle for the book is hosted on GitHub at `https://github.com/PacktPublishing/React-18-Design-Patterns-and-Best-Practices-Fourth-Edition/`.

We also have other code bundles from our rich catalog of books and videos available at `https://github.com/PacktPublishing/`. Check them out!

Download the color images

We also provide a PDF file that has color images of the screenshots/diagrams used in this book. You can download it here: `https://packt.link/o1WtB`.

Conventions used

There are a number of text conventions used throughout this book.

`CodeInText`: Indicates code words in text, database table names, folder names, filenames, file extensions, pathnames, dummy URLs, user input, and Twitter handles. For example: "After you create this `util`, you need to create the `index.ts` file at `packages/utils/src/index.ts`."

A block of code is set as follows:

```
{
    "name": "api",
    "version": "1.0.0",
    "main": "index.js",
    "author": "",
    "license": "ISC"
}
```

Any command-line input or output is written as follows:

```
cd packages/api
npm init -y
```

Bold: Indicates a new term, an important word, or words that you see on the screen. For instance, words in menus or dialog boxes appear in the text like this. For example: "The first package we need to create to be able to compile other packages is called **devtools**."

Warnings or important notes appear like this.

 Tips and tricks appear like this.

Get in touch

Feedback from our readers is always welcome.

General feedback: Email feedback@packtpub.com and mention the book's title in the subject of your message. If you have questions about any aspect of this book, please email us at questions@packtpub.com.

Errata: Although we have taken every care to ensure the accuracy of our content, mistakes do happen. If you have found a mistake in this book, we would be grateful if you reported this to us. Please visit http://www.packtpub.com/submit-errata, click **Submit Errata**, and fill in the form.

Piracy: If you come across any illegal copies of our works in any form on the internet, we would be grateful if you would provide us with the location address or website name. Please contact us at copyright@packtpub.com with a link to the material.

If you are interested in becoming an author: If there is a topic that you have expertise in and you are interested in either writing or contributing to a book, please visit http://authors.packtpub.com.

Share your thoughts

Once you've read *React 18 Design Patterns and Best Practices, Fourth Edition*, we'd love to hear your thoughts! Scan the QR code below to go straight to the Amazon review page for this book and share your feedback.

https://packt.link/r/1803233109

Your review is important to us and the tech community and will help us make sure we're delivering excellent quality content.

Download a free PDF copy of this book

Thanks for purchasing this book!

Do you like to read on the go but are unable to carry your print books everywhere? Is your eBook purchase not compatible with the device of your choice?

Don't worry, now with every Packt book you get a DRM-free PDF version of that book at no cost.

Read anywhere, any place, on any device. Search, copy, and paste code from your favorite technical books directly into your application.

The perks don't stop there, you can get exclusive access to discounts, newsletters, and great free content in your inbox daily

Follow these simple steps to get the benefits:

1. Scan the QR code or visit the link below

https://packt.link/free-ebook/978-1-80323-310-9

2. Submit your proof of purchase
3. That's it! We'll send your free PDF and other benefits to your email directly

1

Taking Your First Steps with React

Hello, readers!

This book assumes that you already know what React is and what problems it can solve for you. You may have written a small/medium application with React, and you want to improve your skills and answer all your questions. You should know that React is maintained by the developers at Meta and hundreds of contributors within the JavaScript community. React is one of the most popular libraries for creating UIs, and it is well known to be fast, thanks to its smart way of working with the **Document Object Model (DOM)**. It comes with JSX, a new syntax for writing markup in JavaScript, which requires you to change your thinking regarding the separation of concerns. It has many cool features, such as server-side rendering, which gives you the power to write universal applications.

In this chapter, we will go through some basic concepts that are essential to master in order to use React effectively, but are straightforward enough for beginners to figure out:

- The difference between imperative and declarative programming
- React components and their instances, and how React uses elements to control the UI flow
- How React changed the way we build web applications, enforcing a different new concept of separation of concerns, and the reasons behind its unpopular design choice
- Why people feel JavaScript fatigue, and what you can do to avoid the most common errors developers make when approaching the React ecosystem

Technical requirements

To follow this book, you need to have some experience in using the terminal to run a few Unix commands. Also, you need to install **Node.js**. You have two options: the first one is to download Node.js directly from the official website (https://nodejs.org), and the second option (recommended) is to install **Node Version Manager** (**NVM**) from https://github.com/nvm-sh/nvm.

If you decide to go with NVM, you can install any version of Node.js you want and switch the versions with the nvm install command:

- node is an alias for the latest version:

```
nvm install node
```

- You can also install a global version of Node.js (nvm will install the latest version of Node.js locally to a user's computer):

```
nvm install 19
nvm install 18
nvm install 17
nvm install 16
nvm install 15
```

- Or you can install a very specific version:

```
nvm install 12.14.3
```

- After you have installed the different versions, you can switch between them by using the nvm use command:

```
nvm use node # for latest version
nvm use 16 # for the latest version of node 16.X.X
nvm use 12.14.3 # Specific version
```

- Finally, you can specify a default Node.js version by running the following command:

```
nvm alias default node
nvm alias default 16
nvm alias default 12.14.3
```

In short, here is a list of the requirements to complete the chapter:

- **Node.js (19+):** https://nodejs.org

- **NVM:** https://github.com/nvm-sh/nvm
- **VS Code:** https://code.visualstudio.com
- **TypeScript:** https://www.npmjs.com/package/typescript

You can find the code in the book's GitHub repository: https://github.com/PacktPublishing/React-18-Design-Patterns-and-Best-Practices-Fourth-Edition.

Differentiating between declarative and imperative programming

When reading the React documentation or blog posts about React, you will have undoubtedly come across the term **declarative**. One of the reasons why React is so powerful is that it enforces a declarative programming paradigm.

Therefore, to master React, it is essential to understand what declarative programming means and what the main differences between imperative and declarative programming are. The easiest way to approach this is to think about imperative programming as a way of describing how things work, and declarative programming as a way of describing what you want to achieve.

Entering a bar for a beer is a real-life example in the imperative world, where normally you will give the following instructions to the bartender:

1. Find a glass and collect it from the shelf.
2. Place the glass under the tap.
3. Pull down the handle until the glass is full.
4. Hand me the glass.

In the declarative world, you would just say, "Can I have a beer, please?"

The declarative approach assumes that the bartender already knows how to serve a beer, an important aspect of the way declarative programming works.

Let's move into a JavaScript example. Here we will write a simple function that, given an array of lowercase strings, returns an array with the same strings in uppercase:

```
toUpperCase(['foo', 'bar']) // ['FOO', 'BAR']
```

An imperative function to solve the problem would be implemented as follows:

```
const toUpperCase = input => {
  const output = []
```

```
  for (let i = 0; i < input.length; i++) {
    output.push(input[i].toUpperCase())
  }

  return output
}
```

First, an empty array to contain the result is created. Then, the function loops through all the elements of the input array and pushes the uppercase values into the empty array. Finally, the output array is returned.

A declarative solution would be as follows:

```
const toUpperCase = input => input.map(value => value.toUpperCase())
```

The items of the input array are passed to a map function that returns a new array containing the uppercase values. There are some significant differences to note: the former example is less elegant, and it requires more effort to be understood. The latter is terser and easier to read, which makes a huge difference in big code bases, where maintainability is crucial.

Another aspect worth mentioning is that in the declarative example, there is no need to use variables or to keep their values updated during the execution. Declarative programming tends to avoid creating and mutating a state.

As a final example, let's see what it means for React to be declarative. The problem we will try to solve is a common task in web development: creating a toggle button.

Imagine a simple UI component such as a toggle button. When you click it, it turns green (on) if it was previously gray (off), and switches to gray (off) if it was previously green (on).

The imperative way of doing this would be as follows:

```
const toggleButton = document.querySelector('#toggle')

toogleButton.addEventListener('click', () => {
  if (toggleButton.classList.contains('on')) {
    toggleButton.classList.remove('on')
    toggleButton.classList.add('off')
  } else {
    toggleButton.classList.remove('off')
```

```
    toggleButton.classList.add('on')
  }
})
```

It is imperative because of all the instructions needed to change the classes. In contrast, the declarative approach using React would be as follows:

```
// To turn on the Toggle
<Toggle on />

// To turn off the toggle
<Toggle />
```

In declarative programming, developers only describe what they want to achieve, and there's no need to list all the steps to make it work. The fact that React offers a declarative approach makes it easy to use, and consequently, the resulting code is simple, which often leads to fewer bugs and more maintainability.

In the next section, you will learn how React elements work and you will get more context on how props are being passed on a React component.

How React elements work

In this book, we assume that you are familiar with components and their instances, but there is another object you should know about if you want to use React effectively – the element. Elements are lightweight immutable descriptions of what should be rendered, while components are more complex stateful objects responsible for generating elements.

Whenever you call **createClass**, **extend Component**, or **declare a stateless function**, you are creating a component. React manages all the instances of your components at runtime, and there can be more than one instance of the same component in memory at a given point in time.

As mentioned previously, React follows a declarative paradigm, and there's no need to tell it how to interact with the DOM; you declare what you want to see on the screen, and React does the job for you. One of the tools that makes this process more expressive and readable is JSX, which allows you to write HTML-like syntax directly in your JavaScript code. JSX is not mandatory, but it's widely used in the React community.

To control the UI flow, React uses a particular type of object called an element. These elements are created using the `React.createElement()` function, or more commonly, with JSX syntax. Elements contain only the information that is strictly needed to represent the interface.

Here is an example of an element created with JSX:

```
<Title color="red">
    <h1>Hello, H1!</h1>
</Title>
```

This JSX code is converted into JavaScript objects like the following:

```
{
  type: Title,
  props: {
    color: 'red',
    children: {
      type: 'h1',
      props: {
        children: 'Hello, H1!'
      }
    }
  }
}
```

The element's type is crucial because it informs React on how to handle it. If the type is a string, the element represents a DOM node, while if it's a function, the element represents a component.

You can nest DOM elements and components to create a render tree, representing the structure of your application's user interface. By organizing your elements and components in a hierarchical manner, you can create complex and dynamic UIs.

React uses a technique called the Virtual DOM, which is an in-memory representation of the actual DOM. It compares the current and new trees to minimize the number of actual DOM updates. This process is called reconciliation and is used by both React DOM and React Native to create UIs for their respective platforms.

When an element's type is a function, React invokes that function, passing in the element's props to obtain the underlying elements. It recursively repeats this process on the result until it constructs a tree of DOM nodes that can be rendered on the screen.

In summary, elements play a crucial role in React's declarative paradigm, allowing you to create complex user interfaces without manually managing the creation and destruction of DOM elements.

By understanding how elements and components work together, and how React efficiently updates the UI using the Virtual DOM and reconciliation, you'll be well equipped to build dynamic and efficient web applications.

Unlearning everything

When working with React for the first time, it's essential to approach it with an open mind. This is because React represents a new way of designing web and mobile applications, breaking away from many traditional best practices.

In the last two decades, we've learned that separation of concerns is crucial, often involving separating logic from templates. We aim to write JavaScript and HTML in different files, and various templating solutions have been created to aid developers in achieving this goal.

However, the problem with this approach is that it often creates an illusion of separation. In reality, JavaScript and HTML are tightly coupled, no matter where they live. To illustrate this, let's consider an example template:

```
{{#items}}
  {{#first}}
    <li><strong>{{name}}</strong></li>
  {{/first}}
  {{#link}}
    <li><a href="{{url}}">{{name}}</a></li>
  {{/link}}
{{/items}}
```

The preceding snippet is taken from the Mustache website, one of the most popular templating systems.

The first row tells Mustache to loop through a collection of items. Inside the loop, there is some conditional logic to check whether the #first and #link properties exist and, depending on their values, a different piece of HTML is rendered. Variables are wrapped in curly braces.

If your application only has to display some variables, a templating library could represent a good solution, but when it comes to starting to work with complex data structures, things change. Templating systems and their **Domain-Specific Language (DSL)** offer a subset of features, and they try to provide the functionalities of a real programming language without reaching the same level of completeness. As shown in the example, templates highly depend on the models they receive from the logic layer to display the information.

On the other hand, JavaScript interacts with the DOM elements rendered by the templates to update the UI, even if they are loaded from separate files. The same problem applies to styles – they are defined in a different file, but they are referenced in the templates, and the CSS selectors follow the structure of the markup, so it is almost impossible to change one without breaking the other, which is the definition of **coupling**. That is why the classic separation of concerns ended up being more the separation of technologies, which is, of course, not a bad thing, but it doesn't solve any real problems.

React tries to move a step forward by putting the templates where they belong – next to the logic. The reason it does that is that React suggests you organize your applications by composing small bricks called components. The framework should not tell you how to separate the concerns because every application has its own, and only the developers should decide how to limit the boundaries of their applications.

The component-based approach drastically changes the way we write web applications, which is why the classic concept of separation of concerns is gradually being taken over by a much more modern structure. The paradigm enforced by React is not new, and it was not invented by its creators, but React has contributed to making the concept mainstream and, most importantly, popularized it in such a way that it is easier to understand for developers with different levels of expertise.

Rendering a React component looks like this:

```
return (
  <button style={{ color: 'red' }} onClick={handleClick}>
    Click me!
  </button>
)
```

We all agree that it seems a bit weird in the beginning, but that is just because we are not used to that kind of syntax. As soon as we learn it and we realize how powerful it is; we understand its potential. Using JavaScript for both logic and templating not only helps us separate our concerns in a better way, but it also gives us more power and more expressivity, which is what we need to build complex UIs.

That is why even if the idea of mixing JavaScript and HTML sounds weird in the beginning, it is vital to give React 5 minutes. The best way to get started with new technology is to try it on a small side project and see how it goes. In general, the right approach is always to be ready to unlearn everything and change your mindset if the long-term benefits are worth it.

There is another concept that is pretty controversial and hard to accept, and that the engineers behind React are trying to push to the community: moving the styling logic inside the component, too. The end goal is to encapsulate every single technology used to create our components and separate the concerns according to their domain and functionalities. Here is an example of a style object taken from the React documentation:

```
const divStyle = {
  color: 'white',
  backgroundImage: `url(${imgUrl})`,
  WebkitTransition: 'all', // note the capital 'W' here
  msTransition: 'all' // 'ms' is the only lowercase vendor prefix
}


ReactDOM.render(<div style={divStyle}>Hello World!</div>, mountNode)
```

This set of solutions, where developers use JavaScript to write their styles, is known as **#CSSinJS**, and we will talk about it extensively in *Chapter 6, Making Your Components Look Beautiful*.

In the next section, we will see how to avoid JavaScript fatigue, which is caused by the large number of configurations that are needed to run a React application (webpack mainly).

Understanding JavaScript fatigue

There is a prevailing opinion that React consists of a vast set of technologies and tools, and if you want to use it, you are forced to deal with package managers, transpilers, module bundlers, and an infinite list of different libraries. This idea is so widespread and shared among people that it has been clearly defined and given the name **JavaScript fatigue**.

Misconceptions about React

It is not hard to understand the reasons behind JavaScript fatigue. All the repositories and libraries in the React ecosystem are made using shiny new technologies, the latest version of JavaScript, and the most advanced techniques and paradigms. Moreover, there is a massive amount of React boilerplate code on GitHub, each with tens of dependencies to offer solutions for any problem.

However, it is essential to understand that React is a pretty tiny library, and it can be used inside any page (or even inside JSFiddle) in the same way everyone used to use jQuery or Backbone, just by including the script on the page before the closing body element.

Getting started with React without the fatigue

React is split into two packages:

- **react**: Implements the core features of the library
- **react-dom**: Contains all the browser-related features

The reason behind this is that the core package is used to support different targets, such as React DOM in browsers and React Native on mobile devices. Running a React application inside a single HTML page does not require any package manager or complex operation.

Here are the URLs to be included in the HTML to start using React:

- `https://unpkg.com/react@18.2.0/umd/react.production.min.js`
- `https://unpkg.com/react-dom@18.2.0/umd/react-dom.production.min.js`

For a simple UI, we could just use **createElement** (**_jsx** since React 17) and only when we start building something more complex can we include a transpiler to enable JSX and convert it into JavaScript. As the app grows, we may need a router, API endpoints, and external dependencies.

Advantages of the JavaScript ecosystem

Despite the fast pace and constant change in the JavaScript ecosystem, it offers several advantages. The community plays a significant role in driving innovation and rapid evolution. As soon as a specification is announced or drafted, someone in the community implements it as a transpiler plugin or a polyfill, letting everyone else experiment with it while the browser vendors agree and start supporting it.

This makes JavaScript and the browser a unique environment compared to other languages or platforms. The downside is that things change quickly, but it is just a matter of finding the right balance between betting on new technologies versus staying safe.

Bye to Create-React-App, welcome to Vite!

Recently, the React team decided to remove **create-react-app** from their official documentation, indicating that it is no longer the default method for setting up a new React project. Instead, React now recommends using a framework such as Next.js, Remix, or Gatsby for more comprehensive solutions. However, if these frameworks do not fit your needs and you are looking for a simpler alternative, you can opt for build tools like Vite or Parcel.

Vite as a solution

Vite is a build tool and development server created by Evan You, the creator of Vue.js. It leverages the native ES modules feature in modern browsers for fast development and efficient production builds.

To use Vite with React, first, install Vite globally using the following command:

```
npm install -g create-vite
```

Next, create a new Vite project using the React TypeScript template:

```
create-vite my-react-app --template react-ts
```

Finally, move into the newly created project folder and start the development server:

```
cd my-react-app
npm install
npm run dev
```

You should see the project running on port **5173** by default.

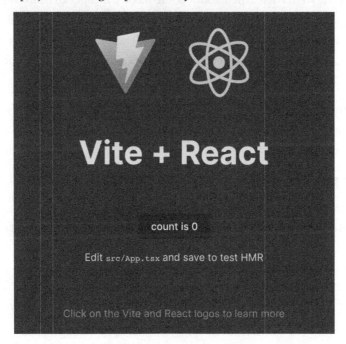

Figure 1.1: Vite default application

If you want to change the port to 3000, you can modify the vite.config.ts file like this:

```
import { defineConfig } from 'vite'
import react from '@vitejs/plugin-react'
// https://vitejs.dev/config/
export default defineConfig({
  plugins: [react()],
  server: {
    port: 3000
  }
})
```

By using Vite, you can scaffold and run a React application with minimal dependencies and still have access to all the features needed to build a complete React application using the most advanced techniques.

Summary

In this first chapter, we have learned about some basic concepts that are very important for following the rest of the book, and that are crucial to working with React daily. We now know how to write declarative code, and we have a clear understanding of the difference between the components we create and the elements that React uses to display their instances on the screen.

We learned the reasons behind the choice of locating logic and templates together, and why that unpopular decision has been a big win for React. We went through the reasons why it is common to feel fatigued in the JavaScript ecosystem, but we have also seen how to avoid those problems by following an iterative approach.

Finally, we have seen what the new create-vite CLI is, and we are now ready to start writing some real code.

In the next chapter, you will learn TypeScript and how to use it in your projects.

Join our community on Discord

Join our community's Discord space for discussion with the author and other readers:

`https://packt.link/React18DesignPatterns4e`

2

Introducing TypeScript

This chapter assumes that you have prior experience with JavaScript and are interested in improving the quality of your code by learning **TypeScript**. TypeScript is a typed superset of JavaScript that compiles to JavaScript. In other words, TypeScript is essentially JavaScript with some additional features.

Designed by Anders Hejlsberg, the creator of C# at Microsoft, TypeScript is an open-source language that enhances the capabilities of JavaScript. By introducing static typing and other advanced features, TypeScript helps developers write more reliable and maintainable code.

In this chapter, we will explore the features of TypeScript and how to convert existing JavaScript code to TypeScript. By the end of this chapter, you will have a solid understanding of TypeScript's benefits and how to leverage them to create more robust and scalable applications.

In this chapter, we will cover the following topics:

- TypeScript's features
- Convert JavaScript code into TypeScript
- Types
- Interfaces
- Extending interfaces and types
- Implementing interfaces and types
- Merging interfaces
- Enums
- Namespaces

- Template literal types
- TypeScript configuration file

Technical requirements

To work through the contents of this chapter, you will need the following:

- Node.js 19+
- Visual Studio Code

TypeScript's features

TypeScript, a popular open-source programming language developed and maintained by Microsoft, is rapidly gaining popularity among developers worldwide. It was introduced as a superset of JavaScript, aiming to facilitate larger-scale applications while enhancing code quality and maintainability. TypeScript leverages static typing and compiles to clean, simple JavaScript code, ensuring compatibility with existing JavaScript environments.

This robust language brings a host of powerful features that set it apart and make it an appealing choice for many programmers. Notably, TypeScript infuses strong typing into JavaScript, providing better error checking and reducing runtime bugs. Moreover, it fully supports object-oriented programming with advanced features like classes, interfaces, and inheritance.

Since any valid JavaScript code is also TypeScript, transitioning from JavaScript to TypeScript can be done gradually, with developers introducing types to their codebase progressively. This makes TypeScript a flexible, scalable solution for both small and large-scale projects.

In this section, we will summarize the essential features of TypeScript that you should take advantage of:

- **TypeScript is JavaScript**: TypeScript is a superset of JavaScript, which means that any JavaScript code you write will work with TypeScript. If you already know how to use JavaScript, you have all the knowledge you need to use TypeScript. You just need to learn how to add types to your code. All TypeScript code is transformed into JavaScript in the end.
- **JavaScript is TypeScript**: This just means that you can rename any valid .js file with the .ts extension, and it will work.
- **Error checking**: TypeScript compiles the code and checks for errors, which helps identify issues before running the code.

- **Strong typing**: By default, JavaScript is not strongly typed. With TypeScript, you can add types to all your variables and functions, and even specify the return value types.

- **Object-oriented programming supported**: TypeScript supports advanced concepts such as classes, interfaces, inheritance, and more. This allows for better organization of code and enhances its maintainability.

After having discussed the key features of TypeScript, let us delve into a practical demonstration of converting JavaScript code into TypeScript.

Converting JavaScript code into TypeScript

In this section, we will see how to transform some JavaScript code into TypeScript.

Let's suppose we have to check whether a word is a palindrome. The JavaScript code for this algorithm will be as follows:

```
function isPalindrome(word) {
   const lowerCaseWord = word.toLowerCase()
   const reversedWord = lowerCaseWord.split('').reverse().join('')


   return lowerCaseWord === reversedWord
}
```

You can name this file palindrome.ts.

As you can see, we are receiving a string variable (word), and we are returning a boolean value. So, how will this be translated into TypeScript?

```
function isPalindrome(word: string): boolean {
   const lowerCaseWord = word.toLowerCase()
   const reversedWord = lowerCaseWord.split('').reverse().join('')


   return lowerCaseWord === reversedWord
}
```

You're probably thinking, "Great, I just specified the string type as word and the boolean type to the function returned value, but now what?"

If you try to run the function with some value that is different from string, you will get a Type-Script error:

```
console.log(isPalindrome('Level')) // true
console.log(isPalindrome('Anna')) // true
console.log(isPalindrome('Carlos')) // false
console.log(isPalindrome(101)) // TS Error
console.log(isPalindrome(true)) // TS Error
console.log(isPalindrome(false)) // TS Error
```

So, if you try to pass a number to the function, you will get the following error:

```
console.log(isPalindrome(   Argument of type 'number' is not assignable to parameter of type
console.log(isPalindrome(   'string'. ts(2345)
console.log(isPalindrome(   Peek Problem (⌥F8)   No quick fixes available
console.log(isPalindrome(101)) // TS Error
console.log(isPalindrome(true)) // TS Error
console.log(isPalindrome(false)) // TS Error
```

Figure 2.1: Type number is not assignable to parameter of type string

That's why TypeScript is very useful, because it will force you to be stricter and more explicit with your code.

Types

In the last example, we saw how to specify some primitive types for our function parameter and returned value, but you're probably wondering how you can describe an object or array with more details. Types can help us to describe our objects or arrays in a better way. For example, let's suppose you want to describe a User type to save the information into the database:

```
type User = {
  username: string
  email: string
  name: string
  age: number
  website: string
  active: boolean
}

const user: User = {
  username: 'czantany',
```

```
    email: 'carlos@milkzoft.com',

    name: 'Carlos Santana',

    age: 33,

    website: 'http://www.js.education',

    active: true

}


// Let's suppose you will insert this data using Sequelize...
models.User.create({ ...user }}
```

We get the following error if we forget to add one of the nodes or put an invalid value in one of them:

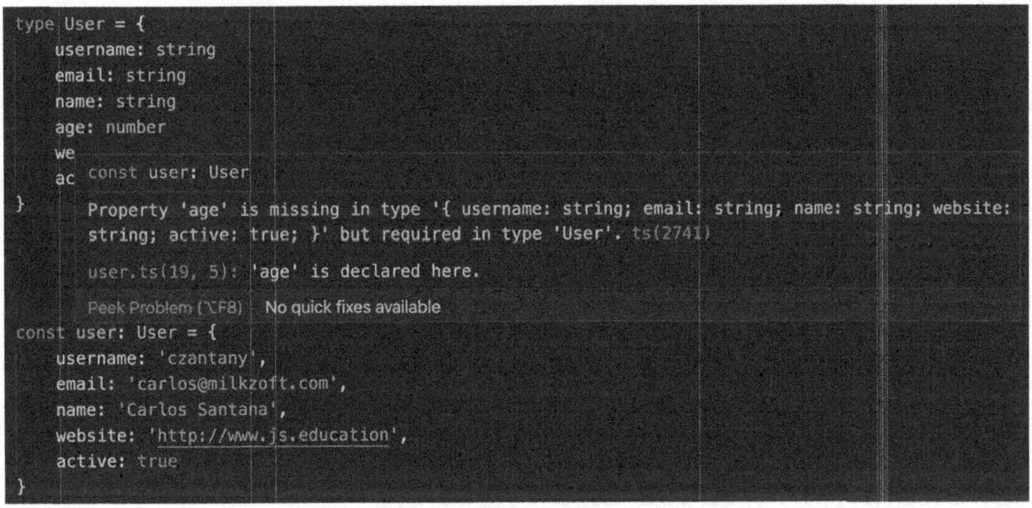

Figure 2.2: Age is missing in type User but is required

If you need optional nodes, you can always put a ? next to the age of the node, as shown in the following code block:

```
type User = {
  username: string
  email: string
  name: string
  age?: number
  website: string
  active: boolean
}
```

You can name type as you want, but a good practice to follow is to add a prefix of T. For example, the User type will become TUser. In this way, you can quickly recognize that it is type and you don't get confused thinking it is a class or a React component.

Interfaces

Interfaces are very similar to types and sometimes developers don't know the differences between them. Interfaces can be used to describe the shape of an object or function signature just like types, but the syntax is different:

```
interface User {
  username: string
  email: string
  name: string
  age?: number
  website: string
  active: boolean
}
```

You can name an interface as you want, but a good practice to follow is to add a prefix of I. For example, the User interface will become IUser. In this way, you can quickly recognize that it is an interface, and you don't get confused thinking it is a class or a React component.

An interface can also be extended, implemented, and merged.

Extending interfaces and types

An interface or type can also be extended, but again, the syntax will differ as shown in the following code block:

```
// Extending an interface
interface IWork {
  company: string
  position: string
}

interface IPerson extends IWork {
  name: string
  age: number
}
```

```typescript
// Extending a type
type TWork = {
  company: string
  position: string
}

type TPerson = TWork & {
  name: string
  age: number
}

// Extending an interface into a type
interface IWork {
  company: string
  position: string
}

type TPerson = IWork & {
  name: string
  age: number
}
```

As you can see, by using the & character, you can extend a type, while you extend an interface using the extends keyword.

Understanding the extension of interfaces and types paves the way for us to delve into their implementation. Let us transition to illustrating how classes in TypeScript can implement these interfaces and types while keeping in mind the inherent constraints when dealing with union types.

Implementing interfaces and types

A class can implement an interface or type alias in the exact same way. But it cannot implement (or extend) a *type alias* that names a union type. For example:

```typescript
// Implementing an interface
interface IWork {
  company: string
  position: string
```

```typescript
}

class Person implements IWork {
  name: 'Carlos'
  age: 35
}

// Implementing a type
type TWork = {
  company: string
  position: string
}

class Person2 implements TWork {
  name: 'Cristina'
  age: 34
}

// You can't implement a union type
type TWork2 = {
  company: string;
  position: string
} | {
  name: string;
  age: number
}

class Person3 implements TWork2 {
  company: 'Google'
  position: 'Senior Software Engineer'
}
```

If you write the preceding code, you will get the following error in your editor:

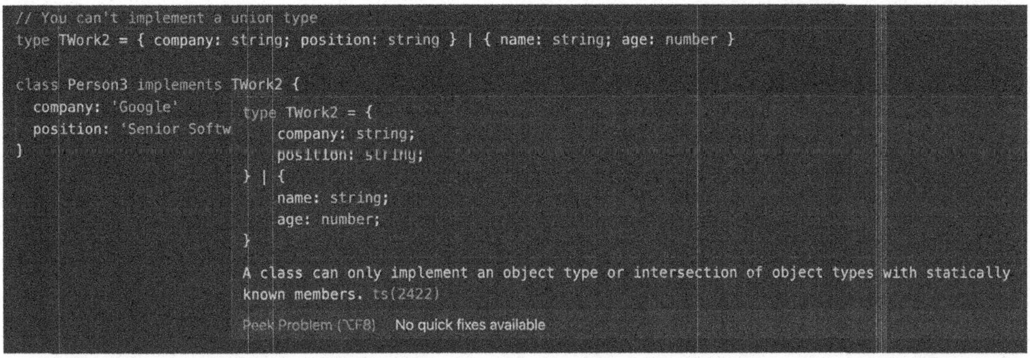

```
// You can't implement a union type
type TWork2 = { company: string; position: string } | { name: string; age: number }

class Person3 implements TWork2 {
  company: 'Google'
  position: 'Senior Softw        type TWork2 = {
}                                   company: string;
                                    position: string;
                                 } | {
                                    name: string;
                                    age: number;
                                 }

                                 A class can only implement an object type or intersection of object types with statically
                                 known members. ts(2422)

                                 Peek Problem (⌥F8)   No quick fixes available
```

Figure 2.3: A class can only implement an object type or intersection of object types with statically known members

As you can see, you are not able to implement a union type.

Merging interfaces

Unlike a type, an interface can be defined multiple times and will be treated as a single interface (all declarations will be merged), as shown in the following code block:

```
interface IUser {
  username: string
  email: string
  name: string
  age?: number
  website: string
  active: boolean
}

interface IUser {
  country: string
}
```

```
const user: IUser = {
  username: 'czantany',
  email: 'carlos@milkzoft.com',
  name: 'Carlos Santana',
  country: 'Mexico',
  age: 35,
  website: 'http://www.js.education',
  active: true
}
```

This is very useful when you need to extend your interfaces in different scenarios by just redefining the same interface.

Enums

Enums are one of the few features TypeScript has that is not a *type*-level extension of JavaScript. Enums permit a developer to define a set of **named constants**. Using enums can make it easier to document intent or create a set of distinct cases.

Enums can store numeric or string values and are normally used to provide predefined values. Personally, I like to use them to define a palette of colors in a theming system, as follows:

```
export enum Base {
  WHITE = '#FFF',
  BLACK = '#000',
  TRANSPARENT = 'transparent'
}

export enum Blue {
  V050 = '#DBEDFF',
  V100 = '#C9E3FF',
  V150 = '#4AA3FF',
  V200 = '#009ED6',
  V250 = '#007BC5',
  V300 = '#004481'
}

export enum Gray {
  V050 = '#EFF2F7',
  V100 = '#F1F4F8',
  V150 = '#74788D',
  V200 = '#636678',
  V250 = '#343A40',
  V300 = '#2C3136'
}

export type ColorPalette = Base | Blue | Gray
```

Figure 2.4: Enums used for color palette

Moving on to another useful feature of TypeScript, let's explore namespaces.

Namespaces

You may have heard of **namespaces** in other programming languages, such as Java or C++. In JavaScript, namespaces are simply named objects in the global scope. They serve as a region in which variables, functions, interfaces, or classes are organized and grouped together within a local scope to avoid naming conflicts between components in the global scope.

While modules are also used for code organization, namespaces are more straightforward to implement for simple use cases. However, modules offer additional benefits such as code isolation, bundling support, re-exporting components, and renaming components that namespaces do not provide.

In my own projects, I find namespaces useful for grouping styles when using `styled-components`, for instance:

```
import styled from 'styled-components'
export namespace CSS {
  export const InputWrapper = styled.div`
    padding: 10px;
    margin: 0;
    background: white;
    width: 250px;

  export const InputBase = styled.input`
    width: 100%;
    background: transparent;
    border: none;
    font-size: 14px;

}
```

Then when I need to use it, I consume it like this:

```
import React, { ComponentPropsWithoutRef, FC } from 'react'
import { CSS } from './Input.styled'
export interface Props extends ComponentPropsWithoutRef<'input'> {
  error?: boolean
}
```

```
const Input: FC<Props> = ({
  type = 'text',
  error = false,
  value = '',
  disabled = false,
  ...restProps
}) => (
    <CSS.InputWrapper style={error ? { border: '1px solid red' } : {}}>
      <CSS.InputBase type={type} value={value} disabled={disabled} {...
restProps} />
    </CSS.InputWrapper>
)
```

This is very useful because I don't need to worry about exporting multiple styled components. I just export the CSS namespace and I can use all the styled components defined inside that namespace.

Template literals

In TypeScript, **template literals** are based on **string literal types** and can be expanded into multiple strings using **unions**. These types are useful for defining a *theme name*, for instance:

```
type Theme = 'light' | 'dark'
```

Theme is a union type that can only be assigned one of the two string literal types: 'light' or 'dark'. This provides type safety and prevents runtime errors caused by passing an invalid value as the theme name.

Using this approach, you can define a set of possible values for a variable, argument, or parameter and ensure that only valid values are used at compile time. This makes your code more reliable and easier to maintain.

TypeScript configuration file

The presence of a tsconfig.json file in a directory indicates that the directory is the root of a TypeScript project. The tsconfig.json file specifies the root files and the compiler options required to compile the project.

You can check all the compiler options at the official TypeScript site: https://www.typescriptlang.org/tsconfig.

This is the `tsconfig.json` file that I normally use in my projects. I've always separated them into two files: the `tsconfig.common.json` file will contain all the shared compiler options, and the `tsconfig.json` file will extend the `tsconfig.common.json` file and add some specific options for that project. This is very useful when you work with **MonoRepos**.

My `tsconfig.common.json` file looks like this:

```json
{
  "compilerOptions": {
    "allowSyntheticDefaultImports": true,
    "alwaysStrict": true,
    "declaration": true,
    "declarationMap": true,
    "downlevelIteration": true,
    "esModuleInterop": true,
    "experimentalDecorators": true,
    "jsx": "react-jsx",
    "lib": ["DOM", "DOM.Iterable", "ESNext"],
    "module": "commonjs",
    "moduleResolution": "node",
    "noEmit": false,
    "noFallthroughCasesInSwitch": false,
    "noImplicitAny": true,
    "noImplicitReturns": true,
    "outDir": "dist",
    "resolveJsonModule": true,
    "skipLibCheck": true,
    "sourceMap": true,
    "strict": true,
    "strictFunctionTypes": true,
    "strictNullChecks": true,
    "suppressImplicitAnyIndexErrors": false,
    "target": "ESNext"
  },
  "exclude": ["node_modules", "dist", "coverage", ".vscode", "**/__
tests__/*"]
}
```

And my `tsconfig.json` looks like this:

```
{
  "extends": "./tsconfig.common.json",
  "compilerOptions": {
    "baseUrl": "./packages",
    "paths": {
      "@web-creator/*": ["*/src"]
    }
  }
}
```

In *Chapter 14*, I will explain how to create a MonoRepos architecture.

Summary

In this chapter, we covered the basics of TypeScript, including creating basic types and interfaces, extending them, and using enums, namespaces, and template literals. We also explored setting up our first TypeScript configuration file (`tsconfig.json`) and splitting it into two parts – one for sharing and the other for extending `tsconfig.common.json`. This approach is particularly useful when working with MonoRepos.

In the next chapter, we will delve into using JSX/TSX code and explore various configurations that can be applied to improve your code style. You will learn how to leverage the power of TypeScript to create efficient and maintainable React applications.

3

Cleaning Up Your Code

This chapter assumes that you have prior experience with **JSX (JavaScript XML)** and are interested in improving your skills to use it effectively. To use JSX/TSX without any issues or unexpected behavior, it's crucial to understand how it works under the hood and the reasons why it's a useful tool for building UIs.

Our objective is to write clean JSX/TSX code, maintain it, and have a good understanding of its inner workings, including how it's translated to JavaScript and the features it provides.

By understanding the intricacies of JSX/TSX, you can leverage its full potential to build efficient and scalable UIs. We will explore various tips and techniques to help you write better code and avoid common mistakes. By the end of this chapter, you will have a solid grasp of how JSX/TSX works and how to use it effectively in your React applications.

In this chapter, we will cover the following topics:

- What is JSX and why should we use it?
- What is Babel and how can we use it to write modern JavaScript code?
- The main features of JSX and the differences between HTML and JSX.
- Best practices to write JSX in an elegant and maintainable way.
- How linting, and ESLint in particular, can make our JavaScript code consistent across applications and teams.
- The basics of functional programming and why following a functional paradigm will make us write better React components.

Technical requirements

To complete this chapter, you will need the following:

- Node.js 19+
- Visual Studio Code

Using JSX

In *Chapter 1*, we saw how React changes the concept of separation of concerns, moving the boundaries inside components. We also learned how React uses the elements returned by the components to display the UI on the screen.

Let's now look at how we can declare elements inside our components.

React provides two ways to define elements. The first one is by using JavaScript functions, and the second one is by using JSX, an optional XML-like syntax. The following is a screenshot of the new official documentation of React.js (https://react.dev):

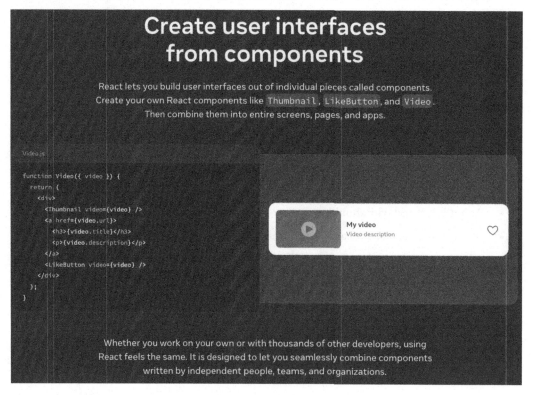

Figure 3.1: New official documentation site of React.js

To begin with, JSX is one of the main reasons why people fail to approach React, because looking at the examples on the home page and seeing JavaScript mixed with HTML for the first time can seem strange to most of us.

As soon as we get used to it, we realize that it is very convenient, precisely because it is similar to HTML and looks very familiar to anyone who has already created UIs on the web. The opening and closing tags make it easier to represent nested trees of elements, something that would have been unreadable and hard to maintain using plain JavaScript.

Let's take a look at JSX in more detail in the following sub-sections.

Babel

Babel is a popular JavaScript compiler widely used in the React community. It allows developers to write code using the latest language features, such as JSX and ES6, that may not yet be supported in all browsers. By transpiling the code into the more widely supported ES5, Babel ensures that your application runs smoothly across different browsers.

To use Babel, you'll first need to install the necessary packages. In older versions (Babel 6.x), you would install the babel-cli package, which included **babel-node** and **babel-core**. However, in more recent versions, these packages have been separated into individual modules: @babel/core, @babel/cli, @babel/node, and so on.

To install Babel, follow these steps:

1. Install the required packages globally (although local installations are generally preferred):

    ```
    npm install -g @babel/core @babel/node
    ```

2. To compile a JavaScript file using Babel, run:

    ```
    babel source.js -o output.js
    ```

3. Babel is highly configurable, and you can customize it using presets. To install the most common presets, run:

    ```
    npm install -g @babel/preset-env @babel/preset-react
    ```

4. Create a .babelrc configuration file in your project's root directory and add the following content to tell Babel to use the installed presets:

    ```
    {
      "presets": [
        "@babel/preset-env",
    ```

```
        "@babel/preset-react"
    ]
  }
```

Now, you can write ES6 and JSX in your source files, and Babel will transpile them into browser-compatible ES5 JavaScript code.

Creating our first element

Now that our environment supports JSX, let's explore a basic example: creating a div element. Using the _jsx function, we can write:

```
_jsx('div', {})
```

However, using JSX, we can simply write:

```
<div />
```

This appears similar to regular HTML, but the crucial difference is that we're writing markup within a .js file. Keep in mind that JSX is only syntactic sugar and gets transpiled into JavaScript before being executed in the browser.

When we run Babel, our <div /> element is translated into _jsx('div', {}). Remember this when crafting templates.

Starting from **React 17**, React.createElement('div') has been deprecated, and the library now uses react/jsx-runtime internally to render JSX. This means that you no longer need to import the React object to write JSX code. Instead, you can write JSX directly, as shown in the previous example.

DOM elements and React components

JSX allows us to create both HTML elements and React components, with the only difference being whether or not they start with a capital letter. For instance, to render an HTML button, we use <button />, while to render the Button component, we use <Button />.

The first button is transpiled into the following:

```
_jsx('button', {})
```

The second one is transpiled into the following:

```
_jsx(Button, {})
```

The key difference is that in the first call, we pass the type of the DOM element as a string, while in the second call, we pass the component itself. As a result, the component should exist in the scope for it to work properly.

JSX also supports self-closing tags, which are useful for keeping the code concise and avoiding unnecessary tag repetition.

Props

JSX is very convenient when your DOM elements or React components have props. Using XML is pretty easy to set attributes on elements:

```
<img src="https://www.ranchosanpancho.com/images/logo.png" alt="Cabañas
San Pancho" />
```

The equivalent in JavaScript would be as follows:

```
_jsx("img", {
  src: "https://www.ranchosanpancho.com/images/logo.png",
  alt: "Cabañas San Pancho"
})
```

This is far less readable, and even with only a couple of attributes, it is harder to read without a bit of reasoning.

Children

JSX allows you to define children to describe the tree of elements and compose complex UIs. A basic example is a link with text inside it, as follows:

```
<a href="https://ranchosanpancho.com">Click me!</a>
```

This would be transpiled into the following:

```
_jsx(
  "a",
  { href: "https://ranchosanpancho.com" },
  "Click me!"
)
```

Our link can be enclosed inside a div element for some layout requirements, and the JSX snippet to achieve that is as follows:

```
<div>
```

```
    <a href="https://ranchosanpancho.com">Click me!</a>
  </div>
```

The JavaScript equivalent is as follows:

```
_jsx(
  "div",
  null,
  _jsx(
    "a",
    { href: "https://ranchosanpancho.com" },
    "Click me!"
  )
)
```

It should now be clear how the *XML-like* syntax of JSX makes everything more readable and maintainable, but it is always important to know the JavaScript parallel to our JSX has control over the creation of elements. The good part is that we are not limited to having elements as children of elements, but we can use JavaScript expressions, such as functions or variables.

To do this, we have to enclose the expression within curly braces:

```
<div>
  Hello, {variable}.
  I'm a {() => console.log('Function')}.
</div>
```

The same applies to non-string attributes, as follows:

```
<a href={someFunction()}>Click me!</a>
```

As you see, any variable or function should be enclosed in curly braces.

Differences with HTML

So far, we have looked at the similarities between JSX and HTML. Let's now look at the little differences between them and the reasons they exist.

Attributes

We must always keep in mind that JSX is not a standard language and that it gets transpiled into JavaScript. Because of this, some attributes cannot be used.

For example, instead of `class`, we have to use `className`, and instead of `for`, we have to use `htmlFor`, as follows:

```
<label className="awesome-label" htmlFor="name" />
```

The reason for this is that `class` and `for` are reserved words in JavaScript.

Style

A pretty significant difference is the way the `style` attribute works. We will look at how to use it in more detail in *Chapter 6, Making Your Components Look Beautiful*, but now we will focus on the way it works.

The `style` attribute does not accept a CSS string as the HTML parallel does, but it expects a JavaScript object where the style names are *camelCased*:

```
<div style={{ backgroundColor: 'red' }} />
```

As you can see, you can pass an object to the `style` prop, meaning you can even have your styles in a separate variable if you want:

```
const styles = {
  backgroundColor: 'red'
}

<div style={styles} />
```

This is the best way to have better control of your inline styles.

Root

One important difference with HTML worth mentioning is that since JSX elements get translated into JavaScript functions, and you cannot return two functions in JavaScript, whenever you have multiple elements at the same level, you are forced to wrap them in a parent.

Let's look at a simple example:

```
<div />
<div />
```

This gives us the following error:

```
Adjacent JSX elements must be wrapped in an enclosing tag.
```

On the other hand, the following works:

```
<div>
  <div />
  <div />
</div>
```

Before, React forced you to return an element wrapped with an `<div>` element or any other tag; since **React 16.2.0**, it is possible to return an array directly as follows:

```
return [
  <li key="1">First item</li>,
  <li key="2">Second item</li>,
  <li key="3">Third item</li>
]
```

Or you can even return a string directly, as shown in the following code block:

```
return 'Hello World!'
```

Also, React now has a new feature called `Fragment` that also works as a special wrapper for elements. It can be specified with `React.Fragment`:

```
import { Fragment } from 'react'
return (
  <Fragment>
    <h1>An h1 heading</h1>
    Some text here.
    <h2>An h2 heading</h2>
    More text here.
    Even more text here.
  </Fragment>
)
```

Or you can use empty tags (`<></>`):

```
return (
  <>
    <ComponentA />
    <ComponentB />
    <ComponentC />
  </>
```

```
  )
```

`Fragment` won't render anything visible on the DOM; it is just a helper tag to wrap your React elements or components.

Spaces

There's one thing that could be a little bit tricky in the beginning and, again, it concerns the fact that we should always keep in mind that JSX is not HTML, even if it has XML-like syntax. JSX handles the spaces between text and elements differently from HTML, in a way that's counter-intuitive.

Consider the following snippet:

```
<div>
  <span>My</span>
  name is
  <span>Carlos</span>
</div>
```

In a browser that interprets HTML, this code would give you `My name is Carlos`, which is exactly what we expect.

In JSX, the same code would be rendered as `MynameisCarlos`, which is because the three nested lines get transpiled as individual children of the `div` element, without taking the spaces into account. A common solution to get the same output is putting a space explicitly between the elements, as follows:

```
<div>
  <span>My</span>
  {' '}
  name is
  {' '}
  <span>Carlos</span>
</div>
```

As you may have noticed, we are using an empty string wrapped inside a JavaScript expression to force the compiler to apply a space between the elements.

Boolean attributes

A couple more things are worth mentioning before really starting regarding the way you define Boolean attributes in JSX.

If you set an attribute without a value, JSX assumes that its value is true, following the same behavior as the HTML disabled attribute, for example.

This means that if we want to set an attribute to false, we have to declare it explicitly as false:

```
<button disabled />
_jsx("button", { disabled: true })
```

The following is another example of the Boolean attribute:

```
<button disabled={false} />
_jsx("button", { disabled: false })
```

This can be confusing in the beginning, because we may think that omitting an attribute would mean false, but it is not like that. With React, we should always be explicit to avoid confusion.

Spread attributes

An important feature is the spread attribute operator (...), which comes from the rest/spread properties for ECMAScript "proposal" and is very convenient whenever we want to pass all the attributes of a JavaScript object to an element.

A common practice that leads to fewer bugs is not to pass entire JavaScript objects down to children by reference, but to use their primitive values, which can be easily validated, making components more robust and error-proof.

Let's see how it works:

```
const attrs = {
  id: 'myId',
  className: 'myClass'
}
return <div {...attrs} />
```

The preceding code gets transpiled into the following:

```
var attrs = {
  id: 'myId',
  className: 'myClass'
}
return _jsx('div', attrs)
```

Template literals

Template literals are string literals that allow for embedded expressions, multiline strings, and string interpolation. They are enclosed by the backtick (` `` `) character instead of single or double quotes.

One of the most useful features of template literals is the ability to include placeholders using the dollar sign and curly braces (`${expression}`). This allows us to easily interpolate variables or complex expressions into our string templates. Here's an example:

```
const name = 'Carlos'
const age = 35
const message = `Hello, my name is ${name} and I am ${age} years old.`
console.log(message)
```

This will log the following output:

```
Hello, my name is Carlos and I am 35 years old.
```

In addition to string interpolation, template literals also support multiline strings, making it easier to write and read complex strings without needing to concatenate multiple strings with the plus (+) operator.

Common patterns

Now that we know how JSX works and can master it, we are ready to see how to use it in the right way following some useful conventions and techniques.

Multiline

Let's start with a very simple one. As stated previously, one of the main reasons we should prefer JSX over React's _jsx function is because of its XML-like syntax, and because balanced opening and closing tags are perfect to represent a tree of nodes.

Therefore, we should try to use it in the right way and get the most out of it. One example is as follows; whenever we have nested elements, we should always go multiline:

```
<div>
  <Header />
  <div>
    <Main content={...} />
  </div>
</div>
```

This is preferable to the following:

```
<div><Header /><div><Main content={...} /></div></div>
```

The exception is if the children are not elements such as text or variables. In that case, it makes sense to remain on the same line and avoid adding noise to the markup, as follows:

```
<div>
  <Alert>{message}</Alert>
  <Button>Close</Button>
</div>
```

Always remember to wrap your elements inside parentheses when you write them on multiple lines. JSX always gets replaced by functions, and functions written on a new line can give you an unexpected result because of automatic semicolon insertion. Suppose, for example, that you are returning JSX from your render method, which is how you create UIs in React.

The following example works fine because the div element is on the same line as the `return`:

```
return <div />
```

The following, however, is not right:

```
return
  <div />
```

The reason for this is that you would then have the following:

```
return
_jsx("div", null)
```

This is why you have to wrap the statement in parentheses, as follows:

```
return (
  <div />
)
```

Multi-properties

A common problem in writing JSX comes when an element has multiple attributes. One solution is to write all the attributes on the same line, but this would lead to very long lines that we do not want in our code (see the following section for how to enforce coding style guides).

A common solution is to write each attribute on a new line, with one level of indentation, and then align the closing bracket with the opening tag:

```
<button
  foo="bar"
  veryLongPropertyName="baz"
  onSomething={this.handleSomething}
/>
```

Conditionals

Things get more interesting when we start working with conditionals, for example, if we want to render some components only when certain conditions are matched. The fact that we can use JavaScript in our conditions is a big plus, but there are many ways to express conditions in JSX, and it is important to understand the benefits and problems of each one of these to write code that is both readable and maintainable.

Suppose we want to show a logout button only if the user is currently logged in to our application.

A simple snippet to start with is as follows:

```
let button

if (isLoggedIn) {
  button = <LogoutButton />
}


return <div>{button}</div>
```

This works, but it is not very readable, especially if there are multiple components and multiple conditions.

In JSX, we can use an inline condition:

```
<div>
  {isLoggedIn && <LoginButton />}
</div>
```

This works because if the condition is false, nothing gets rendered, but if the condition is true, the createElement function of LoginButton gets called, and the element is returned to compose the resulting tree.

If the condition has an alternative (the classic `if...else` statement) and we want, for example, to show a logout button if the user is logged in and a login button otherwise, we can use JavaScript's `if...else` statement as follows:

```
let button

if (isLoggedIn) {
  button = <LogoutButton />
} else {
  button = <LoginButton />
}


return <div>{button}</div>
```

Alternatively, and better still, we can use a ternary condition that makes the code more compact:

```
<div>
  {isLoggedIn ? <LogoutButton /> : <LoginButton />}
</div>
```

You can find the ternary condition used in popular repositories, such as the Redux real-world example (`https://github.com/reactjs/redux/blob/master/examples/real-world/src/components/List.js#L28`), where the ternary is used to show a `Loading` label if the component is fetching the data or `Load More` inside a button depending on the value of the `isFetching` variable:

```
<button [...]>
  {isFetching ? 'Loading...' : 'Load More'}
</button>
```

Let's now look at the best solution for when things get more complicated and, for example, we have to check more than one variable to determine whether to render a component or not:

```
<div>
  {dataIsReady && (isAdmin || userHasPermissions) &&
    <SecretData />
  }
</div>
```

In this case, it is clear that using the inline condition is a good solution, but the readability is strongly impacted. Instead, we can create a helper function inside our component and use it in JSX to verify the condition:

```
const MyComponent = ({ dataIsReady, isAdmin, userHasPermissions }) => {
  const canShowSecretData - () => {
    return dataIsReady && (isAdmin || userHasPermissions)
  }

  return (
    <div>
      {canShowSecretData() && <SecretData />}
    </div>
  )
}
```

As you can see, this change makes the code more readable and the condition more explicit. If you look at this code in 6 months, you will still find it clear just by reading the name of the function.

The same applies to computed properties. Suppose you have two single properties for currency and value. Instead of creating the price string inside render, you can create a function:

```
const MyComponent = ({ currency, value }) => {
  const getPrice = () => {
    return `${currency}${value}`
  }

  return <div>{getPrice()}</div>
}
```

This is better because it is isolated, and you can easily test it if it contains logic.

Going back to conditional statements, we can create a custom component and call it `RenderIf` to render our components conditionally:

```
import React, { FC, ReactElement } from 'react'
interface Props {
  children: ReactElement | string
  isTrue?: Boolean
  isFalse?: Boolean
}
```

```
const RenderIf: FC<Props> = ({ children, isTrue, isFalse }) => {
  if (isTrue === true) {
    return <>{children}</>
  }

  if (isFalse === false) {
    return <>{children}</>
  }
  return null
}
export default RenderIf
```

We can then easily use it in our projects, as follows:

```
import RenderIf from './RenderIf'

const MyComponent = ({ dataIsReady, isAdmin, userHasPermissions }) => {
  return (
    <div>
      <RenderIf isTrue={dataIsReady && (isAdmin || userHasPermissions)}>
        <SecretData />
      </RenderIf>
    </div>
  )
}
```

Loops

A very common operation in UI development is to display lists of items. When it comes to showing lists, using JavaScript as a template language is a very good idea.

If we write a function that returns an array inside our JSX template, each element of the array gets compiled into an element.

As we have seen before, we can use any JavaScript expressions inside curly braces, and the most common way to generate an array of elements, given an array of objects, is to use map.

Let's dive into a real-world example. Suppose you have a list of users, each one with a name property attached to it.

To create an unordered list to show the users, you can do the following:

```
<ul>
  {users.map(user => <li>{user.name}</li>)}
</ul>
```

This snippet is incredibly simple and incredibly powerful at the same time, where the power of HTML and JavaScript converge.

Sub-rendering

It is worth stressing that we always want to keep our components very small and our render methods very clean and simple.

However, that is not an easy goal, especially when you are creating an application iteratively, and in the first iteration, you are not sure exactly how to split the components into smaller ones. So, what should we be doing when the render method becomes too big to maintain? One solution is to split it into smaller functions in a way that lets us keep all the logic in the same component.

Let's look at an example:

```
const renderUserMenu = () => {
  // JSX for user menu
}

const renderAdminMenu = () => {
  // JSX for admin menu
}

return (
  <div>
    <h1>Welcome back!</h1>
    {userExists && renderUserMenu()}
    {userIsAdmin && renderAdminMenu()}
  </div>
)
```

This is not always considered best practice because it seems more obvious to split the component into smaller ones. However, sometimes it helps to keep the render method cleaner. For example, in the Redux real-world examples, a sub-render method is used to render the *load more* button.

Now that we are JSX power users, it is time to move on and see how to follow a style guide within our code to make it consistent.

Styling code

In this section, you will learn how to implement **EditorConfig** and **ESLint** to improve your code quality by validating your code style. It is important to have a standard code style in your team and avoid using different code styles.

EditorConfig

EditorConfig helps developers to maintain consistent coding styles between different IDEs.

EditorConfig is supported by a lot of editors. You can check whether your editor is supported or not on the official website, https://www.editorconfig.org.

You need to create a file called .editorconfig in your root directory – the configuration I use is this one:

```
root = true

[*]
indent_style = space
indent_size = 2
end_of_line = lf
charset = utf-8
trim_trailing_whitespace = true
insert_final_newline = true

[*.html]
indent_size = 4

[*.css]
indent_size = 4

[*.md]
trim_trailing_whitespace = false
```

You can affect all the files with [*], and specific files with [.extension].

Prettier

Prettier is an opinionated code formatter, supported by many languages, that can be integrated with most editors. This plugin is really useful because you can format the code on saving and you don't need to discuss the code style in code reviews, which will save you a lot of time and energy.

If you work with Visual Studio Code, you have to install the Prettier extension first:

Figure 3.2: Prettier – Code formatter

Then, if you want to configure the option to format when you save a file, you need to go to **Settings**, search for Format on Save, and check that option:

Figure 3.3: Configuring option to format when saving a file

This will affect all your projects because it is a global setting. If you want to apply this option just in a specific project, you have to create a .vscode folder inside your project and a settings.json file with the following code:

```
{
    "editor.defaultFormatter": "esbenp.prettier-vscode",
    "editor.formatOnSave": true
}
```

Then you can configure the options you want in your `.prettierrc` file – this is the configuration I normally use:

```
{
  "arrowParens": "avoid",
  "bracketSpacing": true,
  "jsxSingleQuote": false,
  "printWidth": 100,
  "quoteProps": "as-needed",
  "semi": false,
  "singleQuote": true,
  "tabWidth": 2,
  "trailingComma": "none",
  "useTabs": false
}
```

This will help you or your team to standardize the code style.

ESLint

Writing high-quality code is always our goal, but errors can still occur, and spending hours hunting down a bug caused by a simple typo can be incredibly frustrating. Thankfully, there are tools that can help us catch these errors as soon as we type them, allowing us to avoid simple syntactical mistakes.

If you're coming from a statically typed language like C#, you may be used to getting warnings inside your IDE. In the JavaScript world, the popular tool for linting code is ESLint. ESLint is an open-source project released in 2013 that is highly configurable and extensible.

In the fast-paced JavaScript ecosystem, where libraries and techniques change frequently, it's crucial to have a tool that can be easily extended with plugins and rules that can be enabled or disabled as needed. Additionally, with transpilers like Babel and experimental language features that aren't yet part of the standard JavaScript version, we need to be able to tell our linter which rules we're following in our source files. A linter not only helps us catch errors sooner, but it also enforces common coding style guides, which is particularly important in large teams where consistency is key.

In the following sections, we'll take a closer look at ESLint and how it can help us write better, more consistent code.

Installation

First of all, we have to install ESLint and some plugins as follows:

```
npm install -g eslint eslint-config-airbnb eslint-config-prettier eslint-
plugin-import eslint-plugin-jsx-a11y eslint-plugin-prettier eslint-plugin-
react
```

Once the executable is installed, we can run it with the following command:

```
eslint source.ts
```

The output will tell us if there are errors within the file.

When we install and run it for the first time, we do not see any errors because it is completely configurable, and it does not come with any default rules.

Configuration

Let's start configuring ESLint. It can be configured using a `.eslintrc` file that lives in the root folder of the project. To add some rules, let's create a `.eslintrc` file configured for TypeScript and add one basic rule:

```
{
  "parser": "@typescript-eslint/parser",
  "plugins": ["@typescript-eslint", "prettier"],
  "extends": [
    "airbnb",
    "eslint:recommended",
    "plugin:@typescript-eslint/eslint-recommended",
    "plugin:@typescript-eslint/recommended",
    "plugin:prettier/recommended"
  ],
  "settings": {
    "import/extensions": [".js", ".jsx", ".ts", ".tsx"],
    "import/parsers": {
      "@typescript-eslint/parser": [".ts", ".tsx"]
    },
    "import/resolver": {
      "node": {
        "extensions": [".js", ".jsx", ".ts", ".tsx"]
      }
```

```
    }
  },
  "rules": {
    "semi": [2, "never"]
  }
}
```

This configuration file needs a bit of explanation: `"semi"` is the name of the rule and `[2, "never"]` is the value. It is not very intuitive the first time you see it.

ESLint rules have three levels that determine the severity of the problem:

1.   `off` (or 0): The rule is disabled.
2.   `warn` (or 1): The rule is a warning.
3.   `error` (or 2): The rule throws an error.

We are using the value 2 because we want ESLint to throw an error every time our code does not follow the rule. The second parameter tells ESLint that we want the semicolon to never be used (the opposite is *always*). ESLint and its plugins are very well documented, and for any single rule, you can find the description of the rule and some examples of when it passes and when it fails.

Now create an `index.ts` file with the following content:

```
const foo = 'bar';
```

If we run `eslint index.js`, we get the following:

```
Extra semicolon (semi)
```

This is great; we set up the linter and it is helping us follow our first rule.

Here are other rules that I prefer to turn off or change:

```
"rules": {
    "semi": [2, "never"],
    "@typescript-eslint/class-name-casing": "off",
    "@typescript-eslint/interface-name-prefix": "off",
    "@typescript-eslint/member-delimiter-style": "off",
    "@typescript-eslint/no-var-requires": "off",
    "@typescript-eslint/ban-ts-ignore": "off",
```

```
    "@typescript-eslint/no-use-before-define": "off",
    "@typescript-eslint/ban-ts-comment": "off",
    "@typescript-eslint/explicit-module-boundary-types": "off",
    "no-restricted-syntax": "off",
    "no-use-before-define": "off",
    "import/extensions": "off",
    "import/prefer-default-export": "off",
    "max-len": [
      "error",
      {
        "code": 100,
        "tabWidth": 2
      }
    ],
    "no-param-reassign": "off",
    "no-underscore-dangle": "off",
    "react/jsx-filename-extension": [
      1,
      {
        "extensions": [".tsx"]
      }
    ],
    "import/no-unresolved": "off",
    "consistent-return": "off",
    "jsx-a11y/anchor-is-valid": "off",
    "sx-a11y/click-events-have-key-events": "off",
    "jsx-a11y/no-noninteractive-element-interactions": "off",
    "jsx-a11y/click-events-have-key-events": "off",
    "jsx-a11y/no-static-element-interactions": "off",
    "react/jsx-props-no-spreading": "off",
    "jsx-a11y/label-has-associated-control": "off",
    "react/jsx-one-expression-per-line": "off",
    "no-prototype-builtins": "off",
    "no-nested-ternary": "off",
    "prettier/prettier": [
      "error",
```

```
    {
      "endOfLine": "auto"
    }
  ]
}
```

Git Hooks

To avoid having unlinted code in our repository, what we can do is add ESLint at one point of our process using Git Hooks. For example, we can use husky to run our linter in a Git Hook called pre-commit, and it is also useful to run our unit tests on the Hook called pre-push.

To install husky, you need to run the following command:

```
npm install --save-dev husky
```

Then, in our package.json file, we can add this node to configure the tasks we want to run in the Git Hooks.

Edit the package.json > prepare script and run it once:

```
npm pkg set scripts.prepare="husky install"
npm run prepare
```

Add a hook:

```
npx husky add .husky/pre-commit "npm run lint"
git add .husky/pre-commit
```

Make a commit:

```
git commit -m "Keep calm and commit"
# `npm run lint` will run every time you commit
```

There is a special option (flag) for the ESlint command called --fix – with this option, ESLint will try to fix all our linter errors automatically (not all of them). Be careful with this option because sometimes it can affect a little bit of our code style. Another useful flag is --ext to specify the extensions of the files we want to validate – in this case, just the .tsx and .ts files.

In the next section, you will learn about how **functional programming** (**FP**) works and topics such as first-class objects, purity, immutability, currying, and composition.

Functional programming

In addition to following best practices and using a linter to catch errors and enforce consistency, another way to clean up our code is to adopt an **FP** style.

As we discussed in *Chapter 1, Taking Your First Steps with React*, React's declarative programming approach makes our code more readable. FP is a declarative paradigm as well, where side effects are avoided, and data is considered immutable to make the code easier to maintain and reason about.

While we won't cover FP in depth in this section, we'll introduce some concepts commonly used in React that you should be aware of.

FP principles, such as immutability, pure functions, and higher-order functions, can help us write more maintainable and testable code. By treating our data as immutable, we can avoid side effects and make it easier to reason about the flow of our application. Pure functions, which always return the same output for the same input, help us avoid unintended side effects and make our code easier to test. Higher-order functions, which take functions as arguments and/or return functions as output, can help us create more modular and reusable code.

By adopting an FP style, we can write more declarative and less imperative code, making our components easier to read and reason about.

First-class functions

JavaScript has first-class functions because they are treated like any other variable, meaning you can pass a function as a parameter to other functions, or it can be returned by another function and be assigned as a value to a variable.

This allows us to introduce the concept of **Higher-Order Functions (HoFs)**. HoFs are functions that take a function as a parameter, and optionally some other parameters, and return a function. The returned function is usually enhanced with some special behaviors.

Let's look at an example:

```
const add = (x, y) => x + y

const log = fn => (...args) => {
  return fn(...args)
}

const logAdd = log(add)
```

Here, a function is adding two numbers that enhance a function that logs all the parameters and then executes the original function.

This concept is pretty important to understand because, in the React world, a common pattern is to use Higher-Order Components to treat our components as functions, and to enhance them with common behaviors. We will see HOCs and other patterns in *Chapter 4, Exploring Popular Composition Patterns*.

Purity

An important aspect of FP is to write pure functions. You will encounter this concept very often in the React ecosystem, especially if you look into libraries such as Redux.

What does it mean for a function to be pure?

A function is pure when there are no side effects, which means that the function does not change anything that is not local to the function itself.

For example, a function that changes the state of an application, or modifies variables defined in the upper scope, or a function that touches external entities, such as the **Document Object Model (DOM)**, is considered impure. Impure functions are harder to debug, and most of the time it is not possible to apply them multiple times and expect to get the same result.

For example, the following function is pure:

```
const add = (x, y) => x + y
```

It can be run multiple times, always getting the same result, because nothing is stored anywhere, and nothing gets modified.

The following function is not pure:

```
let x = 0
const add = y => (x = x + y)
```

Running add(1) twice, we get two different results. The first time we get 1, but the second time we get 2, even if we call the same function with the same parameter. The reason we get that behavior is that the global state gets modified after every execution.

Immutability

We have seen how to write pure functions that don't mutate the state, but what if we need to change the value of a variable? In FP, a function, instead of changing the value of a variable, creates a new variable with a new value and returns it.

This way of working with data is called **immutability**.

An immutable value is a value that cannot be changed.

Let's look at an example:

```
const add3 = arr => arr.push(3)
const myArr = [1, 2]


add3(myArr); // [1, 2, 3]
add3(myArr); // [1, 2, 3, 3]
```

The preceding function doesn't follow immutability because it changes the value of the given array. Again, if we call the same function twice, we get different results.

We can change the preceding function to make it immutable using concat, which returns a new array without modifying the given one:

```
const add3 = arr => arr.concat(3)
const myArr = [1, 2]
const result1 = add3(myArr) // [1, 2, 3]
const result2 = add3(myArr) // [1, 2, 3]
```

After we have run the function twice, myArr still has its original value.

Currying

A common technique in FP is currying. Currying is the process of converting a function that takes multiple arguments into a function one argument at a time and returning another function. Let's look at an example to clarify the concept.

Let's start with the add function we have seen before and transform it into a curried function.

Say we have the following code:

```
const add = (x, y) => x + y
```

We can instead define the function as follows:

```
const add = x => y => x + y
```

We use it in the following way:

```
const add1 = add(1)
```

```
add1(2); // 3
add1(3); // 4
```

This is a pretty convenient way of writing functions because, since the first value is stored after the application of the first parameter, we can reuse the second function multiple times.

Composition

Finally, an important concept in FP that can be applied to React is **composition**. Functions (and components) can be combined to produce new functions with more advanced features and properties.

Consider the following functions:

```
const add = (x, y) => x + y
const square = x => x * x
```

These functions can be composed together to create a new function that adds two numbers and then doubles the result:

```
const addAndSquare = (x, y) => square(add(x, y))
```

Following this paradigm, we end up with small, simple, testable pure functions that can be composed together.

Summary

In this chapter, we have covered the fundamentals of JSX, including its syntax and features. We have also learned how to configure Prettier and ESLint to maintain consistency and catch errors early on in our codebase. Additionally, we have explored some essential concepts of functional programming, which can help us write more maintainable and testable code.

With our code now clean and well-organized, we are ready to dive deeper into React and learn how to write truly reusable components in the next chapter. By following best practices and adopting good coding habits, we can create React applications that are easier to maintain, scale, and test.

Join our community on Discord

Join our community's Discord space for discussion with the author and other readers:

`https://packt.link/React18DesignPatterns4e`

Exploring Popular Composition Patterns

In this chapter, we will learn how to make components communicate with each other effectively, which is a crucial part of building complex React applications using small, testable, and maintainable components. By mastering the popular composition patterns and tools in React, you will be able to take control of every single part of your application and build scalable and extensible software.

Let's dive in and explore how we can leverage these patterns and tools to build better React applications. We will cover the following topics:

- How components communicate with each other using props and children
- The container and presentational patterns and how they can make our code more maintainable
- What **higher-order components (HOCs)** are and how, thanks to them, we can structure our applications in a better way
- What the function of the child component pattern is and what its benefits are

Technical requirements

To complete this chapter, you will need the following:

- Node.js 19+
- Visual Studio Code

You can find the code for this chapter in the book's GitHub repository at `https://github.com/PacktPublishing/React-18-Design-Patterns-and-Best-Practices-Fourth-Edition/tree/main/Chapter04`.

Communicating components

Composing React components is one of the key benefits of building applications with React. By creating small, **reusable components** with clean interfaces, you can easily compose them together to create complex applications that are both powerful and maintainable.

Small components with a clean interface can be composed together to create complex applications that are powerful and maintainable at the same time.

Composing React components is straightforward; you just have to include them in the render:

```
const Profile = ({ user }) => (
  <>
    <Picture profileImageUrl={user.profileImageUrl} />
    <UserName name={user.name} screenName={user.screenName} />
  </>
)
```

For example, you can create a `Profile` component by simply composing a `Picture` component to display the profile image and a `UserName` component to display the name and the screen name of the user.

In this way, you can produce new parts of the user interface very quickly, writing only a few lines of code. Whenever you compose components, as in the preceding example, you share data between them using props. Props are the way a parent component can pass its data down the tree to every component that needs it (or part of it).

When a component passes some props to another component, it is called the owner, irrespective of the parent-child relationship between them. For example, in the preceding snippet, `Profile` is not the direct parent of `Picture` (the `div` tag is), but `Profile` owns `Picture` because it passes down the props to it.

In the next section, you will learn about the `children` prop and how to use it correctly.

Using the children prop

There is a special prop that can be passed from the owners to the components defined inside their render—children.

In the React documentation, it is described as opaque because it is a property that does not tell you anything about the value it contains. Subcomponents defined inside the render of a parent component usually receive props that are passed as attributes of the component itself in JSX, or as a second parameter of the _jsx function. Components can also be defined with nested components inside them, and they can access those children using the children prop.

Consider that we have a Button component that has a text property representing the text of the button:

```
const Button = ({ text }) => <button className="btn">{text}</button>
```

The component can be used in the following way:

```
<Button text="Click me!" />
```

And this will render the following code:

```
<button class="btn">Click me!</button>
```

Now, suppose we want to use the same button with the same class name in multiple parts of our application, and we also want to be able to display more than a simple string. Our UI consists of buttons with text, buttons with text and icons, and buttons with text and labels.

In most cases, a good solution would be to add multiple parameters to Button or to create different versions of Button, each one with its single specialization, for example, IconButton.

However, we should realize that Button could just be a wrapper, and we are able to render any element inside it and use the children property:

```
const Button = ({ children }) => <button className="btn">{children}</
button>
```

By passing the children prop, we are not limited to a simple single text property, but we can pass any element to Button, and it is rendered in place of the children property.

In this case, any element that we wrap inside the Button component will be rendered as a child of the button element with btn as the class name.

For example, if we want to render an image inside the button and some text wrapped in a span tag, we can do this:

```
<Button>
    <img src="..." alt="..." />
    <span>Click me!</span>
</Button>
```

The preceding snippet gets rendered in the browser as follows:

```
<button class="btn">
    <img src="..." alt="..." />
    <span>Click me!</span>
</button>
```

This is a pretty convenient way to allow components to accept any children elements and wrap those elements inside a predefined parent.

Now, we can pass images, labels, and even other React components inside the Button component, and they will be rendered as its children. As you can see in the preceding example, we defined the children property as an array, which means that we can pass any number of elements as the component's children.

We can pass a single child, as shown in the following code:

```
<Button>
    <span>Click me!</span>
</Button>
```

Let's now explore the container and the presentational pattern in the next section.

Exploring the container and presentational patterns

In the last chapter, we saw how to take a coupled component and make it reusable step by step. Now we will see how to apply a similar pattern to our components to make them clearer and more maintainable.

React components typically contain a mix of *logic* and *presentation*. By logic, we refer to anything that is unrelated to the UI, such as API calls, data manipulation, and event handlers. The presentation is the part of the render where we create the elements to be displayed on the UI.

In React, there are simple and powerful patterns, known as container and presentational, which we can apply when creating components that help us to separate those two concerns.

Creating well-defined boundaries between logic and presentation not only makes components more reusable, but also provides many other benefits, which you will learn about in this section. Again, one of the best ways to learn new concepts is by seeing practical examples, so let's delve into some code.

Suppose we have a component that uses geolocation APIs to get the position of the user and displays the latitude and longitude on the page in the browser.

First, we create a `Geolocation.tsx` file in our `components` folder and define the `Geolocation` component using a functional component:

```
import { useState, useEffect } from 'react'
const Geolocation = () => {}
export default Geolocation
```

We then define our states:

```
const [latitude, setLatitude] = useState<number | null>(null)
const [longitude, setLongitude] = useState<number | null>(null)
```

Now, we can use the useEffect Hook to fire the request to the APIs:

```
useEffect(() => {
    if (navigator.geolocation) {
        navigator.geolocation.getCurrentPosition(handleSuccess)
        }
}, [navigator])
```

When the browser returns the data, we store the result in the state using the following function (place this function before the useEffect Hook):

```
const handleSuccess = ({
    coords: { latitude, longitude }
  }: { coords: { latitude: number; longitude: number }}) => {
    setLatitude(latitude)
    setLongitude(longitude)
}
```

Finally, we show the latitude and longitude values:

```
return (
    <div>
        <h1>Geolocation:</h1>
        <div>Latitude: {latitude}</div>
        <div>Longitude: {longitude}</div>
    </div>
)
```

It is important to note that, during the first render, the latitude and longitude are null because we asked the browser for the coordinates when the component was mounted. In a real-world component, you might want to display a spinner until the data gets returned. To do that, you can use one of the conditional techniques we saw in *Chapter 3, Cleaning Up Your Code*.

Now, this component does not have any problems, and it works as expected. Wouldn't it be nice to separate it from the part where the position gets requested and loaded to iterate faster on it?

We will use the container and presentational patterns to isolate the presentational part. In this pattern, every component is split into two smaller ones, each one with its clear responsibilities. The container knows everything about the logic of the component and is where the APIs are called. It also deals with data manipulation and event handling.

The presentational component is where the UI is defined, and it receives data in the form of props from the container. Since the presentational component is usually logic-free, we can create it as a functional, stateless component.

There are no rules that say that the presentational component must not have a state (for example, it could keep a UI state inside it). In this case, we need a component to display the latitude and longitude, so we are going to use a simple function.

First of all, we should rename our `Geolocation` component `GeolocationContainer`:

```
const GeolocationContainer = () => {...}
```

We will also change the filename from `Geolocation.tsx` to `GeolocationContainer.tsx`.

This rule is not strict, but it is a best practice that's widely used in the React community to append Container to the end of the Container component name and give the original name to the presentational one.

We also have to change the implementation of render and remove all the UI parts of it, as follows:

```
return <Geolocation latitude={latitude} longitude={longitude} />
```

As you can see in the preceding snippet, instead of creating the HTML elements inside the return of the container, we just use the presentational one (which we will create next), and we pass the state to it. The states are the latitude and longitude, which are null by default, and they contain the real position of the user when the browser fires the callback.

Let's create a new file, called Geolocation.tsx, where we define the functional component as follows:

```
import { FC } from 'react'
type Props = {
  latitude: number
  longitude: number
}
const Geolocation: FC<Props> = ({ latitude, longitude }) => (
  <div>
    <h1>Geolocation:</h1>
    <div>Latitude: {latitude}</div>
    <div>Longitude: {longitude}</div>
  </div>
)
export default Geolocation
```

Functional components are an incredibly elegant way to define UIs. They are pure functions that, given a state, return the elements of it. In this case, our function receives the latitude and longitude from the owner, and it returns the markup structure to display it.

The first time you run the components in the browser, the browser will require your permission to allow it to know your location.

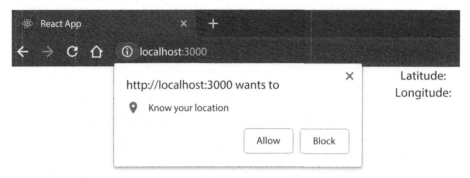

Figure 4.1: Browser will require your permission to access your location

After you allow the browser to know your location, you will see something like this:

Figure 4.2: Displaying latitude and longitude

In adherence to the container and presentational pattern, we have created a "dumb" or presentational component that is reusable and can be effortlessly integrated into our components. This enables us to conveniently pass mock coordinates for testing or demonstration purposes. If a similar data structure is needed elsewhere in the application, it eliminates the necessity of building a new component from scratch. Instead, we can encapsulate this existing component within a new container. This container could, for example, be designed to retrieve latitude and longitude information from a separate endpoint.

At the same time, other developers in our team can improve the container that uses geolocation by adding some error-handling logic, without affecting its presentation. They can even build a temporary presentational component just to display and debug data and then replace it with the real presentational component when it is ready.

Being able to work in parallel on the same component is a big win for teams, especially for those companies where building interfaces is an iterative process.

This pattern is simple but very powerful, and when applied to big applications, it can make a difference when it comes to the speed of development and the maintainability of the project. On the other hand, applying this pattern without a real reason can give us the opposite problem and make the code base less useful as it involves the creation of more files and components.

So, we should think carefully when we decide that a component has to be refactored following the container and presentational patterns. In general, the right path to follow is starting with a single component and splitting it only when the logic and the presentation become too coupled where they shouldn't be.

In our example, we began with a single component, and we realized that we could separate the API call from the markup. Deciding what to put in the container and what goes into the presentation is not always straightforward; the following points should help you make that decision:

The following are the characteristics of container components:

- They are more concerned with behavior.
- They render their presentational components.
- They make API calls and manipulate data.
- They define event handlers.

The following are the characteristics of presentational components:

- They are more concerned with the visual representation.
- They render the HTML markup (or other components).
- They receive data from the parents in the form of props.
- They are often written as stateless functional components.

As you can see, these patterns form a really powerful tool that will help you to develop your web applications faster. Let's see what HOCs are in the next section.

Understanding HOCs

In the *functional programming* section of *Chapter 3, Cleaning Up Your Code*, we introduced the concept of **higher-order functions (HOFs)**. HOFs are functions that accept another function as an argument, enhance its behavior, and return a new function. Applying the idea of HOFs to components results in **higher-order components (HOCs)**.

An HOC looks like this:

```
const HoC = Component => EnhancedComponent
```

HOCs are functions that take a component as input and return an enhanced component as output. Let's start with a simple example to understand what an enhanced component looks like.

Suppose you need to attach the same `className` property to every component. You could manually add the `className` property to each render method, or you could write an HOC like this:

```
const withClassName = Component => props => (
  <Component {...props} className="my-class" />
)
```

In the React community, it's common to use the `with` prefix for HOCs.

The code above might be confusing at first, so let's break it down. We declare a `withClassName` function that takes a `Component` and returns another function. The returned function is a functional component that receives some props and renders the original component. The collected props are spread, and a `className` property with the `"my-class"` value is passed to the functional component.

HOCs typically spread the props they receive on the component because they aim to be transparent and only add new behavior.

While this example is simple and not particularly useful, it should give you a better understanding of what HOCs are and what they look like. Now, let's see how we can use the `withClassName` HOC in our components.

First, create a stateless functional component that receives the `className` and applies it to a `div` tag:

```
const MyComponent = ({ className }) => <div className={className} />
```

Instead of using the component directly, we pass it to an HOC like this:

```
const MyComponentWithClassName = withClassName(MyComponent)
```

Wrapping our components in the `withClassName` function ensures that they receive the `className` property.

Now, let's create a more exciting HOC to detect the `innerWidth`. First, create a function that receives a `Component`:

```
import { useEffect, useState } from 'react'
const withInnerWidth = Component => props => <Component {...props} />
```

It's common practice to prefix HOCs that provide information to the components they enhance using the with pattern.

Next, define the innerWidth state and the handleResize function:

```
const withInnerWidth = Component => props => {
  const [innerWidth, setInnerWidth] = useState(window.innerWidth)
  const handleResize = () => {
    setInnerWidth(window.innerWidth)
  }
  return <Component {...props} />
}
```

Then, add the effects:

```
useEffect(() => {
  window.addEventListener('resize', handleResize)
  return () => {
    window.removeEventListener('resize', handleResize)
  }
}, [])
```

Finally, render the original component like this:

```
return <Component {...props} innerWidth={innerWidth} />
```

Here, we spread the props as before, but we also pass the innerWidth state.

We store the innerWidth value as a state to achieve the original behavior without polluting the component's state. Instead, we use props. Using props is an excellent way to promote reusability.

Now, using an HOC and getting the innerWidth value is straightforward. The new React Hooks can easily replace an HOC by creating custom Hooks. Create a functional component that expects innerWidth as a property:

```
const MyComponent = ({ innerWidth }) => {
  console.log('window.innerWidth', innerWidth)
  // ...
}
```

Enhance it as follows:

```
const MyComponentWithInnerWidth = withInnerWidth(MyComponent)
```

By using HOCs, we avoid polluting any state and don't require the component to implement any function. This means the component and HOC are not coupled, and both can be reused throughout the application.

Using props instead of state allows us to create a "dumb" component that can be used in our style guide, ignoring complex logic and just passing down the props.

In this specific case, we could create a component for each of the different innerWidth sizes we support. Consider the following example:

```
<MyComponent innerWidth={320} />
```

Or the following:

```
<MyComponent innerWidth={960} />
```

As you can see, by using HOCs, we can pass a component and then return a new component with additional functionalities. Some common HOCs are connect from Redux and createFragmentContainer from Relay.

Understanding FunctionAsChild

The FunctionAsChild pattern is gaining consensus within the React community. It is widely used in popular libraries like **react-motion**, which we will explore in *Chapter 5, Writing Code for the Browser*.

The main concept is that instead of passing a child as a component, we define a function that can receive parameters from the parent. Let's see what it looks like:

```
const FunctionAsChild = ({ children }) => children()
```

As you can see, FunctionAsChild is a component with a children property defined as a function. Instead of being used as a JSX expression, it gets called.

The preceding component can be used like this:

```
<FunctionAsChild>
  {() => <div>Hello, World!</div>}
</FunctionAsChild>
```

This example is quite simple: the children function is executed within the parent's render method, returning the Hello, World! text wrapped in a div tag, which is displayed on the screen.

Now, let's explore a more meaningful example where the parent component passes some parameters to the children function.

Create a Name component that expects a function as children and passes it the 'World' string:

```
const Name = ({ children }) => children('World')
```

The preceding component can be used like this:

```
<Name>
  {name => <div>Hello, {name}!</div>}
</Name>
```

The snippet renders Hello, World! again, but this time the name has been passed by the parent. It should now be clear how this pattern works. Let's look at the advantages of this approach:

- The primary advantage is the ability to encapsulate components, delivering variables dynamically, as opposed to utilizing static properties, which is a common practice with HOCs. An excellent illustration of this is a Fetch component, designed to retrieve data from a specific API endpoint and subsequently return it to its child function:

  ```
  <Fetch url="...">
    {data => <List data={data} />}
  </Fetch>
  ```

- Secondly, composing components with this approach does not force children to use predefined prop names. Since the function receives variables, developers who use the component can decide on their names. This flexibility makes the Function as Child solution more versatile.

- Lastly, the wrapper is highly reusable because it does not make any assumptions about the children it receives—it just expects a function. Due to this, the same FunctionAsChild component can be used in different parts of the application to serve various children components.

By adopting the Function as Child pattern, you can create more flexible, versatile, and reusable components in your React applications.

Summary

In this chapter, we learned how to effectively compose and communicate between our reusable components using props. By using props, we can create well-defined interfaces and decouple our components from each other.

We also explored two popular composition patterns: the container and presentational pattern, which help us separate our logic and presentation for more specialized and focused components. Additionally, we discovered **Higher-Order Components (HOCs)** as a way to handle context without tightly coupling our components to it, and the Function as Child pattern for composing components dynamically.

In the next chapter, we will dive into controlled vs. uncontrolled components, refs, handling events, and animations in React.

5

Writing Code for the Browser

There are some specific operations we can conduct when we work with React and the browser. For example, we can ask our users to enter some information using forms. In this chapter, we will look at how we can apply different techniques to deal with forms. We can implement **uncontrolled components** and let the fields keep their internal states, or we can use controlled ones where we have full control over the state of the fields.

In this chapter, we will also look at how events in React work and how the library implements some advanced techniques to give us a consistent interface across different browsers. We will look at some interesting solutions that the React team has implemented to make the event system very performant.

After events, we will jump into **refs** to look at how we can access the underlying **DOM** nodes in our React components. This represents a powerful feature, but it should be used carefully because it breaks some of the conventions that make React easy to work with.

After refs, we will look at how we can implement animations easily with the React add-ons. Finally, we will learn how easy it is to work with **Scalable Vector Graphics** (**SVG**) in React, and how we can create dynamically configurable icons for our applications.

In this chapter, we will go through the following topics:

- Using different techniques to create forms with React
- Listening to DOM events and implementing custom handlers
- A way of performing imperative operations on DOM nodes using refs

- Creating simple animations that work across different browsers
- The React way of generating SVG

Technical requirements

To complete this chapter, you will need the following:

- Node.js 19+
- Visual Studio Code

You can find the code for this chapter in the book's GitHub repository: `https://github.com/`
`PacktPublishing/React-18-Design-Patterns-and-Best-Practices-Fourth-Edition/tree/`
`main/Chapter05`.

Understanding and implementing forms

In this section, we are going to learn how to implement forms with React. As soon as we start
building a real application with React, we need to interact with the users. If we want to ask for
information from our users within the browser, forms are the most common solution. Due to
the way the library works and its declarative nature, dealing with input fields and other form
elements is non-trivial with React, but as soon as we understand its logic, it will become clear.
In the next sections, we are going to learn how to use uncontrolled and controlled components.

Uncontrolled components

Uncontrolled components are like regular HTML form inputs for which you will not be able to
manage the value yourself but instead, the DOM will take care of handling the value and you can
get this value by using a React ref. Let's start with a basic example—displaying a form with an
input field and a Submit button.

The code is pretty straightforward:

```
import { FC, useState, ChangeEvent, MouseEvent } from 'react'
const Uncontrolled: FC = () => {
  const [value, setValue] = useState<string>('')
  return (
    <form>
        <input type="text" />
        <button>Submit</button>
    </form>
  )
```

```
}
export default Uncontrolled
```

If we run the preceding snippet in the browser, we will see exactly what we expect—an input field in which we can write something and a clickable button. This is an example of an uncontrolled component, where we do not set the value of the input field, but we let the component manage its own internal state.

Most likely, we want to do something with the value of the element when the Submit button is clicked. For example, we may want to send the data to an API endpoint.

We can do this easily by adding an onChange listener (we will talk more about event listeners later in this chapter). Let's look at what it means to add a listener.

We need to create the handleChange function:

```
const handleChange = (e: ChangeEvent<HTMLInputElement>) => {
    console.log(e.target.value)
}
```

The event listener is receiving an event object, where the target represents the field that generated the event, and we are interested in its value. We start by just logging it because it is important to proceed with small steps, but we will store the value into the state soon.

Finally, we render the form:

```
return (
  <form>
    <input type="text" onChange={handleChange} />
    <button>Submit</button>
  </form>
)
```

If we render the component inside the browser and type the word React into the form field, we will see something like the following inside the console:

```
R
Re
Rea
Reac
React
```

The handleChange listener is fired every time the value of the input changes. Therefore, our function is called once for each typed character. The next step is to store the value that's entered by the user and make it available when the user clicks the Submit button.

We just have to change the implementation of the handler to store it in the state instead of logging it, as follows:

```
const handleChange = (e: ChangeEvent<HTMLInputElement>) => {
  setValue(e.target.value)
}
```

Getting notified of when the form is submitted is very similar to listening to the change event of the input field; they are both events that are called by the browser when something happens.

Let's define the handleSubmit function, where we just log the value. In a real-world scenario, you could send the data to an API endpoint or pass it to another component:

```
const handleSubmit = (e: MouseEvent<HTMLButtonElement>) => {
  e.preventDefault()

  console.log(value) // Here we are logging the value state
}
```

This handler is pretty straightforward; we just log the value currently stored in the state. We also want to overcome the default behavior of the browser when the form is submitted, to perform a custom action. This seems reasonable, and it works very well for a single field. The question now is, *what if we have multiple fields? Suppose we have tens of different fields?*

Let's start with a basic example, where we create each field and handler manually and look at how we can improve it by applying different levels of optimization.

Let's create a new form with first and last name fields. We can reuse the Uncontrolled component and add some new states:

```
const [firstName, setFirstName] = useState('')
const [lastName, setLastName] = useState('')
```

We initialize the two fields inside the state, and we define an event handler for each one of the fields as well. As you may have noticed, this does not scale very well when there are lots of fields, but it is important to understand the problem clearly before moving to a more flexible solution.

Now, we implement the new handlers:

```
const handleChangeFirstName = ({ target: { value } }) => {
  setFirstName(value)
}


const handleChangeLastName = ({ target: { value } }) => {
  setLastName(value)
}
```

We also have to change the submit handler a little bit so that it displays the first and the last name when it gets clicked:

```
const handleSubmit = (e: MouseEvent<HTMLButtonElement>) => {
  e.preventDefault()

  console.log(`${firstName} ${lastName}`) // Logging the firstName and
LastName states
}
```

Finally, we render the form:

```
return (
  <form onSubmit={handleSubmit}>
    <input type="text" onChange={handleChangeFirstName} />
    <input type="text" onChange={handleChangeLastName} />
    <button>Submit</button>
  </form>
)
```

We are ready to go: if we run the preceding component in the browser, we will see two fields, and if we type Carlos into the first one and Santana into the second one, we will see the full name displayed in the browser console when the form is submitted.

Again, this works fine, and we can do some interesting things this way, but it does not handle complex scenarios without requiring us to write a lot of boilerplate code.

Let's look at how we can optimize it a little bit. Our goal is to use a single change handler so that we can add an arbitrary number of fields without creating new listeners.

Let's go back to the component and let's change our states:

```
const [values, setValues] = useState({ firstName: '', lastName: '' })
```

We may still want to initialize the values, and later in this section, we will look at how to provide prefilled values for the form.

Now, the interesting bit is the way in which we can modify the onChange handler implementation to make it work in different fields:

```
const handleChange = ({ target: { name, value } }) => {
  setValues({
    ...values,
    [name]: value
  })
}
```

As we have seen previously, the target property of the event we receive represents the input field that has fired the event, so we can use the name of the field and its value as variables.

We then have to set the name for each field:

```
return (
  <form onSubmit={handleSubmit}>
    <input
      type="text"
      name="firstName"
      onChange={handleChange}
    />
    <input
      type="text"
      name="lastName"
      onChange={handleChange}
    />
    <button>Submit</button>
  </form>
)
```

That's it! We can now add as many fields as we want without creating additional handlers.

Controlled components

A controlled component is a React component that controls the values of input elements in a form by using the component state.

Here we are going to look at how we can prefill the form fields with some values, which we may receive from the server or as props from the parent. To understand this concept fully, we will start again from a very simple stateless function component, and we will improve it step by step.

The first example shows a predefined value inside the input field:

```
const Controlled = () => (
  <form>
    <input type="text" value="Hello React" />
    <button>Submit</button>
  </form>
)
```

If we run this component inside the browser, we realize that it shows the default value as expected, but it does not let us change the value or type anything else inside it.

The reason it does this is that in React, we declare what we want to see on the screen, and setting a fixed-value attribute always results in rendering that value, no matter what other actions are taken. This is unlikely to be a behavior we want in a real-world application.

If we open the console, we get the following error message. React itself is telling us that we are doing something wrong:

```
You provided a `value` prop to a form field without an `onChange` handler.
This will render a read-only field.
```

Now, if we just want the input field to have a default value and we want to be able to change it by typing, we can use the `defaultValue` property:

```
import { useState } from 'react'
const Controlled = () => {
  return (
    <form>
      <input type="text" defaultValue="Hello React" />
      <button>Submit</button>
    </form>
  )
```

```
}
export default Controlled
```

In this way, the field is going to show Hello React when it is rendered, but then the user can type anything inside it and change its value. Now let's add some states:

```
const [values, setValues] = useState({ firstName: 'Carlos', lastName:
'Santana' })
```

The handlers are the same as the previous ones:

```
const handleChange = ({ target: { name, value } }) => {
  setValues({
    [name]: value
  })
}

const handleSubmit = (e) => {
  e.preventDefault()

  console.log(`${values.firstName} ${values.lastName}`)
}
```

In fact, we will use the value attributes of the input fields to set their initial values, as well as the updated one:

```
return (
  <form onSubmit={handleSubmit}>
    <input
        type="text"
        name="firstName"
        value={values.firstName}
        onChange={handleChange}
    />
    <input
        type="text"
        name="lastName"
        value={values.lastName}
        onChange={handleChange}
    />
```

```
    <button>Submit</button>
  </form>
)
```

The first time the form is rendered, React uses the initial values from the state as the value of the input fields. When the user types something into the field, the handleChange function is called and the new value for the field is stored in the state.

When the state changes, React re-renders the component and uses it again to reflect the current values of the input fields. We now have full control over the values of the fields, and we call this pattern **controlled components**.

In the next section, we are going to work with events, which are a fundamental part of React to handle data coming from forms.

Handling events

Events work in a slightly different way across various browsers. React tries to abstract the way events work and give developers a consistent interface to deal with. This is a great feature of React because we can forget about the browsers we are targeting and write event handlers and functions that are *vendor-agnostic*.

To offer this feature, React introduced the concept of the synthetic event. A synthetic event is an object that wraps the original event object provided by the browser, and it has the same properties, no matter where it is created.

To attach an event listener to a node and get the event object when the event is fired, we can use a simple convention that recalls the way events are attached to the DOM nodes. In fact, we can use the word on plus the camelCased event name (for example, onKeyDown) to define the callback to be fired when the events happen. A popular convention is to name the event handler functions after the event name and prefix them using handle (for example, handleKeyDown).

We have seen this pattern in action in the previous examples, where we were listening to the onChange event of the form fields. Let's reiterate a basic event listener example to see how we can organize multiple events inside the same component in a nicer way. We are going to implement a simple button, and we start, as usual, by creating a component:

```
const Button = () => {

}
export default Button
```

Then we define the event handler:

```
const handleClick = (syntheticEvent) => {
    console.log(syntheticEvent instanceof MouseEvent)
    console.log(syntheticEvent.nativeEvent instanceof MouseEvent)
  }
```

As you can see here, we are doing a very simple thing: we just check the type of the event object we receive from React and the type of native event attached to it. We expect the first to return false and the second to return true.

You should never need to access the original native event, but it is good to know you can do it if you need to. Finally, we define the button with the onClick attribute to which we attach our event listener:

```
return (
  <button onClick={handleClick}>Click me!</button>
)
```

Now, suppose we want to attach a second handler to the button that listens to the double-click event. One solution would be to create a new separate handler and attach it to the button using the onDoubleClick attribute, as follows:

```
<button
  onClick={handleClick}
  onDoubleClick={handleDoubleClick}
>
  Click me!
</button>
```

Remember that we always aim to write less boilerplate and avoid duplicating code. For that reason, a common practice is to write a single event handler for each component, which can trigger different actions according to the event type.

This technique is described in a collection of patterns by Michael Chan:

http://reactpatterns.com/#event-switch

Let's implement the generic event handler:

```
const handleEvent = (event) => {
  switch (event.type) {
```

```
    case 'click':
        console.log('clicked')
      break

    case 'dblclick':
        console.log('double clicked')
      break

    default:
        console.log('unhandled', event.type)
  }
}
```

The generic event handler receives the event object and switches on the event type to fire the right action. This is particularly useful if we want to call a function on each event (for example, analytics) or if some events share the same logic.

Finally, we attach the new event listener to the onClick and onDoubleClick attributes:

```
return (
  <button
    onClick={handleEvent}
    onDoubleClick={handleEvent}
  >
    Click me!
  </button>
)
```

From this point on, whenever we need to create a new event handler for the same component, instead of creating a new method and binding it, we can just add a new case to the switch.

A couple more interesting things to know about events in React are that synthetic events are reused and that there is a **single global handler**. The first concept means that we cannot store a synthetic event and reuse it later because it becomes null right after the action. This technique is very good in terms of performance, but it can be problematic if we want to store the event inside the state of the component for some reason. To solve this problem, React gives us a persist method on the synthetic events, which we can call to make the event persistent so that we can store it and retrieve it later.

The second very interesting implementation detail is again about performance, and it is to do with the way React attaches the event handlers to the DOM.

Whenever we use the on attribute, we are describing to React the behavior we want to achieve, but the library does not attach the actual event handler to the underlying DOM nodes.

What it does instead attaches a single event handler to the root element, which listens to all the events, thanks to **event bubbling**. When an event we are interested in is fired by the browser, React calls the handler on the specific components on its behalf. This technique is called **event delegation** and is used for memory and speed optimization.

In our next section, we are going to explore React refs and see how we can take advantage of them.

Exploring refs

One of the reasons people love React is that it is declarative. Being declarative means that you just describe what you want to be displayed on the screen at any point in time and React takes care of the communications with the browser. This feature makes React very easy to reason about and very powerful at the same time.

However, there might be some cases where you need to access the underlying DOM nodes to perform some imperative operations. This should be avoided because, in most cases, there is a more React-compliant solution to achieve the same result, but it is important to know that we have the option to do it and to know how it works so that we can make the right decision.

Suppose we want to create a simple form with an input element and a button, and we want it to behave in such a way that when the button is clicked, the input field gets focused. What we want to do is call the focus method on the input node, the actual DOM instance of the input, inside the browser's window.

Let's create a component called Focus; you need to import useRef and create an inputRef constant:

```
import { useRef } from 'react'
const Focus = () => {
  const inputRef = useRef(null)
}
export default Focus
```

Then, we implement the handleClick method:

```
const handleClick = () => {
  inputRef.current.focus()
```

```
  }
```

As you can see, we are referencing the current attribute of `inputRef` and calling the focus method on it.

To understand where it comes from, you just have to check the implementation of the render:

```
return (
  <>
    <input
      type="text"
      ref={inputRef}
    />
    <button onClick={handleClick}>Set Focus</button>
  </>
)
```

Here comes the core of the logic. We create a form with an input element inside it and we define a function on its `ref` attribute.

The callback we defined is called when the component gets mounted, and the element parameter represents the DOM instance of the input. It is important to know that, when the component gets unmounted, the same callback is called with a null parameter to free the memory.

What we are doing in the callback is storing the reference of the element to be able to use it in the future (for example, when the `handleClick` method is fired). Then, we have the button with its event handler. Running the preceding code in a browser will show the form with the field and the button, and clicking on the button will focus the input field, as expected.

As we mentioned previously, in general, we should try to avoid using refs because they force the code to be more imperative, and they become harder to read and maintain.

Understanding forwardRef

`React.forwardRef` is a useful feature that allows you to pass a ref (short for "reference") from a parent component down to a child component. This article will provide a basic introduction to `React.forwardRef` and offer a straightforward example to help you understand its practical usage.

Refs in React are a mechanism to access and interact with the DOM elements rendered by a component. They provide a way to modify the DOM or access DOM properties directly.

React.forwardRef is a higher-order component that allows you to pass a ref down to a child component. This is useful when you need to access the child component's DOM element or instance from the parent component.

To create a component that can accept a forwarded ref, you will use the React.forwardRef function, which takes a render function as an argument. This render function receives two parameters: the component's props and the forwarded ref.

```
import React from 'react'
const TextInputWithRef = React.forwardRef((props, ref) => {
  return <input ref={ref} type="text" {...props} />
})
export default TextInputWithRef
```

To use the forwardRef component, you will create a ref using the useRef() hook and assign it to the forwardRef component.

```
import React, { useRef } from 'react'
import TextInputWithRef from './TextInputWithRef'
function App() {
  const inputRef = useRef()
  const handleClick = () => {
    inputRef.current.focus()
  }
  return (
    <div>
      <TextInputWithRef ref={inputRef} />
      <button onClick={handleClick}>Focus on input</button>
    </div>
  )
}
export default App
```

In this example, we created a TextInputWithRef component that accepts a forwarded ref. In the App component, we use the useRef() hook to create a ref, which we then pass to the TextInputWithRef component. When the "Focus on input" button is clicked, the handleClick function is called, which focuses on the input element.

React.forwardRef is a powerful feature that allows you to pass refs from parent components to child components, providing greater control over the child components' behavior.

By understanding the basics of refs and `forwardRef`, and examining a simple example, you can effectively utilize this feature in your React applications.

With the nuances of utilizing `React.forwardRef` for superior control over components explored, we can now shift our focus toward another pivotal aspect of enhancing user experiences in React applications: implementing animations.

Implementing animations

When we think about UIs and the browser, we must surely think about animations as well. Animated UIs are more pleasant for users, and they are a very important tool to show users that something has happened or is about to occur.

This section does not aim to be an exhaustive guide to creating animations and beautiful UIs; the goal here is to provide you with some basic information about the common solutions we can put in place to animate our React components.

For a UI library such as React, it is crucial to provide an easy way for developers to create and manage animations. React comes with an add-on, called `react-transition-group`, which is a component that helps us build animations in a declarative way. Again, being able to perform operations declaratively is incredibly powerful, and it makes the code much easier to reason about and share with the team.

The first thing we need to do to start building an animated component is to install the add-on:

```
npm install --save react-transition-group @types/react-transition-group
```

Once we have done that, we can import the component:

```
import { TransitionGroup} from 'react-transition-group'
```

Then, we just wrap the component to which we want to apply the animation:

```
const Transition = () => (
  <TransitionGroup
    transitionName="fade"
    transitionAppear
    transitionAppearTimeout={500}
  >
    <h1>Hello React</h1>
  </TransitionGroup>
)
```

As you can see, there are some props that need explaining. First, we are declaring the `transitionName` prop. `ReactTransitionGroup` applies a class with the name of that property to the child element so that we can then use CSS transitions to create our animations.

With a single class, we cannot easily create a proper animation, and that is why the transition group applies multiple classes according to the state of the animation. In this case, with the `transitionAppear` prop, we are telling the component that we want to animate the children when they appear on the screen.

So, what the library does is apply the `fade-appear` class (where fade is the value of the `transitionName` prop) to the component as soon as it gets rendered. On the next tick, the `fade-appear-active` class is applied so that we can fire our animation from the initial state to the new one, using CSS.

We also have to set the `transitionAppearTimeout` property to tell React the length of the animation so that it doesn't remove elements from the DOM before animations are completed.

The CSS to make an element `fade-in` is as follows.

First, we define the opacity of the element in the initial state:

```
.fade-appear {
  opacity: 0.01;
}
```

Then, we define our transition using the second class, which starts as soon as it gets applied to the element:

```
.fade-appear.fade-appear-active {
  opacity: 1;
  transition: opacity .5s ease-in;
}
```

We are transitioning the opacity from 0.01 to 1 in 500ms using the ease-in function. This is pretty easy, but we can create more complex animations, and we can also animate different states of the component. For example, the `*-enter` and `*-enter-active` classes are applied when a new element is added as a child of the transition group. A similar thing applies to remove elements.

After delving into the dynamic world of animations and understanding how they can dramatically enhance our React components, let's now turn our attention to another fascinating facet of web design: the exploration of **Scalable Vector Graphics (SVG)**.

Exploring SVG

Finally, one of the most interesting techniques we can apply in the browser to draw icons and graphs is SVG.

SVG is great because it is a declarative way of describing vectors and it fits perfectly with the purposes of React. We used to use icon fonts to create icons, but they have well-known problems, with the first being that they are not accessible. It is also pretty hard to position icon fonts with CSS, and they do not always look beautiful in all browsers. These are the reasons we should prefer SVG for our web applications.

From a React point of view, it does not make any difference if we output a div or an SVG element from the render method, and this is what makes it so powerful. We also tend to choose SVG because we can easily modify them at runtime using CSS and JavaScript, which makes them an excellent candidate for the functional approach of React.

So, if we think about our components as a function of their props, we can easily imagine how we can create self-contained SVG icons that we can manipulate by passing different props to them. A common way to create SVG in a web app with React is to wrap our vectors into a React component and use the props to define their dynamic values.

Let's look at a simple example where we draw a blue circle, thus creating a React component that wraps an SVG element:

```
const Circle = ({ x, y, radius, fill }) => (
  <svg>
    <circle cx={x} cy={y} r={radius} fill={fill} />
  </svg>
)
```

As you can see, we can easily use a stateless functional component that wraps the SVG markup, and it accepts the same props as SVG does.

An example usage is as follows:

```
<Circle x={20} y={20} radius={20} fill="blue" />
```

We can obviously use the full power of React and set some default parameters so that, if the circle icon is rendered without props, we still show something.

For example, we can define the default color:

```
const Circle = ({ x, y, radius, fill = 'red' }) => (...)
```

This is pretty powerful when we build UIs, especially in a team where we share our icon set and we want to have some default values in it, but we also want to let other teams decide their settings without having to recreate the same SVG shapes.

However, in some cases, we prefer to be stricter and fix some values to keep consistency. With React, this is a super simple task.

For example, we can wrap the base circle component into RedCircle, as follows:

```
const RedCircle = ({ x, y, radius }) => (
  <Circle x={x} y={y} radius={radius} fill="red" />
)
```

Here, the color is set by default, and it cannot be changed, while the other props are transparently passed to the original circle.

The following screenshot shows two circles, blue and red, that are generated by React using SVG:

Figure 5.1: Two circles, blue and red SVGs

We can apply this technique and create different variations of the circle, such as SmallCircle and RightCircle, and everything else we need to build our UIs.

Summary

In this chapter, we explored the different capabilities of React when targeting the browser, from creating forms and handling events to animating SVGs. We also learned about the new useRef Hook, which provides a simple way to access DOM nodes. React's declarative approach simplifies the management of complex web applications. Additionally, React provides a way to access the DOM nodes, allowing for imperative operations if needed, making it easier to integrate React with existing libraries.

In the next chapter, we will delve into CSS and inline styles, and explore the concept of writing CSS in JavaScript.

6
Making Your Components Look Beautiful

Our journey into React best practices and design patterns has now reached the point where we want to make our components look beautiful. To do that, we will go through all the reasons why regular CSS may not be the best approach for styling components, and we will check out various alternative solutions.

Starting with inline styles, then CSS modules, and `styled-components`, this chapter will guide you through the magical world of CSS in JavaScript.

In this chapter, we will cover the following topics:

- Common problems with regular CSS at scale
- What it means to use inline styles in React and their downsides
- How to set up a project from scratch using Webpack and CSS modules
- Features of CSS modules and why they represent a great solution to avoid global CSS
- `styled-components`, a new library that offers a modern approach to styling React components

Technical requirements

To complete this chapter, you will need the following:

- Node.js 19+
- Visual Studio Code

You can find the code for this chapter in the book's GitHub repository: `https://github.com/PacktPublishing/React-18-Design-Patterns-and-Best-Practices-Fourth-Edition/tree/main/Chapter06`.

CSS in JavaScript

In November 2014, Christopher Chedeau, also known as *vjeux*, gave a talk at the NationJS conference (`https://blog.vjeux.com/2014/javascript/react-css-in-js-nationjs.html`) that sparked a revolution in the way React components are styled. As a contributor to React and an employee of Meta, Christopher outlined the many issues Facebook faced with CSS at scale. Understanding these issues is important because they are common in web development and will help us introduce concepts such as inline styles and locally scoped class names.

The following is a list of the issues with CSS, which are basically problems with CSS at scale:

- Global namespace
- Dependencies
- Dead code elimination
- Minification
- Sharing constants
- Non-deterministic resolution
- Isolation

The first well-known problem of CSS is that all the selectors are global. No matter how organized our styles are by using namespaces or a procedure such as the **Block, Element, Modifier (BEM)** methodology, we are always polluting the global namespace, which we all know is wrong. It is not only wrong in principle, but it also leads to many errors in big code bases, and it makes maintainability very hard in the long term. Working with big teams, it is non-trivial to know whether a particular class or element has already been styled, and most of the time, we tend to add more classes instead of reusing existing ones.

The second problem with CSS regards the definition of the dependencies. It is very hard, in fact, to state clearly that a particular component depends on a specific CSS and that the CSS has to be loaded for the style to be applied. Since styles are global, any style from any file can be applied to any element, and losing control is very easy.

The third is that frontend developers tend to use pre-processors to be able to split their CSS into submodules, but in the end, a big, global CSS bundle is generated for the browser.

Since CSS code bases tend to become huge quickly, we lose control over them, and the third problem is to do with **dead code elimination**. It is not easy to quickly identify which styles belong to which component, and this makes deleting code incredibly hard. In fact, due to the cascading nature of CSS, removing a selector or a rule can result in an unintended result within the browser.

Another pain point of working with CSS concerns the minification of the selectors and the class names, both in the CSS and in the JavaScript application. It might seem an easy task, but it is not, especially when classes are applied on the fly or concatenated in the client; this is the fourth problem.

Not being able to minify and optimize class names is bad for performance, and it can make a huge difference to the size of the CSS. Another pretty common operation that is non-trivial with regular CSS is sharing constants between the styles and the client application. We often need to know the height of a header, for example, to recalculate the position of other elements that depend on it.

Usually, we read the value in the client using the JavaScript APIs, but the optimal solution would be to share constants and avoid doing expensive calculations at runtime. This represents the fifth problem that vjeux and the other developers at Facebook tried to solve.

The sixth issue concerns the non-deterministic resolution of CSS. In fact, in CSS, the order matters, and if the CSS is loaded on demand, the order is not guaranteed, which leads to the wrong styles being applied to the elements.

Suppose, for example, that we want to optimize the way we request CSS, loading the CSS related to a particular page only when the users navigate to it. If the CSS related to this last page has some rules that also apply to the elements of different pages, the fact that it has been loaded last could affect the styling of the rest of the app. For example, if the user goes back to the previous page, they might see a page with a UI that is slightly different than the first time they visited it.

It is incredibly hard to control all the various combinations of styles, rules, and navigation paths, but again, being able to load the CSS when needed could have a critical impact on the performance of a web application.

Last but not least, the seventh problem of CSS, according to Christopher Chedeau, is related to isolation. In CSS, it is almost impossible to achieve proper isolation between files or components. Selectors are global, and they can easily be overwritten. It is tricky to predict the final style of an element just by knowing the class names applied to it because styles are not isolated, and other rules in other parts of the application can affect unrelated elements. This can be solved by using inline styles.

In the following section, we will look at what it means to use inline styles with React and the benefits and downsides of it.

Understanding and implementing inline styles

The official React documentation suggests developers use **inline styles** to style their React components. This seems odd because we all learned in past years that separating the concerns is important and we should not mix markup and CSS.

React tries to change the concept of separation of concerns by moving it from the separation of technologies to the separation of components. Separating markup, styling, and logic into different files when they are tightly coupled and where one cannot work without the other is just an illusion. Even if it helps keep the project structure cleaner, it does not give any real benefit.

In React, we compose components to create applications where components are a fundamental unit of our structure. We should be able to move components across the application, and they should provide the same result regarding both logic and UI, no matter where they get rendered.

This is one of the reasons why collocating the styles within our components and applying them using inline styles on the elements could make sense in React.

First, let's look at an example of what it means to use the `style` attribute of the nodes to apply the styling to our components in React. We are going to create a button with the text `Click me!` and we are going to apply a color and background color to it:

```
const style = {
  color: 'palevioletred',
  backgroundColor: 'papayawhip'
}

const Button = () => <button style={style}>Click me!</button>
```

As you can see, it is pretty easy to style elements with inline styles in React. We just have to create an object where the attributes are the CSS rules, and the values are the values we would use in a regular CSS file.

The only differences are that the hyphenated CSS rules must be `camelCased` to be JavaScript-compliant, and the values are strings, so they have to be wrapped in quote marks.

There are some exceptions regarding the vendor prefixes. For example, if we want to define a transition on webkit, we should use the WebkitTransition attribute, where the webkit prefix begins with a capital letter. This rule applies to all the vendor prefixes, except for ms, which is lowercase.

Other use cases are numbers – they can be written without quotes or units of measurement, and by default, they are treated as pixels.

The following rule applies a height of 100 pixels:

```
const style = {
  height: 100
}
```

By using inline styles, we can also do things that are hard to implement with regular CSS. For example, we can recalculate some CSS values on the client at runtime, which is a very powerful concept, as you will see in the following example.

Suppose you want to create a form field in which the font size changes according to its value. So, if the value of the field is 24, the font size is going to be 24 pixels. With normal CSS, this behavior is almost impossible to reproduce without putting in a huge effort and duplicated code.

Let's look at how easy it is to use inline styles instead, by creating a FontSize component first and then declaring a value state:

```
import { useState, ChangeEvent } from 'react'
const FontSize = () => {
  const [value, setValue] = useState<number>(16)
}
export default FontSize
```

We implement a simple change handler, where we use the target attribute of the event to retrieve the current value of the field:

```
const handleChange = (e: ChangeEvent<HTMLInputElement>) => {
  setValue(Number(e.target.value))
}
```

Finally, we render the input file of the number type, which is a controlled component because we keep its value updated by using the state. It also has an event handler, which is fired every time the value of the field changes.

Last but not least, we use the `style` attribute of the field to set its font-size value. As you can see, we are using the `camelCased` version of the CSS rule to follow the React convention:

```
return (
  <input
    type="number"
    value={value}
    onChange={handleChange}
    style={{ fontSize: value }}
  />
)
```

Rendering the preceding component, we can see an input field that changes its font size according to its value. The way it works is that when the value changes, we store the new value of the field inside the state. Modifying the state forces the component to re-render, and we use the new state value to set the display value of the field and its font size; it's easy and powerful.

Every solution in computer science has its downsides, and it always represents a trade-off. In the case of inline styles, unfortunately, the problems are many.

For example, with inline styles, it is not possible to use pseudo-selectors (for example, `:hover`) and pseudo-elements, which is a pretty significant limitation if you are creating a UI with interactions and animations.

There are some workarounds, and, for example, you can always create real elements instead of pseudo-elements, but for the pseudo-classes, it is necessary to use JavaScript to simulate the CSS behavior, which is not optimal.

The same applies to **media queries**, which cannot be defined using inline styles, and it makes it harder to create responsive web applications. Since styles are declared using JavaScript objects, it is also not possible to use `style` fallbacks:

```
display: -webkit-flex;
display: flex;
```

JavaScript objects cannot have two attributes with the same name. Style fallbacks should be avoided, but it is always good to have the ability to use them if needed.

Another feature of CSS that it is not possible to emulate using inline styles is **animations**. The workaround here is to define animations globally and use them inside the style attribute of the elements. With inline styles, whenever we need to override a style with regular CSS, we are always forced to use the `!important` keyword, which is bad practice because it prevents any other style from being applied to the element.

The most difficult thing that happens to work with inline styles is debugging. We tend to use class names to find elements in the browser DevTools to debug and check which styles have been applied. With inline styles, all the styles of the items are listed in their `style` attribute, which makes it very hard to check and debug the result.

For example, the button that we created earlier in this section is rendered in the following way:

```
<button style="color:palevioletred;background-color:papayawhip;">Click
me!</button>
```

By itself, it does not seem very hard to read, but if you imagine you have hundreds of elements and hundreds of styles, you realize that the problem becomes very complicated.

Also, if you are debugging a list where every single item has the same `style` attribute, and if you modify one on the fly to check the result in the browser, you will see that you are applying the styles only to it and not to all the other siblings, even if they share the same style.

Last but not least, if we render our application on the server side (we will cover this topic in *Chapter 12, Server-Side Rendering*), the size of the page is bigger when using inline styles.

With inline styles, we are putting all the content of the CSS into the markup, which adds an extra number of bytes to the file that we send to the clients and makes the web application appear slower. Compression algorithms can help with that because they can easily compress similar patterns, and, in some cases, loading the critical path CSS is a good solution; but in general, we should try to avoid it.

It turns out that inline styles cause more problems than the problems they try to solve. For this reason, the community created different tools to solve the problems of inline styles but keeping the styles inside the components, or local to the components, to get the best of both worlds.

After Christopher Chedeau's talk, a lot of developers started talking about inline styles, and many solutions and experiments have been made to find new ways of writing CSS in JavaScript. In the beginning, there were two or three solutions, while today there are more than 40.

In the next section, we are going to learn how to use the CSS modules.

Using CSS modules

If you feel that inline styles are not a suitable solution for your project and your team, but you still want to keep the styles as close as possible to your components, there is a solution for you, called **CSS modules**. The CSS modules are CSS files in which all class names and animation names are scoped locally by default. Let's see how we can use them in our projects; but first, we need to configure **webpack**.

Webpack 5

Before diving into CSS modules and learning how they work, it is important to understand how they were created and the tools that support them.

In *Chapter 3*, *Cleaning Up Your Code*, we looked at how we can write ES6 code and transpile it by using Babel and its presets. As soon as the application grows, you may want to split your code base into modules as well.

You can use Webpack or Browserify to divide the application into small modules that you can import whenever you need them, while still creating a big bundle for the browser. These tools are called **module bundlers**, and what they do is load all the dependencies of your application into a single bundle that can be executed in the browser, which does not have any concept of modules (yet).

In the React world, Webpack is especially popular because it offers many interesting and useful features, with the first one being the concept of loaders. With Webpack, you can potentially load any dependencies other than JavaScript, if there is a loader for them. For example, you can load JSON files, as well as images and other assets, inside the bundle.

In May 2015, Mark Dalgleish, one of the creators of CSS modules, figured out that you could import CSS inside a Webpack bundle as well, and he pushed the concept forward. He thought that, since the CSS could be imported locally into a component, all the imported class names could be locally scoped as well, this is great because this will isolate the styles.

After tracing the conceptual evolution of locally scoped CSS by one of its pioneers, Mark Dalgleish, and understanding how it revolutionized style isolation in Webpack bundles, let us transition into a more practical arena. The next section will guide us in setting up a project that utilizes these principles.

Setting up a project

In this section, we will look at how to set up a very simple Webpack application, using Babel to transpile the JavaScript and CSS modules to load our locally scoped CSS into the bundle. We will also go through all the features of CSS modules and look at the problems they can solve. The first thing to do is move to an empty folder and run the following command:

```
npm init
```

This will create a package.json file with some defaults.

Now, it is time to install the dependencies, with the first one being Webpack and the second being webpack-dev-server, which we will use to run the application locally and to create the bundle on the fly:

```
npm install --save-dev webpack webpack-dev-server webpack-cli
```

Once Webpack is installed, it is time to install Babel and its loader. Since we are using Webpack to create the bundle, we will use the Babel loader to transpile our ES6 code within Webpack itself:

```
npm install --save-dev @babel/core @babel/preset-env @babel/preset-react
ts-loader
```

Finally, we install style-loader and the CSS loader, which are the two loaders we need to enable the CSS modules:

```
npm install --save-dev style-loader css-loader
```

There is one more thing to do to make things easier, and that is to install html-webpack-plugin, which is a plugin that can create an HTML page to host our JavaScript application on the fly, just by looking into the Webpack configuration and without us needing to create a regular file. Also, we need to install the fork-ts-checker-webpack-plugin package to make TypeScript work with Webpack:

```
npm install --save-dev html-webpack-plugin fork-ts-checker-webpack-plugin
typescript
```

Last but not least, we install react and react-dom to use them in our simple example:

```
npm install react react-dom
```

Now that all the dependencies are installed, it is time to configure everything to make it work.

First, you need to create a `.babelrc` file in your root path:

```
{
  "presets": ["@babel/preset-env", "@babel/preset-react"]
}
```

The first thing to do is add an npm script in `package.json` to run the `webpack-dev-server`, which will serve the application in development:

```
"scripts": {
  "dev": "webpack serve --mode development --port 3000"
}
```

 In Webpack 5, you need to use this way to call webpack instead of `webpack-dev-server` but you still need to have this package installed.

Webpack needs a configuration file to know how to handle the different types of dependencies we are using in our application, and to do so, we must create a file called `webpack.config.ts`, which exports an object:

```
module.exports = {}
```

The object we export represents the configuration object used by Webpack to create the bundle, and it can have different properties depending on the size and the features of the project.

We want to keep our example very simple, so we are going to add three attributes. The first one is `entry`, which tells Webpack where the main file of our application is:

```
entry: './src/index.tsx'
```

The second one is `module`, which is where we tell Webpack how to load the external dependencies. It has an attribute called `rules`, where we set a specific loader for each one of the file types:

```
module: {
  rules: [
    {
        test: /\.(tsx|ts)$/,
        exclude: /node_modules/,
        use: {
            loader: 'ts-loader',
```

```
                options: {
              transpileOnly: true
                  }
            }
      },
      {
          test: /\.css/,
          use: [
                'style-loader',
                'css-loader?modules=true'
          ]
      }
    ]
}
```

We are saying that the files that match the .ts or .tsx regular expression are loaded using ts-loader so that they get transpiled and loaded into the bundle.

You may also have noticed that we added our presets in the .babelrc file. As we saw in *Chapter 3, Cleaning Up Your Code*, the presets are sets of configuration options that instruct Babel on how to deal with the different types of syntax (for example, TSX).

The second entry in the rules array tells Webpack what to do when a CSS file is imported, and it uses css-loader with the modules flag enabled to activate **CSS modules**. The result of the transformation is then passed to style-loader, which injects the styles into the header of the page.

Finally, we enable the HTML plugin to generate the page for us, adding the script tag automatically using the entry path we specified earlier:

```
const HtmlWebpackPlugin = require('html-webpack-plugin')
const ForkTsCheckerWebpackPlugin = require('fork-ts-checker-webpack-
plugin')

plugins: [
  new ForkTsCheckerWebpackPlugin(),
  new HtmlWebpackPlugin({
    title: 'Your project name',
    template: './src/index.html',
```

```
      filename: './index.html'
  })
]
```

The complete webpack.config.ts should be as shown in the following code block:

```
const HtmlWebpackPlugin = require('html-webpack-plugin')
const path = require('path')
const ForkTsCheckerWebpackPlugin = require('fork-ts-checker-webpack-
plugin')

const isProduction = process.env.NODE_ENV === 'production'
module.exports = {
  devtool: !isProduction ? 'source-map' : false, // We generate source
maps
  // only for development
  entry: './src/index.tsx',
  output: { // The path where we want to output our bundles
    path: path.resolve(__dirname, 'dist'),
    filename: '[name].[hash:8].js',
    sourceMapFilename: '[name].[hash:8].map',
    chunkFilename: '[id].[hash:8].js',
    publicPath: '/'
  },
  resolve: {
    extensions: ['.ts', '.tsx', '.js', '.json', '.css'] // Here we add the
    // extensions we want to support
  },
  target: 'web',
  mode: isProduction ? 'production' : 'development', // production mode
  // minifies the code
  module: {
    rules: [
        {
            test: /\.(tsx|ts)$/,
            exclude: /node_modules/,
            use: {
              loader: 'ts-loader',
```

```
                options: {
                    transpileOnly: true
                }
            }
        },
        {
            test: /\.css/,
            use: [
              'style-loader',
              'css-loader?modules=true'
            ]
        }
      ]
    },
    plugins: [
      new ForkTsCheckerWebpackPlugin(),
      new HtmlWebpackPlugin({
        title: 'Your project name',
        template: './src/index.html',
        filename: './index.html'
      })
    ],
    optimization: { // This is to split our bundles into vendor and main
      splitChunks: {
        cacheGroups: {
            default: false,
            commons: {
              test: /node_modules/,
              name: 'vendor',
              chunks: 'all'
            }
        }
      }
    }
}
```

Then, to configure TypeScript, you need this `tsconfig.json` file:

```json
{
  "compilerOptions": {
    "allowJs": true,
    "allowSyntheticDefaultImports": true,
    "baseUrl": "src",
    "esModuleInterop": true,
    "forceConsistentCasingInFileNames": true,
    "isolatedModules": true,
    "jsx": "react-jsx",
    "lib": ["dom", "dom.iterable", "esnext"],
    "module": "esnext",
    "moduleResolution": "node",
    "noEmit": true,
    "noFallthroughCasesInSwitch": true,
    "noImplicitAny": false,
    "resolveJsonModule": true,
    "skipLibCheck": true,
    "sourceMap": true,
    "strict": true,
    "target": "esnext"
  },
  "include": ["src/**/*.ts", "src/**/*.tsx"],
  "exclude": ["node_modules"]
}
```

In order to import CSS files using TypeScript, you need to create a declarations file at `src/declarations.d.ts`:

```typescript
declare module '*.css' {
  const content: Record<string, string>
  export default content
}
```

Then, you need to create the main file at `src/index.tsx`:

```tsx
import { createRoot } from 'react-dom/client'
const App = () => {
  return <div>Hello World</div>
```

```
  }
  createRoot(document.getElementById('root') as HTMLElement).render(
    <React.StrictMode>
      <App />
    </React.StrictMode>
  )
```

Finally, you need to create the initial HTML file at src/index.html:

```html
<!DOCTYPE html>
<html>
  <head>
    <meta charset="UTF-8" />
    <meta name="viewport" content="width=device-width, initial-scale=1.0"
      />
    <meta http-equiv="X-UA-Compatible" content="ie=edge" />
    <title><%= htmlWebpackPlugin.options.title %></title>
  </head>
  <body>
    <div id="root"></div>
  </body>
</html>
```

We are done, and if we run the npm run dev command in the terminal and point the browser to http://localhost:8080, we should be able to see the following markup being served:

```html
<!DOCTYPE html>
<html>
  <head>
    <meta charset="UTF-8">
    <title>Your project name</title>
    <script defer src="/vendor.12472959.js"></script>
    <script defer src="/main.12472959.js"></script>
  </head>
  <body>
    <div id="root"></div>
  </body>
</html>
```

Perfect – our React application is working! Let's see now how we can add some CSS to our project.

Locally scoped CSS

Now it is time to create our app, which will consist of a simple button of the same sort we used in previous examples. We will use it to show all the features of the CSS modules.

Let's update the src/index.tsx file, which is the entry we specified in the Webpack configuration:

```
import { createRoot } from 'react-dom/client'
```

We can then create a simple button. As usual, we are going to start with a non-styled button, and we will add the styles step by step:

```
const Button = () => <button>Click me!</button>
```

Finally, we can render the button into the DOM:

```
createRoot(document.getElementById('root') as HTMLElement).render(<Button
/>)
```

Now, suppose we want to apply some styles to the button – a background color, size, and so on. We create a regular CSS file, called index.css, and we put the following class into it:

```
.button {
  background-color: #ff0000;
  width: 320px;
  padding: 20px;
  border-radius: 5px;
  border: none;
  outline: none;
}
```

Now, we said that with CSS modules we could import the CSS files into JavaScript; let's look at how it works.

Inside our index.ts file where we defined the button component, we can add the following line:

```
import styles from './index.css'
```

The result of this import statement is a styles object, where all the attributes are the classes defined in index.css.

If we run `console.log(styles)`, we can see the following object in the DevTools:

```
{
    button: "_2wpxM3yizfwbWee6k0UlD4"
}
```

So, we have an object where the attributes are the class names and the values are (apparently) random strings. We will see later that they are non-random, but let's check what we can do with that object first.

We can use the object to set the class name attribute of our button, as follows:

```
const Button = () => (
    <button className={styles.button}>Click me!</button>
);
```

If we go back to the browser, we can now see that the styles we defined in `index.css` have been applied to the button. This is not magic, because if we check in DevTools, the class that has been applied to the element is the same string that's attached to the `style` object we imported inside our code:

```
<button class="_2wpxM3yizfwbWee6k0UlD4">Click me!</button>
```

If we look at the header section of the page, we can now see that the same class name has also been injected into the page:

```
<style type="text/css">
  ._2wpxM3yizfwbWee6k0UlD4 {
      background-color: #ff0000;
      width: 320px;
      padding: 20px;
      border-radius: 5px;
      border: none;
      outline: none;
  }
</style>
```

This is how the CSS and the style loaders work. The CSS loader lets you import the CSS files into your JavaScript modules and, when the `module` flag is activated, all the class names are locally scoped to the module they are imported into.

As we mentioned previously, the string we imported was non-random, but it is generated using the hash of the file and some other parameters in a way that is unique within the code base.

Finally, `style-loader` takes the result of the CSS module's transformation and injects the styles inside the header section of the page. This is very powerful because we have the full power and expressiveness of the CSS, combined with the advantages of having locally scoped class names and explicit dependencies.

As mentioned at the beginning of this chapter, CSS is global, and that makes it very hard to maintain in large applications. With CSS modules, class names are locally scoped, and they cannot clash with other class names in different parts of the application, enforcing a deterministic result.

Moreover, explicitly importing the CSS dependencies inside our components helps us see clearly which components need which CSS. It is also very useful for eliminating dead code because when we delete a component for any reason, we can tell exactly which CSS it was using.

CSS modules are regular CSS, so we can use pseudo-classes, media queries, and animations.

For example, we can add CSS rules such as the following:

```css
.button:hover {
  color: #fff;
}

.button:active {
  position: relative;
  top: 2px;
}

@media (max-width: 480px) {
  .button {
    width: 160px;
  }
}
```

This will be transformed into the following code and injected into the document:

```css
._2wpxM3yizfwbWee6k0UlD4:hover {
  color: #fff;
}
```

```css
._2wpxM3yizfwbWee6k0UlD4:active {
  position: relative;
  top: 2px;
}

@media (max-width: 480px) {
  ._2wpxM3yizfwbWee6k0UlD4 {
    width: 160px;
  }
}
```

The class names get created and they get replaced everywhere the button is used, making it reliable and local, as expected.

As you may have noticed, those class names are great, but they make debugging pretty hard because we cannot easily tell which classes generated the hash. What we can do in development mode is add a special configuration parameter, with which we can choose the pattern that's used to produce the scoped class names.

For example, we can change the value of the loader as follows:

```js
{
  test: /\.css/,
  use: [
    {
      loader: 'style-loader'
    },
    {
      loader: 'css-loader',
      options: {
        modules: {
          localIdentName: '[local]--[hash:base64:5]'
        }
      }
    }
  ]
}
```

Here, `localIdentName` is the parameter, and `[local]` and `[hash:base64:5]` are placeholders for the original class name value and a five-character hash. Other available placeholders are `[path]`, which represents the path of the CSS file, and `[name]`, which is the name of the source CSS file.

Activating the previous configuration option, the result we have in the browser is as follows:

```
<button class="button--2wpxM">Click me!</button>
```

This is way more readable and easier to debug.

In production, we do not need class names like this, and we are more interested in performance, so we may want shorter class names and hashes.

With Webpack, it is pretty straightforward because we can have multiple configuration files that can be used in the different stages of our application life cycle. Also, in production, we may want to extract the CSS file instead of injecting it into the browser from the bundle so that we can have a lighter bundle and cache the CSS on a **Content Delivery Network (CDN)** for better performance.

To do that, you need to install another Webpack plugin, called `mini-css-extract-plugin`, which can write an actual CSS file, putting in all the scoped classes that were generated from CSS modules.

There are a couple of features of CSS modules that are worth mentioning.

The first one is the `global` keyword. Prefixing any class with `:global`, in fact, means asking CSS modules not to scope the current selector locally.

For example, let's say we change our CSS as follows:

```
:global .button {
  ...
}
```

The output will be as follows:

```
.button {
  ...
}
```

This is good if you want to apply styles that cannot be scoped locally, such as third-party widgets.

My favorite feature of CSS modules is **composition**. With composition, we can extract classes from the same file or external dependencies and get all the styles applied to the element.

For example, extract the rule to set the background to red from the rules for the button into a separate block, as follows:

```
.background-red {
  background-color: #ff0000;
}
```

We can then compose it inside our button in the following way:

```
.button {
  composes: background-red;
  width: 320px;
  padding: 20px;
  border-radius: 5px;
  border: none;
  outline: none;
}
```

The result is that all the rules of the button and all the rules of the `composes` declaration are applied to the element.

This is a very powerful feature, and it works in a fascinating way. You might expect that all the composed classes are duplicated inside the classes where they are referenced as **SASS @extend** does, but that is not the case. Simply put, all the composed class names are applied one after the other on the component in the DOM.

In our specific case, we would have the following:

```
<button class="_2wpxM3yizfwbWee6k0UlD4 Sf8w9cFdQXdRV_i9dgcOq">Click me!</
button>
```

Here, the CSS that is injected into the page is as follows:

```
.Sf8w9cFdQXdRV_i9dgcOq {
  background-color: #ff0000;
}

._2wpxM3yizfwbWee6k0UlD4 {
  width: 320px;
  padding: 20px;
  border-radius: 5px;
```

```
  border: none;
  outline: none;
}
```

As you can see, our CSS class names have unique names, which is good to isolate our styles. Now, let's take a look at the Atomic CSS modules.

Atomic CSS modules

It should be clear how composition works and why it is a very powerful feature of CSS modules. At Disney, the company where I worked when I started writing this book, we tried to push it a step further, combining the power of composes with the flexibility of **Atomic CSS** (also known as **Functional CSS**).

Atomic CSS is a way to use CSS where every class has a single rule.

For example, we can create a class to set `margin-bottom` to 0:

```
.mb0 {
  margin-bottom: 0;
}
```

We can use another one to set `font-weight` to 600:

```
.fw6 {
  font-weight: 600;
}
```

Then, we can apply all those Atomic classes to the elements:

```
<h2 class="mb0 fw6">Hello React</h2>
```

This technique is controversial and particularly efficient at the same time. It is hard to start using it because you end up having too many classes in your markup, which makes it hard to predict the final result. If you think about it, it is pretty similar to inline styles, because you apply one class per rule, apart from the fact that you are using a shorter class name as a proxy.

The biggest argument against Atomic CSS is usually that you are moving the styling logic from the CSS to the markup, which is wrong. Classes are defined in CSS files, but they are composed in the views, and every time you have to modify the style of an element, you end up editing the markup.

On the other hand, we tried using Atomic CSS for a bit and we found that it makes prototyping incredibly fast.

In fact, when all the base rules have been generated, applying those classes to the elements and creating new styles is a very quick process, which is good. Second, using Atomic CSS, we can control the size of the CSS file, because as soon as we create new components with their styles, we are using existing classes and we do not need to create new ones, which is great for performance.

So, we tried to solve the problems of Atomic CSS using CSS modules and we called the technique **Atomic CSS modules**.

In essence, you start creating your base CSS classes (for example, mb0), and then, instead of applying the class names one by one in the markup, you compose them into placeholder classes using CSS modules.

Let's look at an example:

```
.title {
    composes: mb0 fw6;
}
```

Here's another example:

```
<h2 className={styles.title}>Hello React</h2>
```

This is great because you still keep the styling logic inside the CSS, and the CSS module's composes does the job for you by applying all the single classes in the markup.

The result of the preceding code is as follows:

```
<h2 class="title--3JCJR mb0--21SyP fw6--1JRhZ">Hello React</h2>
```

Here, title, mb0, and fw6 are all applied automatically to the element. They are scoped locally as well, so we have all the advantages of CSS modules.

Implementing styled-components

There is a library that is very promising because it takes into account all the problems other libraries have encountered in styling components. Different paths have been followed for writing CSS in JavaScript, and many solutions have been tried, so now the time is ripe for a library that takes all the learning and then builds something on top of it.

The library is conceived and maintained by two popular developers in the JavaScript community: *Glenn Maddern* and *Max Stoiber*. It represents a very modern approach to the problem, and it uses the edge features of ES2015 and some advanced techniques that have been applied to React to provide a complete solution for styling.

Let's look at how it is possible to create the same button we saw in the previous sections and check whether all the CSS features we are interested in (for example, pseudo-classes and media queries) work with `styled-components`.

First, we have to install the library by running the following command:

```
npm install styled-components
```

Once the library is installed, we have to import it inside our component's file:

```
import styled from 'styled-components'
```

At that point, we can use the styled function to create any element by using `styled.elementName`, where `elementName` can be a div, a button, or any other valid DOM element.

The second thing to do is to define the style of the element we are creating and, to do so, we use an ES6 feature called **tagged template literals**, which is a way of passing template strings to a function without them being interpolated beforehand.

This means that the function receives the actual template with all the JavaScript expressions, and this makes the library able to use the full power of JavaScript to apply the styles to the elements.

Let's start by creating a simple button with a basic styling:

```
const Button = styled.button`
  backgroundColor: #ff0000;
  width: 320px;
  padding: 20px;
  borderRadius: 5px;
  border: none;
  outline: none;
`;
```

This *kind-of-weird* syntax returns a proper React component called `Button`, which renders a button element and applies to it all the styles defined in the template. The way the styles are applied is by creating a unique class name, adding it to the element, and then injecting the corresponding style in the head of the document.

The following is the component that gets rendered:

```
<button class="kYvFOg">Click me!</button>
```

The style that gets added to the page is as follows:

```css
.kYvFOg {
  background-color: #ff0000;
  width: 320px;
  padding: 20px;
  border-radius: 5px;
  border: none;
  outline: none;
}
```

The good thing about styled-components is that it supports almost all the features of CSS, which makes it a good candidate to be used in a real-world application.

For example, it supports pseudo-classes using a SASS-like syntax:

```
const Button = styled.button`
  background-color: #ff0000;
  width: 320px;
  padding: 20px;
  border-radius: 5px;
  border: none;
  outline: none;
  &:hover {
    color: #fff;
  }
  &:active {
    position: relative;
    top: 2px;
  }
```

It also supports media queries:

```
const Button = styled.button`
  background-color: #ff0000;
  width: 320px;
  padding: 20px;
  border-radius: 5px;
```

```
  border: none;
  outline: none;
  &:hover {
    color: #fff;
  }
  &:active {
    position: relative;
    top: 2px;
  }
  @media (max-width: 480px) {
    width: 160px;
  }
`;
```

There are many other features that this library can bring to your project.

For example, once you have created the button, you can easily override its styles and use it multiple times with different properties. Inside the templates, it is also possible to use the props that the component received and change the style accordingly.

Another great feature is **theming**. By wrapping your components in a ThemeProvider component, you can inject a theme property down to the three component's children, which makes it extremely easy to create UIs where part of the style is shared between components and some other properties depend on the currently selected theme.

Without a doubt, the styled-components library is a game-changer when you are taking your styles to the next level. In the beginning, it could seem weird because it involves implementing styles with components, but once you get used to it, I guarantee it will be your favorite styles package.

Summary

In this chapter, we explored important topics that aim to help readers navigate the complexities of styling in React. We discussed the challenges of scaling CSS, using Meta's experiences as examples to highlight the real-world difficulties faced by large organizations. This emphasizes the relevance and applicability of the knowledge we're sharing.

To make styling in React more intuitive and efficient, we examined how inline styles work and the benefits of co-locating styles within components. This approach promotes organized and readable code, which is crucial for developers aiming to master React.

Recognizing the limitations of inline styles, we introduced CSS modules as an alternative. We provided a step-by-step guide to setting up a project, allowing readers to learn through hands-on experimentation.

Importing CSS files into components was also emphasized as an important practice. This helps clarify dependencies and prevents issues by keeping class names scoped locally, ensuring scalable and conflict-free code.

Finally, we introduced readers to `styled-components`, a library that aligns with our book's goal of offering innovative ways to style components and optimize development practices in React.

So far, we have explored various approaches to managing CSS styles in React, each illustrating different aspects of our central proposition. In the next chapter, we will further enhance your understanding of React by delving into the practical implementation and benefits of server-side rendering—a technique that improves application performance and user experience.

Join our community on Discord

Join our community's Discord space for discussion with the author and other readers:

`https://packt.link/React18DesignPatterns4e`

7

Anti-Patterns to Be Avoided

In this book, you've learned how to apply best practices when writing a React application. In the first few chapters, we revisited the basic concepts to build a solid understanding, and then we took a leap into more advanced techniques in the following chapters.

You should now be able to build reusable components, make components communicate with each other, and optimize an application tree to get the best performance. However, developers make mistakes, and this chapter is all about the common anti-patterns we should avoid when using React.

Looking at common errors will help you to avoid them and will aid your understanding of how React works and how to build applications in the React way. For each problem, we will see an example that shows how to reproduce and solve it.

In this chapter, we will cover the following topics:

- Initializing the state using properties
- Using indexes as a key
- Spreading properties on DOM elements

Technical requirements

To complete this chapter, you will need the following:

- Node.js 19+
- Visual Studio Code

You can find the code for this chapter in the book's GitHub repository: `https://github.com/PacktPublishing/React-18-Design-Patterns-and-Best-Practices-Fourth-Edition/tree/main/Chapter07`.

Initializing the state using properties

In this section, we will see how initializing the state using properties received from the parent is usually an anti-pattern. I have used the word *usually* because, as we will see, once we have it clear in our mind what the problems with this approach are, we might still decide to use it.

One of the best ways to learn something is by looking at the code, so we will start by creating a simple component with a + button to increment a counter.

Let's create a functional component named `Counter`, as shown in the following code snippet:

```
import { FC, useState } from 'react'
type Props = {
  count: number
}
const Counter: FC<Props> = (props) => {}
export default Counter
```

Now, let's set our count state:

```
const [state, setState] = useState<number>(props.count)
```

The implementation of the click handler is straightforward – we just add 1 to the current count value and store the resulting value back in the state:

```
const handleClick = () => {
  setState({ count: state.count + 1 })
}
```

Finally, we render and describe the output, which is composed of the current value of the count state and the button to increment it:

```
return (
 <div>
   {state.count}
   <button onClick={handleClick}>+</button>
 </div>
)
```

Now, let's render this component, passing 1 as the count property:

```
<Counter count={1} />
```

It works as expected – each click on the + button increments the current value. So, what's the problem?

There are two main errors, which are outlined as follows:

- We have a duplicated source of truth.
- If the count property passed to the component changes, the state does not get updated.

If we inspect the Counter element using the React DevTools, we notice that Props and State hold a similar value:

```
<Counter>
Props
  count: 1
State
  count: 1
```

This makes it unclear which is the current and trustworthy value to use inside the component and to display to the user.

Even worse, clicking + once makes the values diverge. An example of this divergence is shown in the following code:

```
<Counter>
Props
  count: 1
State
  count: 2
```

At this point, we can assume that the second value represents the current count, but this is not explicit and can lead to unexpected behaviors or wrong values down in the tree.

The second problem centers on how the class is created and instantiated by React. The useState function of the component gets called only once when the component is created.

In our Counter component, we read the value of the count property and we store it in the state. If the value of that property changes during the life cycle of the application (let's say it becomes 10), the Counter component will never use the new value because it has already been initialized. This puts the component in an inconsistent state, which is not optimal and hard to debug.

What if we really want to use the prop's value to initialize the component, and we know for sure that the value does not change in the future?

In that case, it's best practice to make it explicit and give the property a name that makes your intentions clear, such as initialCount. For example, let's say we change the prop declaration of the Counter component in the following way:

```
type Props = {
    initialCount: number
}
const Counter: FC<Props> = (props) => {
    const [count, setState] = useState<Count>({ count: props.initialCount
    })
    ...
}
```

This usage makes it clear that the parent can only initialize the counter, and any subsequent values of the initialCount property will be disregarded:

```
<Counter initialCount={1} />
```

In the next section, we are going to delve into the concept of keys.

Using indexes as a key

In *Chapter 15, Improving the Performance of Your Applications*, which talks about performance and the reconciler, we saw how we can help React figure out the shortest path to update the DOM by using the key prop.

The key property uniquely identifies an element in the DOM and React uses it to check whether the element is new or whether it must be updated when the component properties or state change.

Using keys is always a good idea and if you don't do it, React gives a warning in the console (in development mode). However, it is not simply a matter of using a key; sometimes, the value that we decide to use as a key can make a difference. In fact, using the wrong key can give us unexpected behaviors in some instances. In this section, we will see one of those instances.

Let's again create a List component, as shown here:

```
import { FC, useState } from 'react'
const List: FC = () => {
}
export default List
```

Then we define our state:

```
const [items, setItems] = useState(['foo', 'bar'])
```

The implementation of the click handler is slightly different from the previous one because, in this case, we need to insert a new item at the top of the list:

```
const handleClick = () => {
 const newItems = items.slice()
   newItems.unshift('baz')
   setItems(newItems)
}
```

Finally, in the render, we show the list and the + button to add the baz item at the top of the list:

```
return (
 <div>
   <ul>
    {items.map((item, index) => (
      <li key={index}>{item}</li>
    ))}
   </ul>
  <button onClick={handleClick}>+</button>
 </div>
)
```

If you run the component inside the browser, you will not see any problems; clicking the + button inserts a new item at the top of the list. But let's do an experiment.

Let's change the render in the following way, adding an input field near each item. We then use an input field because we can edit its content, making it easier to figure out the problem:

```
return (
 <div>
   <ul>
     {items.map((item, index) => (
       <li key={index}>
       {item}
     <input type="text" />
   </li>
 ))}
```

```
    </ul>
      <button onClick={handleClick}>+</button>
    </div>
  )
```

If we run this component again in the browser, copy the values of the items in the input fields, and then click +, we will get unexpected behavior.

As shown in the following screenshot, the items shift down while the input elements remain in the same position in such a way that their value does not match the value of the items anymore:

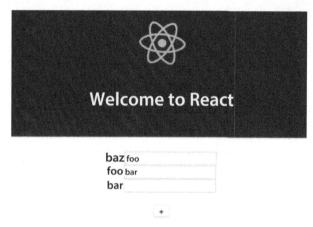

Figure 7.1: Using indexes as a key

Running the component, clicking +, and checking the console should give us all the answers we need.

What we can see is that instead of inserting the new element at the top, React swaps the text of the two existing elements, and inserts the last item at the bottom as if it was new. The reason it does that is that we are using the index of the map function as the key.

In fact, the index always starts from 0, even if we push a new item to the top of the list, so React thinks that we changed the values of the existing two and added a new element at index 2. The behavior is the same as it would have been without using the key property at all.

This is a very common pattern because we may think that providing any key is always the best solution, but it is not like that at all. The key must be unique and stable, identifying one, and only one, item.

To solve this problem, we can, for example, use the value of the item if we expect it not to be repeated within the list, or create a unique identifier, for example:

```
{items.map((item, index) => (
  <li key={`${item}-${index}`}>
    {item}
    <input type="text" />
  </li>
))}
```

Now that we have understood the importance of unique and stable keys in React and explored practical solutions to address this common issue, let's shift our attention to another prevalent practice in React development. The upcoming section will focus on the spreading of properties on DOM elements, a technique that has recently been labeled as an anti-pattern by Dan Abramov.

Spreading properties on DOM elements

There is a common practice that has recently been described as an anti-pattern by Dan Abramov; it also triggers a warning in the console when you do it in your React application.

It is a technique that is widely used in the community, and I have personally seen it multiple times in real-world projects. We usually spread the properties to the elements to avoid writing every single one manually, which is shown as follows:

```
<Component {...props} />
```

This works very well, and it gets transpiled into the following code by Babel:

```
_jsx(Component, props)
```

However, when we spread properties into a DOM element, we run the risk of adding unknown HTML attributes, which is bad practice.

The problem is not related only to the Spread operator; passing non-standard properties one by one leads to the same issues and warnings. Since the Spread operator hides the single properties we are spreading, it is even harder to figure out what we are passing to the element.

To see the warning in the console, a basic operation we can do is render the following component:

```
const Spread = () => <div foo="bar" />
```

The message we get looks like the following because the foo property is not valid for a div element:

```
Unknown prop `foo` on <div> tag. Remove this prop from the element
```

In this case, as we said, it is easy to figure out which attribute we are passing and remove it, but if we use the Spread operator, as in the following example, we cannot control which properties are passed from the parent:

```
const Spread = props => <div {...props} />;
```

If we use the component in the following way, there are no issues:

```
<Spread className="foo" />
```

This, however, is not the case if we do something such as the following. React complains because we are applying a non-standard attribute to the DOM element:

```
<Spread foo="bar" className="baz" />
```

One solution we can use to solve this problem is to create a property called domProps that we can spread safely to the component because we are explicitly saying that it contains valid DOM properties.

For example, we can change the Spread component in the following way:

```
const Spread = props => <div {...props.domProps} />
```

We can then use it as follows:

```
<Spread foo="bar" domProps={{ className: 'baz' }} />
```

As we have seen many times with React, it's always good practice to be explicit.

Summary

Knowing all the best practices is always a good thing, but sometimes, being aware of anti-patterns helps us avoid taking the wrong path. Most importantly, learning the reasons why some techniques are considered bad practice helps us understand how React works, and how we can use it effectively.

In this chapter, we covered four different ways of using components that can harm the performance and behavior of our web applications.

For each one of those, we used an example to reproduce the problem and supplied the changes to apply in order to fix the issue.

We learned why using properties to initialize the state can result in inconsistencies between the state and the properties. We also saw how using the wrong key attribute can produce bad effects on the reconciliation algorithm. Finally, we learned why spreading non-standard properties to DOM elements is considered an anti-pattern.

In the next chapter, we will look into the new React Hooks.

8

React Hooks

React Hooks have revolutionized the way we write React applications, allowing us to use functional components instead of class components, and making coding faster and more efficient. Since their introduction in React 16.8, Hooks have become an essential part of React development and have greatly improved the performance of our applications. With Hooks, we can manage the state, handle side effects, and reuse code in a more concise and readable way. In the next chapter, we will explore the different types of Hooks and how to use them to enhance our React applications.

In this chapter, we will cover the following topics:

- The new React Hooks and how to use them
- The rules of the Hooks
- How to migrate a class component to React Hooks
- Understanding the component life cycle with Hooks and effects
- How to fetch data with Hooks
- How to memoize components, values, and functions with memo, useMemo, and useCallback
- How to implement useReducer

Technical requirements

To complete this chapter, you will require the following:

- Node.js 19+
- Visual Studio Code

You can find the code for this chapter in the book's GitHub repository at https://github.com/
PacktPublishing/React-18-Design-Patterns-and-Best-Practices-Fourth-Edition/tree/
main/Chapter08.

Introducing React Hooks

React Hooks are a new addition to **React 16.8**. They let you use state and other React features
without writing a React class component. React Hooks are also backward-compatible, which
means they do not contain any breaking changes or not replace your knowledge of React concepts.
Over the course of this chapter, we will see an overview of Hooks for experienced React users,
and we are also going to learn about some of the most common React Hooks such as useState,
useEffect, useMemo, useCallback, and memo.

No breaking changes

In the context of React development, it's a common misconception that the introduction of React
Hooks has made class components obsolete. However, this is not true, as there are no plans to
remove classes from React. The Hooks API does not replace your understanding of React concepts,
but rather offers a more streamlined approach to working with those concepts, such as props,
states, context, refs, and life cycles, which you are already familiar with.

Using the State Hook

In old React code, we used this.setState to use the component state. Now we will use the
useState hook to do this.

First, you need to extract the useState Hook from React:

```
import { useState } from 'react'
```

Since React 17, the React object is no longer required to render JSX code.

Then, you need to declare the state you want to use by defining the state and the setter for this
specific state:

```
const Counter = () => {
  const [counter, setCounter] = useState<number>(0)
}
```

As you can see, we are declaring the counter state with the setCounter setter and we are specifying
that we will only accept numbers, and finally, we are setting the initial value to zero.

In order to test our state, we need to create a method that will be triggered by the onClick event:

```
type Operation = 'add' | 'substract'
const Counter = () => {
  const [counter, setCounter] = useState<number>(0)
  const handleCounter = (operation: Operation) => {
    if (operation === 'add') {
      return setCounter(counter + 1)
    }

    setCounter(counter - 1)
  }
}
```

Finally, we can render the counter state and some buttons to increase or decrease the counter state:

```
return (
  <p>
    Counter: {counter} <br />
    <button onClick={() => handleCounter('add')}>+ Add</button>
    <button onClick={() => handleCounter('subtract')}>- Subtract</button>
  </p>
)
```

If you click on the **+ Add** button once, you should see **1** for **Counter:**

Counter: 1
+ Add | - Subtract

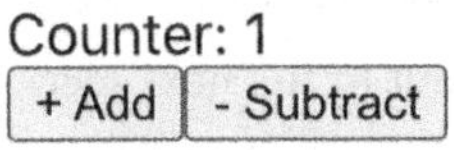

Figure 8.1: Counter 1

And if you click the **- Subtract** button twice, then you should see **-1** for **Counter:**

Counter: -1
+ Add | - Subtract

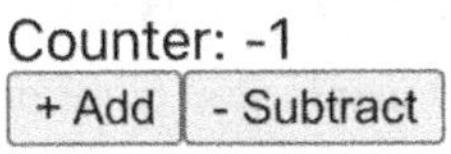

Figure 8.2: Counter -1

As you can see, the useState Hook is a game changer in React and makes it very easy to handle the state in a functional component.

After appreciating how the useState Hook has revolutionized state management in functional components within React, we are now ready to delve deeper into the nuances of Hooks. The following section will discuss the essential *rules of Hooks* that govern their usage in React applications.

Rules of Hooks

React Hooks are basically JavaScript functions, but there are two rules that you need to follow in order to use them. React provides a linter plugin to enforce those rules for you, which you can install by running the following command:

```
npm install --save-dev eslint-plugin-react-hooks
```

Let's look at these two rules.

Rule 1: Only call Hooks at the top level

To ensure the proper functioning of React Hooks, it is important to avoid calling them inside loops, conditions, or nested functions. Instead, it is recommended to always use Hooks at the top level of your React function. This practice ensures that Hooks are called in the same order every time a component is rendered, allowing React to correctly preserve the state of Hooks between multiple useState and useEffect calls. Following this rule will help you write more efficient and maintainable code with React Hooks.

Rule 2: Only call Hooks from React functions

To ensure that all stateful logic in a component is clearly visible from its source code, avoid calling Hooks from regular JavaScript functions. Instead, use Hooks in React function components or custom Hooks (which we'll learn about in the next section). By following this practice, you can ensure that all stateful logic is centralized and easily understandable.

In the next section, we will learn how to migrate a class component to use the new React Hooks.

Migrating a class component to React Hooks

Let's transform code that is currently using class components and is also using some life cycle methods. In this example, we are fetching the issues from a GitHub repository and listing them.

For this example, you will need to install axios to perform the fetch:

```
npm install axios
```

This is the class component version:

```
import axios from 'axios'
import { Component } from 'react'
type Issue = {
  number: number
  title: string
  state: string
}
type Props = {}
type State = { issues: Issue[] }
class Issues extends Component<Props, State> {
  constructor(props: Props) {
    super(props)
    this.state = {
      issues: []
    }
  }
  componentDidMount() {
    axios.get('https://api.github.com/repos/ContentPI/ContentPI/issues')
      .then((response: any) => {
        this.setState({
          issues: response.data
        })
      })
  }
  render() {
    const { issues = [] } = this.state
    return (
      <>
        <h1>ContentPI Issues</h1>
        {issues.map((issue: Issue) => (
          <p key={issue.title}>
            <strong>#{issue.number}</strong>{' '}
            <a
              href={`https://github.com/ContentPI/ContentPI/
issues/${issue.number}`}
```

```
                target="_blank"
          >
            {issue.title}
          </a>{' '}
          {issue.state}
        </p>
      ))}
    </>
  )
 }
}
export default Issues
```

If you render this component, you should see something like this:

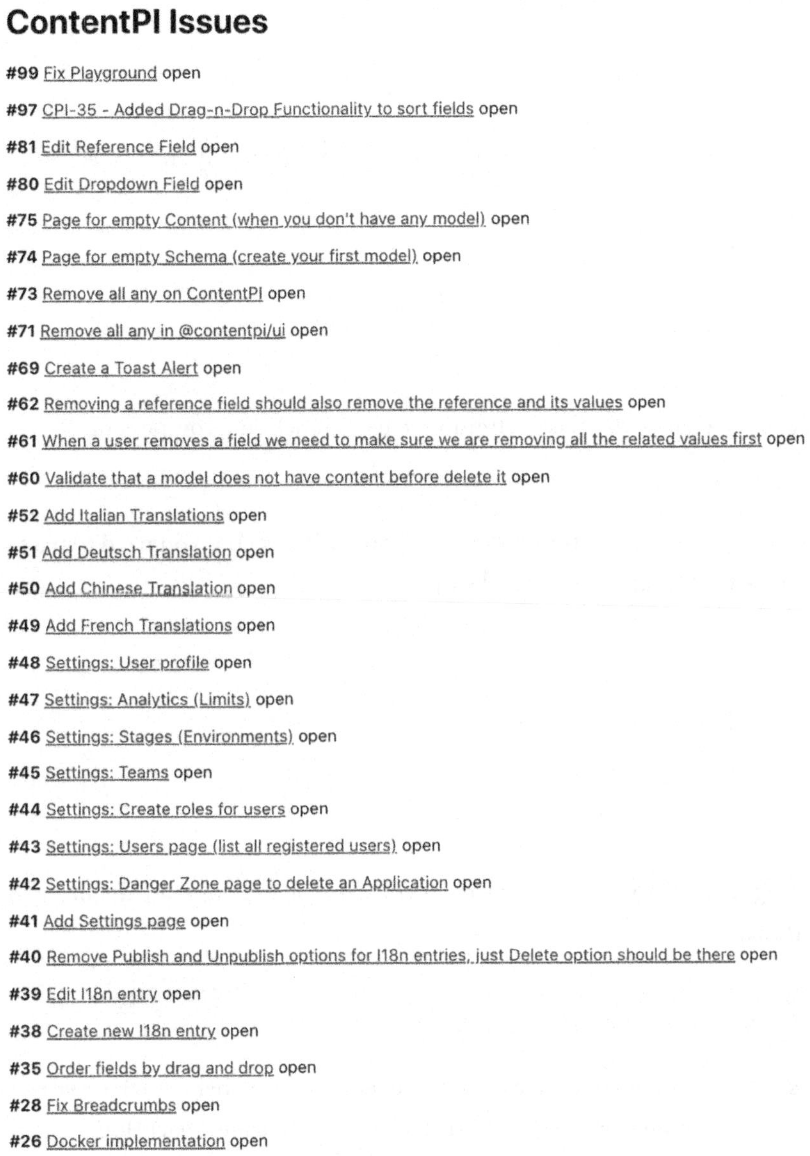

ContentPI Issues

#99 Fix Playground open

#97 CPI-35 - Added Drag-n-Drop Functionality to sort fields open

#81 Edit Reference Field open

#80 Edit Dropdown Field open

#75 Page for empty Content (when you don't have any model) open

#74 Page for empty Schema (create your first model) open

#73 Remove all any on ContentPI open

#71 Remove all any in @contentpi/ui open

#69 Create a Toast Alert open

#62 Removing a reference field should also remove the reference and its values open

#61 When a user removes a field we need to make sure we are removing all the related values first open

#60 Validate that a model does not have content before delete it open

#52 Add Italian Translations open

#51 Add Deutsch Translation open

#50 Add Chinese Translation open

#49 Add French Translations open

#48 Settings: User profile open

#47 Settings: Analytics (Limits) open

#46 Settings: Stages (Environments) open

#45 Settings: Teams open

#44 Settings: Create roles for users open

#43 Settings: Users page (list all registered users) open

#42 Settings: Danger Zone page to delete an Application open

#41 Add Settings page open

#40 Remove Publish and Unpublish options for I18n entries, just Delete option should be there open

#39 Edit I18n entry open

#38 Create new I18n entry open

#35 Order fields by drag and drop open

#28 Fix Breadcrumbs open

#26 Docker implementation open

Figure 8.3: ContentPI Issues

Now, let's transform our code into a functional component using React Hooks. The first thing we need to do is to import some React functions and types:

```
import { FC, useState, useEffect } from 'react'
import axios from 'axios'
```

Now we can remove the Props and State types we created previously and just leave the Issue type:

```
type Issue = {
  number: number
  title: string
  state: string
}
```

After this, you can change the class definition to use a functional component:

```
const Issues: FC = () => {...}
```

The FC type is used to define a **functional component** in React. If you need to pass some props to the component, you can pass them like this:

```
type Props = {
  propX: string
  propY: number
  propZ: boolean
}
const Issues: FC<Props> = () => {...}
```

The next thing we need to do is to replace our constructor and our state definition by using the useState Hook:

```
// The useState hook replace the this.setState method
const [issues, setIssues] = useState<Issue[]>([])
```

We have used the life cycle method called componentDidMount before, which is executed when the component is mounted and is going to run just once. The new React Hook, called useEffect, will now handle all the life cycle methods using different syntax for each one, but for now, let's see how we can get the same *effect* of componentDidMount in our new functional component:

```
// When we use the useEffect hook with an empty array [] on the
// dependencies (second parameter)
// this represents the componentDidMount method (will be executed when the
```

```
// component is mounted).
useEffect(() => {
  axios
    .get('https://api.github.com/repos/ContentPI/ContentPI/issues')
    .then((response: any) => {
      // Here we update directly our issue state
      setIssues(response.data)
    })
}, [])
```

And finally, we just render our JSX code:

```
return (
  <>
    <h1>ContentPI Issues</h1>
    {issues.map((issue: Issue) => (
        <p key={issue.title}>
        <strong>#{issue.number}</strong> {' '}
          <a
          href={`https://github.com/ContentPI/ContentPI/issues/${issue.
number}`}
          target="_blank">{issue.title}
        </a> {' '}
          {issue.state}
        </p>
    ))}
  </>
)
```

As you can see, the new Hooks help us to simplify our code a lot and makes more sense. Also, we reduced our code by 10 lines (the class component code has 53 lines, and the functional component has 43 lines).

Now that we have seen the transformative power of new Hooks in streamlining our code and reducing verbosity, let's shift our focus to another foundational concept in React. In the next section, we will delve into the differences between component life cycle methods used in class components and the innovative React effects.

Understanding React effects

In this section, we will learn the difference between the component life cycle methods that we used in class components and the new React effects. Even if you have read in other places that they are the same, just with a different syntax, this is not correct.

Understanding useEffect

When you work with useEffect, you need to *think in terms of effects*. If you want to perform the equivalent method of componentDidMount using useEffect, you can do the following:

```
useEffect(() => {
  // Here you perform your side effect
}, [])
```

The first parameter is the callback of the effect that you want to execute, and the second parameter is the dependencies array. If you pass an empty array ([ ]) to the dependencies, the state and props will have their original initial values.

However, it is important to mention that even though this is the closest equivalent to componentDidMount, it does not have the same behavior. Unlike componentDidMount and componentDidUpdate, the function that we pass to useEffect fires after layout and paint, during a deferred event. This normally works for many common side effects, such as setting up subscriptions and event handlers, because most types of work shouldn't block the browser from updating the screen.

However, not all effects can be deferred. For example, you will get a blink if you need to mutate the **Document Object Model (DOM)**. This is the reason why you must fire the event synchronously before the next paint. React provides one Hook called useLayoutEffect, which works in the exact same way as useEffect.

Firing an effect conditionally

If you need to fire an effect conditionally, then you should add a dependency to the array of dependencies; otherwise, you will execute the effect multiple times and this may cause an infinite loop. If you pass an array of dependencies, the useEffect Hook will only run if one of those dependencies changes:

```
useEffect(() => {
  // When you pass an array of dependencies the useEffect hook will only
```

```
// run if one of the dependencies changes.
}, [dependencyA, dependencyB])
```

 If you understand how the React class life cycle methods work, basically, `useEffect` behaves in the same way as `componentDidMount`, `componentDidUpdate`, and `componentWillUnmount` combined.

The effects are very important, but let's also explore some other important new Hooks, including useCallback, useMemo, and memo.

Understanding useCallback, useMemo, and memo

In order to understand the difference between useCallback, useMemo, and memo, we will do a to-do list example. You can create a basic application by using create-vite and Typescript as a template:

```
npx create-vite todo --template react-ts
```

Right after that, you can remove all the extra files (App.css, App.test.ts, index.css, logo.svg, reportWebVitals.ts, and setupTests.ts). You just need to keep the App.tsx file, which will contain the following code:

```
import { FC, useState, useEffect, useMemo, useCallback, ChangeEvent } from
'react'
import List, { Todo } from './List'
const initialTodos: Todo[] = [
  { id: 1, task: 'Go shopping' },
  { id: 2, task: 'Pay the electricity bill'}
]
const App: FC = () => {
  const [todoList, setTodoList] = useState<Todo[]>(initialTodos)
  const [task, setTask] = useState<string>('')
  useEffect(() => {
    console.log('Rendering <App />')
  })
  const handleCreate = () => {
    const newTodo = {
        id: Date.now(),
```

```
        task
    }

    // Pushing the new todo to the list
    setTodoList([...todoList, newTodo])

    // Resetting input value
    setTask('')
  }
  return (
    <>
      <input
        type="text"
        value={task}
        onChange={(e: ChangeEvent<HTMLInputElement>) => setTask(e.
target.value)}
      />
      <button onClick={handleCreate}>Create</button>
      <List todoList={todoList} />
    </>
  )
}
export default App
```

Basically, we are defining some initial tasks and creating the todoList state, which we will pass to the List component. Then, you need to create the List.tsx file with the following code:

```
import { FC, useEffect } from 'react'
import Task from './Task'
export type Todo = {
  id: number
  task: string
}
interface Props {
  todoList: Todo[]
}
```

```
const List: FC<Props> = ({ todoList }) => {
  useEffect(() => {
    // This effect is executed every new render
    console.log('Rendering <List />')
  })
  return (
    <ul>
        {todoList.map((todo: Todo) => (
            <Task key={todo.id} id={todo.id} task={todo.task} />
        ))}
    </ul>
  )
}
export default List
```

As you can see, we are rendering each task of the todoList array by using the Task component and we pass the task as a prop. I also added a useEffect Hook to see how many renders we are performing.

Finally, we create our Task.tsx file with the following code:

```
import { FC, useEffect } from 'react'
interface Props {
  id: number
  task: string
}
const Task: FC<Props> = ({ task }) => {
  useEffect(() => {
    console.log('Rendering <Task />', task)
  })
  return (
    <li>{task}</li>
  )
}
export default Task
```

This is how we should see the to-do list:

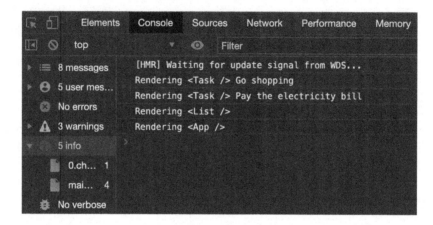

Figure 8.4: To-do list

As you can see, when we render our to-do list, by default, we are performing two renders of the Task component, one render for List, and the other for the App component.

Now, if we try to write a new task in the input, we can see that for each letter we write, we will again see all of those renders:

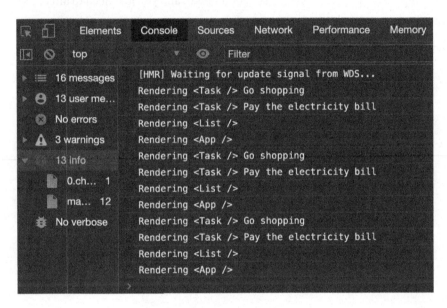

Figure 8.5: Searching in the to-do list

As you can see, by just writing Go, we have two new batches of renders, so we can determine that this component does not have good performance, and this is where memo can help us to improve performance. In the next sections, we are going to learn how to implement memo, useMemo, and useCallback to memoize a component, a value, and a function.

Memoizing a component with memo

The memo **High-Order Component (HOC)** is similar to PureComponent for a React class because it performs a shallow comparison of the props (meaning a superficial check), so if we try to render a component with the same props all the time, the component will render just once and will memoize. The only way to re-render the component is when a prop changes its value.

In order to fix our components to avoid multiple renders when we write in the input, we need to wrap our components in the memo **HOC**.

The first component we will fix is our List component, and you just need to affect import memo and wrap the component in export default:

```
import { FC, useEffect, memo } from 'react'
...
export default memo(List)
```

Then, you need to do the same with the Task component:

```
import { FC, useEffect, memo } from 'react'
...
export default memo(Task)
```

Now, when we try to write Go again in the input, let's see how many renders we get this time:

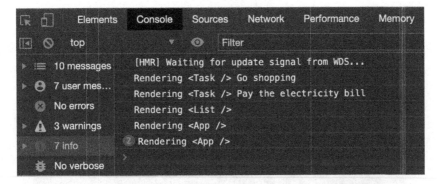

Figure 8.6: Evaluating how many renders our to-do list is performing

Now, we just get the first batch of renders the first time, and then, when we write Go, we just get two more renders of the App component, which is totally fine because the task state (input value) that we are changing is actually part of the App component.

Also, we can see how many renders we are performing when we create a new task by clicking on the **Create** button:

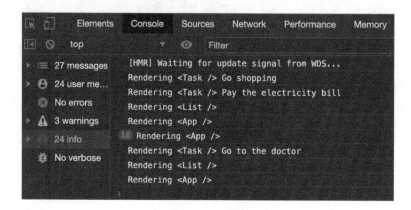

Figure 8.7: Improving performance

If you see, the first 16 renders are the word counting of the Go to the doctor string, and then, when you click on the **Create** button, you should see one render of the Task component, one render of List, and one render of the App component. As you can see, we have improved performance a lot, and we are just performing the exact need that it renders.

At this point, you're probably thinking that the correct thing is to always add memo to our components, or maybe you're thinking, why React doesn't do this by default for us?

The reason is *performance*, which means *it is not a good idea to add* memo *to all our components unless it is totally necessary*; otherwise, the process of shallow comparisons and memorization will have inferior performance than if we don't use it.

I have a rule when it comes to establishing whether it is a good idea to use memo, and this rule is straightforward: **just don't use it.** Normally, when we have small components or basic logic, we don't need this *unless you're working with large data from some API, your component needs to perform a lot of renders (normally huge lists), or when you notice that your app is going slow.* Only in that case would I recommend using memo.

Memoizing a value with useMemo

Let's suppose that we now want to implement a search feature in our to-do list. The first thing we need to do is to add a new state called `term` to the App component:

```
const [term, setTerm] = useState('')
```

Then, we need to create a function called `handleSearch`:

```
const handleSearch = () => {
  setTerm(task)
}
```

Right before the return, we will create `filterTodoList`, which will filter the to-dos based on the task, and we will add a console there to see how many times it is being rendered:

```
const filteredTodoList = todoList.filter((todo: Todo) => {
  console.log('Filtering...')
  return todo.task.toLowerCase().includes(term.toLowerCase())
})
```

Finally, we need to add a new button next to the **Create** button that already exists:

```
<button onClick={handleSearch}>Search</button>
```

At this point, I recommend that you remove or comment `console.log` in the `List` and `Task` components so that we can focus on the performance of filtering:

Figure 8.8: Reviewing filtering performance

When you run the application again, you will see that filtering is being executed twice, and then the App component as well, and everything looks good here, but what's the problem with this?

Try to write Go to the doctor again in the input and let's see how many counts of Rendering...
and Filtering... you get:

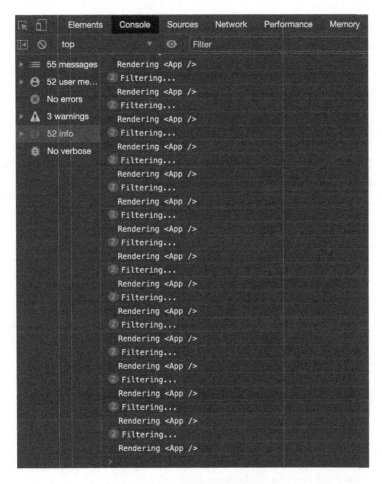

Figure 8.9: Bad performance on filtering

As you can see, for each letter you write, you will get two filtering calls and one App render. You don't need to be a genius to see that this is bad performance; not to mention that if you are working with a large data array, this will be worse, so how can we fix this issue?

The useMemo Hook is our hero in this situation, and basically, we need to move our filter inside useMemo, but first, let's see the syntax:

```
const filteredTodoList = useMemo(() => SomeProcessHere, [])
```

The useMemo Hook will memoize the result (value) of a function and will have some dependencies to listen to. Let's see how we can implement it:

```
const filteredTodoList = useMemo(() => todoList.filter((todo: Todo) => {
    console.log('Filtering...')
    return todo.task.toLowerCase().includes(term.toLowerCase())
}), [])
```

Now, if you write something again in the input, you will see that filtering won't be executed all the time, as was the case previously:

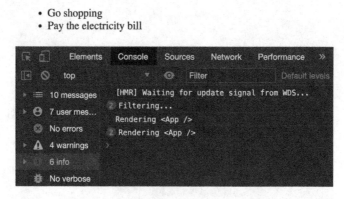

Figure 8.10: Improving the performance of filtering

This is great, but there is still one small problem. If you try to click on the **Search** button, it won't filter, and this is because we missed the dependencies.

Actually, if you see the console warnings, you will see this warning:

Figure 8.11: react-hooks/exhaustive deps

You need to add the `term` and `todoList` dependencies to the array:

```
const filteredTodoList = useMemo(() => todoList.filter((todo: Todo) => {
  console.log('Filtering...')
  return todo.task.toLowerCase().includes(term.toLowerCase())
}), [term, todoList])
```

It should now work if you write Go and click on the **Search** button:

Figure 8.12: After fixing the warning

Here, we have to use the same rule that we used for memo; *just don't use it until absolutely necessary.*

Memoizing a function definition with useCallback

Now we will add a delete task feature to learn how `useCallback` works. The first thing we need to do is to create a new function called `handleDelete` in our App component:

```
const handleDelete = (taskId: number) => {
  const newTodoList = todoList.filter((todo: Todo) => todo.id !== taskId)
  setTodoList(newTodoList)
}
```

And then you need to pass this function to the List component as a prop:

```
<List todoList={filteredTodoList} handleDelete={handleDelete} />
```

Then, in our List component, you need to add the prop to the Props interface:

```
interface Props {
  todoList: Todo[]
  handleDelete: any
}
```

Next, you need to pull it from the props and pass it down to the Task component:

```
const List: FC<Props> = ({ todoList, handleDelete }) => {
  useEffect(() => {
    // This effect is executed every new render
    console.log('Rendering <List />')
  })
  return (
    <ul>
        {todoList.map((todo: Todo) => (
        <Task
          key={todo.id}
          id={todo.id}
          task={todo.task}
          handleDelete={handleDelete}
          />
        ))}
    </ul>
  )
}
```

In the `Task` component, you need to create a button that will execute `handleDelete` `onClick`:

```
interface Props {
  id: number
  task: string
  handleDelete: any
}
const Task: FC<Props> = ({ id, task, handleDelete }) => {
  useEffect(() => {
    console.log('Rendering <Task />', task)
  })
  return (
    <li>{task} <button onClick={() => handleDelete(id)}>X</button></li>
  )
}
```

At this point, I recommend that you remove or comment `console.log` in the `List` and `Task` components so that we can focus on the performance of filtering. Now you should see the **X** button next to the task:

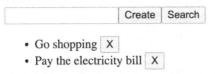

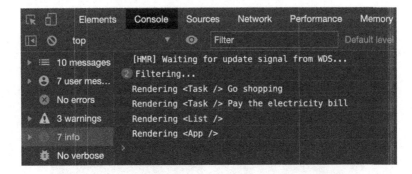

Figure 8.13: Let's delete a task

If you click on the **X** for `Go shopping`, you should be able to remove it:

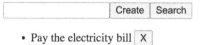

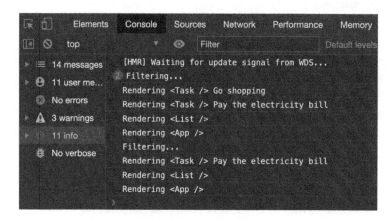

Figure 8.14: Deleting a task

So far, so good, right? But again, we have a little issue with this implementation. If you now try to write something in the input, such as `Go to the doctor`, let's see what happens:

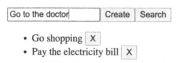

Figure 8.15: Bad performance

As you can see, we are performing 71 renders of all the components again. At this point, you are probably thinking about, *what is going on if we have already implemented the memo HOC to memoize the components?* But the problem now is that our `handleDelete` function is being passed to two components, from `App` to `List` and `Task`, and the issue is that this function is regenerated every time we have a new re-render, in this case, every time we write something. So how do we fix this problem?

The `useCallback` Hook is the hero in this case and is very similar to `useMemo` in the syntax, but the main difference is that instead of memorizing the result value of a function, as `useMemo` does, it is memorizing the **function definition** instead:

```
const handleDelete = useCallback(() => SomeFunctionDefinition, [])
```

Our `handleDelete` function should be like this:

```
const handleDelete = useCallback((taskId: number) => {
  const newTodoList = todoList.filter((todo: Todo) => todo.id !== taskId)
  setTodoList(newTodoList)
}, [todoList])
```

Now, it should work just fine if we write Go to the doctor again:

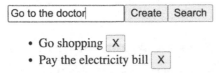

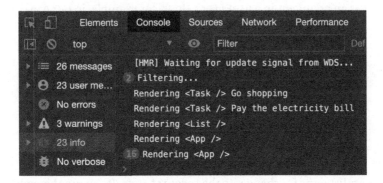

Figure 8.16: Improving performance

Now, instead of 71 renders, we just have 23, which is normal, and we are also able to delete tasks:

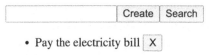

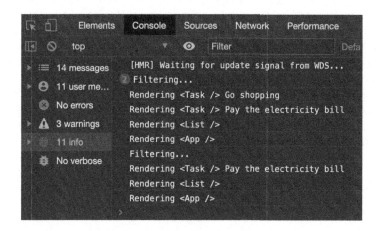

Figure 8.17: Deleting tasks

As you can see, the useCallback Hook helps us to improve performance significantly. In the next section, you will learn how to memoize a function passed as an argument in the useEffect Hook.

Memoizing a function passed as an argument in effect

There is a special case where we will need to use the useCallback Hook, and this is when we pass a function as an argument in a useEffect Hook, for example, in our App component. Let's create a new useEffect block:

```
const printTodoList = () => {
  console.log('Changing todoList')
}
useEffect(() => {
  printTodoList()
}, [todoList])
```

In this case, we are listening for changes to the todoList state. If you run this code and you create or remove a task, it will work just fine (remember to remove all the other consoles first):

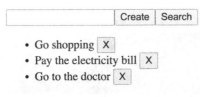

Figure 8.18: Changing the to-do list

Everything works fine, but let's add todoList to the console:

```
const printTodoList = () => {
  console.log('Changing todoList', todoList)
}
```

If you're using Visual Studio Code, you will get the following warning:

```
useEffect(() => {
  // console.log('Rendering <App />')
})
    React Hook useEffect has a missing dependency: 'printTodoList'. Either include it or remove
    the dependency array. eslint(react-hooks/exhaustive-deps)
use
  p  Peek Problem (⌥F8)   Quick Fix... (⌘.)
}, [todoList])
```

Figure 8.19: react-hooks/exhaustive-deps

Basically, it is asking us to add the printTodoList function to the dependencies:

```
useEffect(() => {
  printTodoList()
}, [todoList, printTodoList])
```

But now, after we do that, we get another warning:

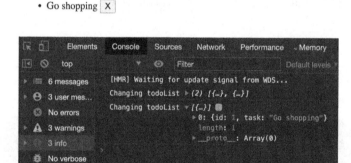

```
▲ ▸ src/App.tsx                                                    webpackHotDevClient.js:138
  Line 17:9:  The 'printTodoList' function makes the dependencies of useEffect Hook (at line 27)
  change on every render. Move it inside the useEffect callback. Alternatively, wrap the
  definition of 'printTodoList' in its own useCallback() Hook   react-hooks/exhaustive-deps
```

Figure 8.20: useCallback warning

The reason why we get this warning is that we are now manipulating the state (consoling the state), which is why we need to add a useCallback Hook to this function to fix this issue:

```
const printTodoList = useCallback(() => {
  console.log('Changing todoList', todoList)
}, [todoList])
```

Now, when we delete a task, we can see that todoList updated correctly:

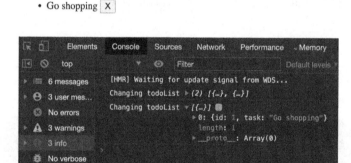

Figure 8.21: Changing to-do list data

At this point, this may be information overload for you, so let's have a quick recap:

- memo:

    - Memoizes a **component**

    - Re-memoizes when props change

    - Avoids re-renders

- useMemo:

    - Memoizes a calculated value

    - For computed properties

- For heavy processes

- `useCallback`:

  - Memoizes a **function definition** to avoid redefining it on each render
  - Use it whenever a function is passed as an effect argument
  - Use it whenever a function is passed by props to a memoized component

And finally, do not forget the golden rule: *Do not use them until absolutely necessary.*

In the next section, we are going to learn how to use the new `useReducer` Hook.

Understanding the useReducer Hook

You probably have some experience using Redux (`react-redux`) with class components, and if that is the case, then you will understand how `useReducer` works. The concepts are basically the same: actions, reducers, dispatch, store, and state. Even if, in general, it seems very similar to react-redux, they have some differences. The main difference is that react-redux provides middleware and wrappers such as **thunk**, **sagas**, and many more besides, while `useReducer` just gives you a `dispatch` method that you can use to dispatch plain objects as actions. Also, `useReducer` does not have a store by default; instead, you can create one using `useContext`, but this is just reinventing the wheel.

Let's create a basic application to understand how `useReducer` works. You can start by creating a new React app:

```
npx create-vite reducer --template react-ts
```

Then, as always, you can delete all files in your `src` folder except `App.tsx` and `index.tsx` to start a brand-new application.

We will create a basic `Notes` application where we can `list`, `delete`, `create`, or `update` our notes using `useReducer`. The first thing you need to do is import the `Notes` component, which we will create later, into your `App` component:

```
import Notes from './Notes'
function App() {
  return (
    <Notes />
  )
}
```

```
}
```

```
export default App
```

Now, in our Notes component, you first need to import useReducer and useState:

```
import { useReducer, useState, ChangeEvent } from 'react'
```

Then we need to define some TypeScript types that we need to use for our Note object, the Redux action, and the **action types**:

```
type Note = {
  id: number
  note: string
}
type Action = {
  type: string
  payload?: any
}
type ActionTypes = {
  ADD: 'ADD'
  UPDATE: 'UPDATE'
  DELETE: 'DELETE'
}
const actionType: ActionTypes = {
  ADD: 'ADD',
  DELETE: 'DELETE',
  UPDATE: 'UPDATE'
}
```

After this, we need to create initialNotes (also known as initialState) with some dummy notes:

```
const initialNotes: Note[] = [
  {
    id: 1,
    note: 'Note 1'
  },
  {
    id: 2,
```

```
    note: 'Note 2'
  }
]
```

If you remember how the reducers work, then this will seem very similar to how we handle the reducer using a switch statement, so as to perform basic operations such as ADD, DELETE, and UPDATE:

```
const reducer = (state: Note[], action: Action) => {
  switch (action.type) {
    case actionType.ADD:
        return [...state, action.payload]
    case actionType.DELETE:
        return state.filter(note => note.id !== action.payload)

    case actionType.UPDATE:
        const updatedNote = action.payload
        return state.map((n: Note) => n.id === updatedNote.id ?
updatedNote : n)

    default:
        return state
  }
}
```

Finally, the component is very straightforward. Basically, you get the notes and the dispatch method from the useReducer Hook (similar to useState), and you need to pass the reducer function and initialNotes (initialState):

```
const Notes = () => {
  const [notes, dispatch] = useReducer(reducer, initialNotes)
  const [note, setNote] = useState<string>('')
  ...
}
```

Then, we have a handleSubmit function to create a new note when we write something in the input. Then, we press *Enter*:

```
const handleSubmit = (e: ChangeEvent<HTMLInputElement>) => {
  e.preventDefault()
  const newNote = {
```

```
    id: Date.now(),
    note
  }
  dispatch({ type: actionType.ADD, payload: newNote })
}
```

Finally, we render our Notes list with map, and we also create two buttons, one for delete and one for update, and then the input should be wrapped into a <form> tag:

```
return (
  <div>
    <h2>Notes</h2>
    <ul>
        {notes.map((n: Note) => (
            <li key={n.id}>
                {n.note} {' '}

              <button onClick={() => dispatch({ type: actionType.DELETE,
payload: n.id })}>
                X
            </button>
            <button
                  onClick={() => dispatch({ type: actionType.UPDATE,
payload: {...n, note} })}
              >
                Update
            </button>
            </li>
        ))}
    </ul>

    <form onSubmit={handleSubmit}>
        <input
            placeholder="New note"
            value={note}
            onChange={e => setNote(e.target.value)}
        />
    </form>
```

```
    </div>
  )

  export default Notes
```

If you run the application, you should see the following output:

Notes

- Note 1 | X | Update |
- Note 2 | X | Update |

New note

Figure 8.22: React DevTools

As you can see in the **React DevTools**, the Reducer object contains the two notes that we have defined as our initial state.

Now, if you write something in the input and you press *Enter*, you should be able to create a new note:

Notes

- Note 1 X Update
- Note 2 X Update
- My new note 3 X Update

My new note 3

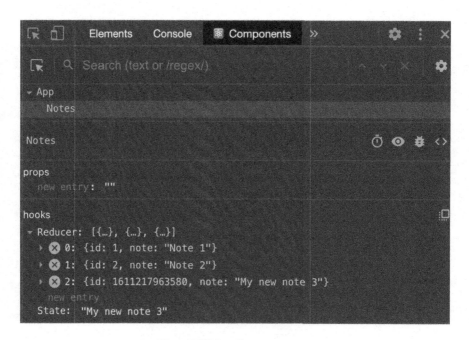

Figure 8.23: Creating a new note

Then, if you want to delete a note, you just need to click on the **X** button. Let's remove **Note 2**:

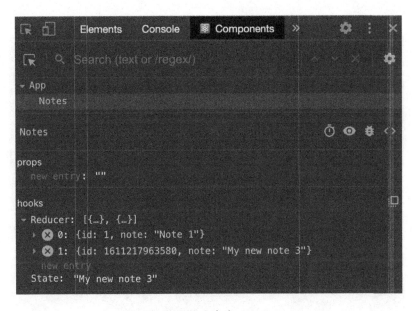

Figure 8.24: Deleting a note

Finally, you can write anything you want in the input, and if you click on the **Update** button, you will change the note value:

Notes

- Note 1 | X | Update |
- My new note 3 UPDATED | X | Update |

| My new note 3 UPDATED |

Figure 8.25: Updating a note

Nice, huh? As you can see, the useReducer Hook is pretty much the same as redux in terms of the dispatch method, actions, and reducers, but the main difference is that this is limited just to the context of your component and its child, so if you need a global store to be accessible from your entire application, then you should use react-redux instead.

Summary

I hope you enjoyed reading this chapter, which is full of very good information pertaining to the new React Hooks. So far, you have learned how the new React Hooks work; how to fetch data with Hooks; how to migrate a class component to **React Hooks**; how the effects work, the difference between `memo`, `useMemo`, and `useCallback`; and finally, you learned how the `useReducer` Hook works and the main difference compared with `react-redux`. This will help you to improve the performance of your React components.

In the next chapter, we will learn about React Router v6 and how to implement it in our projects.

9

React Router

React is a library that provides a lot of useful building blocks for creating web applications, but it doesn't include everything you might need *out of the box*. One key feature that React doesn't provide is routing, which is the ability to handle URLs and navigate between different pages or views in a single-page application. For that, we turn to third-party libraries, and the most popular one for React is **React Router**.

In this chapter, we'll explore React Router and learn how to use it to create dynamic routes and handle navigation in our React applications. By the end of this chapter, you'll have a good understanding of how React Router works and how to use it effectively in your own projects.

In this chapter, we will cover the following topics:

- Understanding the differences between the `react-router`, `react-router-dom`, and `react-router-native` packages
- How to install and configure React Router
- Adding the `<Routes>` component
- Adding parameters to routes
- React Router v6.4 and React Router loaders

Technical requirements

To complete this chapter, you will need the following:

- Node.js 19+
- Visual Studio Code

You can find the code for this chapter in the book's GitHub repository at https://github.com/
PacktPublishing/React-18-Design-Patterns-and-Best-Practices-Fourth-Edition/tree/
main/Chapter09.

Installing and configuring React Router

After you create a new React application using create-react-app, the first thing you need to do
is to install **React Router v6.x**, using the following command:

```
npm install react-router-dom @types/react-router-dom
```

You are probably confused about why we are installing react-router-dom instead of react-
router. React Router contains all the common components of react-router-dom and react-
router-native. That means that if you are using React for the web, you should use react-router-
dom, and if you are using React Native, you need to use react-router-native.

The react-router-dom package was created originally to contain version 4 and react-router
uses version 3. The react-router-dom v6 package has some improvements over react-router.
They are listed here:

- **Simplified route configuration**: React Router v6 has introduced a more straightforward
  route configuration, eliminating the need for Switch and exact props. Routes are now
  implicitly prioritized based on their definition order.

- **Nested routing**: React Router v6 has improved support for nested routing. The Outlet
  component is used to render child routes, allowing for more intuitive and maintainable
  route structures.

- **Simplified navigation**: In v6, the useNavigate hook has replaced the useHistory hook,
  providing a more straightforward and declarative approach to navigation.

- **Route relative links and navigation**: With the introduction of the useLinkProps and Link
  components in v6, it's now easier to create links relative to the current route. This reduces
  the need to hardcode full paths and simplifies route management.

- **Simplified route guards**: React Router v6 introduces a more streamlined approach to
  route guards using the useRoutes hook and the element prop. It allows for easier and
  more maintainable route protection patterns.

 Since React Router v6.4, the approach to creating routes has changed slightly, but it
still supports the "old way." In our final section, we will convert the same example
to the new approach.

Creating our sections

Let's create some sections to test some basic routes. We need to create four stateless components (About, Contact, Home, and Error404) and name them as index.tsx in their directories.

You can add the following to the src/components/Home.tsx component:

```
const Home = () => (
  <div className="Home">
    <h1>Home</h1>
  </div>
)
export default Home
```

The src/components/About.tsx component can be created with the following:

```
const About = () => (
  <div className="About">
    <h1>About</h1>
  </div>
)
export default About
```

The following creates the src/components/Contact.tsx component:

```
const Contact = () => (
  <div className="Contact">
    <h1>Contact</h1>
  </div>
)
export default Contact
```

Finally, the src/components/Error404.tsx component is created as follows:

```
const Error404 = () => (
  <div className="Error404">
    <h1>Error404</h1>
  </div>
)
export default Error404
```

After we have created all the functional components, we need to modify our `index.tsx` file to import our route file, which we will create in the next step:

```
// Dependencies
import { createRoot } from 'react-dom/client'
import { BrowserRouter as Router } from 'react-router-dom'
// Routes
import AppRoutes from './routes'
createRoot(document.getElementById('root') as HTMLElement).render(
  <Router>
    <AppRoutes />
  </Router>
)
```

Now, we need to create the `src/routes.tsx` file, where we will render our Home component when the user accesses the root path (/):

```
// Dependencies
import { Routes, Route } from 'react-router-dom'
// Components
import App from './App'
import Home from './components/Home'
const AppRoutes = () => (
  <App>
   <Routes>
     <Route path="/" element={<Home />} />
   </Routes>
  </App>
)
export default AppRoutes
```

After that, we need to modify our `App.tsx` file to render the route components as children:

```
import { FC, ReactNode } from 'react'
import './App.css'
type Props = {
  children: ReactNode
}
```

```
const App: FC<Props> = ({ children }) => (
  <div className="App">
    {children}
  </div>
)
export default App
```

If you run the application, you will see the Home component in the root (/):

Figure 9.1: Home page

Now, let's add Error404 when the user tries to access any other route:

```
// Dependencies
import { Routes, Route } from 'react-router-dom'
// Components
import App from './App'
import Home from './components/Home'
import Error404 from './components/Error404'
const AppRoutes = () => (
  <App>
    <Routes>
      <Route path="/" element={<Home />} />
      <Route path="*" element={<Error404 />} />
    </Routes>
  </App>
)
export default AppRoutes
```

Now, if you go to /somefakeurl, you will be able to see the **Error404** component:

Error404

Figure 9.2: Error 404 page

Now, we can add our other components (About and Contact):

```
// Dependencies
import { Routes, Route } from 'react-router-dom'
// Components
import App from './App'
import About from './components/About'
import Contact from './components/Contact'
import Home from './components/Home'
import Error404 from './components/Error404'
const AppRoutes = () => (
  <App>
    <Routes>
      <Route path="/" element={<Home />} />
      <Route path="/about" element={<About />} />
      <Route path="/contact" element={<Contact />} />
      <Route path="*" element={<Error404 />} />
    </Routes>
  </App>
)
export default AppRoutes
```

Now, you can visit /about:

Figure 9.3: About page

Alternatively, you can now visit /contact:

Figure 9.4: Contact page

Now that you have implemented your first routes, let's add some parameters to the routes in the next section.

Adding parameters to the routes

So far, you have learned how to use React Router for basic routes (one-level routes). Next, I will show you how to add some parameters to the routes and get them into your components.

For this example, we will create a `Contacts` component to display a list of contacts when we visit the `/contacts` route, but we will show the contact information (name, phone, and email) when the user visits `/contacts/:contactId`.

The first thing we need to do is to create our `Contacts` component. Let's use the following skeleton:

```
const Contacts = () => (
  <div className="Contacts">
    <h1>Contacts</h1>
  </div>
)
export default Contacts
```

Let's use these CSS styles:

```
.Contacts ul {
  list-style: none;
  margin: 0;
  margin-bottom: 20px;
  padding: 0;
}
.Contacts ul li {
  padding: 10px;
}
.Contacts a {
  color: #555;
  text-decoration: none;
}
.Contacts a:hover {
  color: #ccc;
  text-decoration: none;
}
```

Once you have created the `Contacts` component, you need to import it into your route file:

```
import { Routes, Route } from 'react-router-dom'
import App from './App'
import About from './components/About'
import Contact from './components/Contact'
```

```
import Home from './components/Home'
import Error404 from './components/Error404'
import Contacts from './components/Contacts'
const AppRoutes = () => (
  <App>
    <Routes>
      <Route path="/" element={<Home />} />
      <Route path="/about" element={<About />} />
      <Route path="/contact" element={<Contact />} />
      <Route path="/contacts" element={<Contacts />} />
      <Route path="*" element={<Error404 />} />
    </Routes>
  </App>
)
export default AppRoutes
```

Now you will be able to see the Contacts component if you go to the /contacts URL:

Contacts

Figure 9.5: Contacts page

Now that the Contacts component is connected to React Router, let's render our contacts as a list:

```
import { FC, useState } from 'react'
import { Link, useParams } from 'react-router-dom'
import './Contacts.css'
type Contact = {
  id: number
  name: string
  email: string
  phone: string
}
```

```
const data: Contact[] = [
  {
    id: 1,
    name: 'Carlos Santana',
    email: 'carlos.santana@dev.education',
    phone: '415-307-3112'
  },
  {
    id: 2,
    name: 'John Smith',
    email: 'john.smith@dev.education',
    phone: '223-344-5122'
  },
  {
    id: 3,
    name: 'Alexis Nelson',
    email: 'alexis.nelson@dev.education',
    phone: '664-291-4477'
  }
]
const Contacts: FC = () => {
  const { contactId = 0 } = useParams()
  // For now we are going to add our contacts to our
  // local state, but normally this should come
  // from some service.
  const [contacts, setContacts] = useState<Contact[]>(data)
  const renderContacts = () => (
      <ul>
      {contacts.map((contact: Contact, key) => (
      <li key={contact.id}>
        <Link to={`/contacts/${contact.id}`}>{contact.name}</Link>
      </li>
      ))}
      </ul>
  )
  return (
      <div className="Contacts">
```

```
            <h1>Contacts</h1>
            {renderContacts()}
        </div>
    )
}
export default Contacts
```

As you can see, we are using the `<Link>` component, which will generate an `<a>` tag that points to `/contacts/contact.id`, and this is because we will add a new nested route to our route file to match the ID of the contact:

```
const AppRoutes = () => (
  <App>
    <Routes>
      <Route path="/" element={<Home />} />
      <Route path="/about" element={<About />} />
      <Route path="/contact" element={<Contact />} />
      <Route path="/contacts" element={<Contacts />}>
        <Route path=":contactId" element={<Contacts />} />
      </Route>
      <Route path="*" element={<Error404 />} />
    </Routes>
  </App>
)
```

React Router v6 has a special hook called `useParams`, which will give you access to the `contactId` parameter:

```
import { FC, useState } from 'react'
import { Link, useParams } from 'react-router-dom'
import './Contacts.css'
const data = [
{
    id: 1,
    name: 'Carlos Santana',
    email: 'carlos.santana@dev.education',
    phone: '415-307-3112'
},
```

```
{
    id: 2,
    name: 'John Smith',
    email: 'john.smith@dev.education',
    phone: '223-344-5122'
},
{
    id: 3,
    name: 'Alexis Nelson',
    email: 'alexis.nelson@dev.education',
    phone: '664-291-4477'
}
]
type Contact = {
    id: number
    name: string
    email: string
    phone: string
}
const Contacts: FC<any> = () => {
const { contactId = 0 } = useParams()
console.log('contactId', contactId)
```

For now, we are going to add our contacts to our local state, but normally this should come from some service:

```
const [contacts, setContacts] = useState<Contact[]>(data)
```

By default, our selectedNote is false:

```
let selectedContact: any = false
if (contactId > 0) {
```

If the contactId is higher than 0, then we filter it from our contacts array:

```
    selectedContact = contacts.filter((contact) => contact.id ===
    Number(contactId))[0]
  }
  const renderSingleContact = ({ name, email, phone }: Contact) => (
    <>
      <h2>{name}</h2>
      <p>{email}</p>
      <p>{phone}</p>
    </>
  )
  const renderContacts = () => (
    <ul>
    {contacts.map((contact: Contact, key) => (
      <li key={key}>
      <Link to={`/contacts/${contact.id}`}>{contact.name}</Link>
      </li>
    ))}
    </ul>
  )
  return (
    <div className="Contacts">
      <h1>Contacts</h1>
      {/* We render our selectedContact or all the contacts */}
      {selectedContact ? renderSingleContact(selectedContact) :
      renderContacts()}
    </div>
    )
}
export default Contacts
```

As you can see, we are receiving the contactId parameter with useParams.

If you run the application again, you should see your contacts like this:

Contacts

Carlos Santana

John Smith

Alexis Nelson

Figure 9.6: Displaying contacts

If you click on **John Smith** (whose contactId is 2), you will see the contact information:

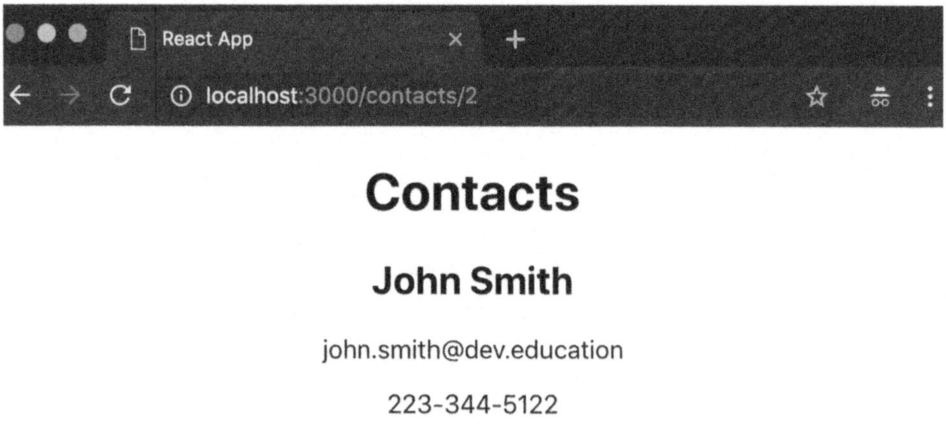

Contacts

John Smith

john.smith@dev.education

223-344-5122

Figure 9.7: Displaying a specific contact

After this, you can add a navbar in the App component to access all the routes:

```
import { Link } from 'react-router-dom'
import './App.css'
const App = ({ children }) => (
```

```
  <div className="App">
    <ul className="menu">
    <li><Link to="/">Home</Link></li>
    <li><Link to="/about">About</Link></li>
    <li><Link to="/contacts">Contacts</Link></li>
     <li><Link to="/contact">Contact</Link></li>
    </ul>
    {children}
  </div>
)
export default App
```

Now, let's modify our App styles:

```
.App {
  text-align: center;
}
.App ul.menu {
  margin: 50px;
  padding: 0;
  list-style: none;
}
.App ul.menu li {
  display: inline-block;
  padding: 0 10px;
}
.App ul.menu li a {
  color: #333;
  text-decoration: none;
}
.App ul.menu li a:hover {
  color: #ccc;
}
```

Finally, you will see something like this:

Home   About   Contacts   Contact

Contacts

Carlos Santana

John Smith

Alexis Nelson

Figure 9.8: Displaying the menu

By the end of this section, you'll know how to add routes with parameters to your application. *This is amazing, right?*

React Router v6.4

As mentioned at the beginning of this chapter, **React Router v6.4** introduces a new way of implementing routes.

Let's rewrite our last example to explore the differences. The first difference is that instead of using AppRoutes as we did previously, we will now add our routes directly to our App.tsx file. Let's begin by modifying our main.tsx and removing AppRoutes:

```
import { createRoot } from 'react-dom/client'
import App from './App'
createRoot(document.getElementById('root') as HTMLElement).render(
  <App />
)
```

Now, in our App.tsx file, we need to import some new functions from react-router-dom and load the components that will be rendered for each URL:

```
import { FC } from 'react'
```

```
import {
  createBrowserRouter,
  createRoutesFromElements,
  Route,
  Link,
  Outlet,
  RouterProvider
} from 'react-router-dom'
import About from './components/About'
import Home from './components/Home'
import Pokemons, { dataLoader } from './components/Pokemons'
import Error404 from './components/Error404'
import './App.css'
```

Afterward, we need to specify our routes by utilizing the `createBrowserRouter` and `createRoutesFromElements` functions:

```
const App: FC<any> = () => {
  const router = createBrowserRouter(
    createRoutesFromElements(
      <Route path="/" element={<Root />}>
        <Route index element={<Home />} />
        <Route path="/about" element={<About />} />
        <Route path="*" element={<Error404 />} />
      </Route>
    )
  )
}
```

As you can see, we are rendering the `<Root />` component, and you might be wondering where this component is located. The `<Root />` component serves the purpose of housing our **Navigation** menu. Additionally, using the new `<Outlet />` component, we can specify the location where we want to render the content of our routes. To accomplish this, you need to create the `<Root />` component before defining the App component (at the top):

```
const Root = () => (
  <>
    <ul className="menu">
      <li><Link to="/">Home</Link></li>
```

```
      <li><Link to="/about">About</Link></li>
      <li><Link to="/pokemons">Pokemons</Link></li>
    </ul>
    <div>
      <Outlet />
    </div>
  </>
)
```

The first route is our Home, which is why we need to utilize the index prop. Next, we have the about route where we specify the path as /about. Lastly, we added an asterisk, which will match any other page that we don't have, rendering a **404 Error page**.

Once we have created the Root component and specified the routes, we need to render the RouterProvider and pass the created router as a parameter:

```
return (
  <div className="App">
    <RouterProvider router={router} />
  </div>
)
```

If you've done everything correctly, you should be able to see the **Home** and **About** pages:

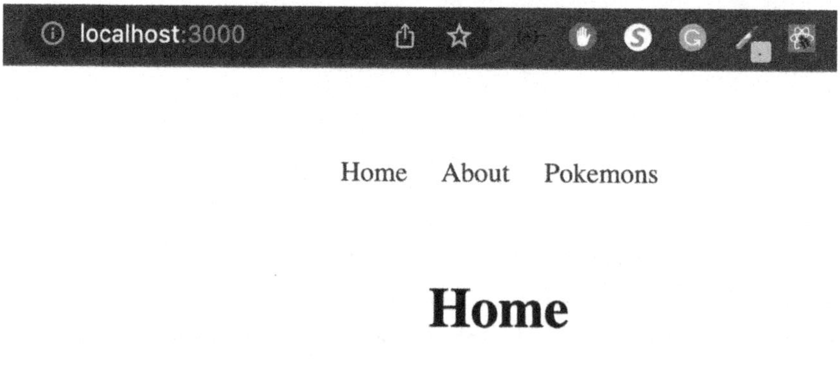

Home   About   Pokemons

Home

Figure 9.9: Home page

If you click on **About**, you should see the page appear as follows:

Home   About   Pokemons

About

Figure 9.10: About page

With this foundational understanding of the changes in React Router v6.4, we'll now venture into looking at implementing the new addition of loaders using the **Pokemons** page as our working example.

React Router loaders

One of the main changes in React Router 6.4 is the addition of **loaders**. These loaders provide a better way to fetch data, eliminating the need for the common pattern of using useEffect and fetch within components.

As you may have noticed in the menu, I have included a **Pokemons** page without specifying the route just yet. The reason for this is that I want to demonstrate how to use the new React Router loaders with this page as an example.

First, let's create our Pokemons component by using the Home component as a template:

```
const Pokemons = () => (
  <div className="Pokemons">
    <h1>Pokemons</h1>
  </div>
)
export default Pokemons
```

Now that we have our base component, we need to create a dataLoader function that is asynchronous. This function will be responsible for fetching the data:

```
export const dataLoader = async () => {
```

```
    const response = await fetch('https://pokeapi.co/api/v2/pokemon?limit=151')
    const data = await response.json()
    return data.results
}
export default Pokemons
```

As you can see, we place the dataLoader before exporting the Pokemons component as the default. Once you have created your dataLoader, you need to import it and specify the route for Pokemons in the App.tsx file. Remember to pass the dataLoader to the loader prop:

```
import Pokemons, { dataLoader } from './components/Pokemons'
...
const router = createBrowserRouter(
  createRoutesFromElements(
  <Route path="/" element={<Root />}>
    <Route index element={<Home />} />
    <Route path="/about" element={<About />} />
    <Route path="/pokemons" element={<Pokemons />} loader={dataLoader} />
    <Route path="*" element={<Error404 />} />
  </Route>
  )
)
```

After connecting our dataLoader to the route, we can now render the data for Pokemons. To retrieve the data, we will utilize the new useLoaderData hook. Additionally, we will use the useNavigation hook to monitor the state of the route, enabling us to determine if the data is still loading. The following is the complete code for the Pokemons component:

```
import { useLoaderData, useNavigation } from 'react-router-dom'
const Pokemons = () => {
  const pokemons: any = useLoaderData()
  const navigation = useNavigation()
    if (navigation.state === 'loading') {
      return <h1>Loading...</h1>
    }
```

```
   const imgUrl = 'https://raw.githubusercontent.com/PokeAPI/sprites/
master/sprites/pokemon/'
  return (
    <div className="Home">
      <h1>Pokemons</h1>
      {pokemons.map((pokemon: any, index: number) => (
        <div key={pokemon.name}>
          <h2>{index + 1} {pokemon.name}</h2>
          <img
            src={`${imgUrl}/${pokemon.url.split('/').slice(-2, -1)}.png`}
            alt={pokemon.name}
          />
          <p>
            <a href={pokemon.url} target="_blank" rel="noreferrer">
              {pokemon.url}
            </a>
          </p>
        </div>
      ))}
    </div>
  )
}
export const dataLoader = async () => {
  const response = await fetch('https://pokeapi.co/api/v2/
pokemon?limit=151')
  const data = await response.json()
  return data.results
}
export default Pokemons
```

Let's test our **Pokemons** page. We should see the first 150 **Pokemons**:

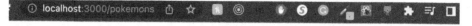

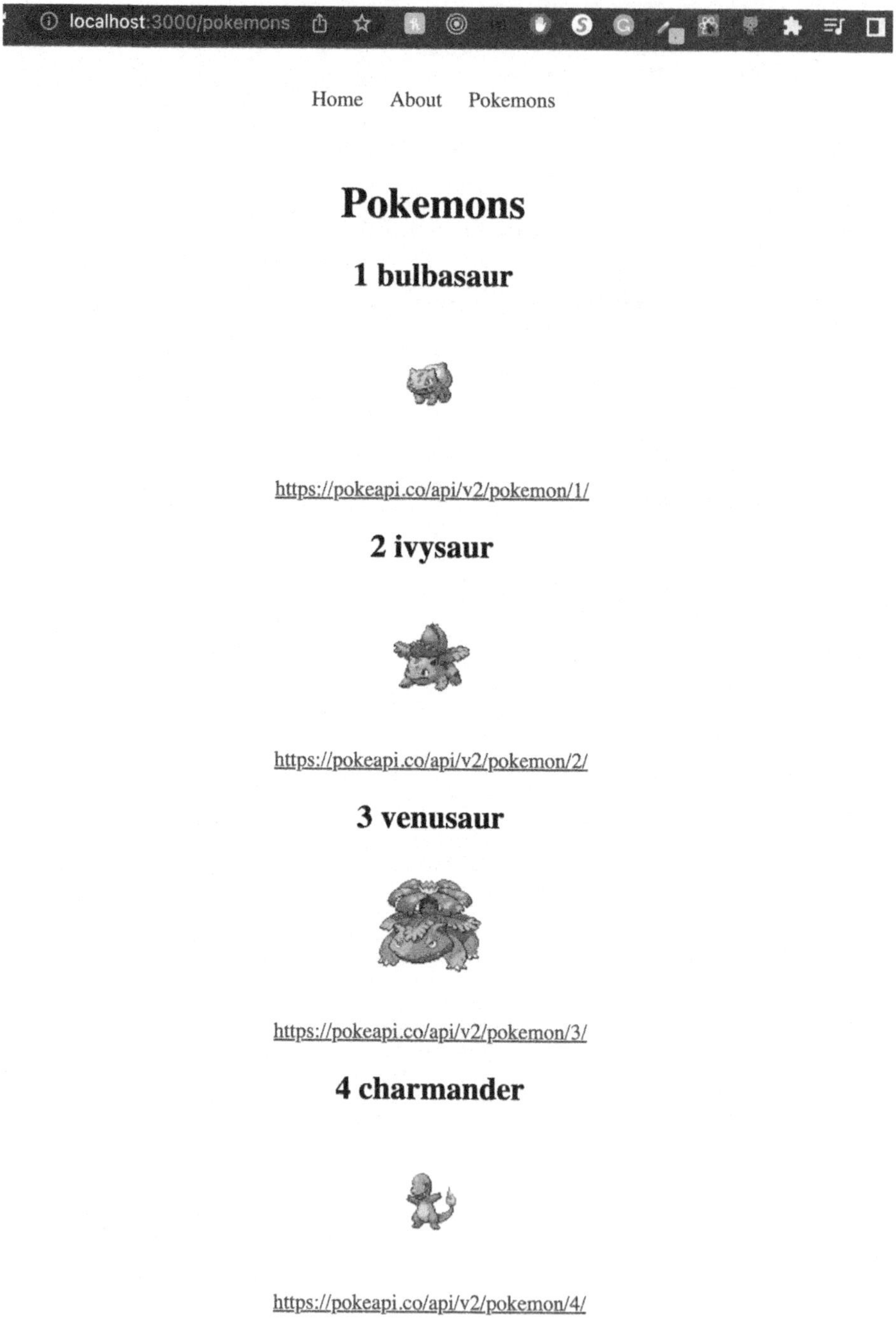
localhost:3000/pokemons
Home
About
Pokemons
Pokemons
1 bulbasaur
https://pokeapi.co/api/v2/pokemon/1/
2 ivysaur
https://pokeapi.co/api/v2/pokemon/2/
3 venusaur
https://pokeapi.co/api/v2/pokemon/3/
4 charmander
https://pokeapi.co/api/v2/pokemon/4/

Figure 9.11: Pokemons page

Through new features like loaders, React Router v6.4 streamlines routing and data fetching in React applications. We created a **Pokemons** page using a dataLoader function, which asynchronously fetched data from an API. We provided a more user-friendly interface by integrating this function into our route configuration and using React Router's useLoaderData and useNavigation hooks. As a result of these enhancements, React Router v6.4 is now more robust, efficient, and intuitive, enabling developers to create more complex, data-driven applications with less effort.

Summary

Good job! By navigating React Router, you have acquired essential skills for installing, configuring, and managing routes, as well as incorporating parameters into nested routes. You will be able to create more dynamic and robust web applications using React Router by utilizing these capabilities. In addition, you have learned about the cutting-edge features of React Router v6.4, particularly its innovative use of loaders.

We are about to embark on the next chapter of this series, where we will explore the exciting new features introduced in React 18. By continuously learning and applying, you will become proficient in React.

Join our community on Discord

Join our community's Discord space for discussion with the author and other readers:

`https://packt.link/React18DesignPatterns4e`

10

React 18 New Features

React 18, the latest version of the popular JavaScript library for building user interfaces, introduces a host of new features and enhancements that aim to improve performance and enhance the developer experience. As a part of the ever-evolving React ecosystem, it is crucial to stay up to date with these advancements. In this chapter, we will provide a succinct overview of the most notable additions in React 18, followed by a brief explanation of the latest features in Node.js 19.

The new features in React 18 include:

- **Automatic Batching of State Updates**: React 18 automatically batches multiple state updates into a single update, which results in improved performance and smoother animations. This automatic batching eliminates the need for manual batching.

- **Concurrent Rendering**: This feature enables React to prioritize the rendering of certain components, leading to faster load times, smoother animations, and better user experiences.

- **Suspense for Data Fetching**: Suspense enables developers to suspend the rendering of a component until the required data is loaded, providing a seamless user experience and improved error handling.

- **Improved Error Handling**: React 18 simplifies error handling by offering more information about errors such as the component and code location where the error occurred, streamlining the debugging process.

- **New Component Types**: React 18 introduces two new component types – portals and components with side effects. Portals enable rendering components outside of their parent components, while components with side effects allow performing side effects without a separate function.

- **No Support for Internet Explorer 11:** To leverage modern web standards and enhance performance, React 18 no longer supports Internet Explorer 11. Developers must ensure their users employ a modern, supported browser like Google Chrome, Mozilla Firefox, Apple Safari, or Microsoft Edge.

We're going to cover the following main topics:

- Concurrent mode
- Automatic batching
- Suspense on the server
- New APIs
- New hooks
- Strict mode
- Node.js latest features

Concurrent mode

React **concurrent mode** is a set of new features in React 18 that enable faster and more responsive user interfaces by allowing React to work on multiple tasks simultaneously.

In traditional React, the rendering process is synchronous, which means that React updates the user interface in a single pass. This can sometimes lead to performance issues, especially when rendering large, complex applications or handling real-time updates.

Concurrent mode allows React to split the rendering process into smaller units of work that can be executed independently and in parallel. This means that React can prioritize certain tasks, such as updating the user interface, while still allowing other tasks to run in the background, such as handling user input or fetching data.

Here are some of the key features of React concurrent mode:

- **Time slicing:** Time slicing is a technique that allows React to break up large chunks of work into smaller pieces and prioritize the most important tasks first. This can help to reduce the perceived latency of an application and make it feel more responsive.
- **Suspense:** Suspense is a new feature in React that allows developers to suspend the rendering of a component until the necessary data has been loaded. This can help to improve the perceived performance of an application and provide a better user experience.

- **Concurrent rendering**: Concurrent rendering is a new rendering mode in React that allows React to update the user interface more frequently, resulting in smoother animations and transitions.

Overall, React concurrent mode is a powerful new set of features that can help developers create faster and more responsive user interfaces. While it may require some adjustments to existing code, adopting concurrent mode can help to improve the user experience of your applications and keep them competitive in a fast-paced digital landscape. Here's an example that demonstrates the use of time slicing and concurrent rendering in React 18:

```
import React, { useState } from 'react'
function Counter() {
  const [count, setCount] = useState(0)

  function handleClick() {
    setCount(count + 1)
  }
  return (
    <button onClick={handleClick}>
      {count}
    </button>
  )
}
function App() {
  return (
    <React.Suspense fallback={<div>Loading...</div>}>
      <Counter />
    </React.Suspense>
  )
}
ReactDOM.createRoot(document.getElementById('root')).render(<App />)
```

Automatic batching

Automatic batching is a new feature in React 18 that improves the performance of updates by automatically batching multiple updates into a single render pass. In traditional React, updates to the user interface are typically processed synchronously, which means that each update triggers a new render pass.

This can be inefficient, especially when multiple updates occur in rapid succession. Automatic batching solves this problem by grouping multiple updates together and processing them in a single render pass.

Here's an example to illustrate how automatic batching works:

```
function MyComponent() {
  const [count, setCount] = useState(0)
  function handleClick() {
    setCount(count + 1)
    setCount(count + 1)
    setCount(count + 1)
  }
  return (
    <div>
      <p>Count: {count}</p>
      <button onClick={handleClick}>Increment</button>
    </div>

  )
}
```

In this example, we have a MyComponent component that uses the useState hook to manage a count state variable. When the user clicks the Increment button, we call the setCount function three times in rapid succession, each time incrementing the count by 1.

In traditional React, each call to setCount would trigger a new render pass, resulting in three separate updates to the user interface. However, with automatic batching in React 18, these updates are automatically grouped together and processed in a single render pass. This can result in significant performance improvements, especially when handling user input or real-time updates.

Overall, automatic batching is a powerful new feature in React 18 that can help to improve the performance and responsiveness of your applications. By automatically batching multiple updates together, React can optimize the rendering process and reduce unnecessary render passes, resulting in faster and more efficient updates to the user interface.

Transitions

React 18 introduces a new feature called **transitions** that allows developers to create smooth, declarative animations and transitions in their applications.

Transitions build on the existing capabilities of React's declarative programming model to provide a simple and intuitive way to animate elements and components.

Here's a simple example to illustrate how transitions work:

```
import { useState } from 'react'
import { Transition } from 'react-transition-group'
function MyComponent() {
  const [show, setShow] = useState(false)
  function handleClick() {
    setShow(!show)
  }
  return (
    <div>
      <button onClick={handleClick}>
        {show ? 'Hide' : 'Show'}
      </button>
      <Transition in={show} timeout={300}>
        {(state) => (
          <div
            style={{
              transition: 'opacity 300ms ease-out',
              opacity: state === 'entered' ? 1 : 0,
            }}
          >
            {show && <p>Hello, world!</p>}
          </div>
        )}
      </Transition>
    </div>
  )
}
```

In this example, we use the `Transition` component from the `react-transition-group` library to animate the appearance and disappearance of a p element. The `Transition` component takes an in prop that determines whether the element should be shown or hidden, and a `timeout` prop that specifies the duration of the transition in milliseconds.

Inside the Transition component, we define a function that takes a state argument and returns the contents of the transitioned element. The state argument is a string that represents the current state of the transition, which can be one of entering, entered, exiting, or exited.

In our example, we use the state argument to set the opacity of the div element based on the current state of the transition. When the state is entered, we set the opacity to 1 to make the element fully visible. When the state is exiting or exited, we set the opacity to 0 to make the element fade out smoothly.

By using the Transition component and the state argument, we can create a smooth, declarative animation that responds to changes in the application state. This can be a powerful way to create engaging and dynamic user interfaces that feel alive and responsive.

Overall, transitions are a powerful new feature in React 18 that allow developers to create declarative animations and transitions with ease. By leveraging the power of React's declarative programming model, developers can create complex animations and transitions with a few lines of code, making it easier than ever to create engaging and dynamic user interfaces.

Suspense on the server

React 18 introduces some improvements to **server-side rendering (SSR)** with **Suspense** that allow developers to create more efficient and scalable server-rendered applications.

Before React 18, Suspense was primarily used in client-side rendering to manage asynchronous data loading and code splitting. However, with React 18, Suspense can also be used on the server to optimize the rendering of server-rendered components.

Here's a high-level overview of how Suspense works on the server:

- During the initial render of a server-rendered component, any Suspense boundaries are registered, and their fallback content is rendered instead of the main content.
- When data loading or code splitting is required, the server can return a "placeholder" HTML response that contains the fallback content for the Suspense boundaries.
- Once the asynchronous data or code has loaded, the client can hydrate the Suspense boundaries with the actual content, replacing the fallback content with the final content.

This approach allows the server to avoid the expensive rendering of component trees that may be blocked by data loading or code splitting. Instead, the server can return a simple HTML response with fallback content, which can be quickly and easily rendered by the client. This can significantly improve the performance and scalability of server-rendered applications.

Here's an example to illustrate how Suspense can be used on the server:

```jsx
import { Suspense } from 'react'
import { fetchUserData } from './api'
function MyComponent() {
  const userData = fetchUserData();
  return (
    <div>
      <p>Name: {userData.name}</p>
      <Suspense fallback={<p>Loading...</p>}>
        <UserProfile userId={userData.id} />
      </Suspense>
    </div>
  )
}
```

In this example, we have a `MyComponent` component that fetches user data from an API and renders it alongside a `UserProfile` component that requires additional data loading. By wrapping the `UserProfile` component in a `Suspense` boundary, we can ensure that the fallback content is displayed until the additional data has been loaded.

When rendering on the server, the server can return a simple HTML response with the fallback content for the Suspense boundary, allowing the client to render the fallback content quickly and easily. Once the data has been loaded, the client can hydrate the Suspense boundary with the actual content, replacing the fallback content with the final content.

Overall, the improvements to SSR with Suspense in React 18 can help to improve the performance and scalability of server-rendered applications, making it easier to create fast and responsive web experiences for users.

New APIs

React 18 has introduced a variety of new APIs that are focused on enhancing the user interface, improving application performance, and providing a better developer experience. Notably, significant additions include `createRoot`, `hydrateRoot`, and `renderToPipeableStream`.

createRoot

React 18 introduces a new API called `createRoot`, which provides a simpler and more explicit way to render React components into the DOM.

Traditionally, when rendering a React application into the DOM, you would use the ReactDOM.render method to specify the root element and the React component to render into it. For example:

```
import React from 'react'
import ReactDOM from 'react-dom'
const App = () => {
  return <div>Hello, world!</div>
}
ReactDOM.render(<App />, document.getElementById('root'))
```

With createRoot, you can create a root element that can be used to **render multiple components**, instead of specifying the root element for each component. Here's an example:

```
const App = () => {
  return <div>Hello, world!</div>
}
const root = ReactDOM.createRoot(document.getElementById('root'))
root.render(<App />)
```

In this example, we first create a root element using createRoot, passing in the DOM element that we want to render our React application into. We then use the render method on the root element to specify the React component to render.

The createRoot API also supports concurrent mode, which allows React to update the UI in a more efficient and responsive way by breaking up large updates into smaller chunks. To use concurrent mode with createRoot, you can pass a mode option:

```
const root = ReactDOM.createRoot(document.getElementById('root'), { mode:
'concurrent' })
root.render(<App />)
```

In this example, we pass the mode option with a value of 'concurrent', indicating that we want to use concurrent mode when rendering our React components.

Overall, the createRoot API provides a simpler and more flexible way to render React components into the DOM and supports the new features introduced in React 18, such as concurrent mode and the improved server-side rendering with Suspense.

hydrateRoot

hydrateRoot is another new API introduced in React 18 that works in conjunction with createRoot.

In the traditional React rendering model, the server would render a static HTML document and send it to the client, which would then create a new React root and render the app on the client side. However, with SSR, React can render the initial HTML on the server and send it to the client, which can then "hydrate" the HTML into a fully functional React app.

hydrateRoot is used for this process of hydrating the initial HTML sent by the server into a React component tree. It allows React to reuse the server-rendered markup so that the initial page load is faster and there's less work for the client to do.

Here's an example of how you can use hydrateRoot to hydrate the initial HTML on the client:

```
import React from 'react'
import { createRoot, hydrateRoot } from 'react-dom'
const App = () => {
  return <div>Hello, world!</div>
}
const root = createRoot(document.getElementById('root'))
if (root.isMounted()) {
  hydrateRoot(document.getElementById('root'), <App />)
} else {
  root.render(<App />)
}
```

In this example, we first create a root element using createRoot as we did in the previous example. We then check if the root is already mounted by calling root.isMounted(). If it is, we use hydrateRoot to hydrate the existing HTML on the page. If not, we use root.render to render the React component as usual.

Note that you need to ensure that the server and client render the same HTML structure, otherwise, hydration may fail, and you may end up with a mismatch between the server-rendered markup and the hydrated React component tree. To avoid this, you can use the Suspense component to handle asynchronous rendering and data fetching on both the server and client and ensure that the HTML structure remains the same.

renderToPipeableStream

renderToPipeableStream is another new API introduced in React 18 that allows you to render a React component tree to a **Node.js** stream. This can be useful for server-side rendering in scenarios where you need to send the rendered content over a network or to a file.

Here's an example of how you can use renderToPipeableStream to render a React component to a stream:

```
import React from 'react'
import { renderToPipeableStream } from 'react-dom/server'
import { createServer } from 'http'
const App = () => {
  return <div>Hello, world!</div>
}
const server = createServer((req, res) => {
  const stream = renderToPipeableStream(<App />)
  stream.pipe(res)
})
server.listen(3000)
```

In this example, we first create a simple React component called App. We then create a Node.js HTTP server using the createServer method. When a request is made to the server, we use renderToPipeableStream to render the App component to a Node.js stream. We then pipe the stream to the response object using the pipe method.

Note that renderToPipeableStream returns a Node.js stream that you can pipe to other streams or write to a file. This allows you to easily generate server-rendered content and send it over a network or save it to disk without having to buffer the entire HTML in memory.

Also note that renderToPipeableStream is asynchronous, so it returns a Promise that resolves to the stream. This means that you can use it with await to wait for the rendering to complete before sending the response.

Overall, renderToPipeableStream is a useful API for SSR in Node.js environments and can help improve the performance and scalability of your server-rendered applications.

New Hooks

In React 18, a set of innovative hooks has been introduced, which provide enhanced techniques for managing IDs, transitions, and optimizing performance. These hooks include useId, useTransition, useDeferredValue, and useInsertionEffect.

useId

useId is a new built-in hook in React 18 that can be used to generate a unique ID. This can be useful in scenarios where you need to generate unique identifiers for elements in a React component, for example, when building forms.

Here's an example of how you can use useId to generate a unique ID:

```
import { useId } from 'react'
const MyComponent = () => {
  const id = useId()
  return <div id={id}>Hello, world!</div>
}
```

In this example, we use the useId hook to generate a unique ID, which we then use as the id attribute of a <div> element.

useId generates a unique ID that is guaranteed to be different on each render. It takes an optional parameter that can be used to specify a prefix for the generated ID, which can be useful for naming elements in a consistent way.

Here's an example of how you can use the prefix parameter to specify a prefix for the generated ID:

```
import { useId } from 'react'
const MyComponent = () => {
  const id = useId('my-prefix')
  return <div id={id}>Hello, world!</div>
}
```

In this example, we use the useId hook with the 'my-prefix' prefix, which generates an ID that starts with the string 'my-prefix'. This can be useful for naming elements in a way that is consistent with your application's naming conventions.

Overall, useId is a useful addition to React 18 and can simplify the process of generating unique identifiers for elements in a React component.

Although the useId hook in React 18 offers unique benefits, it's essential to be aware of certain caveats to avoid potential issues. Firstly, it's not recommended to use useId for generating keys in a list. The preferred approach is to derive keys directly from your data. Secondly, the useId Hook requires a perfect match between the component trees on the server and the client side during server rendering. Any discrepancies between the server and client-rendered trees could lead to inconsistent IDs.

useTransition

useTransition is a new built-in hook in React 18 that allows you to add smooth transitions to your application. It's part of the new concurrent mode feature and is designed to work with Suspense to create loading states and fallbacks for data fetching.

Here's an example of how you can use useTransition to add a loading spinner while data is being fetched:

```
import React, { useState, useTransition } from 'react'
const MyComponent = () => {
  const [data, setData] = useState(null)
  const [startTransition, isPending] = useTransition({ timeoutMs: 3000 })
  const handleClick = () => {
    startTransition(() => {
      const newData = fetchData()
      setData(newData)
    })
  }
  return (
    <div>
      {isPending && <LoadingSpinner />}
      <button onClick={handleClick}>Fetch Data</button>
      {data && <DataDisplay data={data} />}
    </div>
  )
}
```

In this example, we use useState to store the fetched data and useTransition to handle the loading state while the data is being fetched. When the **Fetch Data** button is clicked, the startTransition function is called with a callback that fetches the data and updates the state. The isPending value returned from useTransition is used to conditionally render a loading spinner.

useTransition takes an optional configuration object with a timeoutMs property that specifies the maximum amount of time to spend in the pending state before showing the loading spinner. If the data is fetched before the timeout expires, the loading spinner is not displayed.

Overall, useTransition is a powerful new feature in React 18 that can help you create smoother, more responsive applications with better user experiences.

useDeferredValue

useDeferredValue is a new built-in hook in React 18 that allows you to defer updates to a value until the next frame. This can be useful when working with performance-intensive operations like animations.

Here's an example of how you can use useDeferredValue to animate a component:

```
import { useState, useDeferredValue } from 'react'
function MyComponent() {
  const [x, setX] = useState(0)
  const deferredX = useDeferredValue(x, { timeoutMs: 100 })
  function handleClick() {
    setX(x => x + 100)
  }
  return (
    <div style={{ transform: `translateX(${deferredX}px)` }}
onClick={handleClick}>
      Click me!
    </div>
  )
}
```

In this example, we use useState to store the current position of the component, and useDeferredValue to defer updates to the position until the next frame. When the component is clicked, the position is updated using setX. The deferred value is used to render the component with a transition effect using CSS transforms.

useDeferredValue takes two arguments: the value to defer and an optional configuration object. The configuration object can be used to specify a timeoutMs property that determines the maximum time to defer updates. By default, updates are deferred until the next frame.

Note that useDeferredValue only works in conjunction with the useTransition hook, which provides the timing information necessary to defer updates to the next frame.

useInsertionEffect

useInsertionEffect is a variation of the existing useEffect hook that allows you to perform actions after a DOM node has been inserted into the page. This can be useful for integrating with third-party libraries or for performing actions that require the presence of a DOM node.

Here's an example of how to use useInsertionEffect:

```
import { useInsertionEffect } from 'react'
function MyComponent() {
  useInsertionEffect(() => {
    const canvas = document.createElement('canvas')
    canvas.width = 300
    canvas.height = 200
    canvas.style.backgroundColor = 'red'
    document.body.appendChild(canvas)
    return () => {
      document.body.removeChild(canvas)
    }
  }, [])
  return (
    <div>
      <h1>Hello, world!</h1>
      <p>This is my React component.</p>
    </div>
  )
}
```

In this example, we use useInsertionEffect to create a new canvas element and add it to the DOM when the component is mounted. The cleanup function returned by the hook removes the canvas element when the component is unmounted.

Note that the second argument to useInsertionEffect is an empty array. This is because we only want to perform the insertion action once the component is mounted. If we included any dependencies in the array, the insertion action would be performed every time those dependencies changed.

Strict mode

React 18 introduces a new feature called **Strict Mode,** which allows you to opt in to a stricter set of checks and warnings for your React application. The goal of Strict Mode is to catch potential problems early in development and to encourage best practices that make your code more performant and easier to debug.

Here's an example of how to use Strict Mode:

```
import React from 'react'
function MyComponent() {
  return (
    <React.StrictMode>
      <div>
        <h1>Hello, world!</h1>
        <p>This is my React component.</p>
      </div>
    </React.StrictMode>
  )
}
```

In this example, we wrap our component tree with the React.StrictMode component. This enables several additional checks and warnings during development, such as detecting unsafe lifecycle methods, identifying potential side effects, and highlighting potential performance issues.

Strict Mode does not affect the behavior of your application in production and should only be used during development. Once you are confident that your code is free of any issues highlighted by Strict Mode, you can remove the React.StrictMode component from your code.

It's worth noting that while Strict Mode can be useful for catching potential issues early in development, it is not a replacement for thorough testing and debugging. Always test your code thoroughly before deploying to production and use tools like React's built-in debugging tools to identify and fix any issues that arise.

Node.js latest features

There are some relevant new features in the latest versions of Node (18 and 19); let's see what is new in those versions.

Experimental Fetch API

Node.js 18 (also in version 19) includes an experimental global **Fetch API** that is now available by default. The API's implementation is inspired by **node-fetch**, which is originally based on **undici-fetch** and comes from **undici**. The API's developers aim to make it as close to the specification as possible, but some features require a browser environment and are thus omitted.

Here is an example that hits the Pokémon API:

```javascript
const getPokemons = async () => {
  const response = await fetch('https://pokeapi.co/api/v2/pokemon')
  if (response.ok) {
    const pokemons = await response.json()
    console.log(pokemons)
  } else {
    console.error(`${response.status} ${response.statusText}`)
  }
}
getPokemons()
```

This addition to Node.js 18 (also included in version 19) makes the following global variables available: `fetch`, `FormData`, `Headers`, `Request`, and `Response`. Users can disable the API by specifying the `--no-experimental-fetch` command-line flag.

Experimental test runner module

It's important to note that the test runner module is still in its experimental phase. To write unit tests and generate reports in **Test Anything Protocol** (**TAP**) format, we can import the `node:test` module. In this section, we'll provide a few examples to illustrate how it works. This testing approach bears some similarity to Jest, a widely used JavaScript testing framework.

The `node:test` module simplifies the process of writing JavaScript tests that generate reports in **TAP** format. To access it, simply use the following code:

```javascript
import test from 'node:test'
import assert from 'node:assert'
```

To provide an example, here's a demonstration of a parent test with two subtests:

```
import test from 'node:test'
import assert from 'node:assert'
test('Math tests', async (t) => {
  await t.test('Multiply test', (t) => {
    const n = 2 * 2
    assert.equal(n, 4)
  })
  await t.test('Sum test', (t) => {
    const n = 5 + 3
    assert.equal(n, 8)
  })
})
```

If everything works fine, you should see something like this:

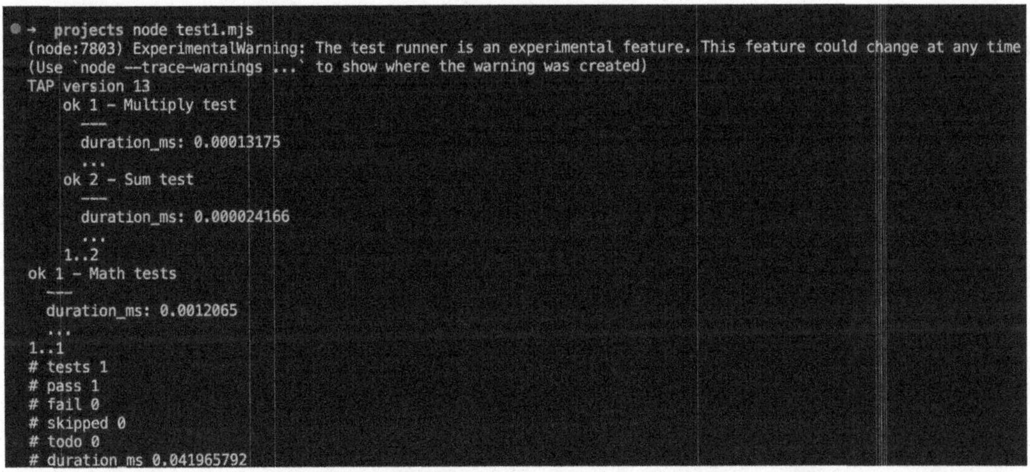

```
● → projects node test1.mjs
(node:7803) ExperimentalWarning: The test runner is an experimental feature. This feature could change at any time
(Use `node --trace-warnings ...` to show where the warning was created)
TAP version 13
    ok 1 - Multiply test
      ---
      duration_ms: 0.00013175
      ...
    ok 2 - Sum test
      ---
      duration_ms: 0.000024166
      ...
    1..2
ok 1 - Math tests
  ---
  duration_ms: 0.0012065
  ...
1..1
# tests 1
# pass 1
# fail 0
# skipped 0
# todo 0
# duration_ms 0.041965792
```

Figure 10.1: Experimental test runner module

Experimental node watch

node --watch was introduced as a direct competitor to nodemon, and is a popular tool used for watching anything, although it has primarily been used for Node.js projects. However, with the code snippet provided below, you can now use it more easily:

```
node --watch <file or directory to observe>
```

This code will automatically detect any changes made to the specified file or directory and restart the server or script accordingly. This feature is available in versions 19.0.0 and 18.11.0+ of Node.js.

Node 18 is now Long-Term Support (LTS)

Following the release of Node.js 19, Node.js 18 became a **LTS** version on October 25, 2022, with the codename *Hydrogen*. This transition marks the end of the active development phase of Node.js 18.x.

The current Node.js 18.x release has moved to **Active LTS** status and will remain so until October 2023. After that, it will enter the **Maintenance** phase and continue to receive necessary security fixes and updates until the end of April 2025.

Summary

In React 18, a wide array of new features and enhancements are introduced, which simplify the development of high-quality and interactive applications. These include automatic batching of state updates, concurrent rendering, the inclusion of Suspense for data fetching, improved error handling, and the addition of new component types. As a result, developers now have the ability to create more responsive and engaging user interfaces. For React developers, considering an upgrade to React 18 holds significant value. Additionally, we have also explored key features in Node.js 18 and 19, which are crucial for enhancing our web projects.

In the next chapter, we will learn how to handle data properly by using React Context API, React Suspense, and **stale-while-revalidate (SWR)**.

11

Managing Data

In this chapter, we will explore two beneficial tools: the **React Context API** and **React Suspense**. The Context API simplifies the process of sharing data across our entire application without the need to pass it down through multiple layers. On the other hand, React Suspense enables specific parts of our app to wait for certain actions before being displayed, resulting in a smoother loading experience.

By utilizing these tools collectively, we can enhance data management and improve the overall performance of our app. Join us on this journey as we delve into the efficient handling of data in React.

We will cover the following topics in this chapter:

- The React Context API
- How to consume a context with `useContext`
- How to use React Suspense with SWR (Stale-While-Revalidate)
- How to use Redux Toolkit

Technical requirements

To complete this chapter, you will need the following:

- Node.js 19+
- Visual Studio Code

You can find the code for this chapter in the book's GitHub repository: `https://github.com/PacktPublishing/React-18-Design-Patterns-and-Best-Practices-Fourth-Edition/tree/main/Chapter11`.

Introducing the React Context API

The **React Context API** has come a long way since it was first introduced as an experimental feature. Since version 16.3.0, it has been officially added to React and has become a game-changer for many developers. In fact, many are now using the new Context API instead of Redux. The Context API allows you to share data between components without having to pass a prop to every child component.

To illustrate how to use the new Context API, let's revisit the example from *Chapter 8*, *React Hooks*, where we fetched GitHub issues using React Hooks, but this time by using the Context API instead.

Creating our first context

The first thing you need to do is to create the issue context. For this, you can create a folder called contexts inside your **src** folder, where you will add the Issue.tsx file.

Then, you need to import some functions from React and axios:

```
import { FC, createContext, useState, useEffect, ReactElement, useCallback
} from 'react'
import axios from 'axios'
```

At this point, it is clear that you should install axios. If you still don't have it, just do the following:

```
npm install axios
npm install --save-dev @types/axios
```

Next, we need to declare our interfaces:

```
export type Issue = {
  number: number
  title: string
  url: string
  state: string
}
interface Issue_Context {
  issues: Issue[]
  url: string
}
interface Props {
  url: string
}
```

The first thing we need to do after this is to create our context by using the createContext function and defining the value we want to export:

```
export const IssueContext = createContext<Issue_Context>({ issues: [],
url: '' })
```

Once we have IssueContext, we need to create a component where we can receive props, set some states, and perform the fetch by using useEffect, and then we render IssueContext.Provider where we specify the context (value) we will export:

```
const IssueProvider: FC<Props> = ({ children, url }) => {
  // State
  const [issues, setIssues] = useState<Issue[]>([])
  const fetchIssues = useCallback(async () => {
    const response = await axios(url)
    if (response) {
      setIssues(response.data)
    }
  }, [url])
  // Effects
  useEffect(() => {
    fetchIssues()
  }, [fetchIssues])
  const context = {
    issues,
    url
  }
  return <IssueContext.Provider value={context}>{children}</IssueContext.
Provider>
}
export default IssueProvider
```

As you know, every time you want to use a function inside the useEffect Hook, you need to wrap your function with the useCallback Hook. A good practice if you want to use async/await is to have it in a separate function and not directly in useEffect.

Once we perform the fetch and get the data in our issues state, we will add all the values we want to export as context, then when we render IssueContext.Provider, we will pass the context on the value prop, and finally, we will render the children of the component.

Wrapping our components with the provider

The way you consume a context is divided into two parts. The first one is where you wrap your app with your context provider, so this code can be added to App.tsx (normally, all the providers are defined in parent components).

Notice here that we are importing the IssueProvider component:

```
// Providers
import IssueProvider from '../contexts/Issue'
// Components
import Issues from './Issues'
const App = () => {
  return (
    <IssueProvider url="https://api.github.com/repos/ContentPI/ContentPI/
issues">
      <Issues />
    </IssueProvider>
  )
}
export default App;
```

As you can see, we are wrapping the Issues component with IssueProvider. This means that inside the Issues component, we can consume our context and get the issues value.

Many people find this concept confusing. If you forget to wrap your components with the provider, you won't be able to access your context within them. The challenging aspect is that you might not receive an error message; instead, you will encounter undefined data, making it difficult to pinpoint the problem.

Now that we comprehend the significance of correctly wrapping our components with providers, let's explore how we can precisely consume our context using the useContext Hook within our Issues component.

Consuming context with useContext

If you've already placed IssueProvider in App.tsx, now you can consume your context in your Issues component by using the useContext Hook.

Notice here that we are importing the IssueContext context (between { }):

```
// Dependencies
import { FC, useContext } from 'react'
// Contexts
import { IssueContext, Issue } from '../contexts/Issue'
const Issues: FC = () => {
  // Here you consume your Context, and you can grab the issues value.
  const { issues, url } = useContext(IssueContext)
  return (
    <>
      <h1>ContentPI Issues from Context</h1>
      {issues.map((issue: Issue) => (
        <p key={`issue-${issue.number}`}>
          <strong>#{issue.number}</strong> {' '}
          <a href={`${url}/${issue.number}`}>{issue.title}</a> {' '}
          {issue.state}
        </p>
      ))}
    </>
  )
}
export default Issues
```

If you did everything correctly, you should be able to see the issues list:

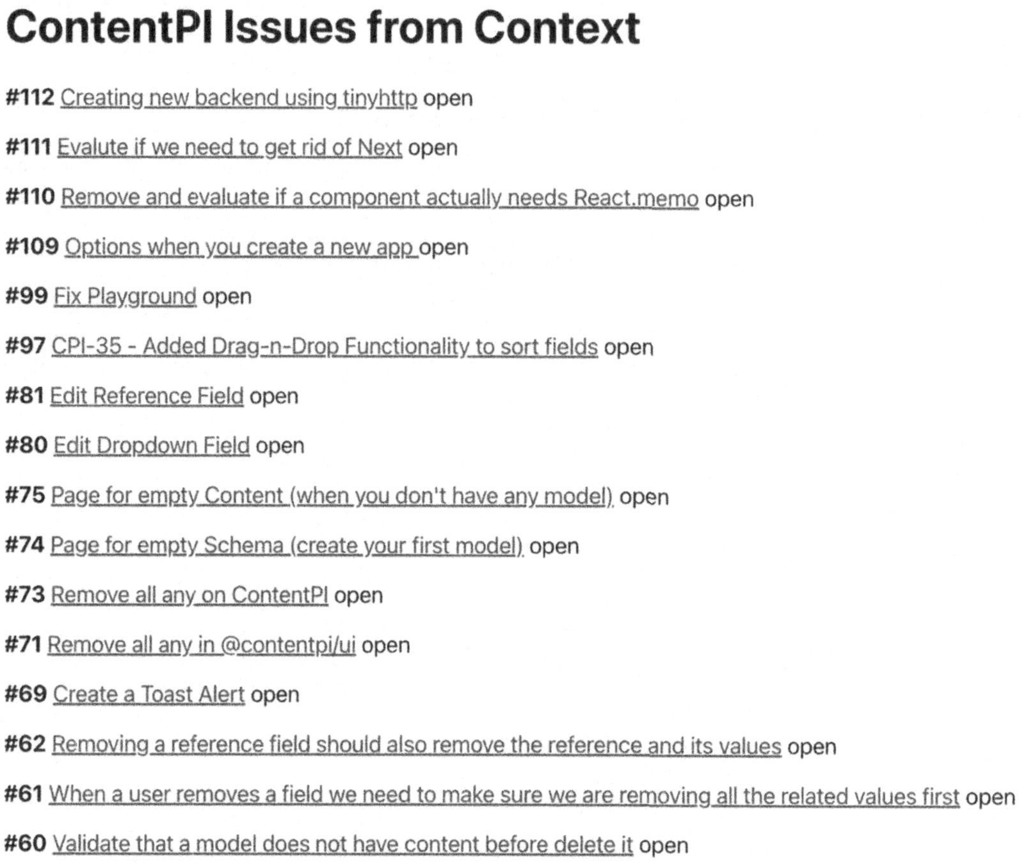

ContentPI Issues from Context

#112 Creating new backend using tinyhttp open

#111 Evalute if we need to get rid of Next open

#110 Remove and evaluate if a component actually needs React.memo open

#109 Options when you create a new app open

#99 Fix Playground open

#97 CPI-35 - Added Drag-n-Drop Functionality to sort fields open

#81 Edit Reference Field open

#80 Edit Dropdown Field open

#75 Page for empty Content (when you don't have any model) open

#74 Page for empty Schema (create your first model) open

#73 Remove all any on ContentPI open

#71 Remove all any in @contentpi/ui open

#69 Create a Toast Alert open

#62 Removing a reference field should also remove the reference and its values open

#61 When a user removes a field we need to make sure we are removing all the related values first open

#60 Validate that a model does not have content before delete it open

Figure 11.1: ContentPI Issues from Context

The **Context API** is super useful when you want to separate your application from your data and do all the fetching in there. Of course, there are multiple uses for the **Context API**, which can also be used for theming or to pass functions; it all depends on your application.

In the next section, we are going to learn how to implement **React Suspense** using the SWR library.

Introducing React Suspense with SWR

React Suspense was introduced in React 16.6. Suspense lets you suspend component rendering until a condition is met. You can render a loading component or anything you want as a fallback of Suspense.

Right now, there are only two use cases for this:

- **Code splitting**: When you split your application and you're waiting to download a chunk of your app when a user wants to access it.
- **Data fetching**: When you're fetching data.

In both scenarios, you can render a fallback, which can normally be a loading spinner, some loading text, or even better, a placeholder skeleton.

Introducing SWR

Stale-While-Revalidate (SWR) is a React Hook for data fetching; it is an HTTP cache invalidation strategy. SWR is a strategy to first return the data from cache (stale), then send the fetch request (revalidate), and finally, return with up-to-date data, and was developed by **Vercel**, the company that created **Next.js**.

Building a Pokedex!

I could not find a better example to explain React Suspense and SWR than building a **Pokedex**. We will use a public Pokemon API (https://pokeapi.co): *gotta catch 'em all*!

The first thing you need to do is to install some packages:

```
npm install swr react-loading-skeleton styled-components
```

For this example, you will need to create the Pokemon directory at src/components/Pokemon. The first thing we need to do to work with SWR is to create a fetcher file where we will perform our requests.

This file should be created at src/components/Pokemon/fetcher.ts:

```
const fetcher = (url: string) => {
  return fetch(url).then((response) => {
    if (response.ok) {
      return response.json()
    }
    return {
      error: true
    }
  })
}
export default fetcher
```

If you notice, we are returning an object with an error if the response is not successful. This is because sometimes we can get a 404 error from the API that can cause the app to break.

Once you have created your fetcher, let's modify `App.tsx` to configure `SWRConfig` and enable Suspense:

```
import { SWRConfig } from 'swr'
import PokeContainer from './Pokemon/PokeContainer'
import fetcher from './Pokemon/fetcher'
import { StyledPokedex, StyledTitle } from './Pokemon/Pokemon.styled'
const App = () => {
  return (
    <>
      <StyledTitle>Pokedex</StyledTitle>
      <SWRConfig value={{ fetcher, suspense: true }}>
        <StyledPokedex>
          <PokeContainer />
        </StyledPokedex>
      </SWRConfig>
    </>
  )
}
export default App
```

As you can see, we need to wrap our `PokeContainer` component inside `SWRConfig` to be able to fetch the data. The `PokeContainer` component will be our parent component, where we will add our first Suspense. This file exists at `src/components/Pokemon/PokeContainer.tsx`:

```
import { FC, Suspense } from 'react'
import Pokedex from './Pokedex'
const PokeContainer: FC = () => {
  return (
    <Suspense fallback={<h2>Loading Pokedex...</h2>}>
      <Pokedex />
    </Suspense>
  )
}
export default PokeContainer
```

As you can see, we are defining a fallback for our first Suspense, which is just Loading Pokedex... text. You can render whatever you want in there, React components or plain text. Then, we have our Pokedex component inside Suspense.

Now let's take a look at our Pokedex component where we are going to fetch data for the first time by using the useSWR Hook:

```
import { FC, Suspense } from 'react'
import useSWR from 'swr'
import LoadingSkeleton from './LoadingSkeleton'
import Pokemon from './Pokemon'
import { StyledGrid } from './Pokemon.styled'
const Pokedex: FC = () => {
  const { data: { results } } = useSWR('https://pokeapi.co/api/v2/
pokemon?limit=150')
  return (
    <>
      {results.map((pokemon: { name: string }) => (
        <Suspense fallback={<StyledGrid><LoadingSkeleton /></StyledGrid>}>
          <Pokemon key={pokemon.name} pokemonName={pokemon.name} />
        </Suspense>
      ))}
    </>
  )
}
export default Pokedex
```

As you can see, we are fetching the first 150 Pokemon because I'm old school and those were the first generation. Right now, I don't know how many Pokemon exist. Also, if you notice, we are grabbing the results variable that comes from the data (this is the actual response from the API). Then we map our results to render each Pokemon, but we add a Suspense component to each one with a <LoadingSkeleton /> fallback (<StyledGrid /> has some CSS styles to make it look nicer), and finally, we pass pokemonName to our <Pokemon> component, and this is because the first fetch just brings us the name of the Pokemon, but we need to do another fetch to bring the actual Pokemon data (name, types, power, and so on).

Then, finally, our Pokemon component will perform a specific fetch by the Pokemon name and will render the data:

```
import { FC } from 'react'
import useSWR from 'swr'
import { StyledCard, StyledTypes, StyledType, StyledHeader } from './
Pokemon.styled'
type Props = {
  pokemonName: string
}
const Pokemon: FC<Props> = ({ pokemonName }) => {
  const { data, error } = useSWR(`https://pokeapi.co/api/v2/
pokemon/${pokemonName}`)
  // Do you remember the error we set on the fetcher?
  if (error || data.error) {
    return <div />
  }
  if (!data) {
    return <div>Loading...</div>
  }
  const { id, name, sprites, types } = data
  const pokemonTypes = types.map((pokemonType: any) => pokemonType.type.
name)
  return (
    <StyledCard pokemonType={pokemonTypes[0]}>
      <StyledHeader>
        <h2>{name}</h2>
        <div>#{id}</div>
      </StyledHeader>
      <img alt={name} src={sprites.front_default} />
      <StyledTypes>
        {pokemonTypes.map((pokemonType: string) => (
          <StyledType key={pokemonType}>{pokemonType}</StyledType>
        ))}
      </StyledTypes>
    </StyledCard>
  )
}
```

```
export default Pokemon
```

Basically, in this component, we put together all the Pokemon data (ID, name, sprites, and types) and we render the information. As you have seen, I'm using styled components, which are amazing, so if you want to know the styles that I'm using for Pokedex, here is the Pokemon.styled.ts file:

```typescript
import styled from 'styled-components'
// Type colors
const type: any = {
  bug: '#2ADAB1',
  dark: '#636363',
  dragon: '#E9B057',
  electric: '#ffeb5b',
  fairy: '#ffdbdb',
  fighting: '#90a4b5',
  fire: '#F7786B',
  flying: '#E8DCB3',
  ghost: '#755097',
  grass: '#2ADAB1',
  ground: '#dbd3a2',
  ice: '#C8DDEA',
  normal: '#ccc',
  poison: '#cc89ff',
  psychic: '#705548',
  rock: '#b7b7b7',
  steel: '#999',
  water: '#58ABF6'
}
export const StyledPokedex = styled.div`
  display: flex;
  flex-wrap: wrap;
  flex-flow: row wrap;
  margin: 0 auto;
  width: 90%;
  &::after {
    content: '';
    flex: auto;
  }
```

```
type Props = {
  pokemonType: string
}
export const StyledCard = styled.div<Props>`
  position: relative;
  ${({ pokemonType }) => `
    background: ${type[pokemonType]} url(./pokeball.png) no-repeat;
    background-size: 65%;
    background-position: center;
  `}
  color: #000;
  font-size: 13px;
  border-radius: 20px;
  margin: 5px;
  width: 200px;
  img {
    margin-left: auto;
    margin-right: auto;
    display: block;
  }

export const StyledTypes = styled.div`
  display: flex;
  margin-left: 6px;
  margin-bottom: 8px;

export const StyledType = styled.span`
  display: inline-block;
  background-color: black;
  border-radius: 20px;
  font-weight: bold;
  padding: 6px;
  color: white;
  margin-right: 3px;
  opacity: 0.4;
  text-transform: capitalize;
```

```
export const StyledHeader = styled.div`
  display: flex;
  justify-content: space-between;
  width: 90%;
  h2 {
    margin-left: 10px;
    margin-top: 5px;
    color: white;
    text-transform: capitalize;
  }
  div {
    color: white;
    font-size: 20px;
    font-weight: bold;
    margin-top: 5px;
  }

export const StyledTitle = styled.h1`
  text-align: center;

export const StyledGrid = styled.div`
  display: flex;
  flex-wrap: wrap;
  flex-flow: row wrap;
  div {
    margin-right: 5px;
    margin-bottom: 5px;
  }
```

Finally, our LoadingSkeleton component should be like this:

```
import { FC } from 'react'
import Skeleton from 'react-loading-skeleton'

const LoadingSkeleton: FC = () => (
  <div>
```

```
    <Skeleton height={200} width={200} />
  </div>
)
export default LoadingSkeleton
```

This library is amazing. It lets you create skeleton placeholders to wait for the data. Of course, you can build as many forms as you want. You have probably seen this effect on sites such as LinkedIn or YouTube.

Testing React Suspense

Once you have all the pieces of the code working, there is a trick you can do in order to see all the Suspense fallbacks. Normally, if you have a high-speed connection, it is hard to see it, but you can slow down your connection to see how everything is being rendered. You can do this by selecting **Slow 3G** in your **Network** tab on your Chrome inspector:

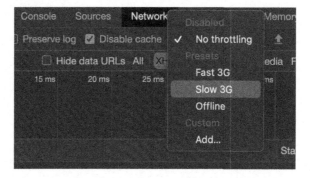

Figure 11.2: Slow 3G connection

Once you set the **Slow 3G** preset and you run your project, the first fallback you will see is **Loading Pokedex...**:

Figure 11.3: Loading Pokedex

Then, you will see the Pokemon fallbacks that are rendering `SkeletonLoading` for each Pokemon that is being loaded:

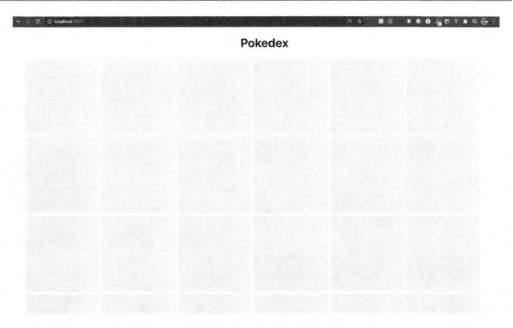

Figure 11.4: SkeletonLoading

Normally those loaders have animation, but you won't see that in this book, of course! And then you will start seeing how the data is rendering and some images start appearing:

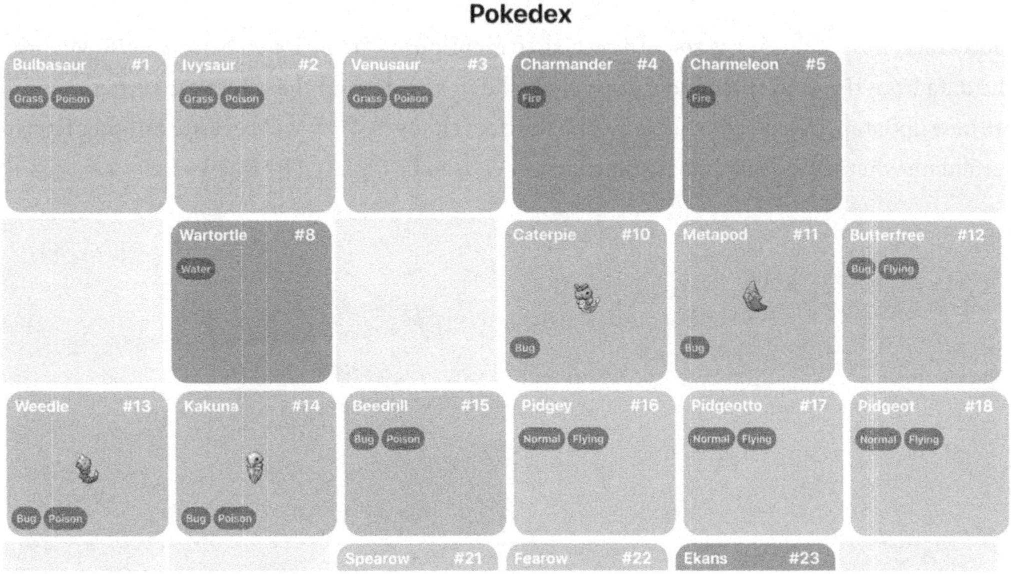

Pokedex

Figure 11.5: Loading Pokedex

If you wait until all the data has downloaded correctly, you should now see the Pokedex with all the Pokemon:

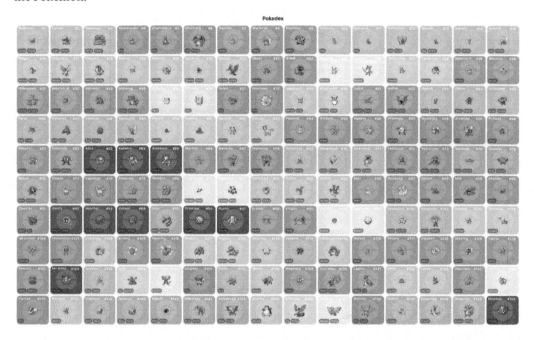

Figure 11.6: Displaying the entire Pokedex

Pretty nice, huh? But there is something else to mention; as I mentioned before, SWR will bring the data from the cache first and then will revalidate the data all the time to see whether there are new updates. This means that any time the data changes, SWR will perform another fetch to revalidate whether the old data is still valid or needs to be replaced by a new one.

You can see this effect even if you move out from the Pokedex tab to another and then come back.
You'll see that your **Network** terminal, for the first time, looks like this:

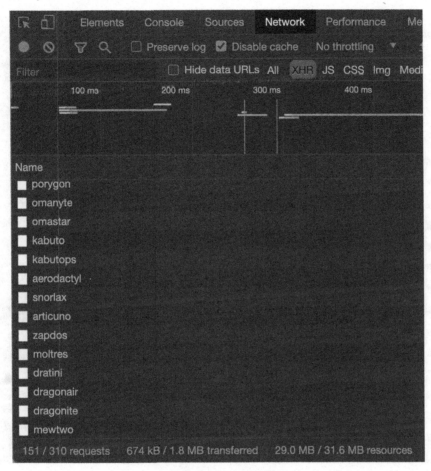

Figure 11.7: Requests

As you can see, we performed 151 initial requests (1 for the Pokemon lists and 150 others, 1 for each Pokemon), but if you change the tab and come back, you will see how SWR is fetching again:

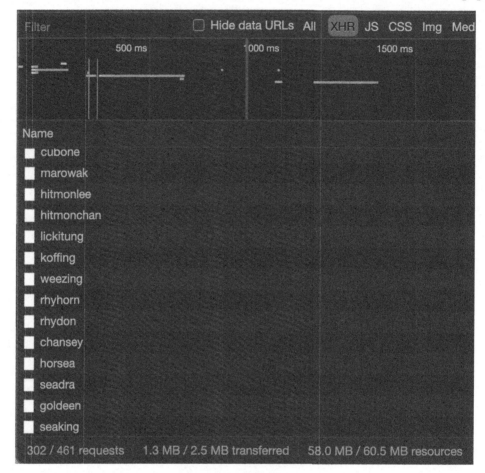

Figure 11.8: 151 requests

Now you can see that it is performing 302 requests (another 151). This is very useful when you have real-time data that you want to fetch every second or every minute.

Currently, React Suspense lacks a defined pattern of use, which implies that there are various ways to utilize it, and there are no established best practices for it yet. I have found that SWR is the easiest and most understandable approach to working with React Suspense. I believe it is a powerful library that can be utilized effectively even without the need for Suspense.

After exploring the flexibility of React Suspense, let's redirect our attention to another formidable tool within the React ecosystem: Redux Toolkit. This tool is revolutionizing the approach to Redux, and in the subsequent section, we will delve into its essential features and demonstrate its application through practical code examples.

Redux Toolkit: a modern approach to Redux

Redux Toolkit is the official, opinionated, and batteries-included toolset for efficient Redux development. It was created to help developers write better and more efficient Redux code with less boilerplate. In this section, we'll explore the key features of Redux Toolkit, along with code examples to demonstrate how to use it in your application.

Key features

Redux Toolkit comes with several key features that simplify the Redux development process:

- **configureStore**: A function that sets up a Redux store with sensible defaults.
- **createSlice**: A function that automatically generates action creators and reducers based on a provided configuration.
- **createAction**: A utility function to create action creators with a specific type and payload.
- **createReducer**: A utility function that simplifies reducer creation using **Immer**, enabling direct state manipulation.

Getting started

First, install Redux Toolkit and its peer dependencies:

```
npm install @reduxjs/toolkit react-redux typescript @types/react @types/
react-redux @types/react-dom
```

Creating a store

To create a store, we'll use the `configureStore` function provided by Redux Toolkit (`store.ts`):

```
import { configureStore } from '@reduxjs/toolkit'
import rootReducer from './rootReducer'
const store = configureStore({
  reducer: rootReducer
})
export type RootState = ReturnType<typeof rootReducer>
export default store
```

Creating a slice

A slice represents a portion of the Redux store that corresponds to a specific feature or domain. To create a slice, use the createSlice function (createSlice.ts):

```
import { createSlice } from '@reduxjs/toolkit'
const counterSlice = createSlice({
  name: 'counter',
  initialState: 0,
  reducers: {
    increment: (state) => state + 1,
    decrement: (state) => state - 1
  }
})
export const { increment, decrement } = counterSlice.actions
export default counterSlice.reducer
```

Combining reducers

If you have multiple slices, you can use the combineReducers function from Redux Toolkit to create a root reducer (rootReducer.ts):

```
import { combineReducers } from '@reduxjs/toolkit'
import counterReducer from './counterSlice'
const rootReducer = combineReducers({
  counter: counterReducer
})
export default rootReducer
```

Connecting components to the store

To connect a React component to the Redux store, use the useSelector and useDispatch Hooks from the react-redux package (Counter.ts):

```
import { useSelector, useDispatch } from 'react-redux'
import { increment, decrement } from './counterSlice'
import { RootState } from './store'
function Counter() {
  const count = useSelector((state: RootState) => state.counter)
  const dispatch = useDispatch()
  return (
```

```
    <div>
      <button onClick={() => dispatch(decrement())}>-</button>
      <span>{count}</span>
      <button onClick={() => dispatch(increment())}>+</button>
    </div>
  )
}
export default Counter
```

Integrating the store with a React application

Finally, wrap your React application with the Provider component from react-redux and pass
your store as a prop:

```
import React from 'react'
import { createRoot } from 'react-dom/client'
import { Provider } from 'react-redux'
import store from './store'
import Counter from './Counter'
createRoot(document.getElementById('root') as HTMLElement).render(
  <Provider store={store}>
    <Counter />
  </Provider>
)
```

In this section, we've explored Redux Toolkit's key features, including configureStore,
createSlice, createAction, and createReducer. By utilizing these features, developers can
write more efficient and maintainable Redux code with less boilerplate. The provided code examples demonstrate how to create a simple counter application using Redux Toolkit, illustrating
the steps required to set up the store, create slices and reducers, and connect components to the
store. By leveraging Redux Toolkit, you can simplify your Redux development process and build
more robust applications.

Summary

I really hope you enjoyed reading this chapter, which contains a lot of information about the
React Context API and how to implement React Suspense with SWR. We covered the basics of the
Context API, including how to create and consume contexts, as well as how to use the useContext
Hook for simpler consumption.

Additionally, we explored React Suspense and how it can improve the user experience by allowing us to handle loading states more effectively. We also learned about SWR and how it can simplify data fetching and caching with React Suspense. Finally, we learned how to implement the new Redux Toolkit. By utilizing these powerful tools, you can build more efficient and user-friendly React applications.

In the next chapter, we will learn how to use **Server-Side Rendering** in React with **Next.js**.

12

Server-Side Rendering

The next step in building React applications is learning how **server-side rendering (SSR)** works and what benefits it can give us. By implementing SSR, we can create **universal applications** that are better for **search engine optimization (SEO)** and enable knowledge-sharing between the frontend and the backend. They can also improve the perceived speed of a web application, which usually leads to increased conversions. However, applying SSR to a React application comes at a cost, and we should think carefully about whether we need it or not.

In this chapter, you will see how to set up a server-side-rendered application, and by the end of the relevant sections, you will be able to build a universal application and understand the pros and cons of the technique.

In this chapter, we will cover the following topics:

- Understanding what a universal application is
- Figuring out the reasons why we may want to enable SSR
- Creating a simple static server-side-rendered application with React
- Adding data fetching to server-side rendering and understanding concepts such as dehydration/hydration
- Using **Next.js** by Zeit to easily create a React application that runs on both the server and the client

Technical requirements

To complete this chapter, you will require the following:

- Node.js 19+
- Visual Studio Code

You can find the code for this chapter in the book's GitHub repository at `https://github.com/PacktPublishing/React-18-Design-Patterns-and-Best-Practices-Fouth-Edition/tree/main/Chapter12`.

Understanding universal applications

A universal application is an application that can run both on the server side and client side with the same code. In this section, we will look at the reasons why we should consider making our applications universal, and we will learn how React components can be easily rendered on the server side.

When we talk about JavaScript web applications, we usually think of client-side code that lives in the browser. The way they usually work is that the server returns an empty HTML page with a script tag to load the application. When the application is ready, it manipulates the DOM inside the browser to show the UI and interact with users. This has been the case for the last few years, and it is still the way to go for a huge number of applications.

In this book, we have seen how easy it is to create applications using React components and how they work within the browser. What we have not seen yet is how React can render the same components on the server, giving us a powerful feature called SSR.

Before going into the details, let's try to understand what it means to create applications that render both on the server and the client. For years, we used to have completely different applications for the server and client: for example, a Django application to render the views on the server, and some JavaScript frameworks, such as Backbone or jQuery, on the client. Those separate apps usually had to be maintained by two teams of developers with different skill sets. If you needed to share data between the server-side-rendered pages and the client-side application, you could inject some variables into a script tag. Using two different languages and platforms, there was no way to share common information, such as models or views, between the different sides of the application.

Since Node.js was released in 2009, JavaScript has gained a lot of attention and popularity on the server side as well, thanks to web application frameworks such as **Express**.

Using the same language on both sides not only makes it easy for developers to reuse their knowledge but also enables different ways of sharing code between the server and the client.

With React in particular, the concept of isomorphic web applications became very popular within the JavaScript community. Writing an **isomorphic application** means building an application that looks the same on the server and the client. The fact that the same language is used to write the two applications means that a big part of the logic can be shared, which opens many possibilities. This makes the code base easier to reason about and avoids unnecessary duplication.

React brings the concept a step forward, giving us a simple API to render our components on the server and transparently applying all the logic needed to make the page interactive (for example, event handlers) on the browser.

The term *isomorphic* does not fit in this scenario because, in the case of React, the applications are the same, and that is why one of the creators of React Router, Michael Jackson, proposed a more meaningful name for this pattern: **universal**.

Before we delve into the specific reasons for implementing universal server-side rendering, let us take a moment to pause and ensure that we possess a solid understanding of when and why this feature might be necessary for our application.

Reasons for implementing SSR

SSR is a great feature, but we should not jump into it just for the sake of it. We should have a real, solid reason to start using it.

Adopting SSR without a clear purpose can introduce unwarranted complexities and issues into your application. The intricacies of SSR can complicate aspects such as managing states, data fetching, and routing, among others. Additionally, SSR puts an increased load on the server as it is responsible for rendering HTML for each request. If not carefully optimized, this can result in slower response times and higher server costs.

Moreover, the added complexity that SSR brings to an application can slow down the development process, complicate debugging, and require maintenance of specific tools and configurations. Furthermore, if your application does not have a significant amount of public content, the SEO benefits that often drive the adoption of SSR may not be substantial.

In essence, while SSR can offer benefits, it is crucial to implement it with a clear understanding of its trade-offs. Carefully assess your application's needs and consider the advantages against the potential disadvantages before deciding to adopt SSR.

Implementing SEO

One of the main reasons why we may want to render our applications on the server side is SEO. If we serve an empty HTML skeleton to the crawlers of the main search engines, they are not able to extract any meaningful information from it. Nowadays, Google seems to be able to run JavaScript, but there are some limitations, and SEO is often a critical aspect of our businesses.

For years, we used to write two applications: an SSR one for the crawlers, and another one to be used on the client side by users. We used to do that because SSR applications could not give us the level of interactivity users expect, while client-side applications did not get indexed by search engines.

Maintaining and supporting two applications is difficult and makes the code base less flexible and less prone to changes. Luckily, with React, we can render our components on the server side and serve the content of our applications to the crawlers in such a way that it is easy for them to understand and index the content.

This is great, not only for SEO but also for social sharing services. Platforms such as Facebook or Twitter give us a way of defining the content of the snippets that is shown when our pages are shared.

For example, using Open Graph, we can tell Facebook that, for a particular page, we want a certain image to be shown and a particular title to be used as the title of the post. It is almost impossible to do that using client-side-only applications because the engine that extracts the information from the pages uses the markup returned by the server.

If our server returns an empty HTML structure for all the URLs, the result is that when the pages are shared on social networks, the snippets of our web application are empty as well, which affects their virality.

A common code base

Utilizing JavaScript on both the client and server sides of an application offers numerous benefits. Firstly, it simplifies matters by employing the same language across all components. This streamlines the process of maintaining a well-functioning system and facilitates knowledge sharing among colleagues within the company.

Moreover, sharing code between the frontend and backend of a website eliminates the need for redundant efforts. As a result, this approach generally reduces the occurrence of mistakes and issues.

Furthermore, maintaining a single code base is more manageable compared to handling two separate ones. Additionally, incorporating JavaScript on the server side enhances collaboration between frontend and backend developers. By leveraging the same language, they can efficiently reuse code and make prompt decisions, thereby enhancing workflow and productivity.

Better performance

Last but not least, we all love client-side applications because they are fast and responsive, but there is a problem—the bundle has to be loaded and run before users can take any action on the application.

This might not be a problem using a modern laptop or a desktop computer with a fast internet connection. However, if we load a huge JavaScript bundle using a mobile device with a 3G connection, users have to wait for a little while before interacting with the application. This is not only bad for the UX in general but it also affects conversions. It has been proven by major e-commerce websites that a few milliseconds added to the page load can have an enormous impact on revenues.

For example, if we serve our application with an empty HTML page and a script tag on the server and we show a spinner to our users until they can click on anything, the perception of the speed of the website is significantly affected.

If we render our website on the server side instead and users start seeing some of the content as soon as they hit the page, they are more likely to stay, even if they have to wait the same amount of time before doing anything for real, because the client-side bundle has to be loaded regardless of the SSR.

This perceived performance is something we can improve greatly using SSR because we can output our components on the server and return some information to users straight away.

Don't underestimate the complexity of SSR

Even though React provides an easy API to render components on the server, creating a universal application has a cost. So, we should consider carefully before enabling it for one of the preceding reasons and check whether our team is ready to support and maintain a universal application.

SSR can incur additional costs, extending development time and adding complexity. It also increases the server load, potentially necessitating costlier infrastructure. Operationally, SSR requires a well-maintained server with a complete setup, leading to increased operational costs. Additionally, testing may become more time-consuming due to the heightened complexity.

It is crucial to strike a balance between these costs and the potential benefits of SSR, such as improved SEO and faster initial page loads.

As we progress through the upcoming sections, we will discover that rendering components is not the sole task involved in creating server-side-rendered applications. We must establish and maintain a server with its routes and logic, manage the server data flow, and perform various other essential tasks to sustain a fully functional universal application. Consider caching content to serve pages more efficiently and address other necessary responsibilities.

Therefore, my recommendation is to initially focus on constructing the client-side version of your web application. Once it is fully functional and performs well on the server, you can then consider incorporating SSR to enhance the user experience. It is essential to enable SSR only when genuinely required. For instance, if improving your website's visibility in search engines (SEO) is a priority, that is when you should begin contemplating the implementation of SSR.

If you realize that your application takes a lot of time to load fully and you have already done all the optimization (refer to *Chapter 16*, *Improving the Performance of Your Applications*, for more on this topic), you can consider using SSR to offer a better experience to your users and improve the perceived speed. Now that we have learned what SSR is and the benefits of universal applications, let's jump into some basic examples of SSR in our next section.

Creating a basic example of SSR

We will now create a very simple server-side application to look at the steps that are needed to build a basic universal setup. It is going to be a minimal and simple setup on purpose because the goal here is to show how SSR works rather than providing a comprehensive solution or a boilerplate, even though you could use the example application as a starting point for a real-world application.

 This section assumes that readers have a basic understanding of Node.js and are familiar with the concepts related to JavaScript build tools, such as **webpack** and its loaders.

The application will consist of two parts:

- On the server side, where we will use Express to create a basic web server and serve an HTML page with the server-side-rendered React application.
- On the client side, where we will render the application, as usual, using react-dom.

Configuring our project from scratch with webpack

Both sides of the application will be transpiled with Babel and bundled with webpack before being run, which will let us use the full power of ES6 and the modules both on Node.js and on the browser.

Let's start by creating a new project folder (you can call it `ssr-project`) and running the following command to create a new package:

```
npm init
```

Once `package.json` is created, it is time to install the dependencies. We can start with webpack:

```
npm install webpack
```

After this is done, it is time to install `ts-loader` and the presets that we need to write an ES6 application using React and TSX:

```
npm install --save-dev @babel/core @babel/preset-env @babel/preset-react
ts-loader typescript
```

In order to create the server bundle, we need to install a dependency. Webpack allows us to define a set of externals, which are dependencies that we do not want to include in the bundle. When generating a build for the server, it is preferable not to include all the `Node.js` packages used; instead, we only want to bundle our server code. Excluding dependencies from the server bundle offers several advantages, including reduced bundle size, faster compilation, and compatibility with the Node.js environment. By leveraging the native module system of Node.js, the server code can directly access the installed packages without the need for bundling. Tools like `webpack-node-externals` assist in defining these dependencies as externals in the webpack configuration, resulting in an optimized server bundle and a streamlined build process. Let's proceed with the installation of this tool:

```
npm install --save-dev webpack-node-externals
```

Great. It is now time to create an entry in the npm scripts section of `package.json` so that we can easily run the `build` command from the terminal:

```
"scripts": {
  "build": "webpack"
}
```

Next, you need to create a `.babelrc` file in your root path:

```
{
  "presets": ["@babel/preset-env", "@babel/preset-react"]
}
```

We now have to create the configuration file, called `webpack.config.js`, to tell webpack how we want our files to be bundled.

Let's start by importing the library we will use to set our node externals. We will also define the configuration for `ts-loader`, which we will use for both the client and the server:

```
const nodeExternals = require('webpack-node-externals')
const path = require('path')
const rules = [{
  test: /\.(tsx|ts)$/,
  use: 'ts-loader',
  exclude: /node_modules/
}]
```

In *Chapter 6, Making Your Components Look Beautiful,* we looked at how we had to export a configuration object from the configuration file. There is one cool feature in webpack that lets us export an array of configurations as well so that we can define both client and server configurations in the same place and use both in one go.

The client configuration shown in the following block should be very familiar:

```
const client = {
  entry: './src/client.tsx',
  output: {
    path: path.resolve(__dirname, './dist/public'),
    filename: 'bundle.js',
    publicPath: '/'
  },
  module: {
    rules
  }
}
```

We are telling webpack that the source code of the client application is inside the `src` folder, and we want the output bundle to be generated in the `dist` folder.

We also set the module loaders using the previous object we created with ts-loader. The server configuration is slightly different; we need to define a different entry, and add some new nodes, such as target, externals, and resolve:

```
const server = {
  entry: './src/server.ts',
  output: {
   path: path.resolve(__dirname, './dist'),
   filename: 'server.js',
   publicPath: '/'
  },
  module: {
   rules
  },
  target: 'node',
  externals: [nodeExternals()],
  resolve: {
   extensions: [".ts", ".tsx", ".js", ".json"]
  }
}
```

As you can see, entry, output, and module are the same, except for the filenames.

The new parameters are the target, where we specify the node to tell webpack to ignore all the built-in system packages of Node.js, such as fs, and externals, where we use the library we imported earlier to tell webpack to ignore the dependencies.

Last but not least, we have to export the configurations as an array:

```
module.exports = [client, server]
```

The configuration is done. We are now ready to write some code, and we will start with the React application, which we are more familiar with.

Creating the application

Let's create an src folder and an app.ts file inside it.

The app.ts file should have the following content:

```
const App = () => <div>Hello React</div>
export default App
```

Nothing complex here; we import React, create an `App` component, which renders the `Hello React` message, and export it.

Let's now create `client.tsx`, which is responsible for rendering the `App` component inside the DOM:

```
import { render } from 'react-dom'
import App from './app'
render(<App />, document.getElementById('root'))
```

Again, this should sound familiar, since we import React, ReactDOM, and the `App` component we created earlier, and we use ReactDOM to render it in a DOM element with the app ID.

Let's now move to the server.

The first thing to do is to create a `template.ts` file, which exports a function that we will use to return the markup of the page that our server will give back to the browser:

```
export default body => `
  <!DOCTYPE html>
  <html>
    <head>
      <meta charset="UTF-8" />
    </head>
    <body>
      <div id="root">${body}</div>
      <script src="/bundle.js"></script>
    </body>
  </html>
```

It should be pretty straightforward. The function accepts body, which we will later see contains the React app, and it returns the skeleton of the page.

It is worth noting that we load the bundle on the client side even if the app is rendered on the server side. SSR is only half of the job that React does to render our application. We still want our application to be a client-side application, with all the features we can use in the browser, such as event handlers, for example.

After this, you need to install express, react, and react-dom:

```
npm install express react react-dom @types/express @types/react @types/
react-dom
```

Now it is time to create `server.tsx`, which has more dependencies and is worth exploring in detail:

```
import React from 'react'
import express, { Request, Response } from 'express'
import { renderToString } from 'react-dom/server'
import path from 'path'
import App from './App'
import template from './template'
```

The first thing that we import is express, the library that allows us to create a web server with some routes easily, and which is also able to serve static files.

Secondly, we import React and ReactDOM to render App, which we import as well. Notice the `/server` path in the `import` statement of ReactDOM. The last thing we import is the template we defined earlier.

Now we create an Express application:

```
const app = express()
```

We tell the application where our static assets are stored:

```
app.use(express.static(path.resolve(__dirname, './dist/public')))
```

As you may have noticed, the path is the same that we used in the client configuration of webpack as the output destination of the client bundle.

Then, here comes the logic of SSR with React:

```
app.get('/', (req: Request, res: Response) => {
  const body = renderToString(<App />)
  const html = template(body)
  res.send(html)
})
```

We are telling Express that we want to listen to the / route, and when it gets hit by a client, we render App to a string using the ReactDOM library. Here comes the magic and simplicity of the SSR of React.

What `renderToString` does is return a string representation of the DOM elements generated by our App component, the same tree that it would render in the DOM if we were using the React-DOM render method.

The value of the body variable is something like the following:

```
<div data-reactroot="" data-reactid="1" data-react-
checksum="982061917">Hello React</div>
```

As you can see, it represents what we defined in the render method of App, except for a couple of data attributes that React uses on the client to attach the client-side application to the server-side-rendered string.

Now that we have the SSR representation of our app, we can use the template function to apply it to the HTML template and send it back to the browser within the Express response.

Last but not least, we have to start the Express application:

```
app.listen(3000, () => {
  console.log('Listening on port 3000')
})
```

We are now ready to go; there are only a few operations left. The first one is to define the start script of npm and set it to run the node server:

```
"scripts": {
  "build": "webpack",
  "start": "node ./dist/server"
}
```

The scripts are ready, so we can first build the application with the following command:

```
npm run build
```

When the bundles are created, we can run the following command:

```
npm start
```

Point the browser to http://localhost:3000 and see the result.

There are two important things to note here. First, when we use the **View Page Source** feature of the browser, we can see the source code of the application being rendered and returned from the server, which we would not see if SSR was not enabled.

Second, if we open DevTools and we have the React extension installed, we can see that the App component has been booted on the client as well.

The following screenshot shows the source of the page:

```
1
2    <!DOCTYPE html>
3    <html>
4      <head>
5        <meta charset="UTF-8">
6      </head>
7      <body>
8        <div id="app"><div data-reactroot="" data-reactid="1" data-react-checksum="982061917">Hello
     React</div></div>
9        <script src="/bundle.js"></script>
10     </body>
11   </html>
12
```

Figure 12.1: Source code page

Great! Now that you have created your first React application using SSR, let's learn how to fetch data in the next section.

Implementing data fetching

The example in the previous section should clearly explain how to set up a universal application in React. It is pretty straightforward, and the main focus is on getting things done. However, in a real-world application, we will likely want to load some data instead of a static React component, such as App in the example.

Let's assume, for example, we want to load Dan Abramov's gists on the server and return the list of items from the Express app we just created.

In the data fetching examples in *Chapter 12, Managing Data*, we looked at how we can use useEffect to fire the data loading. That wouldn't work on the server because components do not get mounted on the DOM and the life cycle Hook never gets fired.

Using Hooks that were executed earlier will not work either because the data fetching operation is async, while renderToString is not. For that reason, we have to find a way to load the data beforehand and pass it to the component as props.

Let's look at how we can take the application from the previous section and change it a bit to make it load gists during the SSR phase.

The first thing to do is to change **App.tsx** to accept a list of `gists` as `props`, and loop through it in the render method to display their descriptions:

```
import { FC } from 'react'
type Gist = {
    id: string
    description: string
 }
 type Props = {
    gists: Gist[]
}
const App: FC<Props> = ({ gists }) => (
  <ul>
    {gists.map(gist => (
    <li key={gist.id}>{gist.description}</li>
  ))}
  </ul>
)
export default App
```

Applying the concept that we learned in the previous chapter, we define a stateless functional component, which receives `gists` as `props` and loops through the elements to render a list of items. Now, we have to change the server to retrieve `gists` and pass them to the component.

To use the `fetch` API on the server side, we have to install a library called `isomorphic-fetch`, which implements the fetch standards. It can be used in Node.js and the browser:

```
npm install isomorphic-fetch @types/isomorphic-fetch
```

We first import the library into `server.tsx`:

```
import fetch from 'isomorphic-fetch'
```

The API call that we want to make looks as follows:

```
fetch('https://api.github.com/users/gaearon/gists')
  .then(response => response.json())
  .then(gists => {})
```

Here, gists are available to be used inside the last `then` function. In our case, we want to pass them down to App.

Therefore, we can change the / route as follows:

```
app.get('/', (req, res) => {
  fetch('https://api.github.com/users/gaearon/gists')
    .then(response => response.json())
    .then(gists => {
    const body = renderToString(<App gists={gists} />)
    const html = template(body)
    res.send(html)
    })
})
```

Here, we first fetch `gists`, and then we render `App` as a string, passing the property.

Once `App` is rendered and we have its markup, we use the template we used in the previous section and return it to the browser.

Run the following command in the console and point the browser to `http://localhost:3000`. You should be able to see a `server-side` render list of `gists`:

```
npm run build && npm start
```

To make sure that the list is rendered from the Express app, you can navigate to `view-source:http://localhost:3000` and you will see the markup and the descriptions of gists.

That is great, and it looks easy, but if we check the DevTools console, we can see `Cannot read property 'map' of undefined error`. The reason we see the error is that, on the client, we are rendering App again, but without passing `gists` to it.

This could sound counter-intuitive in the beginning because we might think that React is smart enough to use `gists` rendered within the server-side string on the client. But that is not what happens, so we have to find a way to make `gists` available on the client side as well.

You may consider that you could execute the fetch again on the client. That would work, but it is not optimal because you would end up firing two HTTP calls, one on the Express server and one in the browser. If we think about it, we already made the call on the server, and we have all the data we need. A typical solution to sharing data between the server and the client is dehydrating the data in the HTML markup and hydrating it back in the browser.

This seems like a complex concept, but it is not. We will now look at how easy it is to implement. The first thing we must do is inject `gists` into the template after we have fetched them on the client.

To do this, we have to change the template slightly, as follows:

```
export default (body, gists) => `
  <!DOCTYPE html>
  <html>
    <head>
      <meta charset="UTF-8" />
    </head>
    <body>
      <div id="root">${body}</div>
      <script>window.gists = ${JSON.stringify(gists)}</script>
      <script src="/bundle.js"></script>
    </body>
  </html>
`
```

The `template` function now accepts two parameters—the body of the app and the collection of gists. The first one is inserted into the app element, while the second is used to define a global gists variable attached to the `window` object so that we can use it in the client.

Inside the Express route (`server.ts`), we just have to change the line where we generate the template passing the body, as follows:

```
const html = template(body, gists)
```

Last but not least, we have to use gists attached to a window inside **client.tsx**, which is pretty easy:

```
ReactDOM.hydrate(
  <App gists={window.gists} />,
  document.getElementById('app')
)
```

The hydrate method was introduced in React 16 and works similarly to render on the client side, irrespective of whether the HTML has server-side-rendered markup or not. If there is no markup previously using SSR, then the hydrate method will fire a warning, which you can silence by using the new `suppressHydrationWarning` attribute.

We read `gists` directly, and we pass them to the App component that gets rendered on the client.

Now, run the following command again:

```
npm run build && npm start
```

If we point the browser window to `http://localhost:3000`, the error is gone, and if we inspect the App component using React DevTools, we can see how the client-side App component receives the collection of gists.

As we have created our first SSR application, let's now see how we can do this more easily by using an SSR framework called Next.js in the next section.

Using Next.js to create a React application

You have looked at the basics of SSR with React, and you can use the project we created as a starting point for a real app. However, you may think that there is too much boilerplate and that you are required to know about too many different tools to run a simple universal application with React. This is a common feeling called **JavaScript fatigue**, as described in the introduction to this book.

Luckily, Meta developers and other companies in the React community are working very hard to improve the DX and make the lives of developers easier. You might have used `create-react-app` at this point to try out the examples in the previous chapters, and you should understand how it makes it very simple to create React applications without requiring developers to learn about many technologies and tools.

Now, `create-react-app` does not support SSR yet, but there's a company called **Vercel** that has created a tool called **Next.js**, which makes it incredibly easy to generate universal applications without worrying about configuration files. It also reduces the boilerplate a lot.

It is important to say that using abstractions is always very good for building applications quickly. However, it is crucial to know how the internals work before adding too many layers, and that is why we started with the manual process before learning Next.js. We have looked at how SSR works and how we can pass the state from the server to the client. Now that the base concepts are clear, we can move on to a tool that hides a little bit of complexity and makes us write less code to achieve the same results.

We will create the same app where all gists from Dan Abramov are loaded, and you will see how clean and simple the code is, thanks to Next.js.

First of all, create a new project folder (you can call it `next-project`) and run the following command:

```
npm init
```

When this is done, we can install the Next.js library and React:

```
npm install next react react-dom typescript @types/react @types/node
```

Now that the project is created, we have to add an npm script to run the binary:

```
"scripts": {
  "dev": "next"
}
```

Perfect! It is now time to generate our App component. Next.js is based on conventions, with the most important one being that you can create pages to match the browser URLs. The default page is index, so we can create a folder called pages and put an index.js file inside it.

We start importing the dependencies:

```
import fetch from 'isomorphic-fetch'
```

Again, we import isomorphic-fetch because we want to be able to use the fetch function on the server side.

We then define a component called App:

```
const App = () => {}
export default App
```

Then we define a static async function, called getInitialProps, which is where we tell Next.js which data we want to load, both on the server side and on the client side. The library will make the object returned from the function available as props inside the component.

The static and async keywords applied to a class method mean that the function can be accessed outside the instance of the class and that the function yields the execution of the wait instructions inside its body.

These concepts are pretty advanced, and they are not part of the scope of this chapter, but if you are interested in them, you should check out the ECMAScript proposals (https://github.com/tc39/proposals).

The implementation of the method we just described is as follows:

```
App.getInitialProps = async () => {
  const url = 'https://api.github.com/users/gaearon/gists'
  const response = await fetch(url)
```

```
    const gists = await response.json()
  return {
    gists
  }
}
```

We are telling the function to fire the `fetch` and wait for the response, then we are transforming the response into JSON, which returns a promise. When the promise is resolved, we can return the props object with `gists`.

The render of the component looks pretty similar to the preceding one:

```
return (
  <ul>
    {props.gists.map(gist => (
      <li key={gist.id}>{gist.description}</li>
    ))}
  </ul>
)
```

Before you run the project, you need to configure `tsconfig.json`:

```
{
  "compilerOptions": {
    "baseUrl": "src",
    "esModuleInterop": true,
    "module": "esnext",
    "noImplicitAny": true,
    "outDir": "dist",
    "resolveJsonModule": true,
    "sourceMap": false,
    "target": "esnext",
    "lib": ["dom", "dom.iterable", "esnext"],
    "allowJs": true,
    "skipLibCheck": true,
    "strict": true,
    "forceConsistentCasingInFileNames": true,
    "noEmit": true,
    "moduleResolution": "node",
```

```
    "isolatedModules": true,
    "jsx": "react-jsx"
  },
  "include": ["src/**/*.ts", "src/**/*.tsx"],
  "exclude": ["node_modules"]
}
```

Now, open the console and run the following command:

```
npm run dev
```

We will see the following output:

```
> Ready on http://localhost:3000
```

If we point the browser to that URL, we can see the universal application in action. It is really impressive how easy it is to set up a universal application with a few lines of code and zero configuration, thanks to Next.js.

You may also notice that if you edit the application inside your editor, you will be able to see the results within the browser instantly without needing to refresh the page. That is another feature of Next.js, which enables hot module replacement. It is incredibly useful in development mode.

If you liked this chapter, go and give it a star on GitHub: `https://github.com/zeit/next.js`.

Summary

The journey through SSR has come to an end. You are now able to create a server-side-rendered application with React, and it should be clear why it can be useful for you. SEO is certainly one of the main reasons, but social sharing and performance are important factors as well. You learned how it is possible to load the data on the server and dehydrate it in the HTML template to make it available to the client-side application when it boots on the browser.

Finally, you looked at how tools such as Next.js can help you reduce the boilerplate and hide some of the complexity that setting up a server-side-rendered React application usually brings to the code base.

In the next chapter, we will talk about how to improve the performance of our React applications.

Join our community on Discord

Join our community's Discord space for discussion with the author and other readers:

`https://packt.link/React18DesignPatterns4e`

13

Understanding GraphQL with a Real Project

GraphQL is a powerful query language designed to work seamlessly with APIs, allowing them to efficiently interact with your existing data. Unlike traditional REST APIs, GraphQL provides a comprehensive overview of the data in your API, making it easy to request only the exact data you need and nothing more. This not only streamlines your API requests but also makes it easier to optimize and improve your APIs when necessary. Additionally, GraphQL comes equipped with powerful developer tools to further enhance your development experience.

In this chapter, we'll delve into the practical application of GraphQL by building a basic login and user registration system for a real-world project. By exploring how GraphQL can be utilized in this context, you'll gain a comprehensive understanding of the language and be able to apply it effectively in your own projects.

We will cover the following topics in this chapter:

- Installing PostgreSQL
- Creating environment variables with a .env file
- Configuring Apollo Server
- Defining GraphQL queries and mutations
- Working with resolvers
- Creating Sequelize models
- Implementing JWT

- Using GraphQL Playground
- Performing authentication

Technical requirements

To complete this chapter, you will need the following:

- Node.js 19+
- Visual Studio Code
- PostgreSQL
- Homebrew (`https://brew.sh`)
- pgAdmin 4 (`https://www.pgadmin.org/download/`)

You can find the code for this chapter in this book's GitHub repository at `https://github.com/PacktPublishing/React-18-Design-Patterns-and-Best-Practices-Fourth-Edition/tree/main/Chapter13`.

Building a backend login system using PostgreSQL, Apollo Server, GraphQL, Sequelize, and JSON Web Tokens

In this section, we will be building a backend login system using PostgreSQL, Apollo Server, GraphQL, Sequelize, and **JSON Web Tokens (JWTs)**. We will utilize PostgreSQL for data storage, Sequelize to perform database operations, Apollo Server to create a GraphQL API, GraphQL to shape our API, and JWTs for user authentication and authorization. Whether you are a beginner or an experienced developer, this guide will offer a comprehensive understanding of how to integrate these technologies into a robust and secure backend login system. Let us dive in.

Installing PostgreSQL

For this example, we will use a PostgreSQL database, so you'll need to install PostgreSQL to be able to run this project on your machine.

PostgreSQL is an excellent choice for our database. *Why?* It excels in keeping data secure and well organized, even in the event of an unexpected issue. It has the capability to handle various types of data, which proves to be extremely convenient. Additionally, PostgreSQL is extensible, enabling it to go beyond the basics. It operates efficiently and can manage a substantial number of users concurrently.

Moreover, it boasts robust security features that ensure the protection of our data. Being an open-source platform, it is not only free but also benefits from a large community actively working toward its improvement. If you have prior experience with other databases, PostgreSQL is easy to comprehend, as it adheres to the same standards. Furthermore, it can handle considerable amounts of data and accommodate numerous users simultaneously. This is precisely why it stands as a reliable choice for projects such as our login system.

If you have a macOS machine, the easiest way to install PostgreSQL is by doing so with Homebrew. You just need to run the following command:

```
brew install postgres
```

Once you've installed it, you need to run the following command:

```
ln -sfv /usr/local/opt/postgresql/*.plist ~/Library/LaunchAgents
```

This command creates a symbolic link (a type of shortcut) from the PostgreSQL `plist` files (which are configuration files used by macOS) to your `~/Library/LaunchAgents` directory. The options used with the `ln -sfv` command are as follows: "**s**" for **symbolic** (to create a symbolic link), "**f**" for **force** (to remove existing destination files), and "**v**" for **verbose** (to display what is happening).

Then, you can create two new aliases to start and stop your PostgreSQL server:

```
alias pg_start="launchctl load ~/Library/LaunchAgents"
alias pg_stop="launchctl unload ~/Library/LaunchAgents"
```

Now, you should be able to start your PostgreSQL server by using `pg_start` or stop it with `pg_stop`. After this, you need to create your first database, like so:

```
createdb `whoami`
```

Now, you can connect to PostgreSQL using the `psql` command. If you get an error stating the role "postgresql" does not exist, you can fix it by running the following command:

```
createuser -s postgres
```

If you did everything correctly, you should see something like this:

Figure 13.1: psql

If you use Windows, you can download PostgreSQL at `https://www.postgresql.org/download/windows/` and for those that use Linux (Ubuntu), you can download it from `https://www.postgresql.org/download/linux/ubuntu/`.

Best tools for PostgreSQL database management

The best tool for PostgreSQL database management is **pgAdmin 4** (`https://www.pgadmin.org/download/`). I like this tool as it can be used to create new servers, users, and databases and can be used to perform SQL queries and work with data. Remember to create a database in order to use it in this example.

Sometimes, you may get an error when you start your PostgreSQL server that could say something like **FATAL lock file "postmaster.pid" already exists.** If you get this error, you can easily fix it by running the following command:

```
rm /usr/local/var/postgres/postmaster.pi
```

With this, you will be able to start your PostgreSQL server.

Now that we have completed the setup of PostgreSQL and have the pgAdmin tool available for easier database management, we can shift our focus to the next task, which is building our backend project.

Creating our backend project

First, you need to create a backend directory in your GraphQL project (`graphql/backend`). After that, let's review the huge list of NPM packages you will need to install (focusing on the most relevant):

```
npm init --yes
npm install @apollo/server@4.7.3 @contentpi/lib@1.0.10 @graphql-tools/
load-files@7.0.0 @graphql-tools/merge@9.0.0 @graphql-tools/schema@10.0.0
body-parser@1.20.2 cors@2.8.5 dotenv@16.1.4 express@4.18.2 graphql-
middleware@6.1.34 graphql-tag@2.12.6 jsonwebtoken@9.0.0 pg@8.11.0 pg-
hstore@2.3.4 pm2@5.3.0 sequelize@6.32.0 ts-node@10.9.1
npm install --save-dev prettier@2.8.8 ts-node-dev@2.0.0 typescript@5.1.3
eslint@8.42.0 @types/jsonwebtoken@9.0.2 @types/cors@2.8.13
```

Please note that some readers of my last book encountered issues with certain code that did not work as intended. This is due to updates to package versions since the time of writing.

To ensure that the code in this book functions correctly, I have specified the specific versions of packages that I use. It's important to note that newer versions of these packages may contain breaking changes that could impact the functionality of the code, so it's recommended that you use the specified versions to avoid any issues.

The scripts you should have in your `package.json` file should be as follows:

```
"scripts": {
  "dev": "ts-node-dev src/index.ts",
  "build": "rm -rf dist && tsc -p . --traceResolution",
  "lint": "eslint . --ext .js,.tsx,.ts",
  "lint:fix": "eslint . --fix --ext .js,.tsx,.ts",
  "test": "jest src"
}
```

In the next section, we are going to configure our environment variables.

Configuring our .env file

A `.env` file (also known as *dotenv*) is a configuration file to specify your application's environment variables. Normally your application won't change in development, staging, or production environments but they normally need a different configuration. The most common variables to change are the base URL, API URL, or even your API keys.

Before we jump into the actual login code, we need to create a file called `.env` (normally, this file is ignored by **.gitignore**), which will allow us to use private data, such as the database connection and security secrets. A file already exists in the repository called **.env.example**; you just need to rename it and put your connection data inside it. The `.env file` will look something like this:

```
DB_DIALECT=postgres
DB_PORT=5432
DB_HOST=localhost
DB_DATABASE=<your-database>
DB_USERNAME=<your-username>
DB_PASSWORD=<your-password>
```

Creating a basic config file

For this project, we need to create a config file to store some security data, which should be created at **/backend/config/config.json**.

Here, we will define some basic configurations, such as our server's port and some security information:

```
{
  "server": {
    "port": 4000
  },
  "security": {
    "secretKey": "C0nt3ntP1",
    "expiresIn": "7d"
  }
}
```

Then, you need to create an **index.ts** file in the config directory. This will bring in all the database connection information we defined in the .env file using the dotenv package and then export three configuration variables called **$db**, **$security**, and **$server**:

```
import dotenv from 'dotenv'
import config from './config.json'
dotenv.config()
type Db = {
  dialect: string
  host: string
  port: string
  database: string
  username: string
  password: string
}
type Security = {
  secretKey: string
  expiresIn: string
}
type Server = {
  port: number
}
const db: Db = {
  dialect: process.env.DB_DIALECT || '',
  port: process.env.DB_PORT || '',
  host: process.env.DB_HOST || '',
```

```
    database: process.env.DB_DATABASE || '',
    username: process.env.DB_USERNAME || '',
    password: process.env.DB_PASSWORD || ''
}
const { security, server } = config
export const $db: Db = db
export const $security: Security = security
export const $server: Server = server
```

If your .env file is not in the root directory or does not exist, all your variables are going to be **undefined**.

Once you have configured your file and verified the security details of your project, the subsequent step toward enhancing our project involves the utilization and setup of Apollo Server. This invaluable tool facilitates the management of data exchanges between your server and client, streamlining the communication process.

Configuring Apollo Server

Apollo Server is a highly popular open-source library for working with GraphQL, both as a server and client. With extensive documentation and straightforward implementation, it has become a go-to choice for many developers. Its intuitive interface and flexible architecture make it easy to customize and adapt to your specific needs, while its robust features and reliable performance ensure seamless integration with your existing code base. Whether you're a seasoned developer or new to GraphQL, Apollo Server is a powerful tool that can help you take your projects to the next level.

The following diagram explains how Apollo Server works in the client and the server:

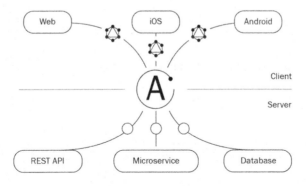

Figure 13.2: Apollo Server

Apollo Server facilitates efficient communication between your app or website and the associated database. By utilizing GraphQL, it enables the frontend part of your app to request specific data from the backend in a single operation, resulting in a faster and smoother data exchange. In essence, it serves as an effective intermediary between your user interface and the database.

For our setup, we will use Express to establish our Apollo Server and the Sequelize **Object Relational Mapper (ORM)** to handle our PostgreSQL database. Express is a popular choice to configure Apollo Server due to its seamless integration with Apollo and its flexibility, which provides developers with greater freedom. Express.js is a lightweight and performance-optimized framework suitable for applications of various sizes, from small to large and scalable ones. Moreover, its maturity and extensive community support make it a reliable option. Its simplicity, especially for those already familiar with JavaScript and Node.js, enables a quick and efficient Apollo Server setup. Therefore, we will begin by importing the necessary components.

The required file can be found at /backend/src/index.ts:

```
import { makeExecutableSchema } from '@graphql-tools/schema'
import { ApolloServer } from '@apollo/server'
import { expressMiddleware } from '@apollo/server/express4'
import { ApolloServerPluginDrainHttpServer } from '@apollo/server/plugin/
drainHttpServer'
import cors from 'cors'
import http from 'http'
import express from 'express'
import { applyMiddleware } from 'graphql-middleware'
import { json } from 'body-parser'
import { $server } from '../config'
import resolvers from './graphql/resolvers'
import typeDefs from './graphql/types'
import models from './models'
```

First, we need to set up our Express.js application and cors:

```
const app = express()
const corsOptions = {
  origin: '*',
  credentials: true
}
app.use(cors(corsOptions))
```

```
app.use((req, res, next) => {
  res.header('Access-Control-Allow-Origin', '*')
  res.header(
    'Access-Control-Allow-Headers',
    'Origin, X-Requested-With, Content-Type, Accept'
  )
  next()
})
```

Then, we need to create our schema using `applyMiddleware` and `makeExecutableSchema` by passing `typeDefs` and `resolvers`:

```
// Schema
const schema = applyMiddleware(
  makeExecutableSchema({
    typeDefs,
    resolvers
  })
)
```

After that, we need to create an instance of Apollo Server, where we need to pass the schema and the plugins:

```
// Apollo Server
const apolloServer = new ApolloServer({
  schema,
  plugins: [ApolloServerPluginDrainHttpServer({ httpServer })]
})
```

Finally, we need to synchronize Sequelize. Here, we pass some optional variables (`alter` and `force`). If `force` is true and you change your Sequelize models, this will delete your tables, including their values, and force you to create the tables again, while if `force` is `false` and `alter` is true, then you will only update the table fields, without this affecting your values. So, you need to be careful with this option, as you can lose all your data by accident. Then, after the sync, we must run our Apollo Server, which listens to port 4000 (**$server.port**):

```
const main = async () => {
  const alter = true
  const force = false
  await apolloServer.start()
```

```
await models.sequelize.sync({ alter, force })
app.use(
  '/graphql',
  cors<cors.CorsRequest>(),
  json(),
  expressMiddleware(apolloServer, {
    context: async () => ({ models })
  })
)
await new Promise<void>((resolve) => httpServer.listen({
  port: $server.port
}, resolve))
console.log(` 🚀 Server ready at http://localhost:${$server.port}/
graphql`)
}
main()
```

This process will help us in synchronizing our database with our models, ensuring that any modifications made to the models will automatically update the corresponding tables.

Defining our GraphQL types, queries, and mutations

Now that you have created your Apollo Server instance, the next step is to create your GraphQL types. When setting up a GraphQL server like Apollo, creating GraphQL types is crucial. These types ensure that the data returned from your API is reliable and conforms to the expected structure. They act as a helpful reference for available data and its expected format. By using types, your application can precisely request the required data, resulting in faster execution and reduced data consumption. Additionally, types help maintain data consistency, resulting in a robust, comprehensible, and efficient API.

Scalar types

The first thing you need to do is define your scalar types at /backend/src/graphql/types/Scalar. ts:

```
import gql from 'graphql-tag'
export default gql`
  scalar UUID
  scalar Datetime
  scalar JSON
```

Now, let's create our User type (backend/src/graphql/types/User.ts):

```
import gql from 'graphql-tag'
export default gql`
  type User {
    id: UUID!
    username: String!
    email: String!
    password: String!
    role: String!
    active: Boolean!
    createdAt: Datetime!
    updatedAt: Datetime!
  }
`
```

As you can see, we use some scalar types such as **UUID** and **Datetime** to define some fields in our User type. In this case, when you define a type in GraphQL, you need to do so with the type keyword, followed by the type's name capitalized. Then, you can define your fields inside the curly braces, {}.

There are some primitive data types in GraphQL such as String, Boolean, Float, and Int. You can define custom scalar types as we did with **UUID**, **Datetime**, and **JSON**, and you can also define custom types such as the User type and specify whether we want an array of that type, for example, [User].

 The ! character after the types means the field is non-nullable.

Queries

GraphQL queries are used to read or fetch values from a data store. Now that you know how to define custom types, let's define our Query type. Here, we will define getUsers and getUser. The first will retrieve a list of users, while the second will bring us the data of the specific user:

```
type Query {
  getUser(at: String!): User!
```

```
    getUsers: [User!]
}
```

In this case, our getUsers query will return an array of users ([User!]), while our getUser query, which requires the at (access token) attribute, will return a single User!. Remember that with any query you add here, you will need to define it under your resolvers later (we will do that in the next section).

Mutations

Mutations are used to write or post values: that is, to modify data in the data store: and return a value if you want to do some comparisons with REST, such as perform any POST, PUT, PATCH, or DELETE actions. The Mutation type works exactly the same as the Query type, in that you need to define your mutations and specify what arguments you will receive and what data you will return:

```
type Mutation {
    createUser(input: CreateUserInput): User!
    login(input: LoginInput): Token!
}
```

As you can see, we have defined two mutations. The first is **createUser**, to register or create a new user in our data store, while the second one is to perform a **login**. As you may have noticed, both receive the input argument with some different values (CreateUserInput and LoginInput), called **input types**, which are used as query or mutation parameters. Finally, they will return the User! and Token! types, respectively. Let's learn how to define those inputs:

```
type Token {
 token: String!
}
input CreateUserInput {
 username: String!
 password: String!
 email: String!
 active: Boolean!
 role: String!
}
input LoginInput {
 emailOrUsername: String!
 password: String!
}
```

The inputs are normally used with mutations, but you can also use them with queries.

Merging type definitions

Now that we've defined all our types, queries, and mutations, we need to merge all our GraphQL files to create our GraphQL schema, which is basically one big file containing all our GraphQL definitions.

For this, you need to create a file called `/backend/src/graphql/types/index.ts` that contains the following code:

```
import { mergeTypeDefs } from '@graphql-tools/merge'
import Scalar from './Scalar'
import User from './User'
export default mergeTypeDefs([Scalar, User])
```

After successfully merging your type definitions into one comprehensive GraphQL schema, the next critical step is to create resolvers. Resolvers are functions that have the responsibility of fetching and generating the data that corresponds to the fields defined in your GraphQL schema.

Creating our resolvers

A resolver is a function that's responsible for generating data for a field in your GraphQL schema. It can normally generate the data in any way you want, in that it can fetch data from a database or by using a third-party API.

To create our user resolvers, you need to create a file called `/backend/src/graphql/resolvers/user.ts`. Let's create a skeleton of what our resolver should look like. Here, we need to specify the functions that are defined under **Query** and **Mutation** in our GraphQL schema. So, your resolver should look like this:

```
export default {
  Query: {
    getUsers: () => {},
    getUser: () => {}
  },
  Mutation: {
    createUser: () => {},
    login: () => {}
  }
}
```

As you can see, we return an object with two main nodes called **Query** and **Mutation**, and we map the queries and the mutations we defined in our GraphQL schema (the User.ts file). Of course, we need to make some changes to receive some parameters and return some data, but I wanted to show you the basic skeleton of a resolver file first.

The first thing you need to do is add some imports to the file:

```
import { doLogin, getUserBy } from '../../lib/auth'
import { getUserData } from '../../lib/jwt'
import { ICreateUserInput, IloginInput, Imodels, Itoken, Iuser } from
'../../types'
```

We will create the **getUsers** and **getUser** functions in the next section.

Creating the getUsers query

Our first method will be the **getUsers** query. Let's see how we need to define it:

```
getUsers: (
    _: any,
    args: any,
    ctx: { models: Imodels }
): Iuser[] => ctx.models.User.findAll(),
```

In any query or mutation method, we always receive four parameters: the parent (defined as _), arguments (defined as args), the context (defined as ctx), and info (which is optional).

If you want to simplify the code a little bit, you can destructure the context, like this:

```
getUsers: (
    _: any,
    args: any,
  { models }: { models: Imodels }
): Iuser[] => ctx.models.User.findAll(),
```

In our next resolver function, we are going to destructure our arguments as well. Just as a reminder, the context is passed in our Apollo Server setup (we did this previously):

```
// Apollo Server
const apolloServer = new ApolloServer({
schema,
context: async () => ({
```

```
    models
  })
})
```

The context is very important when we need to share something globally in our resolvers.

Creating the getUser query

This function needs to be async because we need to perform some asynchronous operations, such as getting the connected user via an at (access token) if a user already has a valid session. Then, we can validate whether this is a real user by looking at our database. This helps stop people from modifying the cookies or trying to do some form of injection. If we don't find a connected user, then we return an object of the user that contains empty data:

```
getUser: async (
    _: any,
    { at }: { at: string },
    { models }: { models: IModels }
): Promise<any> => {
// Get current connected user
const connectedUser = await getUserData(at)
if (connectedUser) {
  // Validating if the user is still valid
  const user = await getUserBy({
    id: connectedUser.id,
    email: connectedUser.email,
    active: connectedUser.active
  },
  [connectedUser.role],
  models
)

if (user) {
  return connectedUser
  }
}
return {
  id: '',
  username: '',
```

```
    password: '',
    email: '',
    role: '',
    active: false
  }
}
```

Creating the mutations

Our mutations are very simple: we just need to execute some functions and pass all our arguments by spreading the input value (this comes from our GraphQL schema). Let's see what our Mutation node should look like:

```
Mutation: {
  createUser: (
    _: any,
    { input }: { input: ICreateUserInput },
    { models }: { models: IModels }
  ): IUser => models.User.create({ ...input }),
  login: (
    _: any,
    { input }: { input: ILoginInput },
    { models }: { models: IModels }
  ): Promise<IToken> => doLogin(input.email, input.password, models)
}
```

You need to pass the **email**, **password**, and **models** to the doLogin function.

Merging our resolvers

As we did with our types definitions, we need to merge all our resolvers using the @graphql-tools packages. You need to create the following file at /backend/src/graphql/resolvers/index.ts:

```
import { mergeResolvers } from '@graphql-tools/merge'
import user from './user'
const resolvers = mergeResolvers([user])
export default resolvers
```

This will combine all your resolvers into an array of resolvers.

Once your resolvers are merged, bringing all your data-fetching functions into one coherent structure, it's time to move on to the next phase: creating Sequelize models. Sequelize is a powerful tool that simplifies the interaction between your application and various databases, translating complex SQL commands into user-friendly JavaScript.

Using the Sequelize ORM

Sequelize is a popular ORM library for Node.js. It enables developers to interact with databases like MySQL, PostgreSQL, SQLite, and Microsoft SQL Server by abstracting the underlying SQL commands into higher-level, easy-to-use JavaScript objects and methods.

Using Sequelize, developers can perform database operations like creating, updating, deleting, and querying records without having to write raw SQL queries. Sequelize also helps with defining data models, managing associations between tables, and handling database migrations.

Some key features of Sequelize ORM include:

- **Model definition**: Sequelize allows you to define models with their attributes, data types, and constraints, which map to tables in the underlying database.
- **Associations**: You can easily define relationships between models, such as one-to-one, one-to-many, and many-to-many, which map to foreign key constraints in the database.
- **Querying**: Sequelize provides a robust querying system that allows you to fetch, filter, sort, and paginate data without writing raw SQL.
- **Transactions**: It supports transactions for performing multiple database operations atomically.
- **Migrations**: Sequelize offers a migration system to manage schema changes over time and keep your database schema in sync with your application's code.

Creating a user model in Sequelize

Before we jump into the authentication functions, we need to create our User model in Sequelize. For this, we need to create a file at `/backend/src/models/User.ts`. Our model will have the following fields:

- `id`
- `username`
- `password`
- `email`

- role

- active

Let's see the code:

```
import { encrypt } from '@contentpi/lib'
import { IDataTypes, IUser } from '../types'
export default (sequelize: any, DataTypes: IDataTypes): IUser => {
  const User = sequelize.define('User', {
    id: {
      primaryKey: true,
      allowNull: false,
      type: DataTypes.UUID,
      defaultValue: DataTypes.UUIDV4()
    },
    username: {
      type: DataTypes.STRING,
      allowNull: false,
      unique: true,
      validate: {
        isAlphanumeric: {
          args: true,
          msg: 'The user just accepts alphanumeric characters'
        },
        len: {
          args: [4, 20],
          msg: 'The username must be from 4 to 20 characters'
        }
      }
    },
    password: {
      type: Datatypes.STRING,
      allowNull: false
    },
    email: {
      type: DataTypes.STRING,
      allowNull: false,
      unique: true,
```

```
            validate: {
              isEmail: {
                args: true,
                msg: 'Invalid email'
              }
            }
          },
          role: {
            type: DataTypes.STRING,
            allowNull: false,
            defaultValue: 'user'
          },
          active: {
            type: DataTypes.BOOLEAN,
            allowNull: false,
            defaultValue: false
          }
        },
        {
          hooks: {
            beforeCreate: (user: IUser): void => {
              user.password = encrypt(user.password)
            }
          }
        }
      )
      return User
}
```

As you can see, we are defining a Sequelize Hook called beforeCreate, which helps us **encrypt** (using **sha1**) the user password right before the data is saved. Finally, we return the User model.

Connecting Sequelize to a PostgreSQL database

Now that we've created the user model, we need to connect Sequelize to our PostgreSQL database and put all our models together.

You need to add the following code to the /backend/src/models/index.ts file:

```
import { Sequelize } from 'sequelize'
import { $db } from '../../config'
import { IModels } from '../types'
// Db Connection
const { dialect, port, host, database, username, password } = $db
// Connecting to the database
const uri =
`${dialect}://${username}:${password}@${host}:${port}/${database}`
const sequelize = new Sequelize(uri)
// Models
const models: IModels = {
  User: require('./User').default(sequelize, Sequelize),
  sequelize
}
export default models
```

Authentication functions

Step by step, we are putting all the puzzle pieces together. Now, let's look at the authentication functions we will use to validate whether a user is connected or not and get the user's data. For this, we need to use JWTs.

JWT is an open standard outlined in RFC 7519 (https://tools.ietf.org/html/rfc7519). It serves as a valuable tool to transmit information between parties as a JSON object. One of the primary advantages of JWTs is their digital signature, which allows them to be easily verified and trusted. The token is signed using the HMAC algorithm and a secret or a public key pair using RSA or ECDSA, ensuring that it remains secure and tamper-proof. This makes JWTs a reliable choice for authentication and authorization purposes in a wide range of applications.

Creating JWT functions

Let's create some functions that will help verify a JWT and get the user data. For this, we need to create the jwtVerify, getUserData, and createToken functions. This file should be created at /backend/src/lib/jwt.ts:

```
import { encrypt, getBase64, setBase64 } from '@contentpi/lib'
import jwt from 'jsonwebtoken'
import { $security } from '../../config'
```

```
import { IUser } from '../types'
const { secretKey } = $security
export function jwtVerify(accessToken: string, cb: any): void {
  // Verifiying our JWT token using the accessToken and the secretKey
  jwt.verify(accessToken, secretKey, (error: any, accessTokenData: any =
  {}) => {
    const { data: user } = accessTokenData
    // If we get an error or the user is not found we return false
    if (error || !user) {
    return cb(false)
    }
    // The user data is on base64 and getBase64 will retreive the
    // information as JSON object
    const userData = getBase64(user)
    return cb(userData)
  })
}
export async function getUserData(accessToken: string): Promise<any> {
  // We resolve the jwtVerify promise to get the user data
  const UserPromise = new Promise((resolve) => jwtVerify(accessToken,
  (user: any) => resolve(user)))
  // This will get the user data or false (if the user is not connected)
  const user = await UserPromise
  return user
}
export const createToken = async (user: IUser): Promise<string[]> => {
  // Extracting the user data
  const { id, username, password, email, role, active } = user
  // Encrypting our password by combining the secretKey and the password
  // and converting it to base64
  const token = setBase64(`${encrypt($security.secretKey)}${password}`)
  // The "token" is an alias for password in this case
  const userData = {
    id,
    username,
    email,
    role,
```

```
    active,
    token
  }
  // We sign our JWT token and we save the data as Base64
  const _createToken = jwt.sign({ data: setBase64(userData) }, $security.
secretKey, {
    expiresIn: $security.expiresIn
  })
  return Promise.all([_createToken])
}
```

As you can see, jwt.sign is used to create a new JWT, while jwt.verify is used to validate our JWT.

Creating authentication functions

Now that we've created the JWT functions, we need to create some functions that will help us log in at /backend/src/lib/auth.ts:

```
import { encrypt, isPasswordMatch } from '@contentpi/lib'
import { IToken, IModels, IUser } from '../types'
import { createToken } from './jwt'
export const getUserBy = async (where: any, models: IModels):
Promise<IUser> => {
```

We find a user by a WHERE condition:

```
const user = await models.User.findOne({
 where,
   raw: true
 })
 return user
}
export const doLogin = async (
   email: string,
   password: string,
   models: IModels
): Promise<IToken> => {
```

Finding a user by email:

```
const user = await getUserBy({ email }, models)
```

If the user does not exist, we return `Invalid Login`:

```
if (!user) {
  throw new Error('Invalid Login')
}
```

We verify that our encrypted password is the same as the `user.password` value:

```
const passwordMatch = isPasswordMatch(encrypt(password), user.password)
```

We validate that the user is active:

```
const isActive = user.active
```

If the password does not match, we return `Invalid Login`:

```
if (!passwordMatch) {
  throw new Error('Invalid Login')
}
```

If the account is not active, we return an error:

```
if (!isActive) {
  throw new Error('Your account is not activated yet')
}
```

If the user exists, the password is correct and the account is active, then we create the JWT:

```
const [token] = await createToken(user)
// Finally we return the token to Graphql
return {
  token
}
}
```

Here, we validate whether the user exists by email, whether the password is correct, and whether the account is active in order to create the JWT.

Defining types and interfaces

Finally, we need to define our types and interfaces for all our Sequelize models and GraphQL inputs. For this, you need to create a file at /backend/src/types/types.ts:

```
export type User = {
  username: string
```

```
  password: string
  email: string
  role: string
  active: boolean
}
export type Sequelize = {
  _defaults?: any
  name?: string
  options?: any
  associate?: any
}
```

Now, let's create our interfaces at /backend/src/types/interfaces.ts:

```
import { Sequelize, User } from './types'
export interface IDataTypes {
    UUID: string
    UUIDV4(): string
    STRING: string
    BOOLEAN: boolean
    TEXT: string
    INTEGER: number
    DATE: string
    FLOAT: number
}
export interface IUser extends User, Sequelize {
    id: string
    token?: string
    createdAt?: Date
    updatedAt?: Date
}
export interface ICreateUserInput extends User {}
export interface ILoginInput {
    email: string
    password: string
}
export interface IToken {
```

```
      token: string
}
export interface IModels {
   User: any
   sequelize: any
}
```

Finally, we need to export both files in /backend/src/types/index.ts:

```
export * from './interfaces'
export * from './types'
```

When you need to add more models, remember to always add your types and interfaces to those files.

Finally, you need to create your tsconfig.json file in the root directory:

```
{
  "compilerOptions": {
    "baseUrl": "./src",
    "esModuleInterop": true,
    "module": "commonjs",
    "noImplicitAny": true,
    "outDir": "dist",
    "resolveJsonModule": true,
    "sourceMap": true,
    "target": "ESNext",
    "typeRoots": ["./src/@types", "./node_modules/@types"]
  },
  "include": ["src/**/*.ts"],
  "exclude": ["node_modules"]
}
```

In the next section, we will run our project and create our tables.

Running our project for the first time

Next up, we're going to start our project for the first time. If we've done everything right, we'll see our Users table being set up and our Apollo Server will start running.

In this part, we'll cover how to start our project. After that, we'll explore how to use our GraphQL API. We'll learn about testing queries, which allow us to retrieve data, and mutations, which enable us to modify data. We'll also discuss validations, which are checks to ensure the correctness of our data. Lastly, we'll delve into the process of user login. Let's get started!

If you followed the previous sections correctly and run the npm run dev command, you should be able to see that the Users table has been created and that Apollo Server is running on port 4000:

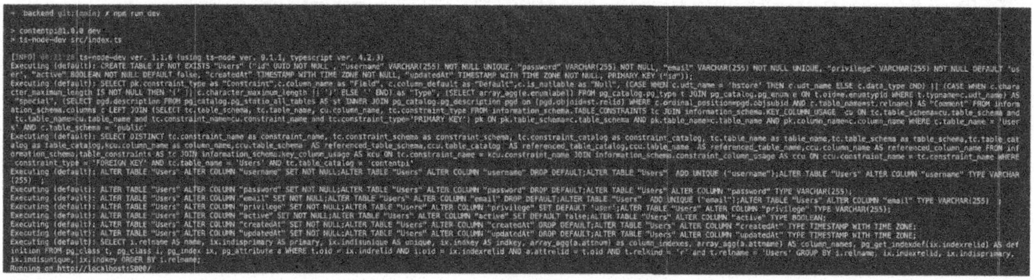

Figure 13.3: Running our project for the first time

Now, let's say that you want to modify your user model and change the "username" field to "username2". Let's see what will happen:

```
[INFO] 23:45:16 Restarting: /Users/czantany/projects/React-Design-
Patterns-and-Best-Practices-Third-Edition/Chapter05/graphql/backend/src/
models/User.ts has been modified
Executing (default): CREATE TABLE IF NOT EXISTS "Users" ("id" UUID NOT
NULL , "username2" VARCHAR(255) NOT NULL UNIQUE, "password" VARCHAR(255)
NOT NULL, "email" VARCHAR(255) NOT NULL UNIQUE, "privilege" VARCHAR(255)
NOT NULL DEFAULT 'user', "active" BOOLEAN NOT NULL DEFAULT false,
"createdAt" TIMESTAMP WITH TIME ZONE NOT NULL, "updatedAt" TIMESTAMP WITH
TIME ZONE NOT NULL, PRIMARY KEY ("id"));
Executing (default): ALTER TABLE "public"."Users" ADD COLUMN "username2"
VARCHAR(255) NOT NULL UNIQUE;
Executing (default): ALTER TABLE "Users" ALTER COLUMN "password" SET NOT
NULL;ALTER TABLE "Users" ALTER COLUMN "password" DROP DEFAULT;ALTER TABLE
"Users" ALTER COLUMN "password" TYPE VARCHAR(255);
```

```
Executing (default): ALTER TABLE "Users" ALTER COLUMN "email" SET NOT
NULL;ALTER TABLE "Users" ALTER COLUMN "email" DROP DEFAULT;ALTER TABLE
"Users" ADD UNIQUE ("email");ALTER TABLE "Users" ALTER COLUMN "email" TYPE
VARCHAR(255) ;
Executing (default): ALTER TABLE "Users" ALTER COLUMN "privilege" SET NOT
NULL;ALTER TABLE "Users" ALTER COLUMN "privilege" SET DEFAULT 'user';ALTER
TABLE "Users" ALTER COLUMN "privilege" TYPE VARCHAR(255);
Executing (default): ALTER TABLE "Users" ALTER COLUMN "active" SET NOT
NULL;ALTER TABLE "Users" ALTER COLUMN "active" SET DEFAULT false;ALTER
TABLE "Users" ALTER COLUMN "active" TYPE BOOLEAN;
Executing (default): ALTER TABLE "Users" ALTER COLUMN "createdAt" SET NOT
NULL;ALTER TABLE "Users" ALTER COLUMN "createdAt" DROP DEFAULT;ALTER TABLE
"Users" ALTER COLUMN "createdAt" TYPE TIMESTAMP WITH TIME ZONE;
Running on http://localhost:4000/graphql
```

This will execute the following SQL query:

```
Executing (default): ALTER TABLE "public"."Users" ADD COLUMN "username2"
VARCHAR(255) NOT NULL UNIQUE;
Executing (default): ALTER TABLE "public"."Users" DROP COLUMN "username";
```

Now, let's suppose you changed the force constant in your index.ts file to true. The following will happen:

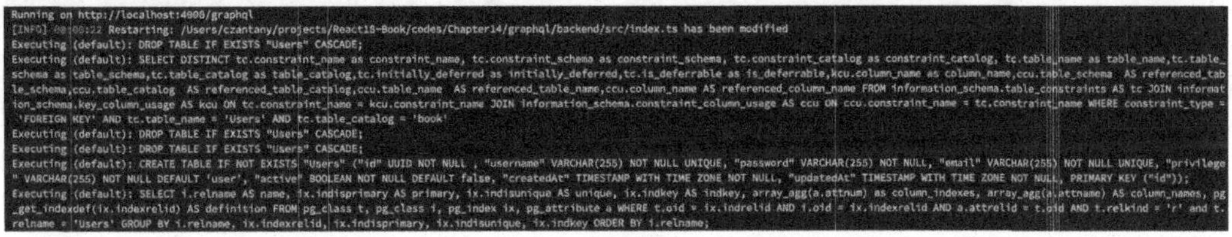

Figure 13.4: DROP TABLE IF EXISTS

As you can see, if force is true, it will execute DROP TABLE IF EXISTS "Users" CASCADE;. This will completely remove your table and values and then recreate your table from scratch. That's why you need to be careful when you use the force option.

At this point, if you open `http://localhost:4000/graphql`, you should be able to see your new GraphQL Explorer:

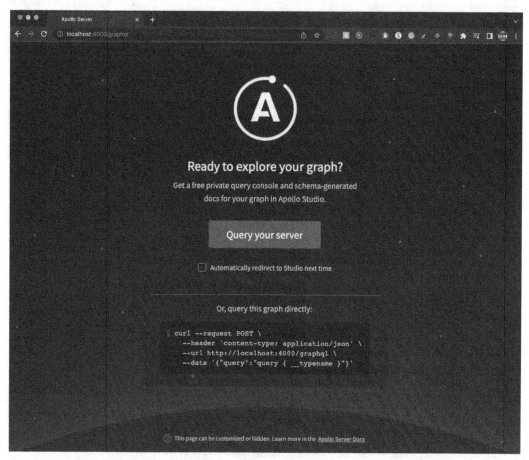

Figure 13.5: GraphQL Explorer

Click on the **Query your server** button and then we are ready to test our queries and mutations.

Testing GraphQL queries and mutations

Great! At this point, you're very close to executing your first GraphQL query and mutation. The first query we will execute is going to be `getUsers`. The following is the correct syntax to run a query:

```
query {
  getUsers {
    id
```

```
        username
        email
        role
    }
}
```

When you don't have any attribute to pass to the query, you just need to specify the name of the query under the query `{...}` block and then specify the fields you want to retrieve once you've executed your query. In this case, we want to fetch the `id`, `username`, `email`, and `role` fields.

If you run this query, you will probably get an empty array of data. This is because we don't have any users registered yet:

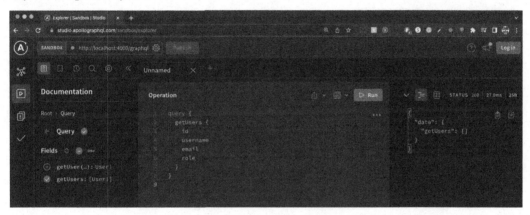

Figure 13.6: getUsers query

This means we need to execute our `createUser mutation` in order to register our first user. One thing I like about GraphQL Explorer is that you have all the schema documentation in the **Schema** icon on the left-hand side. If you click on the **Schema** icon, you will see all your queries and mutations listed.

Let's click there and select our `createUser` mutation to see what needs to be called and what data may be returned:

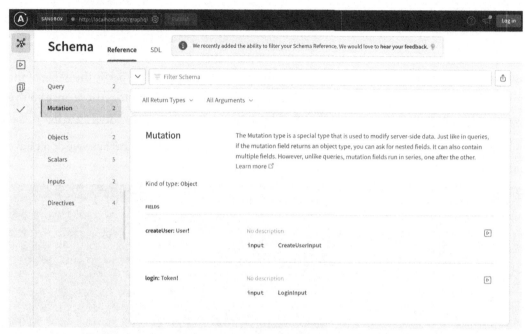

Figure 13.7: Schema

As you can see, the `createUser` mutation needs an `input` argument, which is `CreateUserInput`. Let's click on that input:

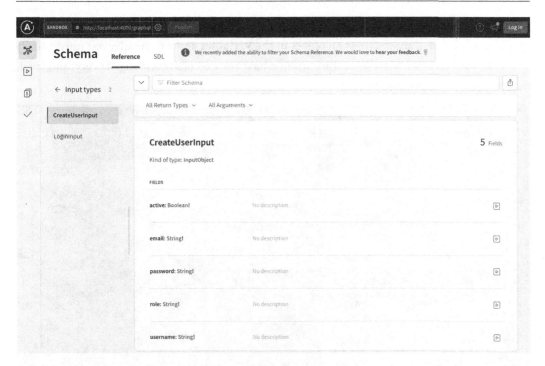

Figure 13.8: CreateUserInput

Awesome! Now, we know that we need to pass the **username**, **password**, **email**, **role**, and **active** fields in order to create a new user. Let's do this!

Create a new tab so that you don't lose the code of your first query and then write the mutation:

```
mutation($input: CreateUserInput) {
  createUser(input: $input) {
    id
    username
    email
    role
    active
  }
}
```

As you can see, your mutation needs to be written under the `mutation {...}` block, and you must pass the `input` argument as an object in the **Variables** section. Finally, you must specify the fields you want to retrieve once the mutation has been executed correctly. If everything is OK, you should see something like this:

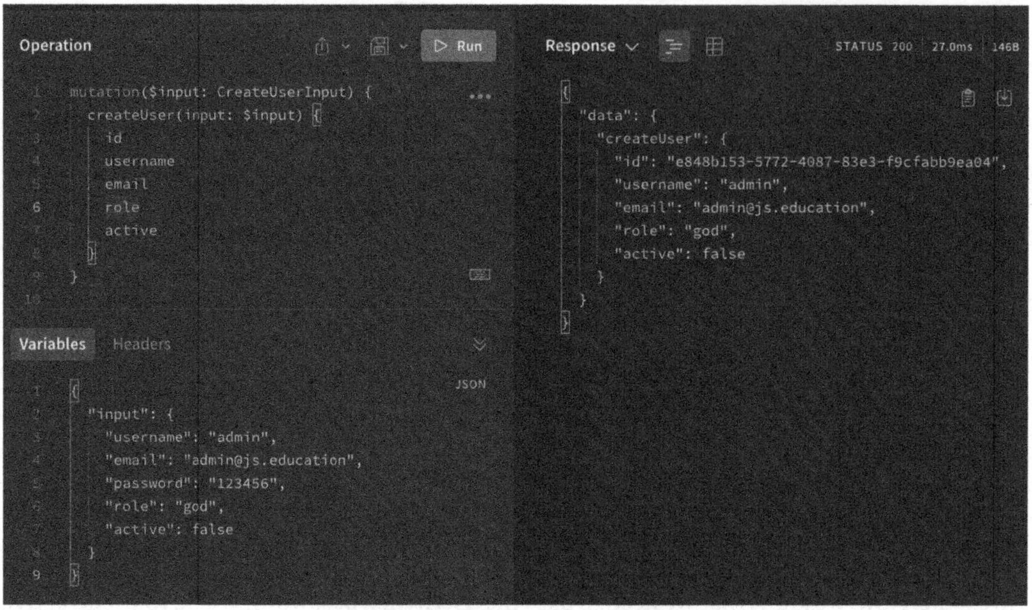

Figure 13.9: CreateUser mutation

If you're curious and wish to take a look at the terminal where you run your Apollo Server, you will see the SQL query that was performed for this user:

```
INSERT INTO "Users"
("id","username","password","email","role","active","createdAt","updatedAt")
VALUES ($1,$2,$3,$4,$5,$6,$7,$8)
```

The `VALUES` variables are handled by Apollo Server, so you won't see the actual values in there, but you can find out which operation is being executed in the database.

Now, go back to your first query (getUsers) and run it again!

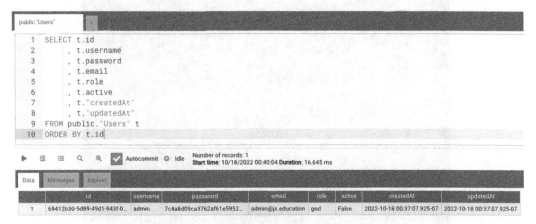

Figure 13.10: getUsers query

Nice: this is your first query and mutation that have been executed correctly in GraphQL. If you want to see this data in your database, you can use OmniDB or PgAdmin4 to view your Users table in your PostgreSQL database:

```
public."Users"

1    SELECT t.id
2         , t.username
3         , t.password
4         , t.email
5         , t.role
6         , t.active
7         , t."createdAt"
8         , t."updatedAt"
9    FROM public."Users" t
10   ORDER BY t.id
```

Number of records: 1
Start time: 10/18/2022 00:40:04 Duration: 16.645 ms

	id	username	password	email	role	active	createdAt	updatedAt
1	69412b30-5d89-49d1-943f-0...	admin	7c4a8d09ca3762af61e5952...	admin@js.education	god	False	2022-10-18 00:37:07.925-07	2022-10-18 00:37:07.925-07

Figure 13.11: Database query

As you can see, our first record has its own id field (UUID) and also has an encrypted password field (remember our beforeCreate Hook in the user model?). By default, Sequelize will create the createdAt and updatedAt fields.

Testing model validations and querying users

As you may recall, regarding our user model, you will want to make sure all the validations we did work fine, such as whether the user is unique or whether their email is valid and unique. You just need to execute the exact same mutation again:

```json
{
  "errors": [
    {
      "message": "Validation error",
      "locations": [
        {
          "line": 2,
          "column": 3
        }
      ],
      "path": [
        "createUser"
      ],
      "extensions": {
        "code": "INTERNAL_SERVER_ERROR",
        "exception": {
          "name": "SequelizeUniqueConstraintError",
          "errors": [
            {
              "message": "username must be unique",
              "type": "unique violation",
              "path": "username",
              "value": "admin",
              "origin": "DB",
              "instance": {
                "id": "38fb8276-b872-40ce-a717-b00f55a0d78c",
                "username": "admin",
                "password": "7c4a8d09ca3762af61e59520943dc26494f8941b",
                "email": "admin@js.education",
                "active": false,
                "role": "god",
                "updatedAt": "2022-10-18T07:41:01.088Z",
                "createdAt": "2022-10-18T07:41:01.088Z"
              },
              "validatorKey": "not_unique",
              "validatorName": null,
              "validatorArgs": []
            }
          ],
        }
      }
    }
  ]
}
```

Figure 13.12: Username must be unique

As you can see, we will get a **"username must be unique"** error message because we've already registered the "admin" username. Now, let's try to change the username to **"admin2"** but leave the email as is (**admin@js.education**):

```
{
  "errors": [
    {
      "message": "Validation error",
      "locations": [
        {
          "line": 2,
          "column": 3
        }
      ],
      "path": [
        "createUser"
      ],
      "extensions": {
        "code": "INTERNAL_SERVER_ERROR",
        "exception": {
          "name": "SequelizeUniqueConstraintError",
          "errors": [
            {
              "message": "email must be unique",
              "type": "unique violation",
              "path": "email",
              "value": "admin@js.education",
              "origin": "DB",
              "instance": {
                "id": "26a3c886-c14f-4992-960b-bb5103d5a20c",
                "username": "admin2",
                "password": "7c4a8d09ca3762af61e59520943dc26494f8941b",
                "email": "admin@js.education",
                "active": false,
                "role": "god",
                "updatedAt": "2022-10-18T07:42:00.657Z",
                "createdAt": "2022-10-18T07:42:00.657Z"
              },
              "validatorKey": "not_unique",
              "validatorName": null,
              "validatorArgs": []
            }
          ],
```

Figure 13.13: Email must be unique

We will also get an **"email must be unique"** error for the email. Now, try to change the email to something invalid, such as **admin@myfakedomain**:

```json
{
  "errors": [
    {
      "message": "Validation error: Invalid email",
      "locations": [
        {
          "line": 2,
          "column": 3
        }
      ],
      "path": [
        "createUser"
      ],
      "extensions": {
        "code": "INTERNAL_SERVER_ERROR",
        "exception": {
          "name": "SequelizeValidationError",
          "errors": [
            {
              "message": "Invalid email",
              "type": "Validation error",
              "path": "email",
              "value": "admin@myfakedomain",
              "origin": "FUNCTION",
              "instance": {
                "id": "8c6fce2a-790d-4c11-84f5-08ecc8e1e564",
                "username": "admin2",
                "password": "123456",
                "email": "admin@myfakedomain",
                "active": false,
                "role": "god",
                "updatedAt": "2022-10-18T07:42:52.494Z",
                "createdAt": "2022-10-18T07:42:52.494Z"
              },
```

Figure 13.14: Invalid email

Now, we're getting an `"Invalid email"` error message. This is just amazing, don't you think? Now, let's stop playing with the validations and add a new valid user (**username:** admin2 and **email:** admin2@js.education). Once you've created your second user, run our **getUsers** query once more. However, this time, add the `active` field to the list of fields we want to return:

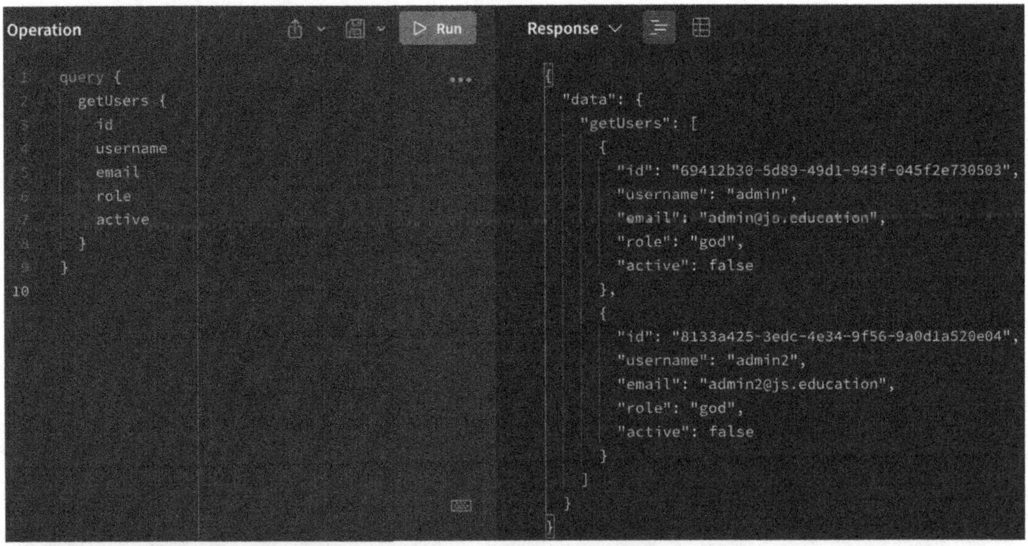

Figure 13.15: getUsers query

Now, we have two registered users, and both are inactive accounts ("active" = false).

One thing I love about GraphQL is that when you're writing your queries or mutations and you don't remember a certain field, GraphQL will always show you the list of available fields for that query or mutation. For example, if you just write the letter p for the password, you will see something like this:

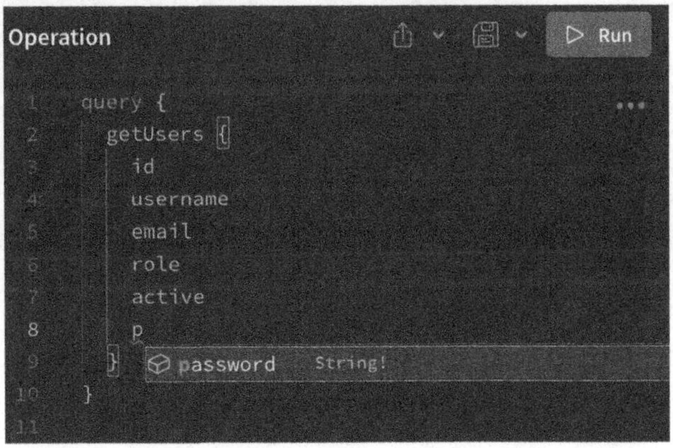

Figure 13.16: Autocomplete

Now, we are ready to try and log in!

Performing a login

I want to congratulate you for getting to this point in this book: I know we have covered a lot, but we are almost there! Now, we are going to try and log in with GraphQL (how crazy is that?).

First, we need to write our login mutation:

```
mutation($input: LoginInput) {
  login(input: $input) {
    token
  }
}
```

Then, we need to log our user in by using "fake@email.com" as our email and "123456" as our password. These do not exist in our database:

Figure 13.17: Invalid login after using non-existent login details

Because the email does not exist in our database, an `Invalid Login` error message will be returned. Now, let's add the correct email but use a fake password:

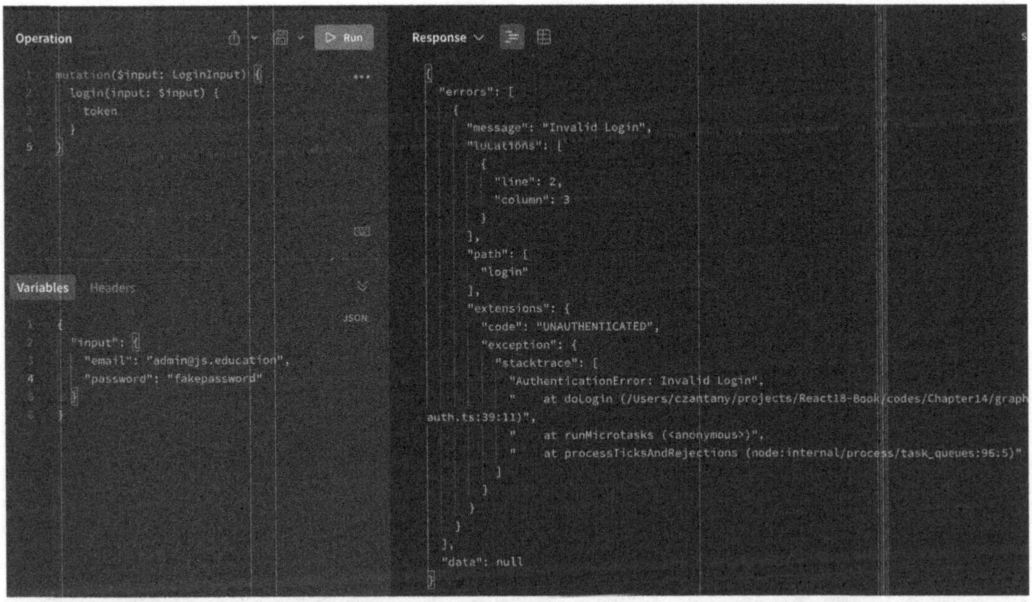

Figure 13.18: Invalid login after inputting the correct email but a fake password

As you can see, we receive the exact same error (`Invalid Login`). This is because we don't want to provide too much information about what's wrong with the login, as someone may be trying to hack into your system. If we say something such as `Invalid password` or `Your email does not exist in our system`, we give the attackers extra information that they may find useful.

Now, let's try to connect with the correct user and password (admin@js.education and 123456) and see what happens:

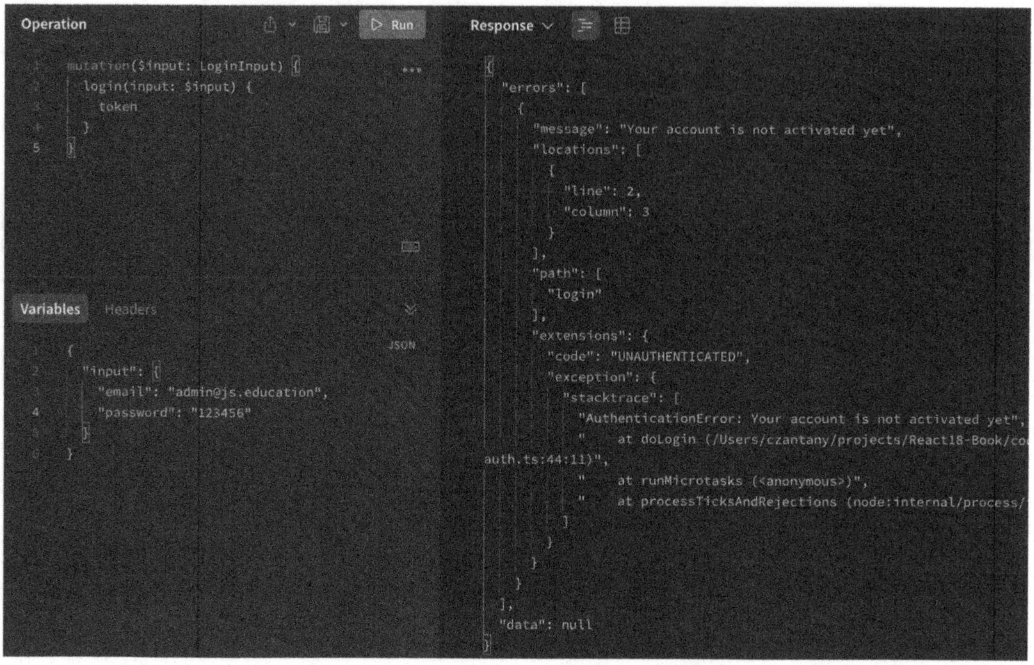

Figure 13.19: Your account is not activated yet

Now, we receive an error stating Your account is not activated yet. This is OK because our user has not been activated yet. Normally, when a user is registered in a system, you need to send a link to their email so that they can activate their account. We don't have this feature at the moment, but let's suppose we sent that email, and the user has already activated their account. We can simulate this by manually changing the value in our database using OnmiDB or PgAdmin4.

We can do this by performing an UPDATE SQL query:

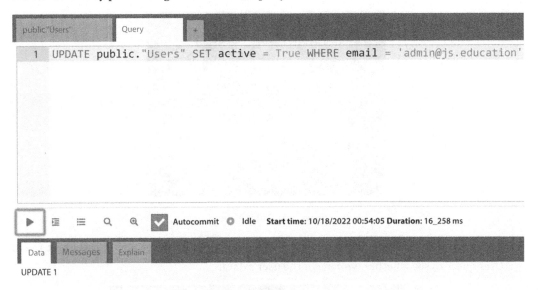

Figure 13.20: UPDATE SQL query

Now, let's try to log in again!

Figure 13.21: Login token

Nice: we are in, baby! This is you at this point:

Figure 13.22: Anonymous

Now that we've logged in and retrieved our JWT, let's copy that huge string and use it in our **getUser** query to see whether we can get the user's data:

Figure 13.23: Access token

If everything went well, then you should get the user's data:

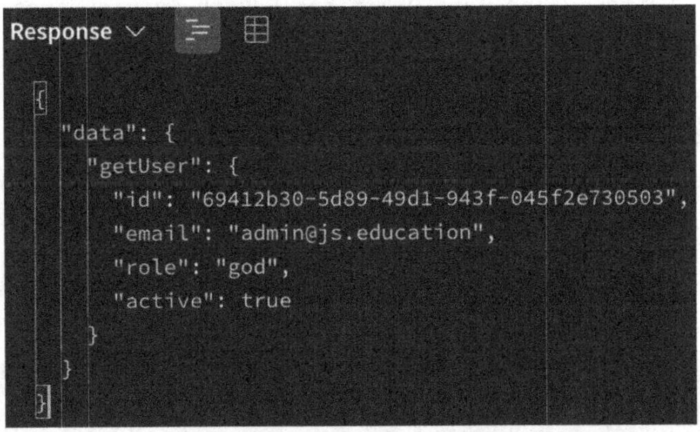

```
{
  "data": {
    "getUser": {
      "id": "69412b30-5d89-49d1-943f-045f2e730503",
      "email": "admin@js.education",
      "role": "god",
      "active": true
    }
  }
}
```

Figure 13.24: getUser data

If you change or remove any letter from the string (meaning the token is invalid), then you should get empty user data:

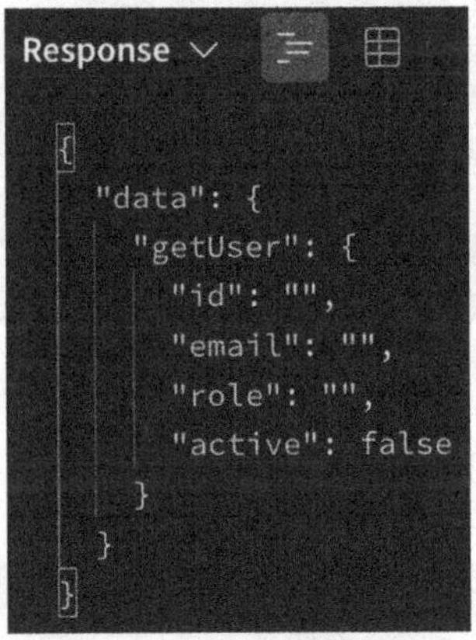

```
{
  "data": {
    "getUser": {
      "id": "",
      "email": "",
      "role": "",
      "active": false
    }
  }
}
```

Figure 13.25: Empty getUser data

Now that our login system works perfectly in the backend, it is time to implement this in the frontend application. We'll do this in the next section.

Building a frontend login system with Apollo Client

In the previous section, we learned how to build the backend for a login system using Apollo Server to create our GraphQL queries and mutations. You are probably thinking, *Great, I have the backend working, but how can I use this on the frontend?* And you're right: I always like to explain things with full examples and not just show basic things, even if this will take longer to do. So let's get started!

You can find the code for the example in this section at https://github.com/PacktPublishing/
React-18-Design-Patterns-and-Best-Practices-Fourth-Edition/tree/main/Chapter13/
graphql/frontend.

Configuring Webpack 5

Instead of using a **vite** project, we will configure a React project from scratch using Webpack 5
and Node.js.

The first thing we need to do is create the frontend directory and install all the packages inside.
To do this, we will execute the following commands:

```
npm init --yes
npm install @apollo/client@3.7.0 @contentpi/lib@1.0.10 cookie-parser@1.4.6
cors@2.8.5 dotenv-webpack@8.0.1 express@4.18.2 jsonwebtoken@8.5.1
pm2@5.2.2 react@18.2.0 react-dom@18.2.0 react-cookie@4.1.1 react-router-
dom@6.4.2 run-script-webpack-plugin@0.1.1 styled-components@5.3.6
typescript-plugin-styled-components@2.0.0 webpack-node-externals@3.0.0
npm install --save-dev @babel/core@7.19.3 @babel/preset-env@7.19.4 @babel/
preset-react@7.18.6 @types/node@18.11.3 buffer@6.0.3 cross-env@7.0.3
crypto-browserify@3.12.0 dotenv@16.0.3 html-webpack-plugin@5.5.0 npm-
run-all@4.1.5 prettier@2.7.1 stream-browserify@3.0.0 ts-loader@9.4.1
ts-node@10.9.1 ts-node-dev@2.0.0 typescript@4.8.4 webpack@5.74.0 webpack-
cli@4.10.0 webpack-dev-server@4.11.1 webpackbar@5.0.2
```

The buffer, crypto-browserify, and stream-browserify are polyfills that were included by
default in Webpack up to and including version 4. However, in the latest version (Webpack 5),
these are not included anymore, so you will get the following error:

```
ERROR in ./node_modules/@contentpi/lib/dist/security/index.js 8:33-50
Module not found: Error: Can't resolve 'crypto' in '/Users/czantany/projects/React-Design-Patterns-and-Best-Practices-Third-Edition/Chapter05/graph
ql/frontend/node_modules/@contentpi/lib/dist/security'

BREAKING CHANGE: webpack < 5 used to include polyfills for node.js core modules by default.
This is no longer the case. Verify if you need this module and configure a polyfill for it.

If you want to include a polyfill, you need to:
        - add a fallback 'resolve.fallback: { "crypto": require.resolve("crypto-browserify") }'
        - install 'crypto-browserify'
If you don't want to include a polyfill, you can use an empty module like this:
        resolve.fallback: { "crypto": false }
```

Figure 13.26: Webpack < 5 used to include polyfills for Node.js core modules by default

You need to have those scripts in your package.json:

```
"scripts": {
  "build": "npm-run-all clean build:production:*",
```

```
    "build:production:client": "webpack --env mode=production --env
presets=client",
    "build:production:server": "webpack --env mode=production --env
presets=server",
    "clean": "rm -rf dist",
    "dev": "cross-env DEBUG=server:* npm-run-all clean serve:dev",
    "analyze": "cross-env ANALYZE=true cross-env DEBUG=server:* npm-run-all
clean serve:*",
    "start": "pm2 start apps.json",
    "stop": "pm2 stop apps.json",
    "restart": "pm2 restart apps.json",
    "serve:dev": "cross-env NODE_ENV=development ts-node ./src/server/
devServer.ts",
    "webpack": "cross-env NODE_ENV=production webpack",
    "lint": "eslint . --ext .js,.tsx,.ts",
    "lint:fix": "eslint . --fix --ext .js,.tsx,.ts",
    "test": "jest src",
    "test:coverage": "jest src --coverage"
}
```

I like to split my Webpack configuration into separate files to identify more easily what is for the client, for the server, for development, and for production. First let's create our presets directory under /frontend/webpack/presets, and then create our webpack.client.ts to specify our client configuration:

```
import HtmlWebpackPlugin from 'html-webpack-plugin'
import { Configuration } from 'webpack'
import { BundleAnalyzerPlugin } from 'webpack-bundle-analyzer'
import WebpackBar from 'webpackbar'
const isAnalyze = Boolean(process.env.ANALYZE) // This is to analyze the
bundles sizes
const webpackClientConfig: (args: { mode: string }) => Configuration = ({
mode }) => {
  const isProductionMode = mode === 'production'
  const title = 'My Website Title'
  const webpackConfig: Configuration = {
    entry: {
      main: './src/client/index.tsx' // Entry for the client app
    },
```

```
      output: {
        publicPath: 'http://localhost:3001/' // This is for webpack-dev-server
      },
      plugins: [
        new HtmlWebpackPlugin({
          title,
          template: './src/client/index.html',
          filename: './index.html'
        }),
        new WebpackBar({
          name: 'client',
          color: '#2EA1F8'
        })
      ]
    }
    if (isProductionMode) {
      webpackConfig.output = {
        filename: '[name].js',
        chunkFilename: '[name].js',
        publicPath: '/'
      }
    }
    if (isAnalyze) {
        webpackConfig.plugins = [
          ...(webpackConfig.plugins || []),
          new BundleAnalyzerPlugin({
            analyzerPort: 9001
          })
        ]
    }
    return webpackConfig
}
export default webpackClientConfig
```

That is our client preset; now let's create the server preset under /frontend/webpack/presets/
webpack.server.ts:

```
import { resolve } from 'path'
```

```
import { RunScriptWebpackPlugin } from 'run-script-webpack-plugin'
import { Configuration, IgnorePlugin, optimize } from 'webpack'
import { BundleAnalyzerPlugin } from 'webpack-bundle-analyzer'
import nodeExternals from 'webpack-node-externals'
import WebpackBar from 'webpackbar'
const isAnalyze = Boolean(process.env.ANALYZE)
const webpackServerConfig: (args: { mode: string }) => Configuration = ({
mode }) => {
  const isDevelopment = mode === 'development'
  const webpackConfig: Configuration = {
    target: 'node', // Target node is only for server
    entry: './src/server/index.ts', // Entry for the server app
    output: {
      libraryTarget: 'commonjs2',
      filename: 'server.js',
      path: resolve('dist')
    },
    externals: [nodeExternals()], // Ignoring all node_modules
    plugins: [
      new optimize.LimitChunkCountPlugin({
        maxChunks: 1
      }),
      new IgnorePlugin({
        resourceRegExp: /\.((sc|c)ss|jpe?g|png|gif|svg)$/i
      }),
      new WebpackBar({
        name: 'server',
        color: '#2EA1F8',
        profile: true,
        basic: false
      })
    ]
  }
  if (isDevelopment) {
    webpackConfig.watch = true
    if (webpackConfig.entry instanceof Array) {
      webpackConfig.entry.unshift('webpack/hot/poll?300') // This is for HMR
```

```
    }
    if (webpackConfig.plugins instanceof Array) {
      webpackConfig.plugins.push(
        new RunScriptWebpackPlugin({
          name: 'server.js',
          nodeArgs: ['--inspect']
        })
      )
    }
    webpackConfig.externals = [
      nodeExternals({
        allowlist: ['webpack/hot/poll?300']
      })
    ]
  }
  if (isAnalyze) {
    webpackConfig.plugins = [
      ...(webpackConfig.plugins || []),
      new BundleAnalyzerPlugin({
        analyzerPort: 9002
      })
    ]
  }
  return webpackConfig
}
export default webpackServerConfig
```

After you've created the presets, you need to create the loadPresets.ts file that will handle those presets. This file must exist under /frontend/webpack/loadPresets.ts:

```
import { Configuration } from 'webpack'
import { merge } from 'webpack-merge'
import { ConfigArgs } from './webpack.types'
const loadPresets: (mode: ConfigArgs) => Promise<Configuration> = async
(env) => {
  const presets: string[] = ([] as string[]).concat(...[env.presets])
  const webpackConfigs = await Promise.all(
    presets.map(async (presetName: string) => {
```

```
    try {
      // Dynamically loading the presets
      const {default: webpackConfig} = await import(`./presets/
webpack.${presetName}`)
      return Promise.resolve(webpackConfig(env))
    } catch (err) {
      return Promise.resolve({})
    }
  })
)
return merge({}, ...webpackConfigs)
}
export default loadPresets
```

Besides the client and server presets, we need to create some other configuration files: one for development, another for production, and a file that will contain a common configuration between both. First let's create the common configuration at /frontend/webpack/webpack.common.ts:

```
import Dotenv from 'dotenv-webpack'
import { resolve } from 'path'
import createStyledComponentsTransformer from 'typescript-plugin-styled-
components'
import { Configuration } from 'webpack'
const styledComponentsTransformer = createStyledComponentsTransformer()
const webpackCommonConfig: () => Configuration = () => {
  const webpackConfig: Configuration = {
    output: {
      path: resolve('dist') // Output by default will be dist directory
    },
    resolve: {
      extensions: ['.ts', '.tsx', '.js', '.jsx', '.json'],
      alias: {
        '~': resolve(__dirname, '../src') // Alias for src
      },
    },
    fallback: {
      crypto: require.resolve('crypto-browserify'),
      buffer: require.resolve('buffer/'),
      stream: require.resolve('stream-browserify')
```

```
    }
  },
  optimization: { // This is to split the bundle in main.js (app) and
vendor.js (node_modules)
    splitChunks: {
      cacheGroups: {
        default: false,
        commons: {
          test: /node_modules/,
          name: 'vendor',
          chunks: 'all'
        }
      }
    }
  },
  module: {
    rules: [
      {
        test: /\.(woff|woff2)$/, // For loading fonts
        use: {
          loader: 'url-loader'
        }
      },
      {
        test: /\.(ts|tsx)$/, // For loading TypeScript files
        exclude: /node_modules/,
        use: [
          {
            loader: 'ts-loader',
            options: {
              transpileOnly: true,
              getCustomTransformers: () => ({
                before: [styledComponentsTransformer]
              })
            }
          }
        ]
```

```
      }
    ]
  },
  plugins: [new Dotenv()] // This will load our .env variables into
Webpack
  }
  return webpackConfig
}
export default webpackCommonConfig
```

Then we need to create the development configuration at /frontend/webpack/webpack.development.ts:

```
import { Configuration, HotModuleReplacementPlugin, NoEmitOnErrorsPlugin }
from 'webpack'
const webpackDevConfig: () => Configuration = () => {
  const webpackConfig: Configuration = {
    mode: 'development',
    devtool: 'source-map',
    output: {
      filename: '[name].js'
    },
    plugins: [new HotModuleReplacementPlugin(), new NoEmitOnErrorsPlugin()]
  }
  return webpackConfig
}
export default webpackDevConfig
```

As you can see in development, we include the HotModuleReplacementPlugin for the **HMR** to reload the site every time we make a change. After this, you need to create the production configuration file at /frontend/webpack/webpack.production.ts:

```
import { Configuration } from 'webpack'
const webpackProdConfig: (args: { presets: string[] }) => Configuration =
() => {
  const webpackConfig: Configuration = {
    mode: 'production' // By default this mode minifies all code
  }
```

```
    return webpackConfig
  }
export default webpackProdConfig
```

Finally, we have to create our Webpack types file at /frontend/webpack/webpack.types.ts. These are the TypeScript types we will use for Webpack:

```
export type WebpackMode = 'production' | 'development'
export type ConfigArgs = {
  mode: WebpackMode
  presets: string[]
}
```

At this point, you need to create the index.html file, which should be at /frontend/src/client/index.html. This will be our initial HTML file handled by HtmlWebpackPlugin:

```
<!DOCTYPE html>
<html>
<head>
<meta charset="UTF-8" />
  <title><%= htmlWebpackPlugin.options.title %></title>
</head>
<body>
  <div id="root"></div>
</body>
</html>
```

In the next section, we will configure our TypeScript.

Configuring our TypeScript

TypeScript is a special version of JavaScript, the language typically used to write web apps. What makes TypeScript interesting is its ability to identify mistakes in our code earlier, potentially saving us significant time. This feature becomes particularly valuable when working on large-scale projects. Therefore, we will utilize TypeScript for our project. Let's now delve into the process of setting it up.

Our tsconfig.json file should look like this:

```
{
  "compilerOptions": {
```

```
      "sourceMap": true,
      "target": "ESNext",
      "lib": ["dom", "dom.iterable", "esnext"],
      "allowJs": true,
      "skipLibCheck": true,
      "esModuleInterop": true,
      "allowSyntheticDefaultImports": true,
      "strict": true,
      "forceConsistentCasingInFileNames": true,
      "noFallthroughCasesInSwitch": true,
      "module": "commonjs",
      "moduleResolution": "node",
      "resolveJsonModule": true,
      "isolatedModules": true,
      "noEmit": true,
      "jsx": "react-jsx",
      "noImplicitAny": false,
      "paths": {
        "~/*": ["./src/*"]
      }
    },
  "include": ["src"],
  "exclude": ["node_modules", "**/*.test.tsx"]
}
```

Now, let's learn how to configure the Express server.

Configuring the Express server

Our application requires a Express server so that we can perform validations. These will help us find out whether the user is connected (using a custom middleware, which I'll explain later) and can also configure our Express sessions. We have four main routes on our site:

- /: Our home page (handled by React).
- /dashboard: Our dashboard, which is protected. Only connected users with god or admin permissions are allowed (handled by Express first then by React).
- /login: Our login page (handled by React).

- /logout: This will delete our existing session (handled by Express).

Let's look at our server code. The following file should exist at /frontend/src/server.ts. This is in order to create our Express app and run our React app:

```ts
import cookieParser from 'cookie-parser'
import cors from 'cors'
import express, { Application, Request, Response } from 'express'
import { resolve } from 'path'
import * as config from '../config'
import html from './html'
import { isConnected } from './lib/middlewares/user'
// Express application
const app: Application = express()
const distDir = resolve('dist')
const staticDir = resolve('src', 'static')
// Middlewares
app.use(express.json())
app.use(express.urlencoded({ extended: true }))
app.use(cookieParser(config.security.secretKey))
app.use(cors({ credentials: true, origin: true }))
// Static directories
app.use(express.static(distDir))
app.use(express.static(staticDir))
// Routes
app.get('/login', isConnected(false), (req: Request, res: Response) => {
  res.send(html({ title: 'My Website' }))
})
app.get(`/logout`, (req: Request, res: Response) => {
  const redirect: any = req.query.redirectTo || '/'
  res.clearCookie('at')
  res.redirect(redirect)
})
app.get('*', (req: Request, res: Response) => {
  res.send(html({ title: 'My Website' }))
})
export default app
```

As you can see, we protect our dashboard route with the `isConnected` middleware. Here, we validate that we only accept users that are not connected in the login route.

Creating our frontend configuration

Now, we need to create our frontend configuration. So, let's create the configuration at `/frontend/src/config.ts`. This file will assist us to manage our GraphQL port and server, as well as incorporate security configurations such as our secret key and the expiration options:

```typescript
// Types
type API = {
  uri: string
}
type Security = {
  secretKey: string
  expiresIn: string
}
// Environment Configuration
export const isProduction: boolean = process.env.NODE_ENV === 'production'
export const isDevelopment: boolean = process.env.NODE_ENV !==
'production'
// Server Configuration
const devUrl = 'localhost'
const prodUrl = 'localhost' // change this to your production url
export const PORT: number = Number(process.env.PORT) || 3000
export const DEV_SERVER_PORT = 3001
export const GRAPHQL_PORT = 4000
export const GRAPHQL_SERVER = isDevelopment ? devUrl : prodUrl
// Paths Configuration
export const domain: string = devUrl
export const baseUrl: string = isProduction
  ? `https://${domain}:${PORT}`
  : `http://${domain}:${PORT}` // Remove port in actual production
export const publicPath: string = isProduction
  ? ''
  : `http://${domain}:${DEV_SERVER_PORT}/`
// API Configuration
export const api: API = {
```

```
    uri: `http://${GRAPHQL_SERVER}:${GRAPHQL_PORT}/graphql`
 }
 // Security Configuration
 export const security: Security = {
   secretKey: process.env.SECURITY_SECRET_KEY || '',
   expiresIn: '7d'
 }
```

Next, we need to create a user-called middleware and the **jwt** functions to validate whether the user is connected and has the correct privileges.

Creating the user middleware

In web development, a middleware is a function that has access to the request object (**req**), the response object (**res**), and the next function in the application's request-response cycle. The next function is a function in the Express router that, when invoked, executes the middleware succeeding the current middleware. This creates a chain of functions, each of which can perform a specific task or modify the request and response objects as needed. By utilizing middleware, you can streamline your code and simplify complex processes.

The following diagram provides a visual representation of the middleware flow:

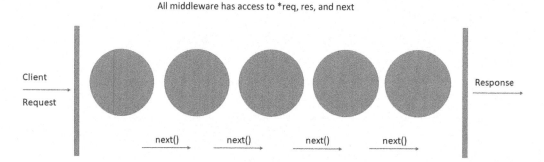

Figure 13.27: Visual representation of the middleware flow

In our case, we will create the **isConnected** middleware to validate if a user is connected and has the correct privileges. If not, we will break the flow and redirect them to the login page. If the user is valid, we will execute the next piece of middleware, which will render our React application. The following diagram describes this process:

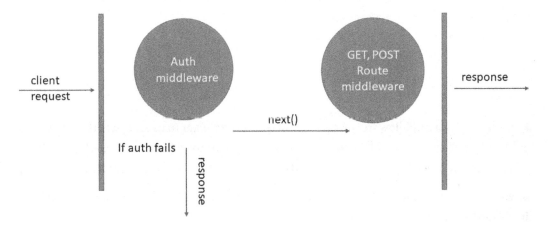

Figure 13.28: Auth middleware

Let's apply the theoretical part to our code. The required file should exist at /frontend/src/server/lib/middlewares/user.ts:

```
import { NextFunction, Request, Response } from 'express'
import { getUserData } from '../jwt'
export const isConnected = (isLogged = true, roles = ['user'], redirectTo
= '/') =>
  async (req: Request, res: Response, next: NextFunction): Promise<void>
=> {
    const user = await getUserData(req.cookies.at)
    if (!user && !isLogged) {
      return next()
    }
    if (user && isLogged) {
      if (roles.includes('god') && roles.role === 'god') {
        return next()
      }
      if (roles.includes('admin') && user.role === 'admin') {
        return next()
      }
      if (roles.includes('user') && user.role === 'user') {
        return next()
      }
    }
```

```
      res.redirect(redirectTo)
    } else {
      res.redirect(redirectTo)
    }
  }
```

Basically, with this middleware, we can control whether we want to validate whether the user is connected (`isLogged = true`). Then, we can validate specific roles (`roles = ['god', 'admin']`) and redirect the user if they are not connected or do not have the correct roles (`redirectTo = '/'`).

As you can see, we are using the `getUserData` function from `jwt`. We'll create our `jwt` functions in the next section.

Creating JWT functions

Earlier, when I explained the backend code, I talked about JWTs. In the frontend, we need those functions to validate our token and get the user's data. Let's create a file containing the following code at `/frontend/src/server/lib/jwt.ts`:

```
import { getBase64 } from '@contentpi/lib'
import jwt from 'jsonwebtoken'
import * as config from '~/config'
const { security: { secretKey } } = config
export function jwtVerify(accessToken: string, cb: any) {
  jwt.verify(accessToken, secretKey, (error: any, accessTokenData: any =
{}) => {
    const { data: user } = accessTokenData
    if (error || !user) {
      return cb(null)
    }
    const userData = getBase64(user)
    return cb(userData)
  })
}
export async function getUserData(accessToken: string): Promise<any> {
  const UserPromise = new Promise(
    (resolve) => jwtVerify(accessToken, (user: any) => resolve(user))
  )
```

```
    const user = await UserPromise
    return user
}
```

As you can see, our getUserData function will retrieve the user data using accessToken, which we grabbed from the cookies.

A JWT must be valid for security reasons and to ensure that the user's identity is verified. The server verifies this token whenever a user makes a request. If the token is invalid, the server will not fulfill the user's request. Additionally, the token helps protect user information, as it cannot be altered without the server's knowledge. Moreover, these tokens have an expiration time, requiring users to log in again. This prevents unauthorized individuals from using a stolen token to impersonate the user. Hence, ensuring the validity of a JWT is of utmost importance.

Creating our GraphQL queries and mutations

We've already created the required queries and mutations in our backend project. At this point, however, we need to create some files that will execute them in our frontend project. For now, we just need to define our getUserData query and our login mutation to perform the login in the frontend.

Let's create our getUser query at /frontend/src/client/graphql/user/getUser.query.ts:

```
import { gql } from '@apollo/client'
  export default gql`
  query getUser($at: String!) {
   getUser(at: $at) {
    id
    email
    username
    role
    active
   }
  }
```

Our login mutation should be at /frontend/src/graphql/user/login.mutation.ts:

```
import { gql } from '@apollo/client'
export default gql`
```

```
mutation login($email: String!, $password: String!) {
  login(input: { email: $email, password: $password }) {
   token
  }
 }
```

Now that we have defined our query and mutation, let's create the user context so that we can use them.

Creating user context to handle login and connected user

In our user context, we will have a login method that will execute our mutation and validate whether the email and password are correct. We will also export the user data.

Let's create this context at /frontend/src/client/contexts/user.tsx:

```
import { useMutation, useQuery } from '@apollo/client'
import { getGraphQlError, redirectTo } from '@contentpi/lib'
import { createContext, FC, ReactElement, useEffect, useState } from 'react'
import { useCookies } from 'react-cookie'
import GET_USER_QUERY from '../graphql/user/getUser.query'
import LOGIN_MUTATION from '../graphql/user/login.mutation'
// Interfaces
interface IUserContext {
  login(input: any): any
  connectedUser: any
}
interface IProps {
  page?: string
  children: ReactElement
}
// Creating context
export const UserContext = createContext<IUserContext>({
  login: () => null,
  connectedUser: null
})
const UserProvider: FC<IProps> = ({ page = '', children }) => {
  const [cookies, setCookie] = useCookies()
  const [connectedUser, setConnectedUser] = useState(null)
```

```
// Mutations
const [loginMutation] = useMutation(LOGIN_MUTATION)
// Queries
const { data: dataUser } = useQuery(GET_USER_QUERY, {
  variables: {
    at: cookies.at || ''
  }
})
// Effects
useEffect(() => {
  if (dataUser) {
    if (!dataUser.getUser.id && page !== 'login') {
      // If the user session is invalid and is on a different page
      // than login
      // we redirect them to login
      redirectTo('/login?redirectTo=/dashboard')
    } else {
      // If we have the user data available we save it in our
      // connectedUser state
      setConnectedUser(dataUser.getUser)
    }
  }
}, [dataUser, page])
async function login(input: { email: string; password: string }):
Promise<any> {
  try {
    // Executing our loginMutation passing the email and password
    const { data: dataLogin } = await loginMutation({
      variables: {
      email: input.email,
      password: input.password
    }
  })
    if (dataLogin) {
      // If the login was success, we save the token in our "at" cookie
      setCookie('at', dataLogin.login.token, { path: '/' })
      return dataLogin.login.token
    }
```

```
    } catch (err) {
      // If there is an error we return it
      return getGraphQlError(err)
    }
  }
  // Exporting our context
  const context = {
    login,
    connectedUser
  }
  return <UserContext.Provider value={context}>{children}</UserContext.
Provider>
}
export default UserProvider
```

As you can see, we handle the login and have the `connectedUser` data in our context. Here, we execute `GET_USER_QUERY` all the time to verify whether the user is connected (validating against the database and not just with the cookies).

Configuring Apollo Client

So far, we have created a lot of code, but none of it is going to work if we don't configure Apollo Client. To configure Apollo Client, we need to add it to our index file at `/frontend/src/client/index.tsx`:

```
import { ApolloClient, ApolloProvider, InMemoryCache } from '@apollo/
client'
import { render } from 'react-dom'
import * as config from '../config'
import AppRoutes from './AppRoutes'
const client = new ApolloClient({
  uri: config.api.uri,
  cache: new InMemoryCache()
})
render(
  <ApolloProvider client={client}>
  <AppRoutes />
  </ApolloProvider>,
```

```
    document.querySelector('#root')
  )
```

Basically, we pass `config.api.uri`, which is where GraphQL Playground is running (`http://localhost:4000/graphql`), and then wrap our `AppRoutes` component with the `ApolloProvider` component.

Creating our app routes

We will use `react-router-dom` to create our application routes. Let's create the required code at `/frontend/src/client/AppRoutes.tsx`:

```
import { BrowserRouter as Router, Route, Routes } from 'react-router-dom'
import DashboardPage from './pages/dashboard'
import Error404 from './pages/error404'
import HomePage from './pages/home'
import LoginPage from './pages/login'
const AppRoutes = () => (
  <>
    <Router>
      <Routes>
        <Route path="/" element={<HomePage />} />
        <Route path="/dashboard" element={<DashboardPage />} />
        <Route path="/login" element={<LoginPage />} />
        <Route element={<Error404 />} />
      </Routes>
    </Router>
  </>
)
export default AppRoutes
```

As you can see, we are adding some pages to our routes, such as `HomePage`, `DashboardPage` (protected), and `LoginPage`. If the user tries to access a different URL, then we will display an `Error404` component. We'll create these pages in the next section.

Creating our pages

The `Home` page should be at `/frontend/src/client/pages/home.tsx`:

```
const Page = () => (
  <div className="home">
```

```
    <h1>Home</h1>
    <ul>
      <li><a href="/dashboard">Go to Dashboard</a></li>
    </ul>
  </div>
)
export default Page
```

The Dashboard page should be at /frontend/src/client/pages/dashboard.tsx:

```
import DashboardLayout from '../components/dashboard/DashboardLayout'
import UserProvider from '../contexts/user'
const Page = () => (
  <UserProvider>
    <DashboardLayout />
  </UserProvider>
)
export default Page
```

The Login page should be at /frontend/src/client/pages/login.tsx:

```
import { isBrowser } from '@contentpi/lib'
import { FC, ReactElement } from 'react'
import LoginLayout from '../components/users/LoginLayout'
import UserProvider from '../contexts/user'
interface IProps {
  currentUrl?: string
}
const Page: FC<IProps> = ({
  currentUrl = isBrowser() ? window.location.search.
replace('?redirectTo=', '') : ''
}) => (
  <UserProvider page="login">
    <LoginLayout currentUrl={currentUrl} />
  </UserProvider>
)
export default Page
```

Finally, we need to create our Error404 page (`/frontend/src/client/pages/error404.tsx`):

```
const Page = () => (
  <div className="error404">
    <h1>Error404</h1>
  </div>
)
export default Page
```

We are almost done. The last piece of this puzzle is to create the Login and Dashboard components. We'll do that in the next section.

Creating our login components

I created some basic components for our login and our dashboard. Of course, their styles can be improved, but let's see how they work and how our login system is going to look.

The first file you need to create is called `LoginLayout.tsx` at `/frontend/src/client/components/users/LoginLayout.tsx`:

```
import { FC, useContext } from 'react'
import { UserContext } from '../../contexts/user'
import Login from './Login'
// Interfaces
interface IProps {
  currentUrl: string
}
const Layout: FC<IProps> = ({ currentUrl }) => {
  const { login } = useContext(UserContext)
  return <Login login={login} currentUrl={currentUrl} />
}
export default Layout
```

The layout file is useful when we want to add a specific layout to our components. It is also useful to consume data from a context and pass the data or functions as props.

Our Login component should look like this (`/frontend/src/client/components/users/Login.tsx`):

```
import { redirectTo } from '@contentpi/lib'
import { ChangeEvent, FC, useState } from 'react'
```

```typescript
import { IUser } from '../../types'
import { StyledLogin } from './Login.styled'
interface IProps {
  login(input: any): any
  currentUrl: string
}
const Login: FC<IProps> = ({ login, currentUrl }) => {
  const [values, setValues] = useState({
    email: '',
    password: ''
  })
  const [errorMessage, setErrorMessage] = useState('')
  const [invalidLogin, setInvalidLogin] = useState(false)
  const onChange = (e: ChangeEvent<HTMLInputElement>): void => {
    const { target: { name, value } } = e
    if (name) {
      setValues((prevValues: any) => ({
        ...prevValues,
        [name]: value
      }))
    }
  }
  const handleSubmit = async (user: IUser): Promise<void> => {
    // Here we execute the Login mutation
    const response = await login(user)
    if (response.error) {
      setInvalidLogin(true)
      setErrorMessage(response.message)
    } else {
      redirectTo(currentUrl || '/')
    }
  }
  return (
    <>
      <StyledLogin>
        <div className="wrapper">
```

```
            {invalidLogin && <div className="alert">{errorMessage}</div>}
            <div className="form">
              <p>
                <input
                  autoComplete="off"
                  type-"email"
                  className="email"
                  name="email"
                  placeholder="Email"
                  onChange={onChange}
                  value={values.email}
                />
              </p>
              <p>
                <input
                  autoComplete="off"
                  type="password"
                  className="password"
                  name="password"
                  placeholder="Password"
                  onChange={onChange}
                  value={values.password}
                />
              </p>
              <div className="actions">
                <button name="login" onClick={() => handleSubmit(values)}>
                  Login
                </button>
              </div>
            </div>
          </div>
        </StyledLogin>
      </>
    )
  }
}
export default Login
```

We'll create the dashboard components next.

Creating our dashboard components

When creating our dashboard components, the first one should be the `DashboardLayout.tsx` file at `/frontend/src/client/components/dashboard/DashboardLayout.tsx`:

```tsx
import { FC, useContext } from 'react'
import { UserContext } from '../../contexts/user'
import Dashboard from './Dashboard'
const Layout: FC = () => {
  const { connectedUser } = useContext(UserContext)
  // We only render the Dashboard if the user is connected
  if (connectedUser) {
    return <Dashboard connectedUser={connectedUser} />
  }
  return <div />
}
export default Layout
```

This is how we protect our dashboard page to allow only connected users. Now, let's create our dashboard component at `/frontend/src/components/dashboard/Dashboard.tsx`:

```tsx
interface IProps {
  connectedUser: any
}
const Dashboard = ({ connectedUser }) => (
  <div className="dashboard">
    <h1>Welcome, {connectedUser.username}!</h1>
    <ul>
      <li><a href="/logout">Logout</a></li>
    </ul>
  </div>
)
export default Dashboard
```

And with that, we're done! We'll test the login system in the next section.

Testing our login system

If you followed the previous sections correctly, then you should be able to run the login system successfully. To do this, we need to open three terminals:

- In the first one, you need to run your backend project (**npm run dev**).

- In the other, you need to run the Node.js server in the frontend project (**npm run dev**).

The third terminal is that when you open http://localhost:3000 for the first time, you should be able to see the Home page:

Home

- Go to Dashboard

Figure 13.29: Home page

Then, if you click on the **Go to Dashboard** (http://localhost:3000/dashboard) link, you will be redirected to http://localhost:3000/login?redirectTo=/dashboard, as shown in the following screenshot:

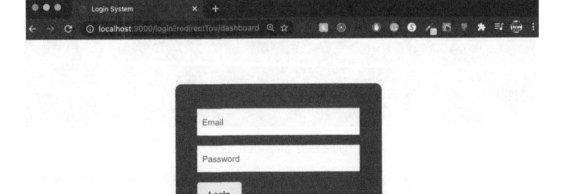

Figure 13.30: Login page

This is our login form. If you try to log in with fake credentials, you should get an error:

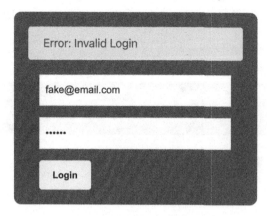

Figure 13.31: Invalid login

If you want to see the GraphQL request, you can do so on the **Headers** tab:

Figure 13.32: GraphQL request

Here, you can see the query you execute and the variables you send (email and password). You can see the response on the **Preview** tab:

Figure 13.33: Invalid login

As you can see, we get an "Invalid Login" error message, and that's why we render it in our login component.

Now, let's try to connect with the correct account (**admin@js.education** and **123456**). If your login is correct, then you should be redirected to the dashboard, where you will see the following page:

Welcome, admin!

- Logout

Figure 13.34: Welcome, admin! page

Additionally, you can take a look at the query being executed to retrieve the user data (**getUser**):

```
▼ Request Payload          view source
 ▼{operationName: "getUserData", variables: {,…},…}
    operationName: "getUserData"
    query: "query getUserData($at: String!) {  getUserData(at: $at) {   id  email  username  privilege  active  __typename
  ▼ variables: {,…}
       at: "eyJhbGciOiJIUzI1NiIsInR5cCI6IkpXVCJ9.eyJkYXRhIjoiZXLKcFpD5TZJalEzTnpsaU16QTJMV1U0TW1NdE5HVmtNUzFoWldNM0xXSXdaVEl5TWpSaU5UUTNlU01lz5
```

Figure 13.35: getUser data

Here, you will see that the payload is returned:

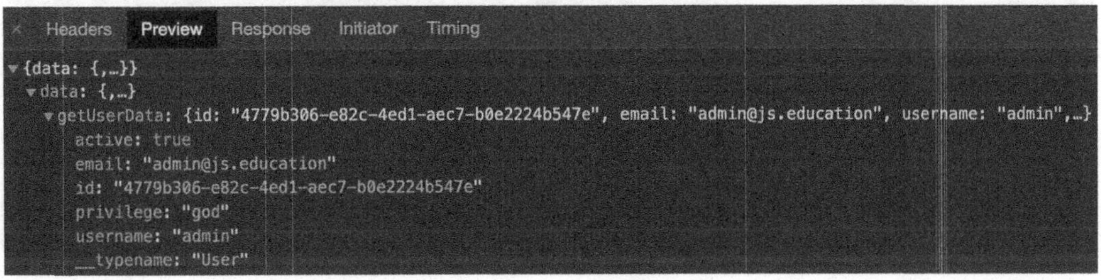

```
 ×  Headers   Preview   Response   Initiator   Timing
▼{data: {,…}}
  ▼data: {,…}
    ▼getUserData: {id: "4779b306-e82c-4ed1-aec7-b0e2224b547e", email: "admin@js.education", username: "admin",…}
        active: true
        email: "admin@js.education"
        id: "4779b306-e82c-4ed1-aec7-b0e2224b547e"
        privilege: "god"
        username: "admin"
        __typename: "User"
```

Figure 13.36: getUserData payload

We get the user information from the access token (**at**). If you refresh the page, you should remain connected to the page. This is because we saved a cookie containing our token:

Figure 13.37: Cookies

Now, let's try to modify the cookie by changing any letter of the token. For example, let's change the first two letters (**ey**) to **XX**:

Figure 13.38: Updating a cookie

Here, you will receive empty data for the user. This will invalidate the session and redirect you to the login page again:

Figure 13.39: Empty data

Now, you have learned how to implement GraphQL in a backend and how to consume queries and mutations in the frontend.

This login system is part of a course I'm doing on YouTube, where I'm teaching viewers how to develop a headless CMS from scratch, so if you're eager to learn more, you can check out the course at https://www.youtube.com/watch?v=4n1AfD6aV4M.

Summary

I hope you found this chapter on GraphQL, JWT creation, login functionality, and Sequelize model creation informative and engaging. It provided a wealth of valuable insights and practical tips that you can apply to your own projects, helping you to streamline your development process and achieve your goals more efficiently. By mastering these concepts, you'll be better equipped to build robust, scalable applications that meet the needs of your users and drive your success.

Thank you for reading, and I look forward to sharing more with you in the next chapter, where you will learn how to create a monorepository and a multi-site project.

14

MonoRepo Architecture

When we think about building apps, we usually talk about an app, a `git` repository, and a build output. However, this configuration of an application and a repository does not always reflect the real-world experience of developers. Often organizations will use a single repository with all the applications, components, and libraries that could be used in common development. These are called a monorepository or single repository, and they are starting to become very popular.

So, what makes a monorepository interesting for organizations? Why put all the code in one place? Why not have a single `git` repository where you have many small and separate repositories? If we keep all our code in one project.

By keeping all the code in one repository, you keep all dependencies up to date across the organization. This is probably the biggest benefit of a single repository. This way we will stop having to waste time updating all the dependencies of several different projects.

In this chapter, we'll be walking through how to create a monorepository with multiple packages using TypeScript, webpack, and NPM Workspaces.

We will look at the following topics:

- Advantages of a monorepository and the problems it solves
- How to create a monorepository
- Implementing TypeScript in the monorepository
- Creating a `devtools` package to compile other packages with Webpack
- Creating a `utils` package
- How to create a multi-site system

Technical requirements

To complete this chapter, you will need the following:

- Node.js 19+
- Visual Studio Code

You can find the code for this chapter in the book's GitHub repository: `https://github.com/PacktPublishing/React-18-Design-Patterns-and-Best-Practices-Fourth-Edition/tree/main/Chapter14`.

Advantages of a monorepository and the problems it solves

Some of the advantages of a **MonoRepo (monorepository)** are:

- **Sharing is made easy**: With all the code in one place, it becomes easier to utilize the same code or tools across multiple projects, saving valuable time and effort.

- **No mix-ups**: In a MonoRepo, every project utilizes the same version of shared components, eliminating concerns about compatibility issues between different versions.

- **Change everything at once**: In a MonoRepo, making changes across all projects simultaneously becomes a straightforward task, as opposed to the complexity of managing individual projects in separate repositories.

- **Grouped changes**: Modifying multiple projects simultaneously within a MonoRepo ensures that all related components stay synchronized, allowing for efficient and cohesive updates.

- **Everyone can see everything**: With all the code centralized in one repository, all developers have access to it, fostering a better understanding of the entire system and facilitating effective collaboration.

Now let's explore some of the real-life problems that a MonoRepo solves:

- **Faster updates**: With a MonoRepo, you can update all projects at once. Without it, you'd have to update each project separately, which can take a lot of time.

- **No more confusion**: Without a MonoRepo, different projects might use different versions of the same thing, which can cause problems. With a MonoRepo, everything uses the same version, so there's no confusion.

- **Better teamwork**: With all the code in one place, developers can easily see and understand what others have done. This can help them work together better.

- **Easier start for newbies**: For new team members, it's easier to get started when all the code is in one place. They can quickly understand the whole system, rather than having to search through different places.

It is important to remember that MonoRepos may not always be the optimal choice. They can introduce their own challenges, such as potential performance issues and increased complexity when they become excessively large. Whether adopting a MonoRepo is a suitable approach depends on the specific needs of the team and the scale of their projects.

In the following image you can see how the structure of a **MonoRepo** is different from that of a **Multi Repo**:

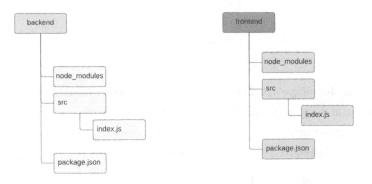

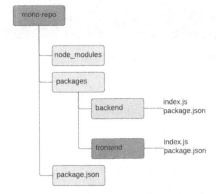

Figure 14.1: MultiRepo vs MonoRepo

Now that we've shed light on the concept of a monorepository and explored why it is becoming increasingly popular for organizations, we will delve into the practical implementation of a monorepository using NPM Workspaces.

Creating a MonoRepo with NPM Workspaces

NPM Workspaces was introduced in NPM 7 and is a generic term that refers to the set of features in the npm CLI that provides support for managing multiple packages from your local filesystem, from within a singular top-level root package.

The first thing you need to do in order to create a monorepository is to create a root package.json file, which should contain the following code:

```
{
  "name": "web-creator",
  "private": true,
  "workspaces": [
    "packages/*"
  ]
}
```

We will name our MonoRepo web-creator. We need to specify that web-creator will be private (only the root), and we need to specify the workspaces where our packages will live, which is on "packages/*"; the * means that we will include any directory that exists under the packages folder. After this, you need to create the packages directly.

Let's create two directories inside our new packages folder: "packages/api" and "packages/frontend". Now go to your api project and run npm init -y:

```
cd packages/api
npm init -y
```

Once you run that command it will create a package.json like this:

```
{
  "name": "api",
  "version": "1.0.0",
  "main": "index.js",
  "author": "",
  "license": "ISC"
}
```

As you can see, the name of that package by default will be `"api"`, but in order to connect that package to our main monorepository, we need to call it with a special format; in this case, you need to rename it `"@<name_of_root_package>/api"`, which in our example will be `"@web-creator/api"`. Your `package.json` should be like this:

```
{
    "name": "@web-creator/api",
    "version": "1.0.0",
    "main": "index.js",
    "author": "",
    "license": "ISC"
}
```

Now you need to create a file (`packages/api/index.js`) inside your api directory (later we will change this to TypeScript) with the following code:

```
module.exports = () => console.log("I'm the API package")
```

After this, you need to go to your `frontend` package (`packages/frontend`) and run the same npm `init -y` command:

```
cd packages/frontend
npm init -y
```

Also, you will need to rename that package `@web-creator/frontend`:

```
{
    "name": "@web-creator/frontend",
    "version": "1.0.0",
    "main": "index.js",
    "author": "Carlos Santana",
    "license": "ISC"
}
```

The monorepository now is ready to share packages. Let's suppose you now want to consume your api package in your `frontend` package. To do this, you need to specify the api package as a dependency and put the same version we have in that api package; in this case, the version will be 1.0.0. You need to be very careful and not change this version unless you really need to, and if you change it then you will need to update it on the `dependencies` node as well.

This will be your package.json from packages/frontend:

```
{
  "name": "@web-creator/frontend",
  "version": "1.0.0",
  "main": "index.js",
  "author": "Carlos Santana",
  "license": "ISC",
  "dependencies": {
    "@web-creator/api": "1.0.0" // this version needs to match with the
API package.json
  }
}
```

After you've specified the api package as a dependency, you need to run npm install inside the frontend project. One very interesting thing you will notice is that even if you run the npm install command inside the frontend package (packages/frontend), your node_modules folder will be created at the root level, and it will look like this:

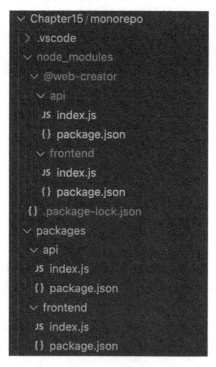

Figure 14.2: Monorepo structure

If everything worked as expected, you can consume your api package in your frontend package. For this, you need to create an index.js file inside packages/frontend/index.js with the following code:

```
const api = require('@web-creator/api')
api()
```

Now you can execute your index file with node and see the console message that comes from the api package:

```
→  frontend git:(main) ✗ node index.js
  I'm the API package
```

Figure 14.3: Running frontend

One of the biggest advantages of a monorepository is that if you update your API index.js, the change will be reflected right away without you having to compile anything or publish any package to the NPM registry. This is very helpful and saves a lot of time for developers when coding large projects. Let's change our message now to I'm the API package UPDATED in the packages/api/index.js and run the index.js again with node:

```
→  frontend git:(main) ✗ node index.js
  I'm the API package UPDATED
```

Figure 14.4: Updating the API

Congratulations, you have created your first MonoRepo successfully! In the next section, we will transform our MonoRepo to use TypeScript.

Implementing TypeScript in our MonoRepo

 In the following sections, I will outline the steps to create a multi-site project. Due to the substantial amount of code involved, I'm unable to include it all in this book. However, I invite you to review the complete code in the repository available at https://github.com/PacktPublishing/React-18-Design-Patterns-and-Best-Practices-Fourth-Edition/tree/main/Chapter14/web-creator.

The first thing you need to do in order to add TypeScript to your project is to install the typescript package at the root level:

```
npm install -D typescript
```

After this, you need to create the `tsconfig.json` file at the root level as well with the following code:

```
{
  "extends": "./tsconfig.common.json",
  "compilerOptions": {
    "baseUrl": "./packages",
    "paths": {
      "@web-creator/*": ["*/src"]
    }
  }
}
```

As you can see, we extend the `tsconfig.json` file to `tsconfig.common.json`, and this is because we don't want to to repeat each package that we want to transform to TypeScript. The only `compilerOptions` we want to specify is the `baseUrl` on our packages directory, and in the paths we will specify the name of our MonoRepo to be able to do imports in the code. This is the `tsconfig.common.json` file that you need to create:

```
{
  "compilerOptions": {
    "allowSyntheticDefaultImports": true,
    "alwaysStrict": true,
    "declaration": true,
    "declarationMap": true,
```

```
        "downlevelIteration": true,
        "esModuleInterop": true,
        "experimentalDecorators": true,
        "jsx": "react-jsx",
        "lib": ["DOM", "DOM.Iterable", "ESNext"],
        "module": "commonjs",
        "moduleResolution": "node",
        "noEmit": false,
        "noFallthroughCasesInSwitch": false,
        "noImplicitAny": true,
        "noImplicitReturns": true,
        "outDir": "dist",
        "resolveJsonModule": true,
        "skipLibCheck": true,
        "sourceMap": true,
        "strict": true,
        "strictFunctionTypes": true,
        "strictNullChecks": true,
        "suppressImplicitAnyIndexErrors": false,
        "target": "ESNext"
    },
    "exclude": ["node_modules", "dist", "coverage", ".vscode", "**/__
tests__/*"]
}
```

The architecture of our project will look like this:

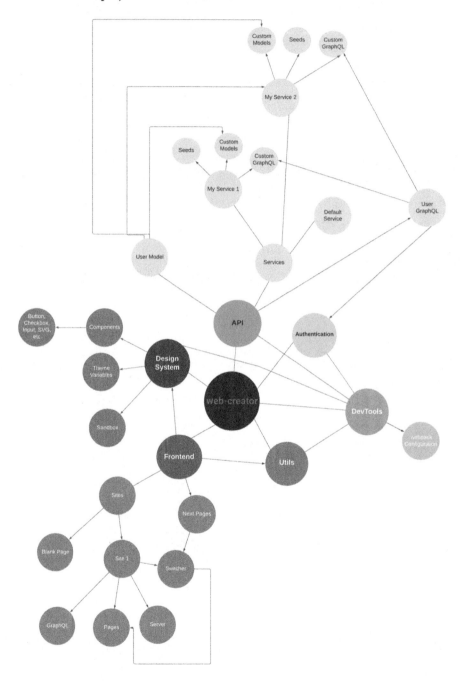

Figure 14.5: Web creator architecture

Now that we have explored the project's architecture, let's dive into the first package that will manage our Webpack configurations. This package will be referred to as devtools.

Creating a devtools package to compile packages with Webpack

The first package we need to create to be able to compile other packages is called devtools and should be created in packages/devtools. Let's see how it should look in its package.json file:

```json
{
  "name": "@web-creator/devtools",
  "version": "1.0.0",
  "main": "dist/index.js",
  "types": "dist/index.d.ts",
  "files": [
    "dist"
  ],
  "scripts": {
    "build": "npm-run-all clean compile",
    "clean": "rm -rf ./dist",
    "compile": "tsc",
    "lint": "npm run --prefix ../../ lint",
    "lint:fix": "npm run --prefix ../../ lint:fix"
  },
  "author": "Carlos Santana",
  "license": "MIT",
  "devDependencies": {
    "@types/cli-color": "^2.0.2",
    "@types/ip": "^1.1.0",
    "@types/webpack-bundle-analyzer": "^4.6.0",
    "@types/webpack-node-externals": "^2.5.3"
  },
  "dependencies": {
    "@svgr/webpack": "^6.5.1",
    "@types/file-loader": "^5.0.1",
    "cli-color": "^2.0.3",
    "css-loader": "^6.7.3",
    "dotenv": "^16.0.3",
```

```
    "file-loader": "^6.2.0",
    "html-webpack-plugin": "^5.5.0",
    "path-browserify": "^1.0.1",
    "run-script-webpack-plugin": "^0.1.1",
    "style-loader": "^3.3.1",
    "ts-loader": "^9.4.2",
    "typescript-plugin-styled-components": "^2.0.0",
    "webpack": "^5.75.0",
    "webpack-bundle-analyzer": "^4.7.0",
    "webpack-dev-server": "^4.11.1",
    "webpack-node-externals": "^3.0.0",
    "webpackbar": "^5.0.2"
  }
}
```

After you create the package.json, you need to create the tsconfig.json file for devtools. Each package will have its own tsconfig.json file. Basically we will extend our tsconfig.common.json from root and just specify the outDir and include the files inside the src folder:

```
{
  "extends": "../../tsconfig.common.json",
  "compilerOptions": {
    "outDir": "./dist"
  },
  "include": ["src/**/*"]
}
```

Creating a colorful log

We need to create a log function that will help us highlight the Webpack configuration that we will implement, and for this we will use the cli-color package, which adds colors to the logs. You need to create the file under packages/devtools/src/cli/log.ts:

```
import cliColor from 'cli-color'
type Args = {
  text?: string
  tag?: string
  json?: any
```

```
    type?: 'info' | 'error' | 'warning'
}
export const log = (args: Args | any) => {
  const blockColor: any = {
    info: cliColor.bgCyan.whiteBright.bold,
    error: cliColor.bgRed.whiteBright.bold,
    warning: cliColor.bgYellow.blackBright.bold
  }
  const textColor: any = {
    info: cliColor.blue,
    error: cliColor.red,
    warning: cliColor.yellow
  }
  if (typeof args === 'string') {
    console.info(textColor.info(args))
  }
  const { tag, json, type } = args
  if (tag && json) {
    console.info(blockColor[type](`<<< BEGIN ${tag.toUpperCase()}`))
    console.info(textColor[type](JSON.stringify(json, null, 2)))
    console.info(blockColor[type](`END ${tag.toUpperCase()} >>>`))
  }
}
```

Webpack common configuration

Now that we have our log function ready, we will continue creating the Webpack configuration. We will break our Webpack configuration into three files: webpack.common.ts, webpack.development.ts, and webpack.production.ts. The common configuration will be merged with the development and production separately. However, before creating our common configuration, we need to create our Webpack types, and you need to add this file to packages/devtools/src/webpack/webpack.types.ts:

```
export type WebpackMode = 'production' | 'development'
export type ConfigType = 'web' | 'package'
export type Package = 'api' | 'design-system' | 'frontend' | 'utils'
export type ConfigArgs = {
  mode: WebpackMode
```

```
  type: ConfigType
  sandbox?: 'true' | 'false'
  packageName: Package
}
export type ModeArgs = {
  configType: ConfigType
  packageName: Package
  mode?: WebpackMode
  sandbox?: boolean
  devServer?: boolean
  isAnalyze?: boolean
  port?: number
  analyzerPort?: number
  color?: string
  htmlOptions?: {
    title: string
    template: string
  }
}
```

Now let's create our webpack.common.ts file, starting with the packages we need to import:

```
import HtmlWebPackPlugin from 'html-webpack-plugin'
import path from 'path'
import createStyledComponentsTransformer from 'typescript-plugin-styled-
components'
import { Configuration } from 'webpack'
import { BundleAnalyzerPlugin } from 'webpack-bundle-analyzer'
import nodeExternals from 'webpack-node-externals'
import { ModeArgs } from './webpack.types'
```

Next we need to create the getWebpackCommonConfig function, which will receive arguments from the terminal to compile each package via the NPM script:

```
const getWebpackCommonConfig = (args: ModeArgs): Configuration => {
  const {
    configType, // it can be "web" or "package"
    isAnalyze,
    port = 3000,
```

```
        mode,
        analyzerPort = 9001,
        packageName,
        htmlOptions,
        sandbox,
        devServer
    } = args
    // Here goes the next block of codes
}
export default getWebpackCommonConfig
```

The blocks of code that you will see next from this chapter's GitHub repository need to be added where the comment is located in the previous code: `// Here goes the next block of codes`.

First let's check if we are running a sandbox (this will be for our design-system package). If yes, we will use port 8080, and if not, we will use the port + 1 (3001 by default):

```
const devServerPort = sandbox && devServer ? 8080 : port + 1
```

The first configuration option we need to create is `entry`, which will define the index file that we will use to compile our project, based on the `packageName` we specify in our script. We can create `entry` by running the following code:

```
// Client Entry
const entry = configType !== 'web'
    ? path.resolve(__dirname, `../../../${packageName}/src/index.ts`)
    : path.resolve(__dirname, `../../../${packageName}/src/index.tsx`)
```

When our `configType` is "package" (or different than 'web'), we will specify the `index.ts` as entry, and for the web packages, we will use `index.tsx`.

The second configuration option we need to create is going to be the `resolve` node, which will include the extensions we want to support and the alias for each package (~). In Webpack 5, we must turn off some fallback packages that are not enabled by default anymore:

```
// Resolve
const resolve = {
    extensions: ['*', '.ts', '.tsx', '.js', '.jsx'],
    alias: {
        '~': path.resolve(__dirname, `../../../${packageName}/src`)
    },
```

```
    fallback: {
      buffer: false,
      crypto: false,
      stream: false,
      querystring: false,
      os: false,
      zlib: false,
      http: false,
      https: false,
      url: false,
      path: require.resolve('path-browserify')
    }
  }
```

The third configuration option is the output, which will specify where we will place the compiled project (the dist directory), which will be the dynamic filename ([name].js). If we want to compile a package, we will add the necessary options to be able to export that package (libraryTarget, library, umdNamedDefine, and globalObject):

```
// Output
const output = {
  path: path.resolve(__dirname, `../../../${packageName}/dist`),
  filename: '[name].js',
    ...(sandbox && {
      publicPath: '/',
      chunkFilename: '[name].js'
    }),
    ...(configType === 'package' && !sandbox && {
      filename: 'index.js',
      libraryTarget: 'umd',
      library: 'lib',
      umdNamedDefine: true,
      globalObject: 'this'
    })
}
```

The fourth configuration option is the `plugins`, which will be applied based on some conditions, depending on if we want to analyze our bundle sizes (`BundleAnalyzerPlugin`) and add a template with `HtmlWebPackPlugin`:

```
// Plugins
const plugins = []
if (isAnalyze) {
  plugins.push(
    new BundleAnalyzerPlugin({
      analyzerPort
    })
  )
}
if (mode === 'development' && htmlOptions?.title && htmlOptions.template)
{
  plugins.push(
    new HtmlWebPackPlugin({
      title: htmlOptions.title,
      template: path.resolve(__dirname,
`../../../${packageName}/${htmlOptions.template}`),
      filename: './index.html'
    })
  )
}
```

The fifth configuration option is the `rules`, which we will define depending on the extension file we want to process. We will also use Webpack loaders like `ts-loader` to load TypeScript files or `svg-url-loader` and `@svgr/webpack` to load SVG files:

```
// Rules
const rules = []
rules.push({
  test: /\.(tsx|ts)$/,
  exclude: /node_modules/,
  loader: 'ts-loader',
  options: {
```

```
      getCustomTransformers: () => ({
        before: [
          createStyledComponentsTransformer({
            displayName: true,
            ssr: true,
            minify: true
          })
        ]
      })
    }
  })
  if (packageName === 'design-system') {
    const svgUrlLoaderInclude: Record<string, string[]> = {
      'design-system': [
        path.resolve(__dirname, '../../../design-system/src/components/
Spinner/loaders'),
        path.resolve(__dirname, '../../../design-system/src/components/
Dialog/icons'),
        path.resolve(__dirname, '../../../design-system/src/icons')
      ]
    }
    const svgrWebpackInclude: Record<string, string[]> = {
      'design-system': [
        path.resolve(__dirname, '../../../design-system/src/components/Icon/
icons')
      ]
    }
    rules.push({
      test: /\.svg$/,
      oneOf: [
        {
          use: 'svg-url-loader',
          include: configType === 'package' ?
svgUrlLoaderInclude[packageName] ?? [] : []
        },
        {
          use: '@svgr/webpack',
```

```
            include: configType === 'package' ? svgrWebpackInclude[packageName]
?? [] : []
          }
        ]
    })
}
if (configType === 'package' && sandbox) {
    rules.push({
        test: /\.(jpe?g|png|gif|svg)$/i,
        use: [{ loader: 'file-loader', options: {} }]
    })
}
```

Finally, we put all the options together in the `webpackConfig` object:

```
const webpackConfig = {
    entry,
    ...(configType === 'package' && sandbox && {
        entry: path.resolve(__dirname, `../../../${packageName}/sandbox/
index.tsx`)
    }),
    ...(devServer && {
        devServer: {
            historyApiFallback: true,
            static: output.path,
            port: devServerPort
        }
    }),
    ...(!sandbox && {
        externals: [nodeExternals()]
    }),
    output,
    resolve,
    plugins,
    module: {
        rules
    },
    ...(configType !== 'web' && !sandbox && {
```

```
      target: 'node'
    })
  }
  return webpackConfig as Configuration
```

Webpack development configuration

After creating our Webpack common configuration file, we now need to create our `webpack.development.ts` file, which is way smaller than the common one and will extend that configuration (on `webpack.config.ts`), specifying the development mode for Webpack, adding the source map, and passing the HMR plugin:

```
import {
  Configuration as WebpackConfiguration,
  HotModuleReplacementPlugin,
  NoEmitOnErrorsPlugin
} from 'webpack'
import { Configuration as WebpackDevServerConfiguration } from 'webpack-dev-server'
interface Configuration extends WebpackConfiguration {
  devServer?: WebpackDevServerConfiguration
}
const getWebpackDevelopmentConfig = (): Configuration => {
  const webpackConfig: Configuration = {
    mode: 'development',
    devtool: 'source-map',
    plugins: [new HotModuleReplacementPlugin(), new NoEmitOnErrorsPlugin()]
  }
  return webpackConfig
}
export default getWebpackDevelopmentConfig
```

Webpack production configuration

The last file we need to create is the `webpack.production.ts`, which will will use external libraries when we try to compile a package that uses shared libraries like **React**, **Apollo Server**, or **JSON Web Tokens**, put the mode as production, and disable the source map:

```
import { Configuration } from 'webpack'
import { ModeArgs } from './webpack.types'
```

```
const getWebpackProductionConfig = (args: ModeArgs): Configuration => {
  const { configType } = args
  // Externals
    const externals = configType === 'package'
      ? {
        react: {
          commonjs: 'react',
          commonjs2: 'react',
          amd: 'React',
          root: 'React'
        },
        'react-dom': {
          commonjs: 'react-dom',
          commonjs2: 'react-dom',
          amd: 'ReactDOM',
          root: 'ReactDOM'
        },
        jsonwebtoken: 'jsonwebtoken'
      }
    : {}
  const webpackConfig = {
    mode: 'production',
    devtool: false,
    externals
  }
  return webpackConfig as Configuration
}
export default getWebpackProductionConfig
```

That's all for our devtools package. Now we only need to create the index.ts file in packages/ devtools/src/index.ts to export all the Webpack configuration and be able to compile our devtools package:

```
// CLI
export * from './cli/log'
// Webpack
```

```
export { default as getWebpackCommonConfig } from './webpack/webpack.
common'
export { default as getWebpackDevelopmentConfig } from './webpack/webpack.
development'
export { default as getWebpackProductionConfig } from './webpack/webpack.
production'
export * from './webpack/webpack.types'
```

Since this will be the base package that will compile other packages, first we need to build it, and for this, we will just use the tsc command to transform TypeScript into JavaScript files. For this, you just need to run the build command inside packages/devtools:

```
npm run build
```

If everything is correct, you should see something like this:

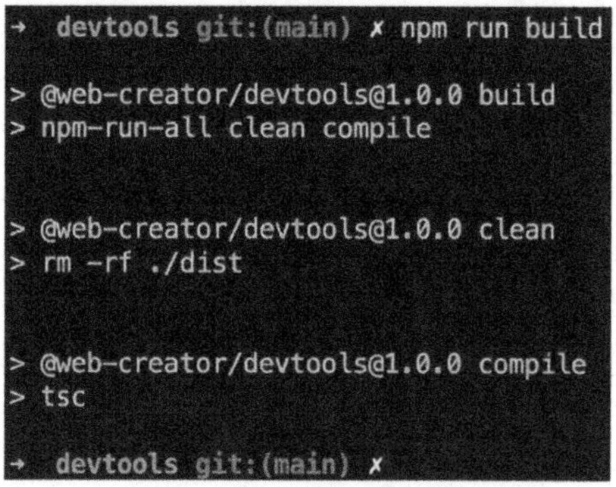

Figure 14.6: npm run build

Finally, we need to create the webpack.config.ts file at the root level where we will consume our brand-new devtools package and merge the configurations (development + common or production + common) using webpack-merge:

```
import {
  ConfigArgs,
  getWebpackCommonConfig,
  getWebpackDevelopmentConfig,
  getWebpackProductionConfig,
  log
} from '@web-creator/devtools'
import { Configuration } from 'webpack'
```

```
import { merge } from 'webpack-merge'
// Mode Config
const getModeConfig = {
  development: getWebpackDevelopmentConfig,
  production: getWebpackProductionConfig
}
// Mode Configuration (development/production)
const modeConfig: (args: ConfigArgs) => Configuration = ({mode, type,
packageName}) => {
  const getWebpackConfiguration = getModeConfig[mode]
  return getWebpackConfiguration({
    configType: type,
    packageName,
    sandbox: true,
    devServer: true
  })
}
// Merging all configurations
const webpackConfig: (args: ConfigArgs) => Promise<Configuration> = async
({
  mode, type, sandbox, packageName
  } = {
    mode: 'production',
    type: 'web',
    sandbox: 'false',
    packageName: 'design-system'
  }) => {
  const isSandbox = type === 'package' && sandbox === 'true'
  const commonConfiguration = getWebpackCommonConfig({
    configType: type,
    packageName,
    mode,
    ...(isSandbox && {
      htmlOptions: { title: 'Sandbox', template: 'sandbox/index.html' },
      sandbox: isSandbox,
      devServer: isSandbox
    })
  })
```

```
  // Mode Configuration
  const modeConfiguration = mode && type ? modeConfig({ mode, type,
packageName }) : {}
  // Merging all configurations
  const webpackConfiguration = merge(commonConfiguration, modeConfiguration)
  // Logging Webpack Configuration
  log({ tag: 'Webpack Configuration', json: webpackConfiguration, type:
'warning' })
  return webpackConfiguration
}
export default webpackConfig
```

Creating the utils package

After we've created the devtools package, it is time to add a basic utils package to test the Web-pack compilation with devtools. For this, you will need to create a directory at packages/utils. For the example in the book, we will just add one util file to test our devtools, but in the actual repository you will find way more util files that have been added to the project.

As always let's start creating our package.json in the utils package:

```
{
  "name": "@web-creator/utils",
  "version": "1.0.0",
  "main": "dist/index.js",
  "types": "dist/index.d.ts",
  "files": [
    "dist"
  ],
  "scripts": {
    "build": "cross-env NODE_ENV=production npm-run-all clean compile
webpack:production",
    "build:dev": "cross-env NODE_ENV=development npm-run-all clean compile
webpack:development",
    "clean": "rm -rf ./dist",
    "compile": "tsc",
    "lint": "npm run --prefix ../../ lint",
    "lint:fix": "npm run --prefix ../../ lint:fix",
    "prepublishOnly": "npm run lint && npm run build",
```

```
      "webpack:development": "webpack --config=../../webpack.config.ts --env
  mode=development --env type=package --env packageName=utils",
      "webpack:production": "webpack --config=../../webpack.config.ts --env
  mode=production --env type=package --env packageName=utils"
    },
    "author": "Carlos Santana",
    "license": "MIT",
    "dependencies": {
      "currency-formatter": "^1.5.9",
      "slug": "^8.2.2",
      "uuid": "^9.0.0"
    },
    "devDependencies": {
      "@types/currency-formatter": "^1.5.1",
      "@types/slug": "^5.0.3",
      "@types/uuid": "^9.0.0"
    }
  }
}
```

There are some important elements in this package.json that I want to mention:

- The first one is the name of the package, which is @web-creator/utils. As I mentioned before, this is the correct format to name packages inside our MonoRepo.

- The second node is version, which always will be 1.0.0 (unless you want to publish this package to the NPM registry; for now you don't need to worry about that).

- main is to specify where our utils code will exist, which will always be in dist/index.js.

- The types node is to be able to load our TypeScript types; if you don't specify this, it won't be possible to see the types you add to your utils package when you consume this package.

- Finally the files node is an array that will contain the dist directory that will contain the compiled package.

Additionally, the scripts have some interesting things that you should know. Our build command will run multiple scripts using npm-run-all, which is a library that helps us run multiple scripts one after the other. In this case, we always execute the script clean first to remove our dist folder and start fresh. Then we compile the code with TypeScript (tsc), then we execute webpack:production. This will execute webpack, specifying the configuration file that exists at the root (two levels behind). We also use the --env flag to pass values as variables.

These variables are defined in our `webpack.config.ts` file. In this case, we're passing `mode=production`, `type=package`, and `packageName=utils`.

If you notice, some scripts contain `npm run --prefix ../../`, and I'm pretty sure you are wondering what exactly the `--prefix` flag is in this command. It is essentially a way to tell NPM that we want to run a script from a different `package.json`. In this specific example, we are going back two levels to run the script `lint` that exists in our root `package.json`.

Now let's create our first `util` file, which is going to be called `is.tsx`, and you must save it in packages/utils/src/utils/is.tsx with the following code:

```
const is = {
  Array(v: unknown) {
    return v instanceof Array
  },
  Defined(v: unknown) {
    return typeof v !== 'undefined' && v !== null
  },
  Email(email: string) {
    const regex = /^[^\s@]+@[^\s@]+\.[^\s@]+$/
    return regex.test(email)
  },
  False(v: unknown) {
    return (this.Defined(v) && v === false) || v === 'false'
  },
  Number(v: unknown) {
    return typeof v === 'number'
  },
  Function(v: unknown) {
    return typeof v === 'function'
  },
  Object(v: unknown) {
    return this.Defined(v) && typeof v === 'object' && !this.Array(v)
  },
  String(v: unknown) {
    return this.Defined(v) && typeof v === 'string'
  },
  Undefined(v: unknown) {
```

```
      return typeof v === 'undefined' || v === null
    },
    JSON(str: string) {
      if (!str || str === null) {
        return false
      }
      try {
        JSON.parse(str)
      } catch (e) {
        return false
      }
      return true
    },
    Password(password: string, min = 8) {
      return Boolean(password && password.length >= min)
    },
    PasswordMatch(p1: string, p2: string) {
      return this.Password(p1) && this.Password(p2) && p1 === p2
    },
    Browser() {
      return typeof window !== 'undefined'
    },
    Device() {
      if (!this.Browser()) {
        return false
      }
      const ua = navigator.userAgent
      if (/(tablet|ipad|playbook|silk)|(android(?!.*mobi))/i.test(ua)) {
        return true
      }
      if (/Mobile|Android|iP(hone|od)|IEMobile|BlackBerry|Kindle|Silk-
Accelerated|(hpw|web)OS|Opera M(obi|ini)/.test(ua)) {
        return true
      }
      return false
    },
    EmptyObject(v: any) {
```

```
        return v ? Object.keys(v).length === 0 : true
    }
}
export default is
```

After you create this util, you need to create the index.ts file in packages/utils/src/index.
ts, where you will export all your utils:

```
export { default as is } from './utils/is'
```

Finally, you must add a script to your root package.json to be able to compile your brand-new
utils package. Here is how your root package.json file should look:

```
{
  "name": "web-creator",
  "private": true,
  "workspaces": [
    "packages/*"
  ],
  "scripts": {
    "lint": "eslint --ext .tsx,.ts ./packages/**/src",
    "lint:fix": "eslint --ext .tsx,.ts ./packages/**/src",
    "build": "npm-run-all build:*",
    "build:devtools": "cd ./packages/devtools && npm run build",
    "build:utils": "cd ./packages/utils && npm run build",
    "build:authentication": "cd ./packages/authentication && npm run
build",
    "build:design-system": "cd ./packages/design-system && npm run build",
    "build:api": "cd ./packages/api && npm run build",
  },
  "devDependencies": {
    "@typescript-eslint/eslint-plugin": "^5.49.0",
    "@typescript-eslint/parser": "^5.49.0",
    "cross-env": "^7.0.3",
    "eslint": "^8.33.0",
    "eslint-config-airbnb": "^19.0.4",
    "eslint-config-airbnb-typescript": "^17.0.0",
    "eslint-config-prettier": "^8.6.0",
    "eslint-import-resolver-typescript": "^3.5.3",
```

```
      "eslint-plugin-import": "^2.27.5",
      "eslint-plugin-jsx-a11y": "^6.7.1",
      "eslint-plugin-prettier": "^4.2.1",
      "eslint-plugin-react": "^7.32.2",
      "eslint-plugin-react-hooks": "^4.6.0",
      "npm-run-all": "^4.1.5",
      "prettier": "^2.8.3",
      "ts-node": "^10.9.1",
      "typescript": "^4.9.5",
      "webpack-cli": "^5.0.1"
    },
    "dependencies": {
      "webpack": "^5.75.0",
      "webpack-merge": "^5.8.0"
    }
  }
```

As you can see, we need to add a build:package_name (in this case, build:utils) script for each package that we want to build, and then our build script will execute all of them using npm-run-all build:*.

Now you can build your utils package by running the npm run build script inside the utils directory; you should see something like this:

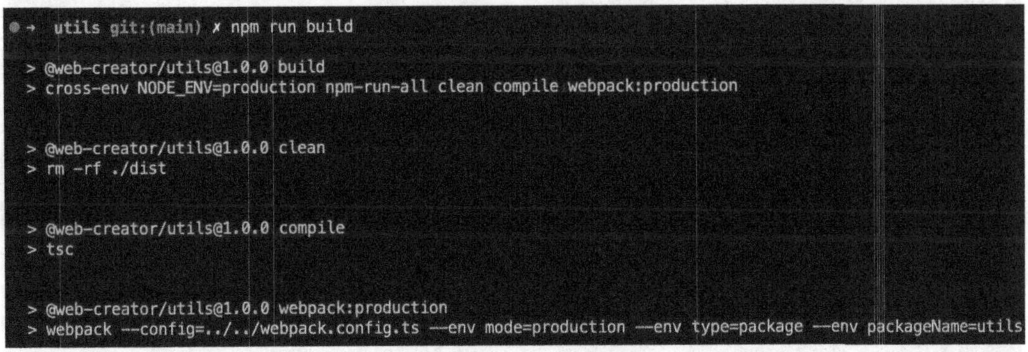

Figure 14.7: Building utils

Following this, you should see the Webpack configuration log that we use to compile this package:

```
<<< BEGIN WEBPACK CONFIGURATION
{
  "entry": "/Users/czantany/projects/React18-Book/codes/Chapter15/web-creator/packages/utils/src/index.ts",
  "externals": {
    "react": {
      "commonjs": "react",
      "commonjs2": "react",
      "amd": "React",
      "root": "React"
    },
    "react-dom": {
      "commonjs": "react-dom",
      "commonjs2": "react-dom",
      "amd": "ReactDOM",
      "root": "ReactDOM"
    },
    "apollo-server-express": "apollo-server-express",
    "jsonwebtoken": "jsonwebtoken"
  },
  "output": {
    "path": "/Users/czantany/projects/React18-Book/codes/Chapter15/web-creator/packages/utils/dist",
    "filename": "index.js",
    "libraryTarget": "umd",
    "library": "lib",
    "umdNamedDefine": true,
    "globalObject": "this"
  },
  "resolve": {
    "extensions": [
      "*",
      ".ts",
      ".tsx",
      ".js",
      ".jsx"
    ],
    "alias": {
      "~": "/Users/czantany/projects/React18-Book/codes/Chapter15/web-creator/packages/utils/src"
    },
    "fallback": {
      "buffer": false,
      "crypto": false,
      "stream": false,
      "querystring": false,
      "os": false,
      "zlib": false,
      "http": false,
      "https": false,
      "url": false,
      "path": "/Users/czantany/projects/React18-Book/codes/Chapter15/web-creator/node_modules/path-browserify/index.js"
    }
  },
  "plugins": [],
  "module": {
    "rules": [
      {
        "test": {},
        "exclude": {},
        "loader": "ts-loader",
        "options": {}
      }
    ]
  },
  "target": "node",
  "mode": "production",
  "devtool": false
}
END WEBPACK CONFIGURATION >>>
```

Figure 14.8: Webpack configuration

Then at the end, you will see the compiled files by Webpack:

```
assets by path utils/ 11.2 KiB
  assets by path utils/*.ts 5.41 KiB
    asset utils/dates.d.ts 778 bytes [compared for emit]
    asset utils/is.d.ts 597 bytes [compared for emit]
    asset utils/graphql.d.ts 497 bytes [compared for emit]
    + 20 assets
  assets by path utils/*.map 5.74 KiB
    asset utils/graphql.d.ts.map 553 bytes [compared for emit]
    asset utils/values.d.ts.map 491 bytes [compared for emit]
    asset utils/url.d.ts.map 429 bytes [compared for emit]
    asset utils/dates.d.ts.map 321 bytes [compared for emit]
    + 19 assets
asset index.js 61.8 KiB [emitted] [minimized] (name: main) 1 related asset
asset index.d.ts.map 1 KiB [compared for emit]
asset index.d.ts 1020 bytes [compared for emit]
orphan modules 9.85 KiB [orphan] 15 modules
runtime modules 937 bytes 4 modules
javascript modules 78.9 KiB
  modules by path ./src/ 29.2 KiB
    modules by path ./src/utils/*.ts 23.6 KiB 22 modules
    ./src/index.ts 3.81 KiB [built] [code generated]
    ./src/utils/is.tsx 1.79 KiB [built] [code generated]
  modules by path ../../node_modules/ 49.6 KiB
    modules by path ../../node_modules/locale-currency/*.js 3.52 KiB 2 modules
    + 5 modules
  external "crypto" 42 bytes [built] [code generated]
json modules 26 KiB
  ../../node_modules/currency-formatter/currencies.json 25 KiB [built] [code generated]
  ../../node_modules/currency-formatter/localeFormats.json 1.03 KiB [built] [code generated]
webpack 5.75.0 compiled successfully in 1560 ms
```

Figure 14.9: Compiled files by Webpack

Now that we have created our first package, which is compiled with devtools, and understand the structure of a package, it's time to start working on our API.

Creating the API package

In this package, we will implement a multi-service system that will help us have more than one service to connect to multiple databases. Let's see how our package.json file should look for the api package:

```
{
  "name": "@web-creator/api",
  "version": "1.0.0",
  "main": "index.js",
  "scripts": {
    "build": "cross-env NODE_ENV=production npm-run-all clean compile
webpack:production",
```

```
    "build:dev": "cross-env NODE_ENV=development npm-run-all clean compile
webpack:development",
    "clean": "rm -rf ./dist",
    "compile": "tsc",
    "dev": "ts-node-dev src/index.ts",
    "lint": "npm run --prefix ../../ lint",
    "lint:fix": "npm run --prefix ../../ lint:fix",
    "webpack:development": "webpack --config=../../webpack.config.ts --env
mode=production --env type=api --env packageName=api",
    "webpack:production": "webpack --config=../../webpack.config.ts --env
mode=development --env type=api --env packageName=api"
  },
  "author": "Carlos Santana",
  "license": "MIT",
  "dependencies": {
    "@graphql-tools/merge": "8.3.18",
    "@graphql-tools/schema": "9.0.16",
    "@web-creator/authentication": "1.0.0",
    "@web-creator/utils": "^1.0.0",
    "@apollo/server": "^4.7.3",
    "cookie-parser": "^1.4.6",
    "cors": "^2.8.5",
    "dotenv": "^16.0.3",
    "express": "^4.18.2",
    "graphql": "16.6.0",
    "graphql-middleware": "6.1.33",
    "graphql-tag": "2.12.6",
    "isomorphic-fetch": "^3.0.0",
    "jsonwebtoken": "^9.0.0",
    "pg": "^8.9.0",
    "pg-hstore": "^2.3.4",
    "pg-native": "^3.0.1",
    "sequelize": "^6.28.0",
    "sequelize-typescript": "^2.1.5"
  },
  "devDependencies": {
    "@types/body-parser": "^1.19.2",
```

```
    "@types/express-jwt": "^6.0.4",
    "@types/jsonwebtoken": "^9.0.1",
    "@types/cors": "^2.8.13",
    "@types/node": "^18.11.18",
    "@types/pg": "^8.6.6",
    "ts-node-dev": "2.0.0"
  }
}
```

In this case, we will use Sequelize (an ORM) and PostgreSQL for the database, but feel free to use MySQL or any other type of database supported by Sequelize.

In the following sections, we'll guide you through each of these steps in detail. We'll demonstrate how to integrate all the components and successfully operate your CRM service. If it appears complex, there's no need to worry. We'll proceed at a steady pace and provide explanations along the way.

Creating a user-shared model

The first thing we need to create is our shared model, which for now will be only the User model, to be able to create a shared authentication system for all our sites.

You must create the User model file in packages/api/src/models/User.ts, which will create a table with the following fields: id (UUID), username (STRING), password (STRING), Email (STRING), Role (STRING), and active (BOOLEAN):

```
import { security } from '@web-creator/utils'
import { DataType, Sequelize, User } from '../types'
export default (sequelize: Sequelize, dataType: DataType): User => {
  const user = sequelize.define('User', {
    id: {
      primaryKey: true,
      allowNull: false,
      type: dataType.UUID,
      defaultValue: dataType.UUIDV4()
    },
    username: {
      type: dataType.STRING,
      allowNull: false,
      unique: true,
```

```
      validate: {
        isAlphanumeric: {
          args: true,
          msg: 'The user just accepts alphanumeric characters'
        },
        len: {
          args: [4, 20],
          msg: 'The username must be from 4 to 20 characters'
        }
      }
    },
    password: {
      type: dataType.STRING,
      allowNull: false
    },
    email: {
      type: dataType.STRING,
      allowNull: false,
      unique: true,
      validate: {
        isEmail: {
          args: true,
          msg: 'Invalid email'
        }
      }
    },
    role: {
      type: dataType.STRING,
      allowNull: false
    },
    active: {
      type: dataType.BOOLEAN,
      allowNull: false,
      defaultValue: false
    }
  },
```

```
    {
      hooks: {
        beforeCreate: (u: User): void => {
          u.password = security.encrypt(u.password)
        }
      }
    }
  )
  return user
}
```

Creating a user-shared GraphQL type and resolver

Besides the User-shared model, we need to create a shared GraphQL **type** and **resolver**, in order to handle the authentication using GraphQL on all our sites.

First we need to create another shared GraphQL type called error, which will help us handle errors on any of the queries or mutations we will create later. This file exists in packages/api/src/graphql/types/Error.ts:

```
import gql from 'graphql-tag'
export default gql`
type ErrorResponse {
  code: Int
  message: String!
}

type Error {
  error: ErrorResponse
}
`
```

Another shared type that we need to create is the scalar one, which will define scalar types like UUID, Datetime, and JSON. This file exists in packages/api/src/graphql/types/Scalar.ts:

```
import gql from 'graphql-tag'
export default gql`
scalar UUID
scalar Datetime
```

```
scalar JSON
```

Finally, we need to create our User type, which will include some queries to get a specific user via an access token (at), get all users, and get some mutations to create a new user and also to log in. This file should be placed in packages/api/src/graphql/types/User.ts:

```
import gql from 'graphql-tag'
export default gql`
  "User type"
  type User {
    id: UUID!
    username: String!
    email: String!
    role: String!
    active: Boolean!
    createdAt: Datetime!
    updatedAt: Datetime!
  }
  "Token type"
  type Token {
    token: String!
  }
  "User Query"
  type Query {
    getUser(at: String!): User!
    getUsers: [User!]
  }
  "User Mutation"
  type Mutation {
    createUser(input: ICreateUser): User!
    login(input: ILogin): Token!
  }
  "CreateUser Input"
  input ICreateUser {
    username: String!
    password: String!
    email: String!
```

```
    active: Boolean!
    role: String!
  }
  "Login Input"
  input ILogin {
    emailOrUsername: String!
    password: String!
  }
```

After you create the preceding types, you need to create the user resolver. For this we will use the authentication package (please check the code at https://github.com/PacktPublishing/ React-18-Design-Patterns-and-Best-Practices-Fourth-Edition/tree/main/Chapter14/ web-creator/packages/authentication). Do you remember the authentication system we created in *Chapter 13*? It is the same code, but now it will have its own package. This resolver should be created in packages/api/src/graphql/resolvers/user.ts:

```
import { authenticate, getUserBy, getUserData } from '@web-builder/
authentication'
import { ICreateUser, ILogin, Model } from '../../types'
const getUsers = (_: any, _args: any, { models }: { models: Model }) =>
models.User.findAll()
  const getUser = async (_: any, { at }: { at: string }, { models }:
{models: Model}) => {
const connectedUser = await getUserData(at)
  if (connectedUser) {
    // Validating if the user is still valid
    const user = await getUserBy(
      {
        id: connectedUser.id,
        email: connectedUser.email,
        active: connectedUser.active
      },
      [connectedUser.role],
      models
    )
    if (user) {
      return {
```

```
        ...connectedUser
      }
    }
  }
  return {
    id: '',
    username: '',
    email: '',
    role: '',
    active: false
  }
}
const createUser = (_:any, {input}: {input: ICreateUser}, {models}:
{models: Model}) =>
models.User.create({ ...input })
const login = (_: any, { input }: { input: ILogin }, { models }: { models:
Model }) =>
authenticate(input.emailOrUsername, input.password, models)
export default {
  Query: {
    getUser,
    getUsers
  },
  Mutation: {
    createUser,
    login
  }
}
```

Creating custom services

Now it is time to create our custom services; for this we will create one default service (just to have an empty service) and one for a **CRM** project (it will be called crm).

The first thing we need to do is to create our service configuration, and for this we will create some types that will help us to be very strict in the options that our configuration will receive. This file needs to be created in packages/api/src/types/config.ts:

```
import { ValueOf } from '@web-creator/utils'
```

```
// Here you need to add all the services you want to create
export const Service = {
  CRM: 'crm'
} as const
export type Service = ValueOf<typeof Service>
export type Mode = 'production' | 'development'
export enum DeploymentType {
  PRODUCTION = 'production',
  STAGING = 'staging',
  DEVELOPMENT = 'development'
}
export interface ServiceConfiguration {
  domainName: string
  port: number
  database?: {
    engine?: string
    port?: number
    host?: string
    database?: string
    username?: string
    password?: string
  }
}
export interface ServiceBuilderConfiguration extends ServiceConfiguration
{
  service: Service
}
```

Our default configuration should be like this (packages/api/src/services/default/config.ts):

```
import { ServiceConfiguration } from '../../types/config'
export const config: ServiceConfiguration = {
  domainName: 'localhost',
  port: 4000,
  database: {
    engine: 'postgresql',
    port: 5432,
    host: 'localhost',
```

```
      database: '',
      username: '',
      password: ''
    }
  }
}
```

After that let's create our CRM configuration (custom service). This should be placed in packages/api/src/services/crm/config.ts:

```
import { ServiceConfiguration } from '../../types/config'
export const config: ServiceConfiguration = {
  domainName: 'ranchosanpancho.com',
  port: 4000,
  database: {
    database: 'crm'
  }
}
```

I'm pretty sure you're wondering where the other options of the database node (engine, port, host, username, and password) are. Those will be overwritten in the main config file that we will create later, but those values will be grabbed from our .env file (you must rename the .env.example file). Hence, let's create that file in packages/api/.env:

```
DB_ENGINE=postgresql
DB_PORT=5432
DB_HOST=localhost
DB_USERNAME=<YourDBUserName>
DB_PASSWORD=<YourDBPassword>
```

Building our service configuration

Now that we have our custom service (**CRM**) ready, let's build our configuration. For this you need to create the config file in packages/api/src/config.ts:

```
// This package will load the environment variables from our .env file
import dotenv from 'dotenv'
// Here you can add your custom services configuration
import { config as crmConfig } from './services/crm/config'
import { config as blankServiceConfig } from './services/default/config'
```

```
import { Service, ServiceBuilderConfiguration, ServiceConfiguration } from
'./types/config'
// Loading Env vars
dotenv.config()
const getServiceConfig = (service: Service): ServiceConfiguration => {
  switch (service) {
    // Add your custom services here
    case Service.CRM:
      return crmConfig
    default:
      return blankServiceConfig
  }
}
const buildConfig = (): ServiceBuilderConfiguration => {
  const service = process.env.SERVICE as Service
  if (!service) {
    throw 'You must specify a service (E.g., SERVICE=crm npm run dev)'
  }
  const serviceConfig = getServiceConfig(service)
  const config: ServiceBuilderConfiguration = {
    ...serviceConfig,
    database: {
      ...serviceConfig.database,
      engine: process.env.DB_ENGINE,
      host: process.env.DB_HOST,
      port: Number(process.env.DB_PORT),
      username: process.env.DB_USERNAME,
      password: process.env.DB_PASSWORD
    },
    service
  }
  return config
}
// Building the config.
const Config = buildConfig()
export default Config
```

Creating our custom models

Once we've created the configuration correctly, we need to create our custom models for our CRM service, which are created specifically for that service, and they will not be shared with other services. In this case, we will add just one and call it Guest. This model needs to be saved in packages/api/src/services/crm/models/Guest.ts:

```
import { DataType } from '../../../types'
export default (sequelize: any, dataType: DataType) => {
  const Guest = sequelize.define('Guest', {
    id: {
      primaryKey: true,
      allowNull: false,
      type: dataType.UUID,
      defaultValue: dataType.UUIDV4()
    },
    fullName: {
      type: dataType.STRING,
      allowNull: false
    },
    email: {
      type: dataType.STRING,
      allowNull: false,
      unique: true
    },
    photo: {
      type: dataType.STRING,
      allowNull: true
    },
    phone: {
      type: dataType.STRING,
      allowNull: true
    },
    socialMedia: {
      type: dataType.STRING,
      allowNull: true
    },
```

```
      location: {
        type: dataType.STRING,
        allowNull: true
      },
      gender: {
        type: dataType.STRING,
        allowNull: true
      },
      birthday: {
        type: dataType.STRING,
        allowNull: true
      }
    })
  return Guest
}
```

After we create the Guest model, we need to connect to our database and join our global models (User) and our local models (Guest) in order to create our service tables. This file needs to be created in packages/api/src/services/crm/models/index.ts:

```
import { keys, ts } from '@web-creator/utils'
import pg from 'pg'
import { Sequelize } from 'sequelize'
import Config from '../../../config'
// Db Connection
const { engine, port, host, database, username, password } = Config.
database ?? {}
const uri =
`${engine}://${username}:${password}@${host}:${port}/${database}`
const sequelize = new Sequelize(uri, {
  dialectModule: pg
})
// Models
const addModel = (path: string) => require(path).default(sequelize,
Sequelize)
const models: any = {
  User: addModel('../../../models/User'), // Global model
  Guest: addModel('./Guest'), // Local model
```

```
  sequelize // We must pass the sequelize object here
}
// Relationships
keys(models).forEach((modelName: string) => {
  if (ts.hasKey(models, modelName)) {
    if (models[modelName].associate) {
      models[modelName].associate(models)
    }
  }
})
export default models
```

Creating model seeds

Seeds are the initial data for our models (tables). Most of the time we want to clear all the model values but keep some of them as default values, but in this case we will add some default data for our User model and our Guest model:

```
import models from '../models'
async function createFirstUser(): Promise<any> {
  const existingUsers = await models.User.findAll()

  if (existingUsers.length === 0) {
    const newUser: any = await models.User.create({
      username: 'admin',
      password: '12345678',
      email: 'admin@ranchosanpancho.com',
      role: 'god',
      active: true
    })
    return newUser
  }
  return null
}
async function createGuests(): Promise<any> {
  const existingGuests = await models.Guest.findAll()
  if (existingGuests.length === 0) {
    const newGuests: any = await models.Guest.bulkCreate([
```

```
      {
        fullName: 'Carlos Santana',
        email: 'carlos@ranchosanpancho.com',
        photo: 'carlos.jpg',
        phone: '+1 555 555 5555',
        socialMedia: 'https://www.facebook.com/carlos.santana',
        location: 'Colima, Mexico',
        gender: 'Male',
        birthday: '11/21/1987'
      },
      {
        fullName: 'Cristina Santana',
        email: 'cristina@ranchosanpancho.com',
        photo: 'cristina.jpg',
        phone: '+1 444 444 4444',
        socialMedia: 'https://www.facebook.com/cristina.santana',
        location: 'Colima, Mexico',
        gender: 'Female',
        birthday: '1/20/1989'
      }
    ])
    return newGuests
  }
  return null
}
function setInitialSeeds(): void {
  createFirstUser()
  createGuests()
}
export default setInitialSeeds
```

Creating our custom GraphQL types and resolvers

For our CRM, we will create a Guest type and resolver just to illustrate how we can use GraphQL in different services that we create; the first file you need to create is the Guest type, which must be saved in packages/api/src/services/crm/graphql/types/Guest.ts:

```
import gql from 'graphql-tag'
export default gql`
```

```
type Guest {
  id: UUID!
  fullName: String!
  email: String!
  photo: String!
  socialMedia: String!
  location: String!
  phone: String!
  gender: String!
  birthday: String
  createdAt: Datetime!
  updatedAt: Datetime!
}
type GuestResponse {
  guests: [Guest!]!
}
union GuestResult = GuestResponse | Error
type Query {
  getGuests: GuestResult
}
```

As you can see, we define our Guest type with some personal fields such as fullName, email, photo, etc. Then we create a GuestResponse type that represents an array of guests ([Guest!]!). The square brackets indicate that it's an array, and the exclamation mark (!) denotes that it cannot contain null values. After that, we create a union type, which enables the schema field to return one of multiple object types. In this case, it can return GuestResponse when we have guests or the Error type if we don't have guests or encounter any other issues. If something else occurs, we define the response of these types in our resolver.

After you create this type file (or more), it is time to merge all your **Type Definitions (TypeDefs)**. For this, we will create an index.ts file inside our types directory and import our global types (Error, Scalar, and User). We will also include our local type (Guest) and merge it with a function provided by @graphql-tools/merge. This file is placed in packages/api/src/services/crm/types/index.ts:

```
import { mergeTypeDefs } from '@graphql-tools/merge'
// Global Types
```

```
import Error from '../../../../graphql/types/Error'
import Scalar from '../../../../graphql/types/Scalar'
import User from '../../../../graphql/types/User'
// Local Types
import Guest from './Guest'
export default mergeTypeDefs([Error, Scalar, User, Guest])
```

Now once you have merged your types, you need to create the Guest resolver. This file should be placed in packages/api/src/services/crm/graphql/resolvers/guest.ts:

```
export default {
  Query: {
    getGuests: async (_: any, _args: any, { models }: { models: any }):
Promise<any> => {
      const guests = await models.Guest.findAll({
        order: [['fullName', 'ASC']]
      })
      // If there are guests, return them with a GuestResponse type
      if (guests.length > 0) {
        return {
          __typename: 'GuestResponse',
          guests
        }
      }
      // If there are no guests, return an Error type with a 404 code and
message
      return {
        __typename: 'Error',
        error: {
          code: 404,
          message: 'No guests found'
        }
      }
    }
  }
}
```

As you can see, when we find guests (or data), we return them and add the __typename property (which is a GraphQL property) with a value of GuestResponse. This property is necessary to resolve the query with the correct type, since we are using a union. Here is where we define what we will return, whether it's the GuestResponse type or the Error type. On the other hand, if we don't find any guests, we return an error object with a code and message, and the __typename is set to 'Error'.

Now, we need to do the same with the resolvers. We need to merge our resolvers, both the global ones and the local ones. To do this, create an index.ts file in the same resolvers directory and add the following code:

```
import { mergeResolvers } from '@graphql-tools/merge'
import user from '../../../../graphql/resolvers/user'
import guest from './guest'
const resolvers = mergeResolvers([user, guest])
export default resolvers
```

We have done a similar thing with our resolvers as we did with the TypeDef. Now, we need to import the global user resolver and merge it with our guest resolver.

Synchronizing our models and starting Apollo Server

Now that we have created our custom configs, models, seeds, types, and resolvers, it's time to put everything together, synchronize our models, and start our Apollo Server. This file should be placed in packages/api/src/index.ts:

```
import { makeExecutableSchema } from '@graphql-tools/schema'
import { ts } from '@web-creator/utils'
import { ApolloServer } from '@apollo/server'
import { expressMiddleware } from '@apollo/server/express4'
import { ApolloServerPluginDrainHttpServer } from '@apollo/server/plugin/
drainHttpServer'
import bodyParser from 'body-parser'
import http from 'http'
import cookieParser from 'cookie-parser'
import cors from 'cors'
import express, { NextFunction, Request, Response } from 'express'
import { applyMiddleware } from 'graphql-middleware'
import { json } from 'body-parser'
import { Service } from './types/config'
```

After importing all the packages we need, first we need to check if we received the SERVICE variable from the terminal; otherwise, we will choose our default service. We will also check if our service is valid (exists in our Service type):

```
// Service
const service: any = process.env.SERVICE ?? 'default'
// Validating service
if (!ts.includes(Service, service)) {
  throw 'Invalid service'
}
```

Once we are sure that our service is valid, then we will dynamically import the resolvers, types, models, and seeds:

```
// We are importing the service files dynamically
const resolvers = require(`./services/${service}/graphql/resolvers`).
default
const typeDefs = require(`./services/${service}/graphql/types`).default
const models = require(`./services/${service}/models`).default
const seeds = require(`./services/${service}/seeds`).default
```

Then we create our Express app and configure cors, cookieParser, and bodyParser:

```
const app = express()
const httpServer = http.createServer(app)
const corsOptions = {
  origin: '*',
  credentials: true
}
app.use(cors(corsOptions))
app.use(cookieParser())
app.use(bodyParser.json())
// CORS
app.use((req: Request, res: Response, next: NextFunction) => {
  res.header('Access-Control-Allow-Origin', '*')
  res.header('Access-Control-Allow-Headers', 'Origin, X-Requested-With,
Content-Type, Accept')
  next()
})
```

We need to create our GraphQL schema with makeExecutableSchema and use the applyMiddleware:

```
// Schema
const schema = applyMiddleware(
  makeExecutableSchema({
    typeDefs,
    resolvers
  })
)
```

Finally, we create our ApolloServer instance passing the schema and the plugins.

```
// Apollo Server
const apolloServer = new ApolloServer({
  schema,
  plugins:[ApolloServerPluginDrainHttpServer({ httpServer })]
})
```

Now we need to sync our models. The alter option enables us to listen to changes in our models and modify them:

 If you change something, BE VERY CAREFUL with the force option. If it is true, it will truncate all your tables (meaning all your data will be deleted). Hence, only use it when totally necessary.

```
// Database Sync
  const main = async () => {
    const alter = true
    const force = false

    await apolloServer.start()
    await models.sequelize.sync({ alter, force })
    // Setting up initial seeds
    console.log('Initializing Seeds...')
    seeds()
```

```
    app.use(
      '/graphql',
      cors<cors.CorsRequest>(),
      json(),
      expressMiddleware(apolloServer, {
        context: async () => ({ models })
      })
    )
    await new Promise<void>((resolve) => httpServer.listen({ port: 4000 },
  resolve))
    console.log(' Server ready at http://localhost:4000/graphql')
  }
  main()
```

Testing our CRM service

If you did everything correctly, you can run the command SERVICE=crm npm run dev inside your
api package. and you should see something like this:

Figure 14.10: SERVICE=crm npm run dev

If you check your database, you will see the two tables created from your models (Guests and Users), and you should be able to see the seeds you added as well:

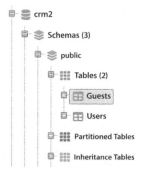

Figure 14.11: Database query

As you can see, the createdAt and updatedAt fields are automatically created by Sequelize. After this, you can try to hit http://localhost:4000/graphql to see if your Apollo Server works fine.

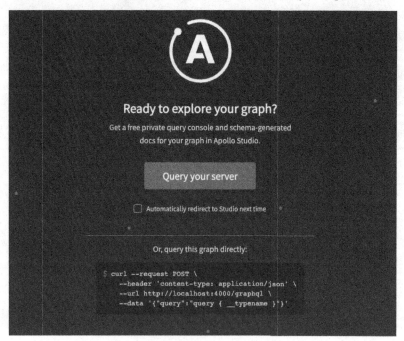

Figure 14.12: GraphQL Explorer

We can start testing our service queries like getGuests; let's see what it returns:

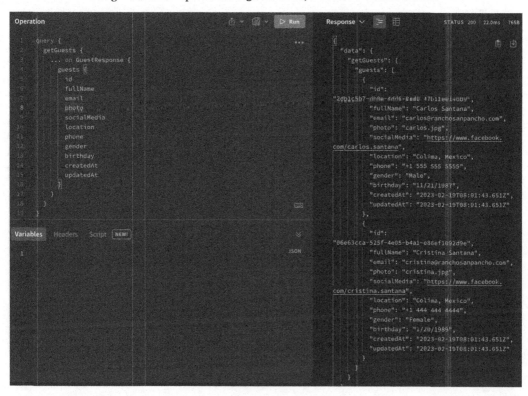

Figure 14.13: getGuests query

Also, you can test the getUsers query:

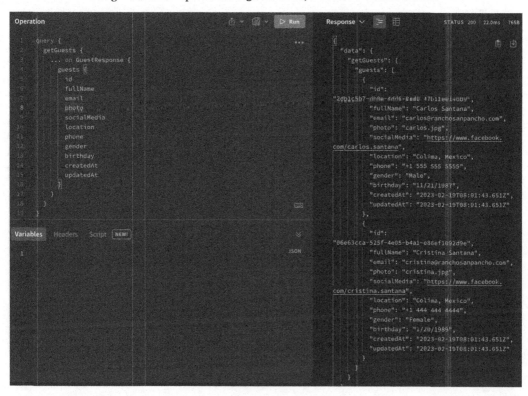

Figure 14.14: getUsers query

Finally, you can also test the login mutation to make sure your global authentication system works fine:

Figure 14.15: The login mutation

Creating the frontend package

In this package, we will implement a multi-site system that will help us have more than one site with the same code base.

Let's see how our package.json file should look for this package:

```
{
  "name": "@web-creator/frontend",
  "version": "1.0.0",
  "scripts": {
    "dev": "cross-env NODE_ENV=development npm run next:dev",
    "build": "next build",
    "next": "ts-node src/server.ts",
    "next:dev": "ts-node src/server.ts",
    "lint": "npm run --prefix ../../ lint",
    "lint:fix": "npm run --prefix ../../ lint:fix",
```

```
      "typecheck": "tsc --noEmit"
  },
  "author": "Carlos Santana",
  "license": "ISC",
  "peerDependencies": {
    "react": ">=17.0.2",
    "react-dom": ">=17.0.2"
  },
  "devDependencies": {
    "@babel/core": "^7.20.12",
    "@babel/node": "^7.20.7",
    "@types/cookie-parser": "^1.4.3",
    "@types/isomorphic-fetch": "^0.0.36",
    "@types/styled-components": "^5.1.26",
    "babel-plugin-jsx-remove-data-test-id": "^3.0.0",
    "babel-plugin-styled-components": "^2.0.7"
  },
  "dependencies": {
    "@apollo/client": "^3.7.7",
    "@web-creator/authentication": "1.0.0",
    "@web-creator/devtools": "1.0.0",
    "@web-creator/utils": "^1.0.0",
    "babel-preset-next": "^1.4.0",
    "cookie-parser": "^1.4.6",
    "dotenv": "^16.0.3",
    "express": "^4.18.2",
    "isomorphic-fetch": "^3.0.0",
    "next": "^13.1.6",
    "react-cookie": "^4.1.1",
    "styled-components": "^5.3.6",
    "webpack": "^5.75.0"
  }
}
```

Our frontend package works a little bit differently from our other packages because we use **Next. js**, which takes care of its own Webpack configuration. We do not compile it using our devtools like the other packages, and the TypeScript configuration differs slightly.

This is the `tsconfig.json` file for our frontend package:

```json
{
  "extends": "../../tsconfig.common.json",
  "compilerOptions": {
    "outDir": "./dist",
    "baseUrl": ".",
    "isolatedModules": true,
    "noEmit": false,
    "allowJs": true,
    "forceConsistentCasingInFileNames": true,
    "incremental": true,
    "jsx": "preserve",
    "paths": {
      "~/*": ["./src/*"]
    }
  },
  "include": ["src/**/*"]
}
```

As you can see, we define the ~ path. This is handled by `devtools` in other packages but in our case, we need to modify the next Webpack configuration directly. For this, you need to create the file `next.config.js` (yes, `.js`, not `.ts`), and the code should look like:

```js
const path = require('path')
module.exports = {
  reactStrictMode: true,
  webpack: (config, { isServer }) => {
    // Fixes npm packages that depend on `fs` module
    if (!isServer) {
      config.resolve.fallback.fs = false
    }
    // Aliases
    config.resolve.alias['~'] = path.resolve(__dirname, './src')
    return config
  }
}
```

Another configuration we need to set up is to add `styled-components` plugins to our `.babelrc` file. We will also use the `next/babel` preset. This file exists in `packages/frontend/.babelrc`:

```
{
  "presets": ["next/babel"],
  "plugins": [["styled-components", { "ssr": true, "preprocess": false
}]],
  "env": {
    "production": {
      "plugins": ["babel-plugin-jsx-remove-data-test-id"]
    }
  }
}
```

Now that we have completed this portion of the chapter, we will proceed to create a universal `User` model. This model will serve as a template that can be utilized across all our websites for anyone who signs up.

Next, our focus will shift toward developing a `Sites` system, which can be visualized as a master control room responsible for managing our websites. Just like changing TV channels, we will also build a **Page Switcher** that enables users to seamlessly switch between different pages on our websites.

Subsequently, we will construct a common `Login` system that ensures a consistent login experience across all our websites. To enhance customization and functionality, we will set up a `Sites` configuration, which acts as a rulebook or settings panel for each individual site, dictating its behavior and features.

To consolidate all these components, we will bundle them together in a single file named `server.ts`, which will function as the command center for our system.

Once the setup is complete, we will proceed to test our work by running the program and examining the outcomes using various examples. If any issues arise, our system will provide error messages to indicate and assist in troubleshooting.

In the upcoming sections, you will witness all these steps in action, enabling you to comprehend how they integrate within our larger system. Rest assured, although it may sound intricate at the moment, we will break it down and guide you through each step, ensuring a clear understanding of the process.

Creating our Sites system

The Sites system is pretty much the same as the services system we created in our API packages, but in this case instead of managing databases, we manage websites. So, like we did before, the first thing we need to do is create the configuration of each site. In this scenario, we will also have a **default** site, which is called `'blank-page'`, just to avoid the system breaking when no site has been provided.

Let's create the config file for this site in `packages/frontend/src/sites/blank-page/config.ts`, and this is the content of that file:

```
import { SiteConfiguration } from '../../types/config'
export const config: SiteConfiguration = {
  siteTitle: 'Blank Page',
  domainName: 'localhost',
  api: {
    uri: 'http://localhost:4000/graphql'
  },
  pages: ['index']
}
```

For this example, I'll use two personal sites, `san-pancho` and `codejobs`, but feel free to add any site you want to the project.

As part of the site, we need to create the `graphql` files, to consume our API queries and mutations, and the specific pages for this site. The only query we will add for now is the `getGuests` query that we previously created in the API package. This file should be in `packages/frontend/src/sites/san-pancho/graphql/guest/getGuests.query.ts`. If, at some point, you want to create a mutation, you may want to use the `myMutation.mutation.ts` format for the filename:

```
import { gql } from '@apollo/client'
export const getGuestsQuery = `
  getGuests {
    on GuestResponse {
      guests {
        id
        fullName
        email
        photo
        socialMedia
```

```
        location
        gender
        birthday
        note
      }
    }
    on Error {
      error {
        code
        message
      }
    }
  }


export default gql`
  query getGuests {
    ${getGuestsQuery}
  }
```

Creating our Page Switcher

If you have used Next.js in the past, you'll know how the **Next** page system works. Essentially, you have your pages directory, and the files or directories you add to that will represent the route of a page. For our example, we will need to create some Next pages that will "switch" or render a custom page from each site. I know it sounds a little bit complicated, but let's break this down into parts.

The first thing to do is to create our index.tsx page in packages/frontend/src/pages/ index.tsx (this is a Next page):

```
import React, { FC } from 'react'
import Config from '~/config'
const SwitcherPage = require(`~/sites/${Config.site}/switcher`).default
const getRouterParams = require(`~/sites/${Config.site}/server/
routerParams`).default
type Props = {
  siteTitle: string
}
const Page: FC<Props> = ({ siteTitle }) => {
```

```
      const routerParams = getRouterParams({})
      return <SwitcherPage routerParams={routerParams} siteTitle={siteTitle} />
}
export default Page
```

Another Next.js page that we must create is one that has a special name and needs to be created in packages/frontend/src/pages/[page]/[...params].tsx. The [page] will be a dynamic path. The [...params].tsx file will receive any additional parameters passed in the URL. If we have more than two nested routes, these additional routes will be added as an array to the params variable:

```
import { useRouter } from 'next/router'
import React, { FC } from 'react'
import Config from '~/config'
const SwitcherPage = require('~/sites/${Config.site}/switcher').default
const getRouterParams = require('~/sites/${Config.site}/server/
routerParams').default
type Props = {
  siteTitle: string
  serverData: any
}
const Page: FC<Props> = ({ siteTitle, serverData }) => {
  const router = useRouter()
  const routerParams = getRouterParams(router.query)
  return (
    <SwitcherPage
      routerParams={routerParams}
      siteTitle={siteTitle}
      props={{ serverData }}
    />
  )
}
export default Page
```

On each Next.js page, we will import a SwitcherPage component that exists on each site. We also import the routerParams, which will control the routing for each site as well, and we will receive the siteTitle via props. In other words, we just render the SwitcherPage component and pass the props.

Let's see how the `Switcher` component from our `san-pancho` site looks (`packages/frontend/src/sites/san-pancho/switcher.tsx`):

```
import dynamic from 'next/dynamic'
import React from 'react'
import Switcher, { Props } from '~/components/Switcher'
const dynamicPages: Record<string, Record<string, any>> = {
  index: {
    index: dynamic(() => import('./pages/index'))
  },
  login: {
    index: dynamic(() => import('./pages/login'))
  },
  dashboard: {
    index: dynamic(() => import('./pages/dashboard/index'))
  }
}
export default ({ routerParams, siteTitle, props }: Props) => (
  <Switcher
    routerParams={routerParams}
    siteTitle={siteTitle}
    props={props}
    dynamicPages={dynamicPages}
  />
)
```

The `next/dynamic` is a composite extension of `React.lazy` and `Suspense`. These components can delay hydration until the `Suspense` boundary is resolved. In our case, we are dynamically loading pages from this site, specifically the `index.index`, `login.index`, and `dashboard.index`. You're probably wondering why we have a nested index page for each of them. This is because we can have nested pages; for example, `index.index` will refer to `http://localhost:3000/`, `login.index` to `http://localhost:3000/login`, and `dashboard.index` to `http://localhost:3000/dashboard`. However, suppose you want to add a page inside the dashboard like `guests`. You will then add `dashboard.guests`, which will point to `http://localhost:3000/dashboard/guests`.

Each `switcher.ts` file from the `sites` directories uses the `Switcher` component. Hence, let's create it. This file is located in `packages/frontend/src/components/Switcher.tsx`:

```
import React, { FC } from 'react'
```

```
import ErrorPage from '~/components/ErrorPage'
type Route = {
  page: string
  section?: string
  subSection?: string
  urlParams?: string[]
  queryParams?: Record<string, string>
}
export type Props = {
  routerParams: Route
  siteTitle: string
  props?: Record<string, any>
  dynamicPages: any
}
const Switcher: FC<Props> = ({ routerParams, props = {}, dynamicPages:
sitePages }) => {
  const {
    page,
    section = 'index',
    subSection = '',
    urlParams,
    queryParams = {}
  } = routerParams
  const extraProps = {
    queryParams,
    router: {
      section,
      subsection
    },
    ...urlParams
  }
  const pageName = page
  let PageToRender // This will be a dynamic React Component
  let sectionPages: any = {}
  // We validate if our main page exists (index, login or dashboard)
  if (sitePages[pageName]) {
```

```
    // If exists we get our sectionsPages (index.index, login.index and
dashboard.index)
    sectionPages = sitePages[pageName]
    // By default we will try to render the index of each page
    PageToRender = sectionPages.index
    // If we have subsection, we render it (dashboard.guests)
    if (sectionPages[section][subSection]) {
      PageToRender = sectionPages[section][subSection]
    } else if (section !== 'index') {
      // This is to render nested routes that only have index
      PageToRender = sectionPages[section].index
    }
  } else {
  // If we can't find any of the pages, then we render an ErrorPage
  PageToRender = ErrorPage
  }
  return <PageToRender {...props} {...extraProps} />
}
export default Switcher
```

Let's now create the index page for our San Pancho site. This page serves a simple purpose: to display the site's title, providing confirmation that we are currently on the San Pancho site. This file should exist in packages/frontend/src/sites/san-pancho/pages/index.tsx:

```
import React from 'react'
export default () => <h1>San Pancho Index Page</h1>
```

After this, we can create our index page for our dashboard (packages/frontend/src/sites/san-pancho/pages/dashboard/index.tsx):

```
import React from 'react'
export default () => (
<>
  <h1>Dashboard for San Pancho</h1>
  <a href="/logout">Logout</a>
</>
)
```

Finally, we need to create our login page for san-pancho, which will share the Login component for all the sites (packages/frontend/src/sites/san-pancho/pages/login.tsx):

```
import React from 'react'
import Login from '~/components/Login'
export default () => <Login />
```

Creating our Login system

All our sites will use the same login page because we share the authentication system. Let's create our Login component and see how we can perform the login:

```
import { Button, Input, RenderIf } from '@web-creator/design-system'
import { getRedirectToUrl, redirectTo } from '@web-creator/utils'
import React, { FC, useContext, useState } from 'react'
import { FormContext } from '~/contexts/form'
import { UserContext } from '~/contexts/user'
import { CSS } from './Login.styled'
type Props = {
  background?: string
}
const Login: FC<Props> = () => {
  const redirectToUrl = getRedirectToUrl()
  // States
  const [values, setValues] = useState({
    emailOrUsername: '',
    password: ''
  })

  const [notification, setNotification] = useState({
    id: Math.random(),
    message: ''
  })
  const [invalidLogin, setInvalidLogin] = useState(false)
  // Contexts
  const { change } = useContext(FormContext)
  const { login } = useContext(UserContext)
  // Methods
  const onChange = (e: any): any => change(e, setValues)
```

```
  const handleSubmit = async (user: any): Promise<void> => {
    const response = await login(user)
    if (response.error) {
      setInvalidLogin(true)
      setNotification({
        id: Math.random(),
        message: response.message
      })
    } else {
      redirectTo(redirectToUrl || '/', true)
    }
  }
  return (
    <>
      <RenderIf isTrue={invalidLogin && notification.message !== ''}>
        {notification.message}
      </RenderIf>
      <CSS.Login>
        <CSS.LoginBox>
          <header>
            <img className="logo" src="/images/isotype.png" alt="Logo" />
<br />
            <h2>Sign In</h2>
          </header>
          <section>
            <Input
              autoComplete="off"
              name="emailOrUsername"
              placeholder="Email Or Username"
              onChange={onChange}
              value={values.emailOrUsername}
            />
            <Input
              name="password"
              type="password"
              placeholder="Password"
              onChange={onChange}
```

```
                value={values.password}
              />
              <div className="actions">
                <Button onClick={(): Promise<void> => handleSubmit(values)}>
                  Login
                </Button>
                <Button color="success">
                  Register
                </Button>
              </div>
            </section>
          </CSS.LoginBox>
        </CSS.Login>
      </>
    )
  }
export default Login
```

As you can see, the `login` function that is executed in the `handleSubmit` comes from our `UserContext`. This will execute the `login` mutation when the user needs to perform a login, and the `getUser` query to validate if a logged user is valid. Let's create that `User Context` (Context API), which should be located in packages/frontend/src/contexts/user.tsx:

```
import { useMutation, useQuery } from '@apollo/client'
import { getGraphQlError, parseDebugData, redirectTo } from '@web-builder/
utils'
import React, { createContext, FC, ReactElement,
useEffect,useMemo,useState} from 'react'
import { useCookies } from 'react-cookie'
import Config from '~/config'
import GET_USER_QUERY from '~/graphql/user/getUser.query'
import LOGIN_MUTATION from '~/graphql/user/login.mutation'
// Interfaces
```

```
interface IUserContext {
  login(input: any): any
  user: any
}
type Props = {
  children: ReactElement
}
// Creating context
export const UserContext = createContext<IUserContext>({
  login: () => null,
  user: null
})
const UserProvider: FC<Props> = ({ children }) => {
  // States
  const [cookies, setCookie] = useCookies()
  const [user, setUser] = useState(null)
  // Mutations
  const [loginMutation] = useMutation(LOGIN_MUTATION)
  // Queries
  const { data: dataUser } = useQuery(GET_USER_QUERY, {
    variables: {
      at: cookies[`at-${Config.site}`] || ''
    }
  })
  // Effects
  useEffect(() => {
    if (dataUser) {
      setUser(dataUser.getUser)
    }
  }, [dataUser])
  async function login(input:{emailOrUsername: string;password: string }):
Promise<any> {
    try {
      const { data: dataLogin } = await loginMutation({
        variables: {
          emailOrUsername: input.emailOrUsername,
          password: input.password
```

```
        }
      })
      if (dataLogin) {
        setCookie(`at-${Config.site}`, dataLogin.login.token, {
          path: '/',
          maxAge: 45 * 60 * 1000
        })
        return dataLogin.login.token
      }
    } catch (err) {
      return getGraphQlError(err)
    }
    return null
  }
  const context = useMemo(() => ({
    login,
    user
  }), [user])
  return <UserContext.Provider value={context}>{children}</UserContext.
Provider>
}
export default UserProvider
```

Now let's create our `login` mutation, which will receive two parameters (`$emailOrUsername` and `$password`). This file should be located in `packages/frontend/src/graphql/user/login.mutation.ts`:

```
import { gql } from '@apollo/client'
export default gql`
  mutation login($emailOrUsername: String!, $password: String!) {
    login(input: { emailOrUsername: $emailOrUsername, password: $password
}) {
      token
    }
  }
```

After that, we need to create the `getUser` query, which will take the `accessToken` (at) as a parameter and validate if the connected user is valid. This file exists in `packages/frontend/src/graphql/user/getUser.query.ts`:

```
import { gql } from '@apollo/client'
export default gql`
  query getUser($at: String!) {
    getUser(at: $at) {
      id
      email
      username
      role
      active
    }
  }
```

There are two more things to do. The first thing is to add our `UserProvider` as a wrapper of our application; we need to do this on a special page called "`_app.tsx`" inside the pages directory:

```
import { ApolloProvider } from '@apollo/client'
import React, { FC } from 'react'
import Config from '~/config'
import GlobalStyle from '~/components/GlobalStyles/GlobalStyles'
import { useApollo } from '~/contexts/apolloClient'
import FormProvider from '~/contexts/form'
import UserProvider from '~/contexts/user'
const App: FC<any> = ({ Component, pageProps }) => {
  const apolloClient = useApollo((pageProps && pageProps.
initialApolloState) || {})
  return (
    <>
      <GlobalStyle />
      <ApolloProvider client={apolloClient}>
        <UserProvider>
          <FormProvider>
            <Component {...pageProps} />
          </FormProvider>
        </UserProvider>
      </ApolloProvider>
    </>
  )
```

```
}
// @ts-ignore
App.getInitialProps = async () => ({
  ...Config
})
export default App
```

Finally, we need to create another special file called "_document.tsx" inside the pages directory. In this file, we will render the ServerStyleSheet from styled-components to be able to use styled-components in the server (Next.js):

```
import { cx } from '@web-creator/utils'
import Document, { Head, Html, Main, NextScript } from 'next/document'
import React from 'react'
import { ServerStyleSheet } from 'styled-components'
import Config from '~/config'
export default class MyDocument extends Document {
  static async getInitialProps(ctx: any) {
    const sheet = new ServerStyleSheet()
    const originalRenderPage = ctx.renderPage
    try {
      ctx.renderPage = () =>
        originalRenderPage({
          enhanceApp: (App: any) => (props: any) => {
            const themeClassname = 'theme--light'
            return sheet.collectStyles(
              <body className={cx.join(themeClassname)}>
                <App {...props} title={Config.siteTitle} />
              </body>
            )
          }
        })
      const initialProps = await Document.getInitialProps(ctx)
      return {
        ...initialProps,
        styles: (
          <>
            {initialProps.styles}
```

```
              {sheet.getStyleElement()}
            </>
          )
        }
      } finally {
        sheet.seal()
      }
    }
    render() {
      return (
        <Html>
          <Head>
            <link rel="icon" type="image/x-icon" href="/images/favicon.png" />
          </Head>
          <Main />
          <NextScript />
        </Html>
      )
    }
}
```

Creating our sites configuration

As we did in our API project, we need to create a configuration for our sites. Let's start by creating our SiteConfiguration type, the file for which will be located in packages/frontend/src/types/config.ts:

```
import { ValueOf } from '@web-creator/utils'
// Here you add your sites
export const Site = {
  SanPancho: 'san-pancho',
  Codejobs: 'codejobs',
  BlankPage: 'blank-page'
} as const
export type Site = ValueOf<typeof Site>
export type Mode = 'production' | 'development'
export enum DeploymentType {
  PRODUCTION = 'production',
  STAGING = 'staging',
```

```
    DEVELOPMENT = 'development'
}
export interface SiteConfiguration {
  siteTitle: string
  domainName: string
  hostname?: string
  mode?: string
  api?: {
    uri: string
}
  pages: string[]
  custom?: any
}
export interface SiteBuilderConfiguration extends SiteConfiguration {
  site: Site
  homeUrl: string
}
```

The configuration we will do is for the san-pancho site, and you should add this file to packages/frontend/src/sites/san-pancho/config.ts:

```
import path from 'path'
import { SiteConfiguration } from '../../types/config'
export const config: SiteConfiguration = {
  siteTitle: 'Cabañas San Pancho',
  domainName: 'ranchosanpancho.com',
  pages: ['index', 'login']
}
```

After this, we must create our main config.ts file, which should be in packages/frontend/src/config.ts:

```
import { is } from '@web-creator/utils'
// Importing sites configurations
import { config as blankPageConfig } from './sites/blank-page/config'
import { config as sanPanchoConfig } from './sites/san-pancho/config'
import { config as codejobsConfig } from './sites/codejobs/config'
import { Site, SiteBuilderConfiguration, SiteConfiguration } from './
types/config'
```

```
const isProduction = process.env.NODE_ENV === 'production'
const isLocal = process.env.LOCAL === 'true'
const isLocalProduction = isProduction && isLocal
// Getting site configuration
const getSiteConfig = (site: Site): SiteConfiguration => {
  switch (site) {
    case Site.SanPancho:
        return sanPanchoConfig
    case Site.Codejobs:
      return codejobsConfig
    default:
      return blankPageConfig
  }
}
// Building configuration
const buildConfig = (): SiteBuilderConfiguration => {
  // Server site
  let site = process.env.SITE as Site
  // On client side we grab the site from Next props
  if (is.Browser()) {
    const { props } = window.__NEXT_DATA__
    if (props && props.site) {
      site = props.site
    }
  } else if (!site) {
    throw 'You must specify a site (E.g. SITE=san-pancho npm run dev)'
  }
  const siteConfig = getSiteConfig(site)
  // Building configuration based on the environment and site configuration
  const config: SiteBuilderConfiguration = {
    ...siteConfig,
    api: {
      uri: isProduction && !isLocalProduction
        ? `https://${siteConfig.domainName}/graphql`
        : `http://localhost:4000/graphql`
    },
```

```
    site,
    homeUrl: `https://${siteConfig.domainName}`,
    hostname: isProduction && !isLocalProduction ? siteConfig.domainName :
'localhost',
    mode: isProduction ? 'production' : 'development'
  }
  return config
}
const Config = buildConfig()
export default Config
```

Putting everything together

The last piece of the puzzle is our server.ts file, which will handle Next.js, our static directories, and routes. Let's break down the file into parts and see each one in detail. This file should be in packages/frontend/src/server.ts.

The first thing we need to do is to import some dependencies and the site configuration:

```
import cookieParser from 'cookie-parser'
import express, { Application, NextFunction, Request, Response } from
'express'
import nextJS from 'next'
import path from 'path'
import { ts } from '@web-creator/utils'
import Config from './config'
import { isConnected } from './lib/middlewares/user'
import { Site } from './types/config'
```

Then we need to check that the SITE being passed in the terminal is actually valid:

```
// Site
const site: string = process.env.SITE ?? 'blank-page'
// Validating service
if (!ts.includes(Site, site)) {
  throw 'Invalid site'
}
```

If the site is valid, then we prepare our Next and Express applications:

```
// Setting up Next App
```

```
const { hostname } = Config
const port = 3000
const dev = process.env.NODE_ENV !== 'production'
const nextApp = nextJS({ dev, hostname, port })
const handle = nextApp.getRequestHandler()
// Running Next App
nextApp.prepare().then(() => {
  // Express application
  const app: Application = express()
```

We also need to configure our cookieParser to be able to use cookies and set up our site's static directories, so we can have a shared public folder and then specific static directories inside each site:

```
  // Cookies
  app.use(cookieParser())
  // Sites static directories
  app.use(express.static(path.join(__dirname, '../public')))
  app.use(express.static(path.join(__dirname, `./sites/${Config.site}/
static`)))
```

Next, we'll handle our custom routes next and add additional protection to specific routes, such as /dashboard. We want to ensure that only connected users can access this route. For this, we will use the isConnected middleware to validate whether a user is connected. If the user is not connected, we will redirect them to the login page:

```
  // Custom Routes
  app.get('/logout', (req: Request, res: Response) => {
    const redirect: any = req.query.redirectTo || '/'
    // The "at (accessToken)" cookie will be per site, like: "at-san-
pancho" or "at-codejobs".
    res.clearCookie(`at-${Config.site}`)
    res.redirect(redirect)
  })
  app.get(
    '/dashboard',
    isConnected(true, ['god', 'admin', 'editor'], '/login?redirectTo=/
dashboard'),
```

```
      (req: Request, res: Response, next: NextFunction) => next()
   )
```

Finally, all other traffic is going to be handled by Next.js; then we listen to port 3000:

```
   // Traffic handling
   app.all('*', (req: Request, res: Response) => handle(req, res))
   // Listening...
   app.listen(3000)
```

Demo time!

After all of those configurations, we are ready to run our project and see if it works. We will need to run it in a similar way to how we did on the API, but instead of the SERVICE variable, we will use the SITE variable. We also need to specify which site we want to run (san-pancho or codejobs). If you try to run some other site that does not exist, you will get an error. Let's try that to test the validation of the sites:

```
→ frontend git:(main) ✗ SITE=fake-site npm run dev

> @web-creator/frontend@1.0.0 dev
> cross-env NODE_ENV=development npm run next:dev


> @web-creator/frontend@1.0.0 next:dev
> ts-node src/server.ts

'Invalid site'
npm ERR! Lifecycle script `next:dev` failed with error:
npm ERR! Error: command failed
npm ERR!   in workspace: @web-creator/frontend@1.0.0
npm ERR!   at location: /Users/czantany/projects/React18-Book/codes/Chapter15/web-creator/packages/frontend
npm ERR! Lifecycle script `dev` failed with error:
npm ERR! Error: command failed
npm ERR!   in workspace: @web-creator/frontend@1.0.0
npm ERR!   at location: /Users/czantany/projects/React18-Book/codes/Chapter15/web-creator/packages/frontend
```

Figure 14.16: getGuests query

The validation works fine. Now, let's run our san-pancho site with the SITE=san-pancho npm run dev command:

San Pancho Index Page

Figure 14.17: San Pancho Index Page

If everything works fine, you should see the preceding. Next, let's run our `codejobs` site with `SITE=codejobs npm run dev`:

Figure 14.18: Codejobs Index Page

Nice, so both our sites work as expected!

Now it's time to test our login page for each site. Let's start with San Pancho:

Figure 14.19: San Pancho Sign In page

Then let's test the Codejobs login page:

Figure 14.20: Codejobs Sign In page

Everything seems good so far. Now let's test the login with our default credentials, which are **username:** admin and **password:** 12345678:

Dashboard for San Pancho

Logout

Figure 14.21: Dashboard for San Pancho

Nice! So now we are connected to San Pancho's dashboard.

One thing I want to highlight here is the cookie name we used for the user session, which is `at-san-pancho`. However, even if you already performed a login in San Pancho, if you try to access the Codejobs dashboard, you will be required to log in again because each site session is independent of the other:

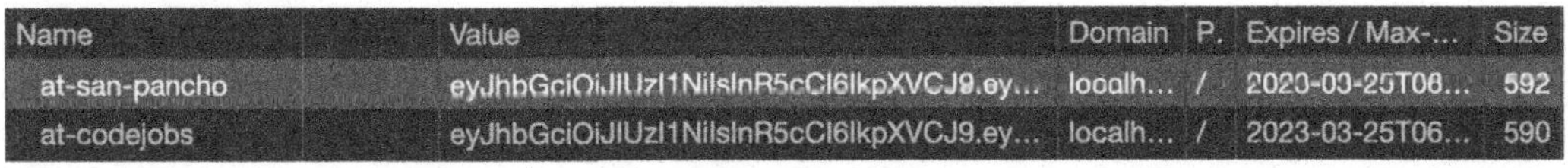

Name	Value	Domain	P.	Expires / Max-...	Size
at-san-pancho	eyJhbGciOiJIUzI1NiIsInR5cCI6IkpXVCJ9.ey...	localh...	/	2020-03-25T06...	592
at-codejobs	eyJhbGciOiJIUzI1NiIsInR5cCI6IkpXVCJ9.ey...	localh...	/	2023-03-25T06...	590

Figure 14.22: Site cookies

Finally, let's test hitting a URL that does not exist on our sites:

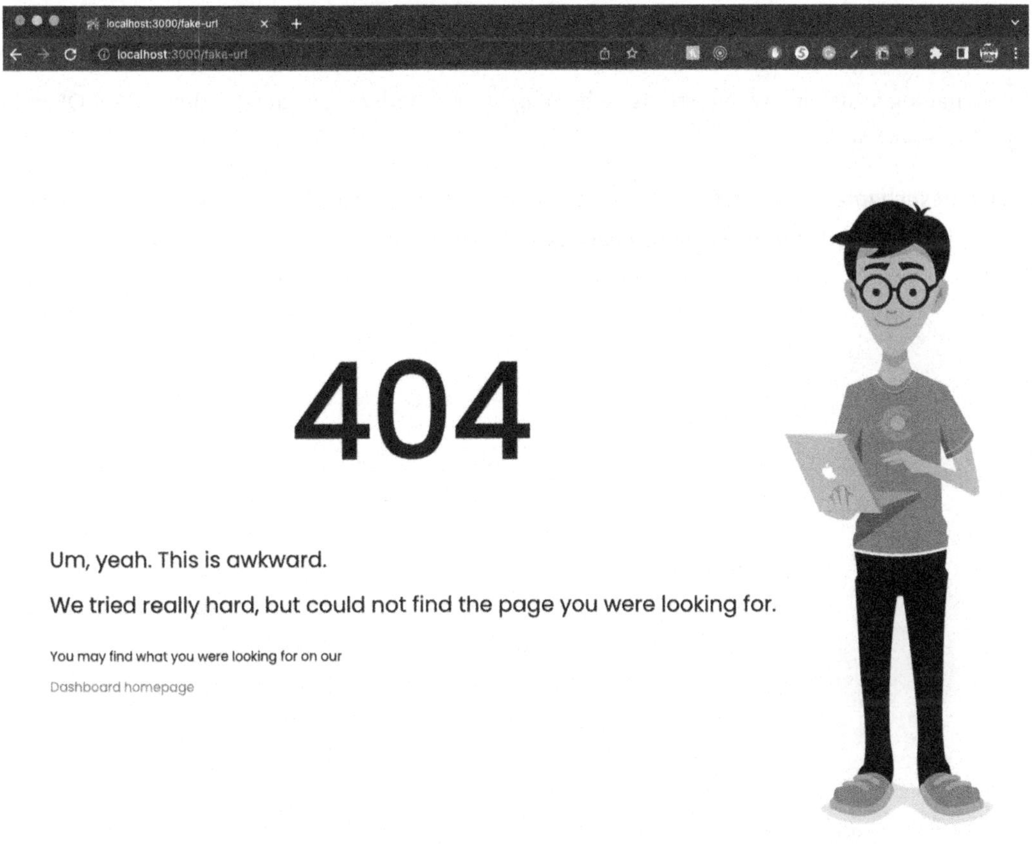

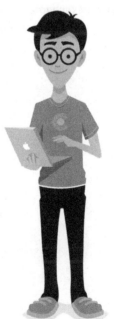

localhost:3000/fake-url
localhost:3000/fake-url
404
Um, yeah. This is awkward.
We tried really hard, but could not find the page you were looking for.
You may find what you were looking for on our
Dashboard homepage

Figure 14.23: 404 error page

You should see a `404` page that will be shared across both sites.

Summary

Congratulations on making it this far! Without a doubt, this chapter has been complex, yet incredibly interesting. Now, you have the bare bones ready to begin working on your personal websites.

Throughout the course of this chapter, you acquired a comprehensive set of skills. You learned how to create User models and GraphQL types, understand error handling, and set up custom services like a CRM. You successfully navigated through the process of building a Sites system, enhanced user experience with a Page Switcher, and established a shared login system. Furthermore, you gained knowledge in managing configurations, working with "seeds" or default data for models, and consolidating components into a command file such as server.ts. As a result, you are now proficient in synchronizing models, starting up the Apollo Server, running tests, and effectively troubleshooting any issues that may arise. In essence, you have established a robust foundation in managing multi-site web systems, enhancing user experience, understanding GraphQL, and troubleshooting.

In the next chapter, you will have the opportunity to expand your skills further as you learn how to improve the performance of your React applications.

15

Improving the Performance of Your Applications

The effective performance of a web application is critical to providing a good user experience and improving conversions. The React library implements different techniques to render our components fast and to touch the **Document Object Model (DOM)** as little as possible. Applying changes to the DOM is usually expensive, so minimizing the number of operations is crucial.

However, there are some scenarios where React cannot optimize the process, and it's up to the developer to implement specific solutions to make the application run smoothly.

In this chapter, we will go through the basic concepts of React and we will learn how to use some APIs to help the library find the optimal path to update the DOM without degrading the user experience. We will also see some common mistakes that can harm our applications and make them slower.

We should avoid optimizing our components for the sake of it, and it is important to apply the techniques that we will see in the following sections only when they are needed.

In this chapter, we will cover the following topics:

- How reconciliation works and how we can help React do a better job using keys
- Common optimization techniques and common performance-related mistakes
- Useful tools and libraries to make our applications run faster
- What it means to use immutable data and how to do it

Technical requirements

To complete this chapter, you will require the following:

- Node.js 19+
- Visual Studio Code

You can find the code for this chapter in the book's GitHub repository at `https://github.com/PacktPublishing/React-18-Design-Patterns-and-Best-Practices-Fourth-Edition/tree/main/Chapter15`.

How reconciliation works

Most of the time, React is fast enough by default, and you do not need to do anything more to improve the performance of your application. React utilizes different techniques to optimize the rendering of the components on the screen.

When React must display a component, it calls its render method and the render methods of its children recursively. The render method of a component returns a tree of React elements, which React uses to decide which DOM operations must be done to update the UI.

Whenever the component state changes, React calls the render method on the nodes again, and it compares the result with the previous tree of React elements. The library is smart enough to figure out the minimum set of operations required to apply the expected changes on the screen. This process is called **reconciliation,** and it is managed transparently by React. Thanks to that, we can easily describe how our components must look at a given point in time in a declarative way and let the library do the rest.

React tries to apply the smallest possible number of operations on the DOM because touching the DOM is an expensive operation.

However, comparing two trees of elements is not free either, and React makes two assumptions to reduce its complexity:

- If two elements have a different type, they render a different tree.
- Developers can use keys to mark children as stable across different render calls.

The second point is interesting from a developer's perspective because it gives us a tool to help React render our views faster.

By default, when coming back to the children of a DOM node, both lists of children are iterated by React at the same time, and whenever there is a difference, it creates a mutation.

Let's look at some examples. Converting between the following two trees will work well when adding an element at the end of the children:

```
<ul>
  <li>Carlos</li>
  <li>Javier</li>
</ul>
<ul>
  <li>Carlos</li>
  <li>Javier</li>
  <li>Emmanuel</li>
</ul>
```

The two `<li>Carlos</li>` trees match the two `<li>Javier</li>` trees by React and then it will insert the `<li>Emmanuel</li>` tree.

Inserting an element at the beginning produces inferior performance if implemented naively. If we look at the example, it works very poorly when converting between these two trees:

```
<ul>
  <li>Carlos</li>
  <li>Javier</li>
</ul>
<ul>
  <li>Emmanuel</li>
  <li>Carlos</li>
  <li>Javier</li>
</ul>
```

Every child will be mutated by React instead of it realizing that it can keep the subtrees line, `<li>Carlos</li>` and `<li>Javier</li>`, intact. This could possibly be an issue. This problem can, of course, be solved and the way to do this is with the key attribute that is supported by React. Let's look at that next.

Using keys

Children possess keys and these keys are used by React to match children between the subsequent tree and the original tree. The tree conversion can be made efficient by adding a key to our previous example:

```
<ul>
```

```
    <li key="2018">Carlos</li>
    <li key="2019">Javier</li>
  </ul>
  <ul>
    <li key="2017">Emmanuel</li>
    <li key="2018">Carlos</li>
    <li key="2019">Javier</li>
  </ul>
```

React now knows that the 2017 key is the new one and that the 2018 and 2019 keys have just moved.

Finding a key is not hard. The element that you will be displaying might already have a unique ID. So, the key can just come from your data:

```
  <li key={element.id}>{element.title}</li>
```

A new ID can be added to your model by you, or the key can be generated by some parts of the content. The key must only be unique among its siblings; it does not have to be unique globally. An item index in the array can be passed as a key, but it is now considered a bad practice. However, if the items are never recorded, this can work well. The reorders will seriously affect performance.

If you are rendering multiple items using a map function and you don't specify the key property, you will get this message: *Warning: Each child in an array or iterator should have a unique key prop.*

Let's learn some optimization techniques in our next section.

Optimization techniques

It is important to notice that, in all the examples in this book, we are using apps that have either been created with **create-react-app** or have been created from scratch, but always with the development version of React.

Using the development version of React is very useful for coding and debugging as it gives you all the necessary information to fix various issues. However, all the checks and warnings come with a cost, which we want to avoid in production.

So, the very first optimization that we should do to our applications is to build the bundle, setting the NODE_ENV environment variable to production. This is easy with webpack, and it is just a matter of using DefinePlugin in the following way:

```
  new webpack.DefinePlugin({
    'process.env': {
```

```
      NODE_ENV: JSON.stringify('production')
    }
  })
```

To achieve the best performance, we not only want to create the bundle with the production flag activated, but we also want to split our bundles, one for our application and one for node_modules.

To do so, you need to use the new optimization node in webpack:

```
optimization: {
  splitChunks: {
   cacheGroups: {
     default: false,
     commons: {
      test: /node_modules/,
      name: 'vendor',
      chunks: 'all'
     }
    }
   }
 }
```

Webpack has two modes, *development* and *production*. By default, production mode is enabled, meaning the code will be minified and compressed when you compile your bundles using production mode; you can specify it with the following code block:

```
{
  mode: process.env.NODE_ENV === 'production' ? 'production' :
'development',
}
```

Your webpack.config.ts file should look like this:

```
module.exports = {
   entry: './index.ts',
   optimization: {
    splitChunks: {
     cacheGroups: {
       default: false,
       commons: {
        test: /node_modules/,
```

```
      name: 'vendor',
      chunks: 'all'
    }
   }
  }
 },
 plugins: [
  new webpack.DefinePlugin({
   'process.env': {
    NODE_ENV: JSON.stringify('production')
   }
  })
 ],
 mode: process.env.NODE_ENV === 'production' ? 'production' :
'development'
}
```

With this webpack configuration, we are going to get very optimized bundles; one for our vendors and one for the actual application.

Tools and libraries

In the next section, we will go through several techniques, tools, and libraries that we can apply to our code base to monitor and improve performance.

Immutability

The new React Hooks, such as React.memo, use a shallow comparison method against the props, which means that if we pass an object as a prop and we mutate one of its values, we do not get the expected behavior.

In fact, a shallow comparison cannot find mutation on the properties and the components never get re-rendered, except when the object itself changes. One way to solve this issue is by using immutable data, data that, once it gets created, cannot be mutated.

For example, we can set the state in the following mode:

```
const [state, setState] = useState({})
const obj = state.obj
obj.foo = 'bar'
setState({ obj })
```

Even if the value of the foo attribute of the object is changed, the reference to the object is still the same and the shallow comparison does not recognize it.

What we can do instead is create a new instance every time we mutate the object, as follows:

```
const obj = Object.assign({}, state.obj, { foo: 'bar' })
setState({ obj })
```

In this case, we get a new object with the foo property set to bar, and the shallow comparison will be able to find the difference. With ES6 and Babel, there is another way to express the same concept in a more elegant way, and it is by using the object spread operator:

```
const obj = {
  ...state.obj,
  foo: 'bar'
}
setState({ obj })
```

This structure is more concise than the previous one, and it produces the same result, but, at the time of writing, it requires the code to be transpiled to be executed inside the browser.

React provides some immutability helpers to make it easy to work with immutable objects, and there is also a popular library called immutable.js, which has more powerful features, but it requires you to learn new APIs.

Babel plugins

There are also a couple of interesting **Babel** plugins that we can install and use to improve the performance of our React applications. They make the applications faster, optimizing parts of the code at build time.

The first one is the React **constant elements transformer**, which finds all the static elements that do not change depending on the props and extracts them from render (or the functional components) to avoid calling _jsx unnecessarily.

Using a Babel plugin is straightforward. We first install it with npm:

```
npm install --save-dev @babel/plugin-transform-react-constant-elements
```

You need to create the .babelrc file and add a plugins key with an array that has a value of the list of plugins that we want to activate:

```
{
```

```
    "plugins": ["@babel/plugin-transform-react-constant-elements"]
}
```

The second Babel plugin that we can choose to use to improve performance is the React inline elements transform, which replaces all the JSX declarations (or the _jsx calls) with a more optimized version of them to make execution faster.

Install the plugin using the following command:

```
npm install --save-dev @babel/plugin-transform-react-inline-elements
```

Next, you can easily add the plugin to the array of plugins in the .babelrc file, as follows:

```
{
    "plugins": ["@babel/plugin-transform-react-inline-elements"]
}
```

Both plugins should be used only in production because they make debugging harder in development mode. So far, we have learned a lot of optimization techniques and how to configure some plugins using webpack.

Summary

Our journey through performance is finished, and we can now optimize our applications to give users a better UX.

In this chapter, we learned how the reconciliation algorithm works and how React always tries to take the shortest path to apply changes to the DOM. We can also help the library to optimize its job by using keys. Once you've found your bottlenecks, you can apply one of the techniques we have seen in this chapter to fix the issue.

We have learned how refactoring and designing the structure of your components in the proper way could provide a performance boost. Our goal is to have small components that do one single thing in the best possible way. At the end of the chapter, we talked about immutability, and we've seen why it's important not to mutate data to make React.memo and shallowCompare do their job. Finally, we ran through different tools and libraries that can make your applications faster.

In the next chapter, we'll look at testing and debugging using Jest, the React Testing Library, and React DevTools.

Join our community on Discord

Join our community's Discord space for discussion with the author and other readers:

`https://packt.link/React18DesignPatterns4e`

16
Testing and Debugging

Thanks to its components, React makes it easy to test our applications. There are many different tools available that we can use to create tests with React. In this chapter, we will cover the most popular ones to understand the benefits they provide.

Jest is an *all-in-one* testing framework solution maintained by Christoph Nakazawa from Meta and contributors within the community and aims to give you the best developer experience.

By the end of this chapter, you'll be able to create a test environment from scratch and write tests for your application's components.

In this chapter, we will look at the following topics:

- Why it is important to test our applications and how they help developers move faster
- How to set up a Jest environment to test components using Enzyme
- What the React Testing Library is and why it is a *must-have* for testing React applications
- How to test events
- How to implement Vitest
- React DevTools and some error-handling techniques

Technical requirements

To complete this chapter, you will need the following:

- Node.js 19+
- Visual Studio Code

You can find the code for this chapter in the book's GitHub repository: `https://github.com/PacktPublishing/React-18-Design-Patterns-and-Best-Practices-Fourth-Edition/tree/main/Chapter16`.

Understanding the benefits of testing

Testing web UIs has always been a difficult job. From unit to end-to-end tests, the fact that the interfaces depend on browsers, user interactions, and many other variables makes it difficult to implement an effective testing strategy.

If you've ever tried to write end-to-end tests for the web, you'll know how complex it is to get consistent results and how the results are often affected by false negatives due to different factors, such as the network. Other than that, user interfaces are frequently updated to improve the experience, maximize conversions, or simply add new features.

If tests are hard to write and maintain, developers are less prone to cover their applications. On the other hand, tests are important because they make developers more confident with their code, which is reflected in speed and quality. If a piece of code is well tested (and the tests are well written), developers can be sure that it works and is ready to ship. Similarly, thanks to tests, it becomes easier to refactor the code because tests guarantee that the functionalities do not change during the rewrite.

Developers tend to focus on the feature they are currently implementing, and sometimes it is hard to know if other parts of the application are affected by those changes. Tests help to avoid regressions because they can tell if the new code breaks the old tests. Greater confidence in writing new features leads to faster releases.

Testing the main functionalities of an application makes the code base more solid, and whenever a new bug is found, it can be reproduced, fixed, and covered by tests so that it does not happen again in the future.

Luckily, React (and the component era) makes testing user interfaces easy and efficient. Testing components, or trees of components, is a less arduous job because every single part of the application has its responsibilities and boundaries. If components are built in the right way, if they are pure and aim for composability and reusability, they can be tested as simple functions.

Another great power that modern tools bring us is the ability to run tests using Node.js and the console. Spinning up a browser for every single test makes tests slower and less predictable, degrading the developer experience; instead, running the tests using the console is faster.

Testing components only in the console can sometimes give unexpected behaviors when they are rendered in a real browser, but in my experience, this is rare. When we test React components, we want to make sure that they work properly and that, given different sets of props, their output is always correct.

We may also want to cover all the various states that a component can have. The state might change by clicking a button, so we write tests to check if all the event handlers are doing what they are supposed to do.

When all the functionalities of the component are covered, but we want to do more, we can write tests to verify the component's behavior on **edge cases**. Edge cases are states that the component can assume when, for example, all the props are null or there is an error. Once the tests are written, we can be pretty confident that the component behaves as expected.

Testing a single component is great, but it does not guarantee that multiple individually tested components will still work once they are put together. As we will see later, with React, we can mount a tree of components and test the integration between them.

There are different techniques that we can use to write tests, and one of the most popular ones is **test-driven development (TDD)**. Applying TDD means writing the tests first and then writing the code to pass the tests.

Following this pattern helps us to write better code because we are forced to think more about the design before implementing the functionalities, which usually leads to higher quality.

So, now that we have covered all of this, let's roll up our sleeves and start writing tests for our React components. We will also learn about a cool way of writing code called test-driven development and use a handy tool called Jest to simplify our JavaScript testing. Are you ready? Let's dive in and start working with real code!

Painless JavaScript testing with Jest

The most important way to learn how to test React components in the right way is by writing some code, and that is what we are going to do in this section.

The React documentation says that Facebook uses Jest to tests its components. However, React does not force you to use a particular test framework, and you can use your favorite one without any problems. To see Jest in action, we are going to create a project from scratch, install all the dependencies, and write a component with some tests. It'll be fun!

The first thing to do is to move into a new folder and run the following:

```
npm init
```

Once package.json is created, we can start installing the dependencies, with the first one being the jest package itself:

```
npm install --save-dev jest
```

To tell npm that we want to use the jest command to run the tests, we must add the following scripts to package.json:

```
"scripts": {
  "build": "webpack",
  "start": "node ./dist/server",
  "test": "jest",
  "test:coverage": "jest --coverage"
}
```

To write components and tests using ES6 and JSX, we must install all Babel-related packages so that Jest can use them to transpile and understand the code.

The second set of dependencies is installed as follows:

```
npm install --save-dev @babel/core @babel/preset-env @babel/preset-react
ts-jest
```

As you may know, we now have to create a .babelrc file, which is used by Babel to know the presets and the plugins that we would like to use inside the project.

The .babelrc file looks like the following:

```
{
  "presets": ["@babel/preset-env", "@babel/preset-react"]
}
```

Now, it is time to install React and ReactDOM, which we need to create and render components:

```
npm install --save react react-dom
```

The setup is ready, and we can run Jest against the ES6 code and render our components in the DOM, but there is one more thing to do.

We need to install `jest-environment-jsdom`, `@testing-library/jest-dom`, and `@testing-library/react`:

```
npm install @testing-library/jest-dom @testing-library/react jest-
environment-jsdom
```

After you have installed these packages, you must create the `jest.config.js` file:

```
module.exports = {
  preset: 'ts-jest',
  setupFilesAfterEnv: ['<rootDir>/setUpTests.ts'],
  testEnvironment: 'jsdom'
}
```

Then, let's create the `setUpTests.ts` file:

```
import '@testing-library/jest-dom/extend-expect'
```

Now, let's imagine we have a `Hello` component (`src/components/Hello/index.tsx`):

```
import React, { FC } from 'react'
type Props = {
  name?: string
}
function Hello({ name }: Props) {
  return <h1 className="Hello">Hello {name || 'World'}</h1>
}
Hello.defaultProps = {
  name: ''
}
export default Hello
```

In order to test this component, we need to create a file with the same name but add the `.test` (or `.spec`) suffix to the new file. This will be our test file:

```
import React from 'react'
import { render, cleanup } from '@testing-library/react'
import Hello from './index'
describe('Hello Component', () => {
  it('should render Hello World', () => {
    const wrapper = render(<Hello />)
```

```
    expect(wrapper.getByText('Hello World')).toBeInTheDocument()
  })
  it('should render the name prop', () => {
    const wrapper = render(<Hello name="Carlos" />)
    expect(wrapper.getByText('Hello Carlos')).toBeInTheDocument()
  })
  it('should has .Home classname', () => {
    const wrapper = render(<Hello />)
    expect(wrapper.container.firstChild).toHaveClass('Hello')
  })
  afterAll(cleanup)
})
```

Then, in order to run the test, you need to execute the following command:

```
npm test
```

You should see this result:

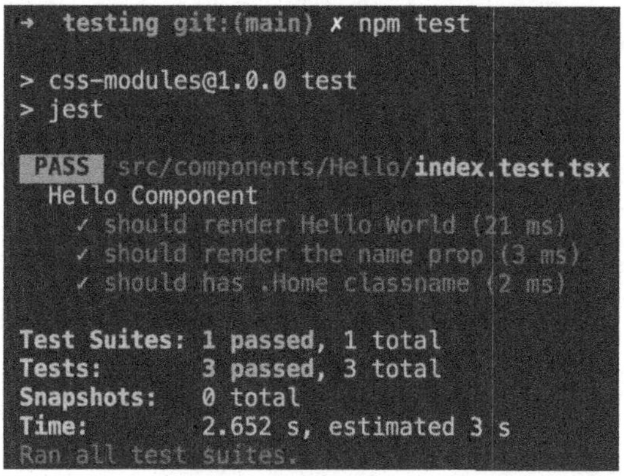

Figure 16.1: npm test

The **PASS** label means that all tests have been passed successfully; if at least one test failed, you will see the **FAIL** label. Let's change one of our tests to make it fail:

```
it('should render the name prop', () => {
  const wrapper = render(<Hello name="Carlos" />)
  expect(wrapper.getByText('Hello World')).toBeInTheDocument()
})
```

This is the result:

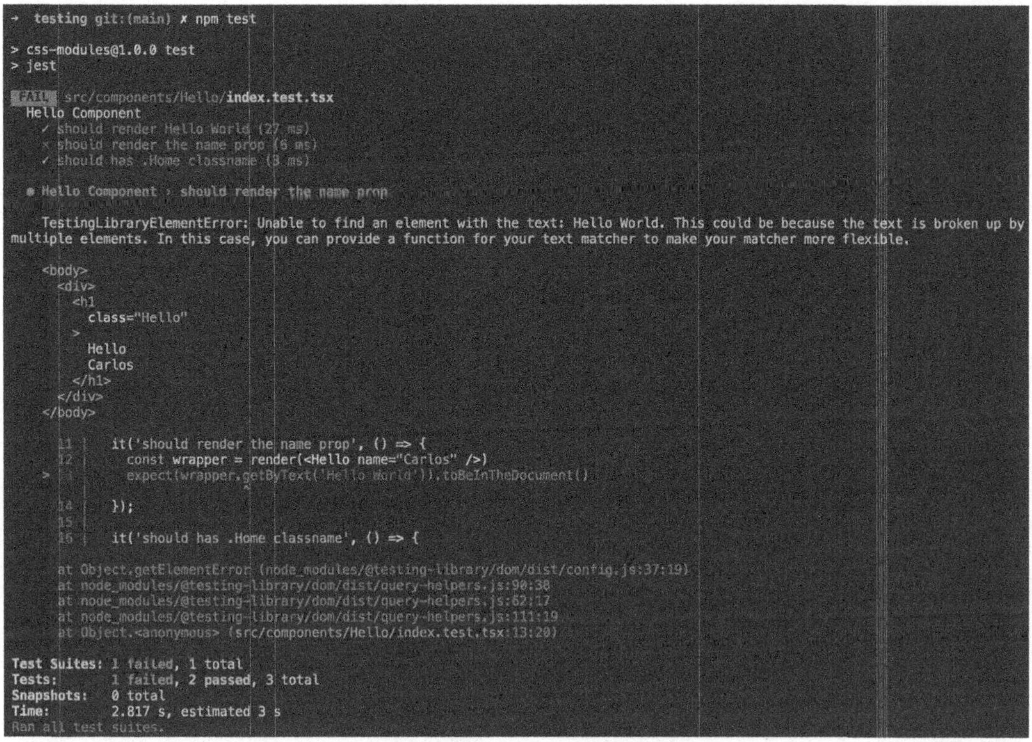

Figure 16.2: Fail tests

As you can see, the **FAIL** label is specified with an **X**. Also, the expected and received values provide useful information, and you can see which value is expected and which value is received.

If you want to see the coverage percentage of all your unit tests, you can execute the following command:

```
npm run test:coverage
```

The result is the following:

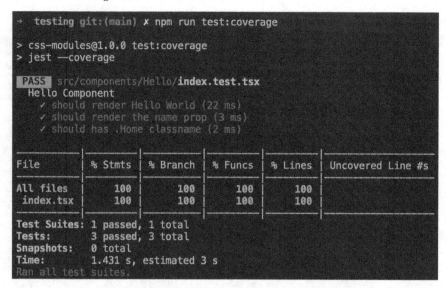

Figure 16.3: Passing tests

The coverage also generates an HTML version of the result; it creates a directory called `coverage` and inside another called `Icov-report`. If you open the `index.html` file in your browser, you will see the HTML version as follows:

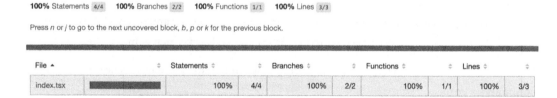

Figure 16.4: Icov-report

Now that you have done your first tests and you know how to collect the coverage data, let's see how we can test events in the next section.

Testing events

Events are very common in any web application, and we need to test them as well, so let's learn how to test events. For this, let's create a new `ShowInformation` component:

```
import { useState, ChangeEvent } from 'react'
```

```
function ShowInformation() {
  const [state, setState] = useState({ name: '', age: 0, show: false })
  const handleOnChange = (e: ChangeEvent<HTMLInputElement>) => {
    const { name, value } = e.target
    setState({
      ...state,
      [name]: value
    })
  }
  const handleShowInformation = () => {
    setState({
      ...state,
      show: true
    })
  }
  if (state.show) {
    return (
      <div className="ShowInformation">
      <h1>Personal Information</h1>
        <div className="personalInformation">
          <p><strong>Name:</strong> {state.name}</p>
          <p><strong>Age:</strong> {state.age}</p>
        </div>
      </div>
    )
  }

  return (
    <div className="ShowInformation">
      <h1>Personal Information</h1>
      <p><strong>Name:</strong></p>
      <p>
      <input name="name" type="text" value={state.name}
onChange={handleOnChange} />
      </p>
      <p>
```

```
        <input name="age" type="number" value={state.age}
onChange={handleOnChange} />
      </p>
      <p><button onClick={handleShowInformation}>Show Information</
button></p>
    </div>
  )
}
export default ShowInformation
```

Now, let's create the test file at src/components/ShowInformation/index.test.tsx:

```
import { render, cleanup, fireEvent } from '@testing-library/react'
import ShowInformation from './index'
describe('Show Information Component', () => {
  let wrapper
  beforeEach(() => {
    wrapper = render(<ShowInformation />)
  })
  it ('should modify the name', () => {
    const nameInput = wrapper.container.
querySelector('input[name="name"]') as HTMLInputElement
    const ageInput = wrapper.container.querySelector('input[name="age"]')
as HTMLInputElement
    fireEvent.change(nameInput, { target: { value: 'Carlos' } })
    fireEvent.change(ageInput, { target: { value: 34 } })
    expect(nameInput.value).toBe('Carlos')
    expect(ageInput.value).toBe('34')
  })
  it ('should show the personal information when user clicks on the
button', () => {
    const button = wrapper.container.querySelector('button')
    fireEvent.click(button)
    const showInformation = wrapper.container.querySelector('.
personalInformation')
    expect(showInformation).toBeInTheDocument()
  })
})
```

```
    afterAll(cleanup)
})
```

If you run the test and it works fine, you should see this:

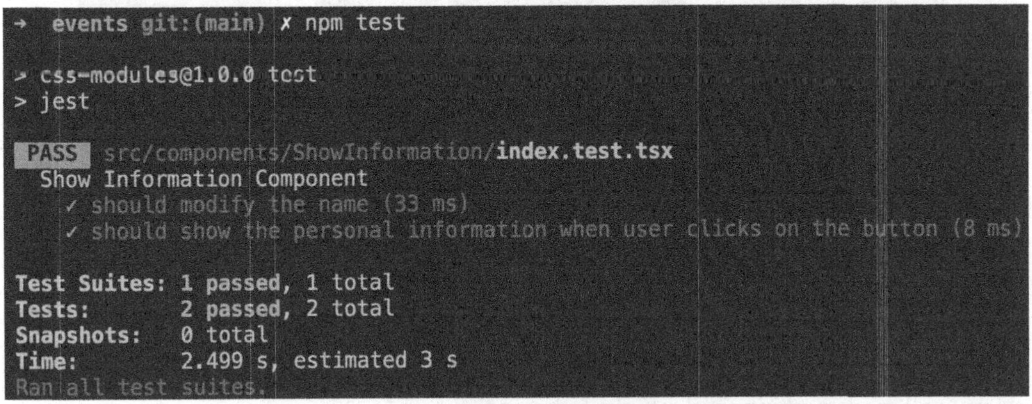

```
→   events git:(main) x npm test

> css-modules@1.0.0 test
> jest

 PASS  src/components/ShowInformation/index.test.tsx
  Show Information Component
    ✓ should modify the name (33 ms)
    ✓ should show the personal information when user clicks on the button (8 ms)

Test Suites: 1 passed, 1 total
Tests:       2 passed, 2 total
Snapshots:   0 total
Time:        2.499 s, estimated 3 s
Ran all test suites.
```

Figure 16.5: Passing tests

Introducing Vitest

Vitest is a unit test framework built on **Vite**, designed for speed and minimal configuration. It serves as a replacement for various testing tools such as Jest, Mocha, and Chai. Since Vitest is built on top of the Jest API, if you already know how to use Jest, it works in a similar manner.

In this context, we will utilize Vite, a build tool that aims to provide a fast and lean development experience for modern web projects.

Firstly, you need to install Vite globally with:

```
npm install vite -g
```

After it's installed, you need to create your first project with the npm command:

```
npm create vite@latest
```

It will ask you for the project name. You can use my-first-vite-project, then for the framework you want to use (React), and finally, choose the variant (TypeScript):

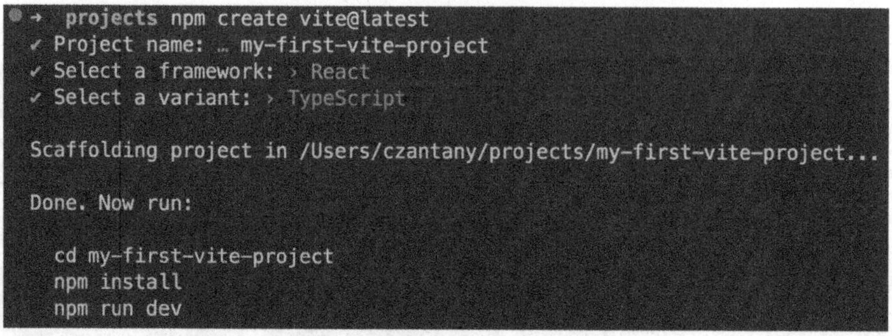

```
→  projects npm create vite@latest
✓ Project name: … my-first-vite-project
✓ Select a framework: › React
✓ Select a variant: › TypeScript

Scaffolding project in /Users/czantany/projects/my-first-vite-project...

Done. Now run:

  cd my-first-vite-project
  npm install
  npm run dev
```

Figure 16.6: npm create vite@latest

Next, you need to install the project dependencies and run the npm run dev command. If you do so, you will see something similar to the following on port 5173:

Figure 16.7: Vite app

Installing and configuring Vitest

Once you have your Vite app running, it is time to install Vitest. To do so, you simply need to run this command in your project terminal:

```
npm install -D vitest @test-library/react
```

After you've installed Vitest, you need to modify the `vite.config.ts` file with the following code:

```
/// <reference types="vitest" />
import react from '@vitejs/plugin-react'
import { defineConfig } from 'vite'

// https://vitejs.dev/config/
export default defineConfig({
  plugins: [react()],
  test: {
    environment: 'jsdom'
  }
})
```

As you can see, we will use the `jsdom` environment, so you'll need to install it as well:

```
npm install -D jsdom
```

Additionally, Vitest offers a plugin called Vitest UI, which enables Vitest to provide a visually appealing user interface for viewing and interacting with your tests in the browser. While it is an optional plugin, we will be using it. You can install it by executing the following command:

```
npm install -D @vitest/ui
```

In order to test your code, you need to add the test script to your `package.json` file using the `vitest --ui` command:

```
"scripts": {
  "dev": "vite",
  "build": "tsc && vite build",
  "preview": "vite preview",
  "test": "vitest --ui"
}
```

We will be using the same `Hello` component that we used for Jest, although there will be a few differences. You need to save this component at `src/components/Hello/index.tsx`:

```
import React, { FC } from 'react'
type Props = {
  name?: string
}
const Hello: FC<Props> = ({ name }) => <h1 className="Hello">Hello {name
|| "World"}</h1>
export default Hello
```

Then you need to create a test file called `index.test.tsx` under the same component directory:

```
import { cleanup, render } from '@testing-library/react'
import { afterAll, describe, expect, it } from 'vitest'
import Hello from './index'
describe("Hello Component", () => {
  it("should render Hello World", () => {
    const wrapper = render(<Hello />)
    expect(wrapper.getByText("Hello World")).toBeDefined()
  })

  it("should render the name prop", () => {
    const wrapper = render(<Hello name="Carlos" />)
    expect(wrapper.getByText("Hello Carlos")).toBeDefined()
  })

  it("should has .Home classname", () => {
    const wrapper = render(<Hello />)
    const firstChild = wrapper.container.firstChild as HTMLElement
    expect(firstChild?.classList.contains("Hello")).toBe(true)
  })

  afterAll(cleanup)
})
```

As you can see, the code is quite similar to Jest. However, one of the main differences is that we are now importing all the testing methods we will use, such as `afterAll`, `describe`, `expect`, and `it`.

If you run the `test` command, you should see something similar to this in your terminal:

```
⊗ → my-first-vite-project npm test

> my-first-vite-project@0.0.0 test
> vitest --ui


  DEV   v0.26.3 /Users/czantany/projects/my-first-vite-project
        UI started at http://localhost:51204/__vitest__/

 ✓ src/components/Hello/index.test.tsx (3)

 Test Files  1 passed (1)
      Tests  3 passed (3)
   Start at  02:03:22
   Duration  1.73s (transform 373ms, setup 0ms, collect 183ms, tests 36ms)


  PASS  Waiting for file changes...
        press h to show help, press q to quit
```

Figure 16.8: npm test

If you have noticed, there is a link that is generated by the Vitest UI plugin we installed earlier. If you click on that link, you will see the following:

Figure 16.9: Vitest UI

Currently, we only have one test file, but if you add more, you will see them listed on the sidebar on the left. Now, let's click on our current `Hello` test:

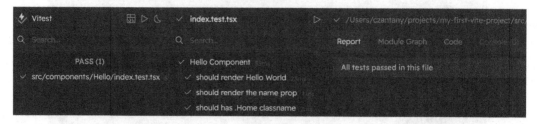

Figure 16.10 – Report

You will be able to see the test cases that are passing correctly. However, one of the most interesting advantages of this UI plugin is that you can even modify the test code directly in the browser by clicking on the **Code** tab:

```
✓ index.test.tsx               ▷    ✓ /Users/czantany/projects/my-first-vite-project/src/components/Hello/index.test.tsx
Q Search...                          Report    Module Graph    Code    Console (0)

✓ Hello Component               1 import { cleanup, render } from '@testing-library/react'
  ✓ should render Hello World   2 import { afterAll, describe, expect, it } from 'vitest'
                                3
  ✓ should render the name prop 4 import Hello from './index'
                                5
  ✓ should has .Home classname  6 describe("Hello Component", () => {
                                7   it("should render Hello World", () => {
                                8     const wrapper = render(<Hello />);
                                9     expect(wrapper.getByText("Hello World")).toBeDefined();
                               10   });
                               11
                               12   it("should render the name prop", () => {
                               13     const wrapper = render(<Hello name="Carlos" />);
                               14     expect(wrapper.getByText("Hello Carlos")).toBeDefined();
                               15   });
                               16
                               17   it("should has .Home classname", () => {
                               18     const wrapper = render(<Hello />);
                               19     const firstChild = wrapper.container.firstChild as HTMLElement;
                               20
                               21     expect(firstChild?.classList.contains("Hello")).toBe(true);
                               22   });
                               23
                               24   afterAll(cleanup);
                               25 });
                               26
```

Figure 16.11: Code

Let's modify our code to intentionally cause some tests to fail. You can change the first test to say "Hello Foo" instead of "Hello World" and make sure to save it (*Cmd + S*):

Figure 16.12: Failing test

As you can see, now our first test fails because it is unable to find the "Hello Foo" text.

Enabling globals

Personally, I prefer importing all the necessary functions or variables in a file. However, I am aware that when creating numerous test files, repeatedly importing global testing variables like describe, it, expect, and so on, can become tedious and cumbersome.

Fortunately, Vitest offers a configuration option to enable `globals`, eliminating the need to import them every time. To enable this feature, you need to modify your `vite.config.ts` file with the following code:

```
/// <reference types="vitest" />
/// <reference types="vite/client" />
import react from '@vitejs/plugin-react'
import { defineConfig } from 'vite'
// https://vitejs.dev/config/
export default defineConfig({
  plugins: [react()],
  test: {
    environment: "jsdom",
    globals: true
  }
})
```

After making the changes mentioned earlier, you also need to update your `tsconfig.json` file by adding the global types:

```
"compilerOptions": {
  "types": ["vitest/globals"]
}
```

After following these steps, you will now be able to remove the import of the `globals` in your test file. If you still encounter any TypeScript errors, it is likely that you will need to restart your TypeScript server or reload the window in your VSCode.

In-source testing

Vitest also offers a way to run tests within your source code alongside the implementation, similar to Rust's module tests.

Personally, I have an old-school approach, and I usually prefer to have a separate test file for my testing. However, there are situations where the component or functions being tested are very small, and creating a new test file may seem excessive.

To enable this feature, you need to modify your `vite.config.ts` file and add the `includeSource` option:

```
export default defineConfig({
```

```
  plugins: [react()],
  test: {
    environment: "jsdom",
    globals: true,
    includeSource: ["src/**/*.{ts,tsx}"]
  }
})
```

To resolve the TypeScript issues, you need to make another change by adding the vitest/importMeta type to your tsconfig.json file:

```
"compilerOptions": {
  "types": ["vitest/globals", "vitest/importMeta"]
}
```

Now, let's move our Hello component test file inside the same Hello component. Again, this is optional and is just to demonstrate that it is possible to do so. In the end, you can decide which testing approach to use.

To achieve this, we need to add an if statement inside our Hello component to check if we are in testing mode. We can accomplish this with the following code: if (import.meta.vitest). Inside this block, we will move all the testing cases, and we will also require the **React Testing Library** methods only within that block. This way, our code will resemble the following:

```
import React, { FC } from 'react'
  type Props = {
  name?: string;
}
const Hello: FC<Props> = ({ name }) => <h1 className="Hello">Hello {name
|| "World"}</h1>
export default Hello;
if (import.meta.vitest) {
  const { cleanup, render } = require('@testing-library/react')

  describe("Hello Component", () => {
    it("should render Hello World", () => {
      const wrapper = render(<Hello />)
      expect(wrapper.getByText("Hello World")).toBeDefined()
    })
```

```
it("should render the name prop", () => {
  const wrapper = render(<Hello name="Carlos" />)
  expect(wrapper.getByText("Hello Carlos")).toBeDefined()
})
it("should has .Home classname", () => {
  const wrapper = render(<Hello />)
  const firstChild = wrapper.container.firstChild as HTMLElement
  expect(firstChild?.classList.contains("Hello")).toBe(true)
})

afterAll(cleanup)
})
}
```

Now you can delete your previous file (index.test.tsx). If you run your tests again, they should work the same.

The difference is that now you will be able to see the entire code (Component and Test cases):

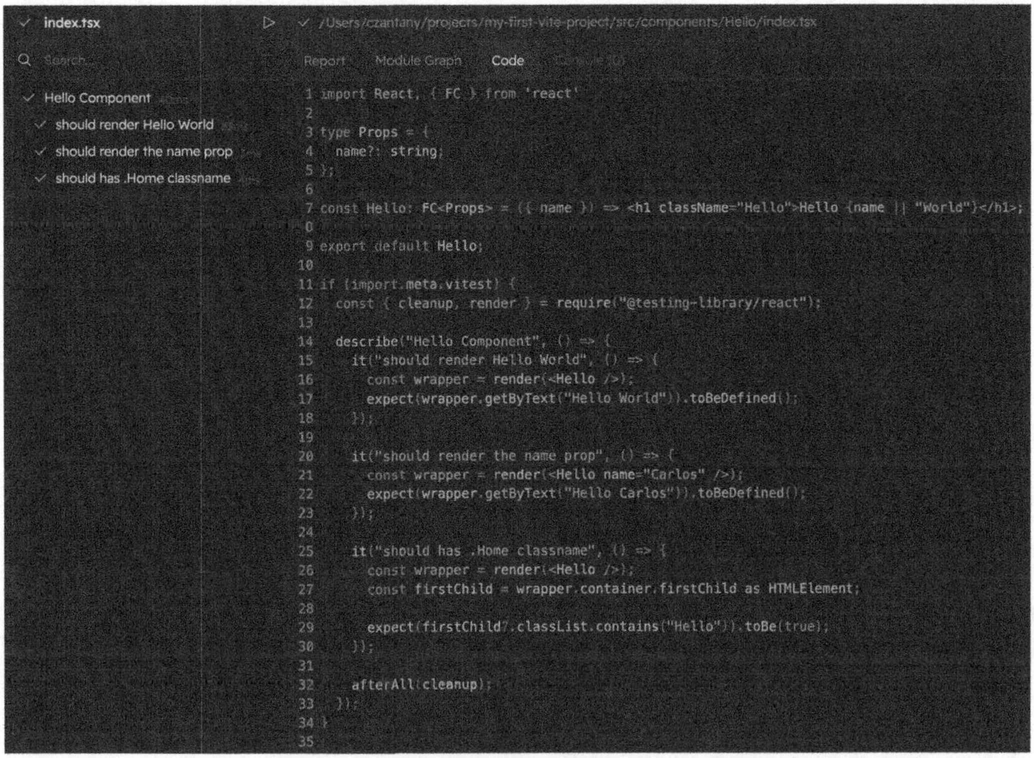

Figure 16.13: Passing test

This approach may potentially speed up the testing process for a component or a function. However, personally, I still prefer to perform testing in a separate test file. Nevertheless, you are free to choose what works best for you and your project.

After exploring the concept of in-source testing, let's proceed to understand how React DevTools can be effectively applied in our development process to optimize our application's performance and ensure it runs smoothly.

Using React DevTools

When testing in the console is not enough, and we want to inspect our application while it is running inside the browser, we can use React DevTools.

 You can install this as a Chrome extension at the following URL: `https://chrome.` `google.com/webstore/detail/react-developer-tools/fmkadmapgo` `fadopljbjfkapdkoienihi?hl=en`.

The installation adds a tab to the Chrome DevTools called **React**, where you can inspect the rendered tree of components and check which properties they have received and what their state is at a particular point in time.

Props and states can be read, and they can be changed in real time to trigger updates in the UI and see the results straight away. This is a must-have tool, and in the most recent versions, it has a new feature that can be enabled by checking the **Trace React Updates** checkbox.

When this functionality is enabled, we can use our application and see which components get updated when we perform a particular action. The updated components are highlighted with colored rectangles, and it becomes easy to spot possible optimizations.

Using Redux DevTools

If you are using Redux in your application, you probably want to use Redux DevTools to be able to debug your Redux flow. You can install it at the following URL: `https://chrome.google.com/` `webstore/detail/redux-devtools/lmhkpmbekcpmknklioeibfkpmmfibljd?hl=es`

Also, you need to install the `redux-devtools-extension` package:

```
npm install --save-dev redux-devtools-extension
```

Once you have installed React DevTools and Redux DevTools, you will need to configure them.

If you try to use Redux DevTools directly, it won't work; this is because we need to pass the composeWithDevTools method into the Redux store; this should be the configureStore.ts file:

```
import { createStore, applyMiddleware } from 'redux';
import thunk from 'redux-thunk';
import { composeWithDevTools } from 'redux-devtools-extension';
import rootReducer from '@reducers';

export default function configureStore({
  initialState,
  reducer
}) {
const middleware = [thunk];
return createStore(
  rootReducer,
  initialState,
  composeWithDevTools(applyMiddleware(...middleware))
  );
}
```

This is the best tool to test our Redux applications.

Summary

In this chapter, you gained a comprehensive understanding of the benefits of testing, as well as the various frameworks and tools available for testing React components. You learned how to implement and test components and events using the React Testing Library and how to use Jest coverage to optimize your testing process. Additionally, you explored tools such as React DevTools and Redux DevTools to further enhance your development experience. It's important to keep in mind common solutions when it comes to testing complex components, such as higher-order components or forms with multiple nested fields, to ensure that your tests accurately reflect the functionality of your application.

In the next chapter, you will learn how to deploy your application to production.

17

Deploying to Production

Now that you have completed your first React application, it is time to learn how to deploy it to the world. For this purpose, we will use the cloud service called **DigitalOcean**.

In this chapter, you will learn how to deploy your React application using Node.js and nginx on an Ubuntu server from DigitalOcean. In a nutshell, we will cover the following topics:

- Creating a DigitalOcean Droplet and configuring it
- Configuring nginx, PM2, and a domain
- Implementing CircleCI for continuous integration

Technical requirements

To complete this chapter, you will need the following:

- Node.js 19+
- Visual Studio Code

Creating our first DigitalOcean Droplet

I have used DigitalOcean for the last seven years, and I can say that it is one of the best cloud services I have tried, not just because of the affordable costs but also because it is super easy and fast to configure, and the community has a lot of updated documentation to fix most of the common issues related to server configuration.

At this point, you will need to invest some money to get this service. I will show you the cheapest way to do this, and if in the future you want to increase the power of your Droplets, you will be able to increase the capacity without redoing the configuration.

The lowest price for a very basic Droplet is \$6.00 per month (\$0.009 per hour).

We are going to use Ubuntu 20.04 (but feel free to use the latest version, 21.04); you will need to know some basic Linux commands to be able to configure your Droplet. If you're a beginner using Linux, don't worry—I'll try to show you each step in a very easy way.

Signing up to DigitalOcean

If you don't have a DigitalOcean account, you can sign up at `https://cloud.digitalocean.com/registrations/new`.

You can sign up with your Google account or by registering manually. Once you register with Google, you will see the **Billing Info** view, as follows:

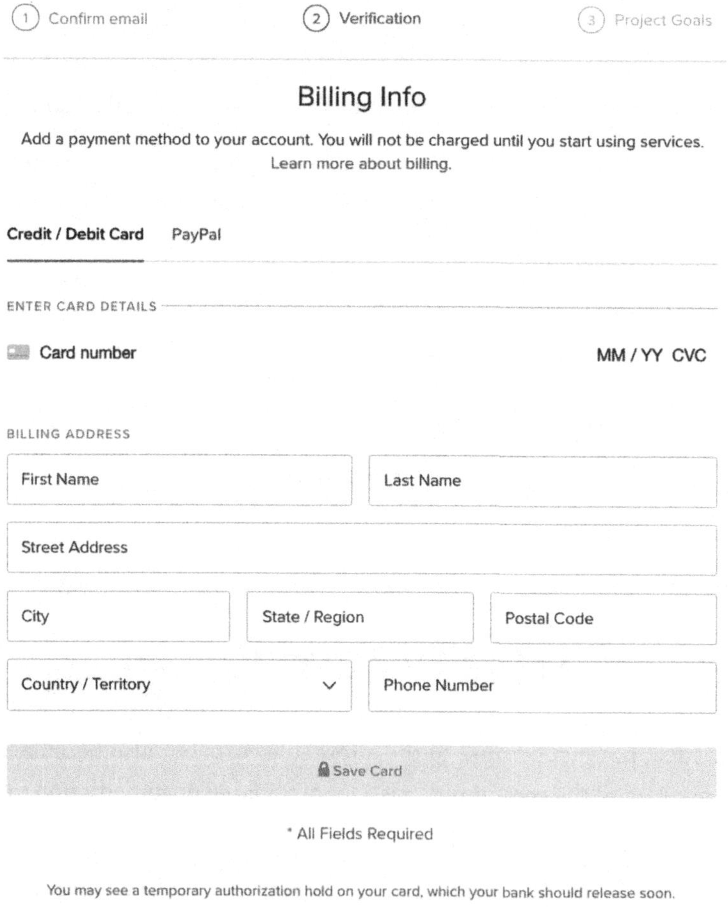

Figure 17.1: Billing Info

You can pay with your credit card or by using PayPal. Once you have configured your payment information, DigitalOcean will ask you for some information about your project so that it can configure your Droplet faster.

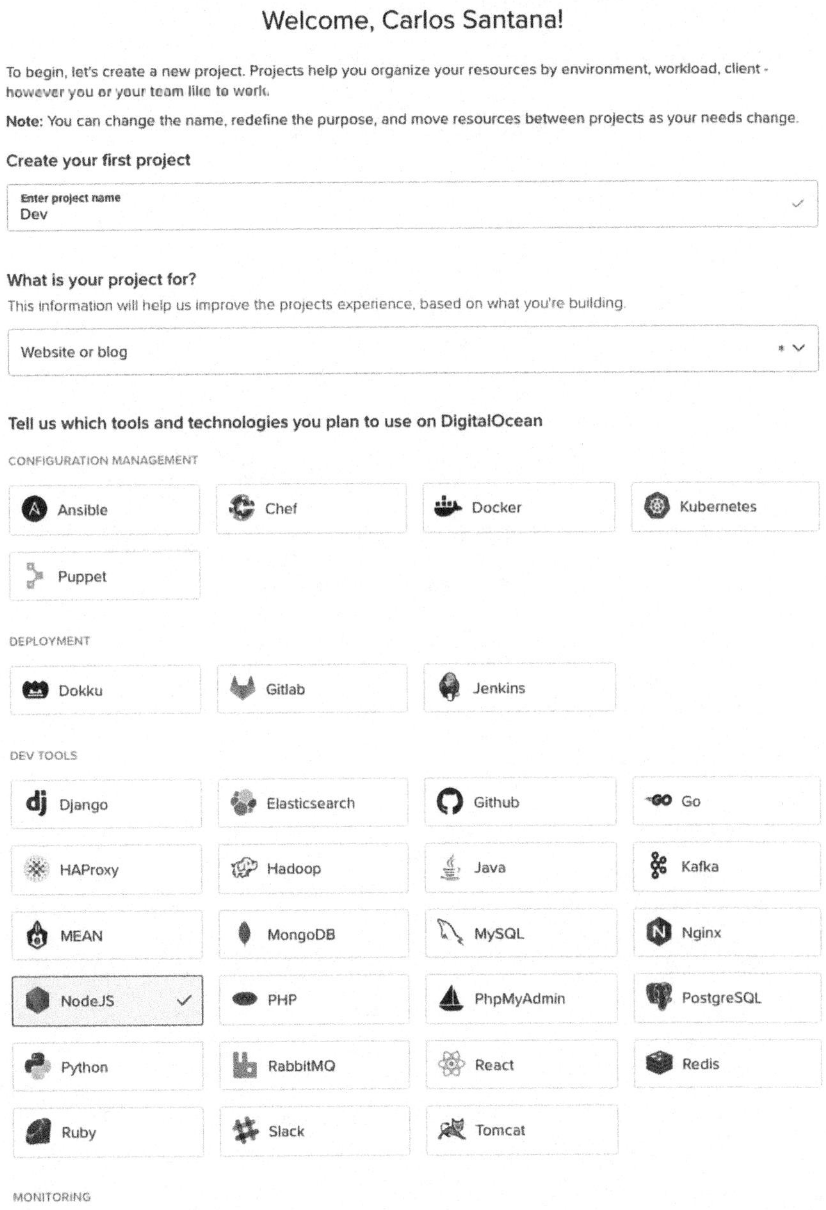

Figure 17.2: First application

Let's go on to create our first Droplet.

Creating our first Droplet

We will create a new Droplet from scratch. Follow these steps to do so:

1. Select the **New Droplet** option, as shown in the following screenshot:

Figure 17.3: New Droplet

2. Choose **Ubuntu 20.04 (LTS) x64**, as follows:

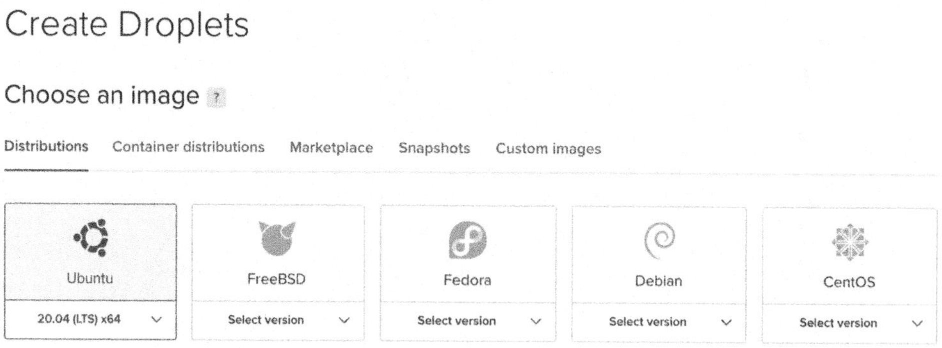

Create Droplets

Choose an image ?

Distributions   Container distributions   Marketplace   Snapshots   Custom images

Ubuntu	FreeBSD	Fedora	Debian	CentOS
20.04 (LTS) x64 ⌄	Select version ⌄	Select version ⌄	Select version ⌄	Select version ⌄

Figure 17.4: Choose an image

3. Then, choose the **Basic** plan, as shown here:

Figure 17.5: Choose a plan

4. You can then choose **$6/mo** from the payment plan options:

Figure 17.6: CPU options

5. Select a region. In this case, we will select the **San Francisco** region:

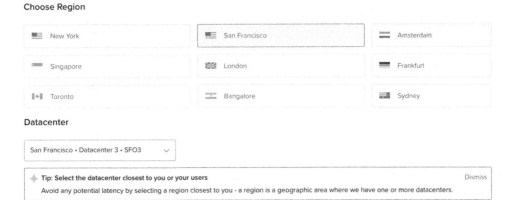

Figure 17.7: Choose Region

6. Create a root password, add the name of your Droplet, and then click on the **Create Droplet** button, as follows:

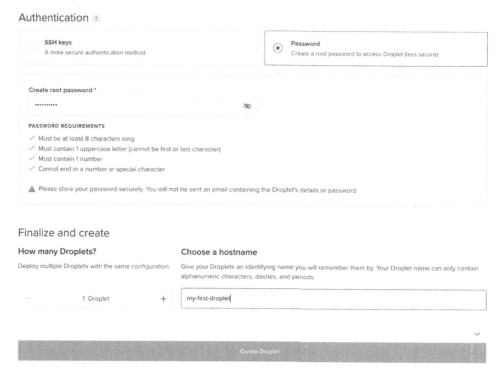

Figure 17.8: Authentication

7. It will take around 30 seconds to create your Droplet. Once it has been created, you will be able to see it:

Figure 17.9: My first Droplet

8. Now, in your Terminal, you can access the Droplet by using the following command:

```
ssh root@THE_DROPLET_IP
```

9. The first time you access it, you will be asked for a fingerprint. You just need to type *Yes*, and then it will require your password (the one you defined when you created your Droplet).

This serves as a security feature specifically designed to prevent *man-in-the-middle* attacks. The server's "fingerprint" acts as a distinctive digital signature that is unique to the server itself. When you observe a fingerprint that matches the expected one, you can proceed by typing yes and pressing *Enter* to continue. Subsequently, the server will prompt you to enter your password. Provide the password you defined when you created your Droplet, and press *Enter*. Please note that, for security purposes, no characters will be displayed on the screen as you enter your password. Upon successful authentication, you will be logged in to your server, ready to initiate commands.

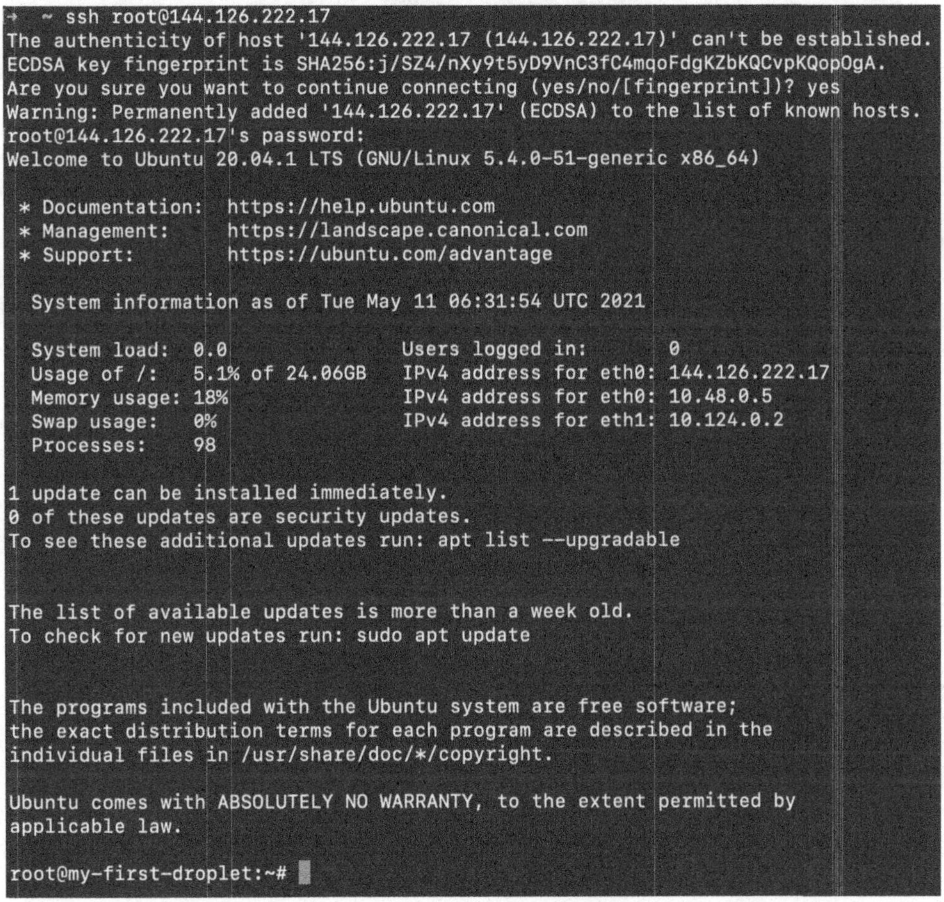

```
→  ~ ssh root@144.126.222.17
The authenticity of host '144.126.222.17 (144.126.222.17)' can't be established.
ECDSA key fingerprint is SHA256:j/SZ4/nXy9t5yD9VnC3fC4mqoFdgKZbKQCvpKQopOgA.
Are you sure you want to continue connecting (yes/no/[fingerprint])? yes
Warning: Permanently added '144.126.222.17' (ECDSA) to the list of known hosts.
root@144.126.222.17's password:
Welcome to Ubuntu 20.04.1 LTS (GNU/Linux 5.4.0-51-generic x86_64)

 * Documentation:  https://help.ubuntu.com
 * Management:     https://landscape.canonical.com
 * Support:        https://ubuntu.com/advantage

  System information as of Tue May 11 06:31:54 UTC 2021

  System load:  0.0                Users logged in:        0
  Usage of /:   5.1% of 24.06GB    IPv4 address for eth0: 144.126.222.17
  Memory usage: 18%                IPv4 address for eth0: 10.48.0.5
  Swap usage:   0%                 IPv4 address for eth1: 10.124.0.2
  Processes:    98

1 update can be installed immediately.
0 of these updates are security updates.
To see these additional updates run: apt list --upgradable


The list of available updates is more than a week old.
To check for new updates run: sudo apt update


The programs included with the Ubuntu system are free software;
the exact distribution terms for each program are described in the
individual files in /usr/share/doc/*/copyright.

Ubuntu comes with ABSOLUTELY NO WARRANTY, to the extent permitted by
applicable law.

root@my-first-droplet:~# █
```

Figure 17.10: Connecting to Droplet

Now we are all set to install Node.js, which we will cover in the next section.

Installing Node.js

Now that you're connected to your Droplet, let's configure it. First, we need to install the latest version of Node.js using a Personal Package Archive. The current version of Node at the time of writing this book is 19.9.x. Follow these steps to install Node.js:

1. If, when you are reading this paragraph, Node has a new version, change the version in the setup_19.x command:

```
cd ~
curl -sL https://deb.nodesource.com/setup_19.x -o nodesource_setup.
sh
```

2. Once you get the nodesource_setup.sh file, run the following command:

```
sudo bash nodesource_setup.sh
```

3. Then, install Node by running the following command:

```
sudo apt install nodejs -y
```

4. If everything works fine, verify the installed version of Node and npm with the following commands:

```
node -v
v19.9.0
npm -v
9.6.3
```

If you need a newer version of Node.js, you can always upgrade it.

Configuring Git and GitHub

I created a special repository to help you to deploy your first React application to production (https://github.com/FoggDev/production).

In your Droplet, you need to clone this Git repository (or your own repository if you have your React application ready to be deployed). The production repository is public, but normally you will use a private repository; in this case, you need to add the SSH key of your Droplet to your GitHub account.

To create this key, follow these steps:

1. Run the `ssh-keygen` command and then press *Enter* three times without entering any passphrase:

```
root@my-first-droplet:~# ssh-keygen
Generating public/private rsa key pair.
Enter file in which to save the key (/root/.ssh/id_rsa):
Enter passphrase (empty for no passphrase):
Enter same passphrase again:
Your identification has been saved in /root/.ssh/id_rsa
Your public key has been saved in /root/.ssh/id_rsa.pub
The key fingerprint is:
SHA256:FzejHaIZaY88/wlVUDocpeEjV+wjwY/RfBowIQenWts root@my-first-droplet
The key's randomart image is:
+---[RSA 3072]----+
|         ooXO+   |
|        . B+O= . |
|       + * &*.+  |
|      o O @oB=   |
|       S = E. .  |
|        + .      |
|         o       |
|          o .    |
|           o     |
+-----[SHA256]-----+
root@my-first-droplet:~#
```

Figure 17.11: ssh-keygen

If you leave your Terminal inactive for more than five minutes, your Droplet connection will probably be closed, and you will need to connect again.

2. Once you have created your Droplet SSH key, you can see it by running the following command:

```
vi /root/.ssh/id_rsa.pub
```

You will see something like this:

```
ssh-rsa AAAAB3NzaC1yc2EAAAADAQABAAABgQCzz49rPKe+dctYr3UG8F+vr3uKZS
rqVKbJjypIzOc2OrrEPyjulL0GEYBRLYNDVFHjmhAhQo45Y86xlIfQn4aC9QODiDcj
sDJZwc+bQ91NqvhP4q5+RHK/yizlcVBZKCw5RIx9AzpQt8bFRWWlP188cnvXhHlBxL
b0eej5xtaL6afdAEUh5z/klXGQO6kIzZlnyEnvqqKfUmUHDyLOyqB1xjkY/Shgf5o1
YdNk2hAFfC4r96mIyfVRR23tYPPE06OqZ1M= root@my-first-droplet
```

Figure 17.12: ssh-rsa

3. Copy your SSH key and then visit your GitHub account. Go to **Settings | SSH and GPG Keys** (`https://github.com/settings/ssh/new`). Then, paste your key in to the text area and add your title to the key:

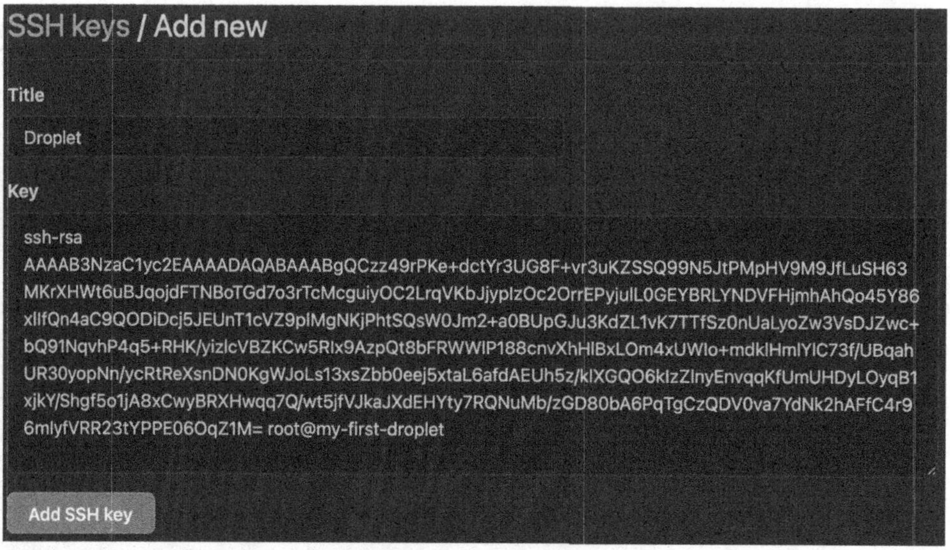

SSH keys / Add new

Title

Droplet

Key

ssh-rsa
AAAAB3NzaC1yc2EAAAADAQABAAABgQCzz49rPKe+dctYr3UG8F+vr3uKZSSQ99N5JtPMpHV9M9JfLuSH63
MKrXHWt6uBJqojdFTNBoTGd7o3rTcMcguiyOC2LrqVKbJjyplzOc2OrrEPyjuIL0GEYBRLYNDVFHjmhAhQo45Y86
xIIfQn4aC9QODiDcj5JEUnT1cVZ9pIMgNKjPhtSQsW0Jm2+a0BUpGJu3KdZL1vK7TTfSz0nUaLyoZw3VsDJZwc+
bQ91NqvhP4q5+RHK/yizlcVBZKCw5Rlx9AzpQt8bFRWWIP188cnvXhHIBxLOm4xUWIo+mdklHmlYIC73f/UBqah
UR30yopNn/ycRtReXsnDN0KgWJoLs13xsZbb0eej5xtaL6afdAEUh5z/klXGQO6kIzZInyEnvqqKfUmUHDyLOyqB1
xjkY/Shgf5o1jA8xCwyBRXHwqq7Q/wt5jfVJkaJXdEHYty7RQNuMb/zGD80bA6PqTgCzQDV0va7YdNk2hAFfC4r9
6mlyfVRR23tYPPE06OqZ1M= root@my-first-droplet

Add SSH key

Figure 17.13: Adding a new SSH key to GitHub

4. Once you click on the **Add SSH key** button, you will see your SSH key, like so:

Droplet
SHA256:FzejHaIZaY88/wlVUDocpeEjV+wjwY/RfBowIQenWts
Added on 10 May 2021
Never used — Read/write

Delete

SSH

Figure 17.14: SSH

5. Now you can clone our repository (or yours) using the following command:

```
git clone git@github.com:FoggDev/production.git
```

6. When you clone it for the first time, you will get a message asking you to allow the RSA key fingerprint:

```
root@my-first-droplet:~# git clone git@github.com:D3vEducation/production.git
Cloning into 'production'...
The authenticity of host 'github.com (192.30.255.113)' can't be established.
RSA key fingerprint is SHA256:nThbg6kXUpJWGl7E1IGOCspRomTxdCARviKw6E5SY8.
Are you sure you want to continue connecting (yes/no/[fingerprint])?
```

Figure 17.15: Cloning repository

7. You have to type Yes and then hit *Enter* to be able to clone it:

```
Warning: Permanently added 'github.com,192.30.255.113' (RSA) to the list of known hosts.
remote: Enumerating objects: 188, done.
remote: Total 188 (delta 0), reused 0 (delta 0), pack-reused 188
Receiving objects: 100% (188/188), 217.06 KiB | 1.07 MiB/s, done.
Resolving deltas: 100% (61/61), done.
root@my-first-droplet:~#
```

Figure 17.16: Known hosts

8. Then, you have to go to the production directory and install the npm packages:

```
cd production
npm install
```

9. If you want to test the application, just run the start script:

```
npm start
```

10. Then open your browser and go to your Droplet IP and add the port number. In my case, it is http://144.126.222.17:3000:

Hello Everyone

Figure 17.17: Project running in development mode

11. This will run the project in development mode. If you want to run it in production mode, use the following command:

```
npm run start:production
```

You should see **Production Process Manager (PM2)** running, as shown in the following screenshot:

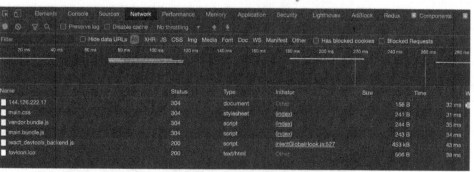

```
^Croot@my-first-droplet:~/production# npm run start:production

> production@1.0.0 start:production /root/production
> npm run stop && npm run build && NODE_ENV=production pm2 start --interpreter babel-node src/backend


> production@1.0.0 stop /root/production
> pm2 kill


                        -------------

__/\\\\\\\\\\\___/\\\_____/\\\\__/\\\_____
_\/\\\/////////\\\_\/\\\\\_____/\\\\\\_\///\\\\\_____
 _\/\\_____\/\\\_\/\\\//\\\____/\\\//\\\____/\\\/\\_____
  _\/\\\\\\\\\\\\\/__\/\\\\///\\\/\\\/_\/\\\___\//\\\\_____
   _\/\\\/////////____\/\\\__\///\\\/___\/\\\____\/\\_____
    _\/\\_____\/\\\____\///_____\/\\\____/\\_____
     _\/\\_____\/\\_____\/\\\__/\\_____
      _\/\\_____\/\\_____\/\\\_\//////////////\\\__
       _\///_____\///_____\///__\/////////////__


                        Runtime Edition

      PM2 is a Production Process Manager for Node.js applications
                    with a built-in Load Balancer.

              Start and Daemonize any application:
              $ pm2 start app.js

              Load Balance 4 instances of api.js:
              $ pm2 start api.js -i 4

              Monitor in production:
              $ pm2 monitor

              Make pm2 auto-boot at server restart:
              $ pm2 startup

              To go further checkout:
              http://pm2.io/

                        -------------
```

Figure 17.18: PM2

12. If you run it and view the **Network** tab in your Chrome DevTools, you will see the bundles being loaded:

Figure 17.19: The Network tab

We now have our React application working in production, but let's see what else we can do with DigitalOcean in the next section.

Turning off our Droplet

To turn off the Droplet, follow these steps:

1. If you want to turn off your Droplet, you can go to the **Power** section, or you can use the **ON/OFF** switch:

Figure 17.20: Turning off the Droplet

2. DigitalOcean will charge you only when your Droplet is **ON**. If you click on the **ON** switch to turn it off, then you will get the following confirmation message:

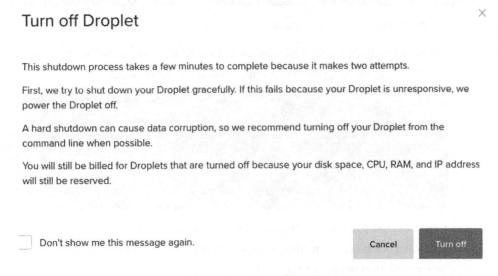

Figure 17.21: Turn off Droplet

In this way, you can control your Droplet and avoid paying unnecessarily when you're not using your Droplet.

Configuring nginx, PM2, and a domain

Our Droplet is ready to be used for production, but as you can see, we are still using port 3000. We need to configure nginx and implement a proxy to redirect the traffic from port 80 to 3000; this means we won't need to specify the port directly anymore.

Node PM2 will help us run the Node server in production securely. Generally, if we run Node directly with the node or babel-node commands, and there is an error in the app, then it will crash and will stop working. PM2 restarts the node server if an error occurs.

First, in your Droplet, you need to install PM2 globally:

```
npm install -g pm2
```

PM2 will help us to run our React app in a very easy way.

Installing and configuring nginx

To install nginx, you need to execute the following command:

```
sudo apt-get update
sudo apt-get install nginx
```

After you have installed nginx, you can start the configuration:

1. We need to adjust the firewall to allow the traffic for port 80. To list the available application configurations, you need to run the following command:

    ```
    sudo ufw app list
    Available applications:
    Nginx Full
    Nginx HTTP
    Nginx HTTPS
    OpenSSH
    ```

2. Nginx Full means that it will allow the traffic from port 80 (HTTP) and port 443 (HTTPS). We haven't configured any domain with SSL, so, for now, we should restrict the traffic to be sent just through port 80 (HTTP):

    ```
    sudo ufw allow 'Nginx HTTP'
    Rules updated
    Rules updated (v6)
    ```

If you try to access the Droplet IP, you should see nginx working:

Welcome to nginx!

If you see this page, the nginx web server is successfully installed and working. Further configuration is required.

For online documentation and support please refer to nginx.org. Commercial support is available at nginx.com.

Thank you for using nginx.

Figure 17.22: Welcome to nginx

3. You can manage the nginx process with these commands:

```
Start server: sudo systemctl start nginx
Stop server: sudo systemctl stop nginx
Restart server: sudo systemctl restart nginx
```

Nginx is an amazing web server that is getting very popular nowadays.

Setting up a reverse proxy server

As I mentioned previously, we need to set up a reverse proxy server to send the traffic from port 80 (HTTP) to port 3000 (the React app). To do this, you need to open the following file:

```
sudo vi /etc/nginx/sites-available/default
```

The steps to set up the reverse proxy server are as follows:

1. In the location / block, you need to replace the code in the file with the following:

```
location / {
    proxy_pass http://localhost:3000;
    proxy_http_version 1.1;
    proxy_set_header Upgrade $http_upgrade;
    proxy_set_header Connection 'upgrade';
    proxy_set_header Host $host;
    proxy_cache_bypass $http_upgrade;
}
```

2. Once you have saved the file, you can verify whether there is a syntax error in the nginx configuration with the following command:

```
sudo nginx -t
```

3. If everything is fine, then you should see this:

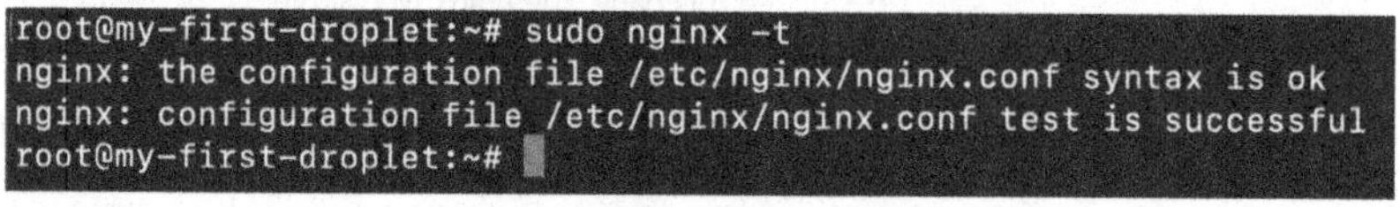

```
root@my-first-droplet:~# sudo nginx -t
nginx: the configuration file /etc/nginx/nginx.conf syntax is ok
nginx: configuration file /etc/nginx/nginx.conf test is successful
root@my-first-droplet:~#
```

Figure 17.23: sudo ngnix-t

4. Finally, you need to restart the nginx server:

```
sudo systemctl restart nginx
```

Now, you should be able to access the React application without the port, as shown in the following screenshot:

Hello Everyone

Figure 17.24: The React application without the port

We are almost done! In the next section, we are going to add a domain to our Droplet.

Adding a domain to our Droplet

Using an IP to access a website is not nice; we always need to use a domain to help users find our website more easily. If you want to use a domain with your Droplet, you need to change the nameservers of your domain to point to the DigitalOcean DNS. I normally use GoDaddy to register my domains.

To do so using GoDaddy, follow these steps:

1. Go to https://dcc.godaddy.com/manage/YOURDOMAIN.COM/dns, and then go to the **Nameservers** section:

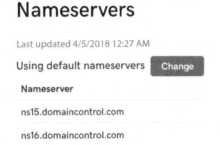

Figure 17.25: Nameservers

2. Click on the **Change** button, select **Custom**, and then specify the DigitalOcean DNS:

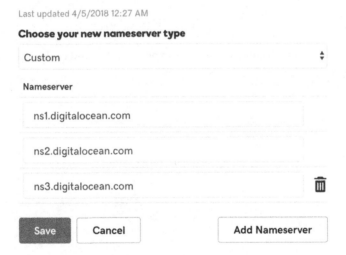

Figure 17.26: DigitalOcean Nameservers

3. Normally, it takes between 15 and 30 minutes for the DNS changes to be reflected; for now, after you have updated your nameservers, go to your **Droplet** dashboard and then choose the **Add a domain** option:

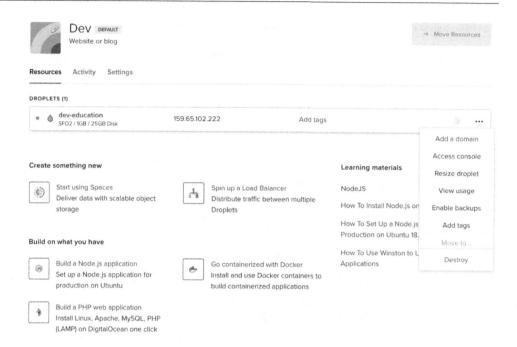

Figure 17.27: Add a domain

4. Then, write your domain name, select your Droplet, and click on the **Add Domain** button:

Networking

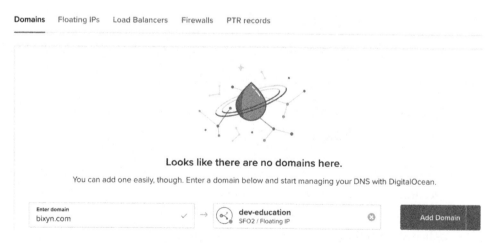

Figure 17.28: Networking

5. Now, you must create a new record for **CNAME**. Select the **CNAME** tab, and in **HOSTNAME**, type www; in the alias field, write @; by default, the TTL is 43200. All of this is to enable access to your domain using the www prefix:

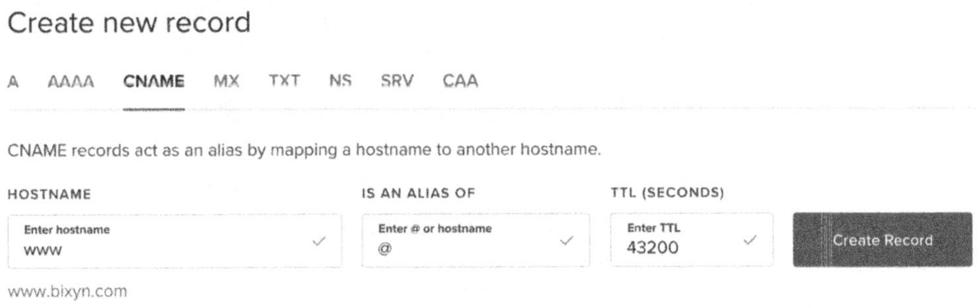

Figure 17.29: Create new record

If you did everything correctly, you should be able to access your domain and see the React application working. As I said before, this process can take up to 30 minutes, but in some cases, it can take up to 24 hours, depending on the DNS propagation speed:

Figure 17.30: React application running on domain

Amazing. Now you have officially deployed your first React application to production!

Implementing CircleCI for continuous integration

I've been using CircleCI for a while, and I can tell you that it is one of the best CI solutions: it is free for personal use, giving you unlimited repositories and users; you have 1,000 build minutes per month, one container, and one concurrent job; if you need more, you can upgrade the plan with an initial price of $50 per month.

The first thing you need to do is sign up on the site using your GitHub account (or Bitbucket, if you prefer).

If you choose to use GitHub, you need to authorize CircleCI in your account, as shown in the following screenshot:

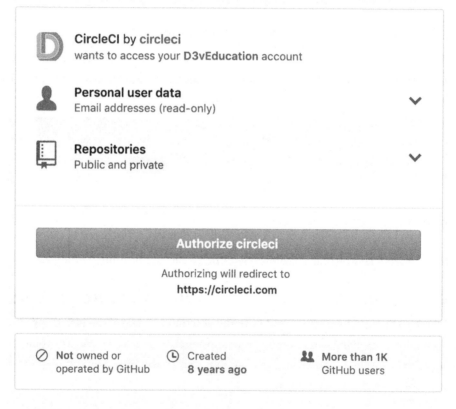

Figure 17.31: Authorize CircleCI

In the next section, we are going to add our SSH key to CircleCI.

Adding an SSH key to CircleCI

Now that you have created your account, CircleCI needs a way to log in to your DigitalOcean Droplet to run the deploy script. Follow these steps to complete this task:

1. Create a new SSH key inside your Droplet using the following command:

```
ssh-keygen -t rsa
# Then save the key as /root/.ssh/id_rsa_droplet with no password.
# After go to .ssh directory
cd /root/.ssh
```

2. After that, let's add the key to our authorized_keys:

```
cat id_rsa_droplet.pub >> authorized_keys
```

3. Now, you need to download the private key. To verify that you can log in with the new key, you need to copy it to your local machine, as follows:

```
# In your local machine do:
scp root@YOUR_DROPLET_IP:/root/.ssh/id_rsa_droplet ~/.ssh/
cd .ssh
ssh-add id_rsa_droplet
ssh -v root@YOUR_DROPLET_IP
```

If you did everything correctly, you should be able to log in to your Droplet without a password, and that means CircleCI can access our Droplet too.

4. Copy the content of your id_rsa_droplet.pub key and then go to your repository settings (https://app.circleci.com/settings/project/github/YOUR_GITHUB_USER/YOUR_REPOSITORY):

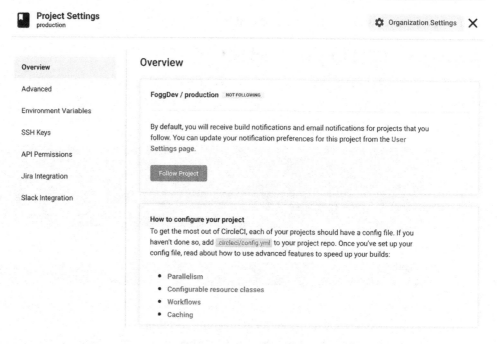

Figure 17.32: Project Settings

5.   Go to **SSH Keys,** as follows:

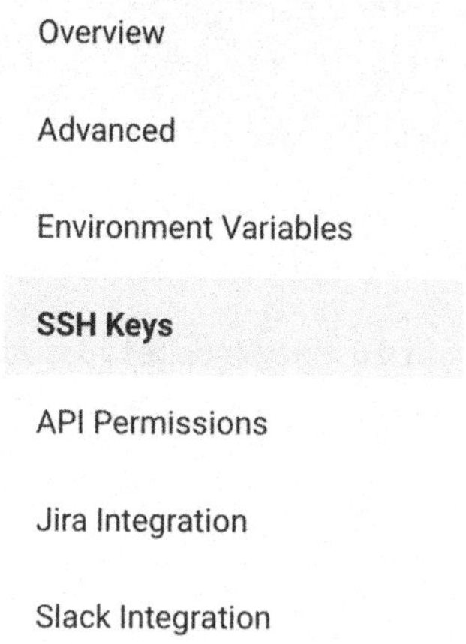

Overview

Advanced

Environment Variables

SSH Keys

API Permissions

Jira Integration

Slack Integration

Figure 17.33: SSH Keys

6. You can also access the URL https://app.circleci.com/settings/project/github/
   YOUR_GITHUB_USER/YOUR_REPOSITORY/ssh, and then click on the **Add SSH Key** button
   at the bottom:

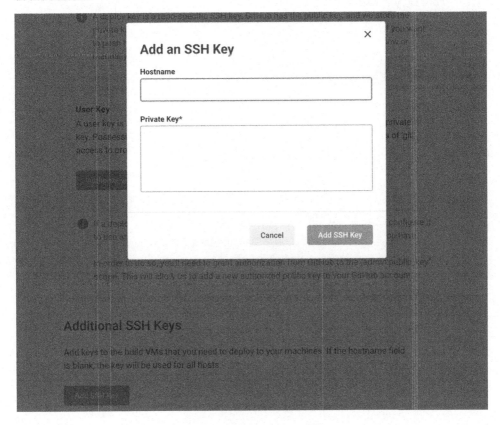

Figure 17.34: Add an SSH key

7. Paste your private key, and then provide a name for the **Hostname** field; we will name it
   DigitalOcean.

Now let's configure our CircleCI instance in the next section.

Configuring CircleCI

Now that you have configured access for CircleCI to your Droplet, you need to add a config file
to your project to specify the jobs you want to execute for the deployment process.

This process is shown in the following steps:

1. For this, you need to create the `.circleci` directory and add the following inside the `config.yml` file:

```
version: 2.1
jobs:
build:
working_directory: ~/tmp
docker:
   - image: cimg/node:14.16.1
steps:
   - checkout
   - run: npm install
   - run: npm run lint
   - run: npm test
   - run: ssh -o StrictHostKeyChecking=no $DROPLET_USER@$DROPLET_IP
'cd production; git checkout master; git pull; npm install; npm run
start:production;'
workflows:
build-deploy:
jobs:
   - build:
filters:
branches:
only: master
```

2. When you have a .yml file, you need to be careful with the indentation; it is similar to Python in that if you don't use indents correctly, you will get an error. Let's see how this file is structured.

3. Specify the CircleCI version we will use. In this instance, you are using version 2.1 (the latest one at the time of writing this book):

```
version: 2.1
```

4. Inside jobs, we will specify that it needs to configure the container; we will create it using Docker and also outline the steps to follow for the deployment process.

5. `working_directory` will be the temporal directory we will use to install the npm packages and run our deploy scripts. In this case, I decided to use the `tmp` directory, as follows:

```
jobs:
build:
working_directory: ~/tmp
```

6. As I said before, we will create a Docker container, and in this instance, I selected an existing image that includes node: `18.12.1`. If you want to know about all the available images, you can visit `https://circleci.com/docs/2.0/circleci-images`:

```
docker:
- image: cimg/node:18.12.1
```

7. For the code case, first do a git `checkout` to master, then in each run sentence, you need to specify the scripts you want to run:

```
steps:
- checkout
- run: npm install
- run: npm run lint
- run: npm test
- run: ssh -o StrictHostKeyChecking=no $DROPLET_USER@$DROPLET_IP
'cd production; git checkout master; git pull; npm install; npm run
start:production;'
```

Here is an explanation of the previous steps:

1. First, you need to install the npm packages using `npm install` to be able to perform the next tasks.

2. Execute the ESLint validation using `npm run lint`. If it fails, it will break the deployment process; otherwise, it continues with the next run.

3. Execute the Jest validations using `npm run test`; if it fails, it will break the deployment process. Otherwise, it continues with the next run.

4. In the last step, we connect to our DigitalOcean Droplet, passing the `StrictHostKeyChecking=no` flag to disable the strict host key checking. We then use the `$DROPLET_USER` and `$DROPLET_IP` ENV variables to connect to it (we will create those in the next step), and finally, we will specify all the commands we will perform inside our Droplet using single quotes.

These commands are listed as follows:

- **cd production:** Grants access to the production (or your Git repository name).
- **git checkout master:** This will check out the master branch.
- **git pull:** Pulls the latest changes from our repository.
- **npm run start:production:** This is the final step, which runs our project in production mode.

Finally, let's add some environment variables to our CircleCI.

Creating environment variables variables in CircleCI

As you saw previously, we are using the **$DROPLET_USER** and **$DROPLET_IP** variables, but how do we define those? Follow these steps:

1. You need to go to your project settings again and select the **Environment Variables** option. Then, you need to create the DROPLET_USER variable:

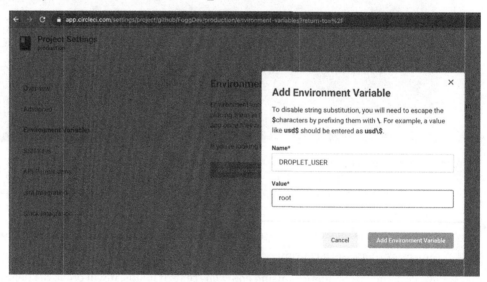

Figure 17.35: Add Environment Variable

2. Then, you need to create the **DROPLET_IP** variable using your Droplet IP:

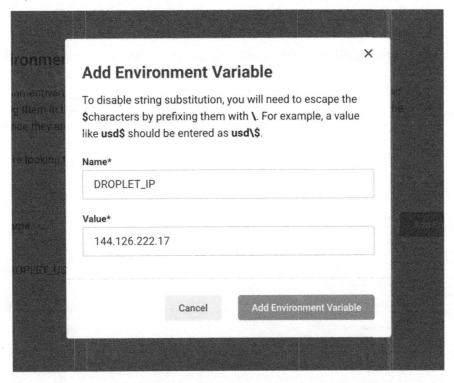

Figure 17.36: DROPLET_IP

3. Now, you need to push the config file to your repository, and you will be ready for the magic. Now that CircleCI is connected to your repository, every time you push changes to master, it will fire a build.

Normally, the first two or three builds can fail due to syntax errors, indent errors in our config, or maybe because we have linter errors or unit test errors. If you have a failure, you will see something like this:

Figure 17.37: Build error

4. As you can see from the preceding screenshot, the first build failures at the bottom say **Build Error**, and the second one says build-deploy under WORKFLOW, as shown in *Figure 17.38*. This basically means that in the first build, I had a syntax error in the config.yml file.

5. After you fix all the syntax errors in the config.yml file and all the issues with the linter or the unit tests, you should see a **Success** build like this:

Figure 17.38: SUCCESS build

6. If you click on the build number, you can see all the steps that CircleCI executed before publishing the new changes in your Droplet:

Figure 17.39: Steps executed by CircleCI

7. As you can see, the order of the steps is the same as we specified in our `config.yml` file; you can even see the output of each step by clicking on it:

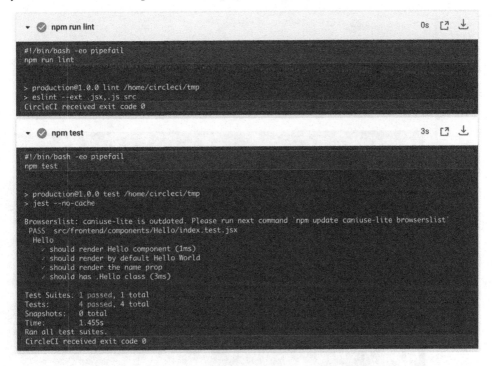

Figure 17.40: Lint and test steps

8. Now, let's suppose you have an error on your linter validation or in some unit tests. Let's see what happens in that case, as follows:

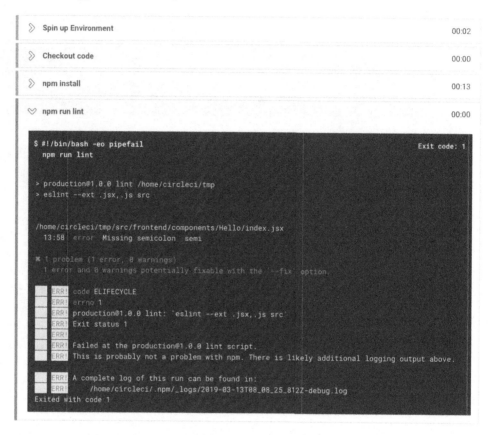

Figure 17.41: Linter error

As you can see, once an error is detected, it will exit with code 1. This means it will abort the deployment and mark it as a failure. Notice that none of the steps after npm run lint are executed.

Another cool thing is that if you now go to your GitHub repository and check your commits, you will see all the commits that had a successful build and all the commits that had a failed build:

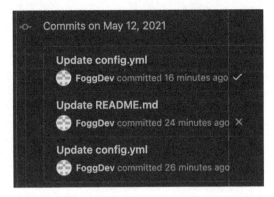

Figure 17.42: GitHub successful build

This is amazing: now you have your project configured to do deployments automatically, and it is connected to your GitHub repository.

Summary

Congratulations! We've reached the end of our journey through the deployment process, and you now have the knowledge and skills needed to deploy your React application to the world (production). You've also learned how to implement CircleCI for continuous integration, streamlining your development process and ensuring that your application remains performant and reliable.

By leveraging the strategies and best practices outlined in this chapter, you can confidently launch your application to a global audience, secure in the knowledge that it has been optimized for speed, scalability, and resilience. Thank you for joining me on this journey. I hope you've enjoyed reading my book.

packt.com

Subscribe to our online digital library for full access to over 7,000 books and videos, as well as industry leading tools to help you plan your personal development and advance your career. For more information, please visit our website.

Why subscribe?

- Spend less time learning and more time coding with practical eBooks and Videos from over 4,000 industry professionals
- Improve your learning with Skill Plans built especially for you
- Get a free eBook or video every month
- Fully searchable for easy access to vital information
- Copy and paste, print, and bookmark content

At www.packt.com, you can also read a collection of free technical articles, sign up for a range of free newsletters, and receive exclusive discounts and offers on Packt books and eBooks.

Other Books You May Enjoy

If you enjoyed this book, you may be interested in these other books by Packt:

Learning Angular, Fourth Edition

Aristeidis Bampakos

ISBN: 9781803240602

- Use the Angular CLI to scaffold, build, and deploy a new Angular application
- Build components, the basic building blocks of an Angular application
- Discover new Angular Material components such as Google Maps, YouTube, and multi-select dropdowns
- Understand the different types of templates supported by Angular
- Create HTTP data services to access APIs and provide data to components
- Learn how to build Angular apps without modules in Angular 15.x with standalone APIs
- Improve your debugging and error handling skills during runtime and development

Angular Projects, Third Edition

Aristeidis Bampakos

ISBN: 9781803239118

- Set up Angular applications using Angular CLI and Nx Console
- Create a personal blog with Jamstack, Scully plugins, and SPA techniques
- Build an issue management system using typed reactive forms
- Use PWA techniques to enhance user experience
- Make SEO-friendly web pages with server-side rendering
- Create a monorepo application using Nx tools and NgRx for state management
- Focus on mobile application development using Ionic
- Develop custom schematics by extending Angular CLI

Web Development with Blazor, Second Edition

Jimmy Engström

ISBN: 9781803241494

- Understand the different technologies that can be used with Blazor, such as Blazor Server, Blazor WebAssembly, and Blazor Hybrid
- Find out how to build simple and advanced Blazor components
- Explore the differences between Blazor Server and Blazor WebAssembly projects
- Discover how Minimal APIs work and build your own API
- Explore existing JavaScript libraries in Blazor and JavaScript interoperability
- Learn techniques to debug your Blazor Server and Blazor WebAssembly applications
- Test Blazor components using bUnit

Blazor WebAssembly by Example, Second Edition

Toi B. Wright

ISBN: 9781803241852

- Discover the power of the C# language for both server-side and client-side web development

- Build your first Blazor WebAssembly application with the Blazor WebAssembly App project template

- Learn how to debug a Blazor WebAssembly app, and use ahead-of-time compilation before deploying it on Microsoft's cloud platform

- Use templated components and the Razor class library to build and share a modal dialog box

- Learn how to use JavaScript with Blazor WebAssembly

- Build a progressive web app (PWA) to enable native app-like performance and speed

- Secure a Blazor WebAssembly app using Azure Active Directory

- Gain experience with ASP.NET Web APIs by building a task manager app

Packt is searching for authors like you

If you're interested in becoming an author for Packt, please visit authors.packtpub.com and apply today. We have worked with thousands of developers and tech professionals, just like you, to help them share their insight with the global tech community. You can make a general application, apply for a specific hot topic that we are recruiting an author for, or submit your own idea.

Share your thoughts

Now you've finished *React 18 Design Patterns and Best Practices, Fourth Edition*, we'd love to hear your thoughts! Scan the QR code below to go straight to the Amazon review page for this book and share your feedback or leave a review on the site that you purchased it from.

https://packt.link/r/1803233109

Your review is important to us and the tech community and will help us make sure we're delivering excellent quality content.

Index

Symbols

A

B

Download a free PDF copy of this book

Thanks for purchasing this book!

Do you like to read on the go but are unable to carry your print books everywhere? Is your eBook purchase not compatible with the device of your choice?

Don't worry, now with every Packt book you get a DRM-free PDF version of that book at no cost.

Read anywhere, any place, on any device. Search, copy, and paste code from your favorite technical books directly into your application.

The perks don't stop there, you can get exclusive access to discounts, newsletters, and great free content in your inbox daily

Follow these simple steps to get the benefits:

1. Scan the QR code or visit the link below

https://packt.link/free-ebook/978-1-80323-310-9

2. Submit your proof of purchase
3. That's it! We'll send your free PDF and other benefits to your email directly

Made in the USA
Las Vegas, NV
05 January 2024